A SUNDAY :

BY

MAURICE BRETT

CIRRUS ASSOCIATES

PUBLISHED BY:
Cirrus Associates (S.W.),
Kington Magna,
Gillingham,
Dorset,
SP8 5EW UK.

ISBN 1 902807 04 9

PRINTED IN ENGLAND BY:
The Book Factory,
35-37 Queensland Road,
London,
N7 7AH.

PHOTO SCANNING BY:
Castle Graphics Ltd,
Nunney,
Nr. Frome,
Somerset,
BA11 4LW.

DISTRIBUTORS:
Vine House Distribution Ltd,
Waldenbury,
North Common,
Chailey,
East Sussex,
BN8 4DR.

COVER: from an original painting by the author.

DEDICATION

To my long-suffering wife Irene for putting up with my various activities so patiently, for so many years: to my enthusiastic co-conspirator on so many occasions, George Cull: to my old friend David Elphick for the many enjoyable 'Tiger nights': and to all my other partners throughout the 24 years' life of the Stevenage Flying Club – life would have seemed very much less full without all of you.

ACKNOWLEDGEMENTS

Chapters 4, 6, 8, 9, 10, 12, 14, 15, 16, 17 were previously published in *"Vintage News,"* the house magazine of the Vintage Aircraft Club.

Chapter 11 was previously published in *"Wingspan."*

Chapter 18 & 23 were previously published in the Herts PFA Strut Newsletter.

CONTENTS

INTRODUCTION

The contents of this book mostly originated as a series of articles written mainly for the Vintage Aircraft Group magazine in the seventies and early eighties, at a time when it *was* a Group and attracted mostly true vintage aircraft and their owners, pilots and admirers. The main purpose of the articles, apart from filling the pages, was to pass on to other members something hopefully of interest and, in some cases, useful experience (much on the lines of the series "I Learned About Flying From That" which has run for many years in a well-known American magazine). When the VAG became the VAC (Vintage Aircraft Club) and the quarterly magazine became annual, there was no longer such a crying need for articles and those earmarked for future issues were shelved. It seemed a shame to bin them, so here they are.

Most of my flying was pretty normal stuff, A to B, mostly to attend weekend Fly-Ins, Rallies and the occasional Air Display – you could actually take part in Public Displays in those days with no more than a PPL (Private Pilot's Licence), provided you were not paid for it and assuming you had a vintage or unusual machine. Such flying was interesting enough to me and the many who accompanied me at various times (the Jackaroo was a great people-mover, slow but reliable, manoeuvrable and great fun), but mostly not the material that makes readers want to turn the page for more (at least I hope those that appear here fall into the latter category). Normally I reckoned I was a very safety-conscious pilot and did things by the book as I was taught to do at Luton Flying Club, but try as one might in those days, something would occasionally happen to catch out the unwary. My motto was: "There are no old, bold pilots."

It should be noted that when I learnt to fly on the Club Austers at Luton they were not fitted with radio, despite Luton having become by that time an International Airport. As with nearly all the major airports in those days, it was sufficient to ring Air Traffic Control before the flight and watch for the Aldis light in conformity with ATC instructions on joining the circuit. No hassle and no accidents that I am aware of in those far-off happy days. Then it was possible to ring RAF Uxbridge at almost any time and talk to the man in charge of the weather: "Well, if you are planning a dawn take-off from Panshanger in a Tiger Moth, there will be a thick ground mist at dawn tomorrow, clearing by about 5.30 am, but it might be OK the next day – give me a ring tomorrow evening at about the same time . . ." (now it costs £19 by Credit Card to talk to an Air Met. Man on the phone!). And in those days of Atlantic Weather Ships you really could trust what the Met. Man gave you – it was a matter of pride to him to get it right.

Much of what is related in the following pages will be dismissed as thoughtless and hazardous flying in today's safety-conscious world (I hope that the Editor of the Flight Safety Bulletin doesn't get a sight of it), succumbing too readily to what is derisively classified as 'pressonitis.' Had I attempted some of such flights in modern high-performance aircraft I agree they should be rightly condemned as such, but the sort of aircraft I flew were, in today's parlance, real 'pussy-cats' – highly man-oeuvrable at low speed, capable of landing when necessary at 40 mph or less (even fully-loaded) in several hundreds rather than thousands of feet – and every normal landing was power-off from a glide approach.

One other important factor was the training we were given in those days. Because we flew non-radio we were taught to map-read and not get lost. We learned about short-field landings and side-slipping to lose height quickly and steeply. We flew always keeping an eye open for a field in which to land in an emergency, progressing from one field to another. We would shut off power at 1,000 ft over an airfield heading in any direction, and show we could get down safely from a power-off approach (not at Luton needless to say – there were plenty of disused RAF airfields in those days). Circuits were always flown within gliding distance of the airfield, even at Luton, and it was not done to touch the throttle once committed to the approach other than to 'clear the plugs' every 300 ft of altitude (the instructor always knew when you gave too long a burst of power in clearing the plugs, and why you were doing it). What has happened to private flying these days when one reads of a pilot running out of fuel on 'finals' and landing in a field four miles short of the airfield!! We took pride in touching down just over the numbers and turning off at the first taxiway without resorting to the use of brakes. Even though the Austers were fitted with brakes, one was being taught to fly any single-engined 'plane and most did not have brakes in those days. This meant that, despite a brand-new PPL and only 33 hours in my Log Book, and a sweaty palm on the stick of a newly-acquired Jackaroo on its delivery flight (four-up) to the 1,250 ft-long grass field which was to be our new home, we made it. What we were not taught was the effect of density altitude (hot and high) and the effects of flying close to ridges in turbulent winds – those, as you may read, we had to learn for ourselves.

It is a matter of great pride that I can say I never caused so much as a scratch to any passengers, only one (of hundreds) was airsick, and the usual reaction was one of great pleasure and enjoyment, even where several of the flights ended in precautionary or emergency landings – universally, they enjoyed the challenge posed by the latter. I remember, when I finally learnt to fly, being a little despondent at having missed what I then judged to be the best days, either before or just after WW2, but on reflection I really don't think they ever came very much better than when I started flying, through to the end of the eighties.

CHAPTER 1
IN THE BEGINNING

There obviously must have been a time when I was not interested in aviation but I honestly cannot remember it. Indeed my very earliest recollection, and one I can positively date, was just before my third birthday, when my grandfather hoisted me onto his shoulder to point out the long, dull-silver, cigar-shaped hull of the Graf Zeppelin, which from that vantage point I could see almost hovering, apparently just above the distant roof tops. The house backed onto Dollis Hill station, in NW London, and the Zeppelin was flying over Wembley Stadium on the occasion of the FA Cup Final in 1929. I suppose that was probably the first time anyone had pointed out to me any form of aircraft, but after that the sky became something more than just the background to clouds. Not only were we close enough to Wembley to see the airship, but we were almost as close to Hendon aerodrome, and suddenly I became aware of other aircraft of a totally different shape, probably formations of DH.9As, Siskins, Grebes and Gamecocks, practising for the Hendon Air Display, which followed soon after.

My next vivid memory, and one that put me off airships and balloons for life, was when I had just started at infants' school at the age of five. One sombre October morning in 1931, we were all assembled in the school hall, and the headmistress, standing on the stage behind a table draped with an enormous Union Jack, told us in grave tones about the tragedy that had befallen the R.101, with the loss of so many lives. It was a national disaster, emphasised by the full-page-width newspaper photographs of the gaunt, burnt-out skeleton grounded on a ridge in Beauvais. A few years later, the Hindenburg went up in flames at Lakehurst, NY, heightening my aversion to lighter-than-air craft; even now I would need a lot of persuasion to fly in a hot-air balloon.

Right through the thirties, my generation of youngsters was brought up on a diet of the thrilling, adventurous, ever faster, ever longer or higher flights of a daring few. No wonder that we were entranced by each new record-breaking attempt, racing home from school to listen to the radio for news of how Amy Johnson, Jim Mollison, Jean Batten, Alex Henshaw, etc. etc. were faring; saddened when the dreaded announcement came, only too often, that someone was now overdue, eventually to be presumed lost. Perhaps the most exciting was the great MacRobertson England–Australia Air Race of 1934. Even at the age of eight, I knew the names of many of the participants, and could recognise most of the aircraft that were entered, particularly the glorious and glamorous DH Comets. As the latter encountered various problems, I can still recall the fear that none of them would finish, to be beaten perhaps by that shiny new Dutch-entered Douglas DC-2 – an airliner! How could that possibly beat the beautiful Comets, flown by the cream of the record-breakers? Each morning, the newspaper was scanned from end to end for the latest snippet of news and the little maps showing the progress of the crews. What relief at the end when the Comet of Scott and Black was announced the winner – the fact that the hated airliner came second, and won the Handicap Section to boot, was ignored; only many years later did I come to appreciate what a remarkable achievement that was.

Like my friends, I was interested in anything mechanical and modern. There was plenty to whet the appetite. Perhaps the most readily available were the cigarette cards put out by most of the cigarette manufacturers. Although each would ring the changes, there seemed always to be at least one brand whose cards dealt with aircraft (or my other love, cars); most of the others covering such as footballers (ugh), Kings & Queens (dead), plants (yuk), etc. etc. were virtually ignored, though trains were just about acceptable even though steam-power was viewed as a thing from the past. Those that spring most readily to mind were Players, who produced a set of 50 covering RAF aircraft around 1938, two sets I believe of civil aircraft from about 1935 and a set of RAF Squadron Badges in 1939. The aircraft were depicted in excellent photographs, coloured by an artist who took care to get the colours right. More importantly for me however, were those in the de Reszke brand; what made these so interesting was that they carried a plan-view silhouette on the reverse so that I soon learned to relate drawn outlines to photographs. All the cards gave details of span, length, engine power and performance. By the time I and my friends had collected all of these sets we knew the shapes and details of around 200 aircraft! You didn't need to know a smoker to collect the cards; we just stood outside the local Underground station and asked all those who looked as if they might be smokers if they had any cigarette cards – most would stop to look in their packets and pass any on to us.

In 1934, my mother bought me most of a set of a children's encyclopedia called the *"Wonderland of Knowledge,"* volumes being issued monthly if you could afford it (which she couldn't always). All pretty mundane stuff until we got to volume four, which covered the history of transport; there was, miraculously, an in-depth section on aircraft – a short history of flight, how an aeroplane flies, how it was controlled, etc. That one volume alone would have been sufficient if only my mother had realised it! Eventually, funds became too scarce to continue and she suggested replacing it with a weekly magazine called *"The Modern Boy"* which kept its readers up-to-date on what was going on in readily-understood diagrams and non-technical terms – and if I recall correctly, introduced me to Biggles. The other important source was the local Public Library (which has been a friend for life). As soon as I was able I became a regular and frequent visitor, soon latching on to a whole range of air books published by John Hamilton Ltd – fiction and fact alike (I still have a few copies on my shelves now). There seemed no end to the books on flying, though in reality they represented only a tiny fraction of what is available to today's enthusiasts.

As if all this was not enough to satisfy the appetite, Hollywood produced many flying films, good, bad and indifferent. It mattered but little as long as there was plenty of flying in them. On Saturday mornings, all the cinemas had children's shows (cost 3d), mostly consisting of comedies from the likes of Charlie Chaplin or Laurel & Hardy, or cowboy films, but with a fair sprinkling of flying films. Who now remembers *"Tail-spin Tommy"* (played by Wallace Beery's son Noah), a sort of barnstormer and stunt pilot flying fabulous Travelair, Pitcairn, Waco, Lincoln etc. biplanes of the early thirties with real wing-walkers? When in the seventies I organised a number of film shows of early films such as *"Wings"* and *"Hell's Angels,"* I tried in vain to track down some Tail-spin Tommy films but alas no one knew of them. I remember seeing *"Hell's Angels"* at the cinema, with the original blue-tinted night scenes – nothing since has sent such a shiver down my spine as did the sinister nose of the Zeppelin emerging from the clouds; alas the postwar copies now available do not have the blue tinting and have lost much in the process. *"Dawn Patrol"* was another favourite which I saw several times and, just before the war, *"Men with Wings,"* the first Technicolor flying film, which brought home the true tragedies of early flying, with horrifying scenes of aircraft crashing and bursting into flames – nothing before had depicted 'flamers' quite so terrifyingly.

For a young boy living in London, there were few air shows available, and how much I envied those living near provincial airports or wherever Cobham's Flying Circus visited. Indeed the only ones I knew of were the RAF's Hendon Air Displays held at the end of June each year until 1937. No one in my family was sufficiently interested to go to any of these until, after much pleading, I persuaded a young aunt to take me to the last one, and finally got to see some aircraft close-up. I remember vividly with what awe I got close enough to an all-yellow Tiger Moth to hesitantly put out my hand and touch it, feeling the smooth, slightly warm, slightly yielding surface of the wing fabric (nowadays it would be described as 'sensuous' though I wouldn't then have known what that meant!). At last I knew they were real – I had actually touched one! Years later at an Air Display where the public were able to walk amongst the aircraft, sitting on the grass with my back to a wheel, that came back to me when a young lad walked up to the Jackaroo, thinking no one was about, and put out a hand to touch it. I felt I knew exactly what he was experiencing, and after watching him for a minute suggested he might like to sit inside. His reaction made my day and after that I never lost an opportunity to encourage anyone, young or old, to do the same.

Another source of aviation knowledge was the Science Museum, which had the trans-Atlantic Vickers Vimy suspended from the roof, along with other exotic aircraft such as the Supermarine S.6B which had won the Schneider Trophy, and a Fokker Eindecker. In those happy prewar days, entrance to all the Museums was free, and once I learned how to get to Kensington, I spent many hours there. In particular, there was a period when a Bristol Bulldog and a Camel (familiar from Biggles books) were suspended over the staircase near the entrance. It was to be another 13 years before I saw that Camel again at Hendon, but 60 years before I saw the Bulldog close up once more, when Skysport's magnificent rebuild was unveiled at the RAF Museum. Had I but known it, the Imperial War Museum was just a few miles from Kensington, but it might have been as distant as the moon – I finally got there after the war, but some of the exhibits such as the Short 184 were, alas, destroyed in the Blitz.

There was little in the way of aeroplane toys that came my way – one I remember particularly well was a beautifully constructed and shaped gull-wing monoplane in tinplate. It was about 15 inches in span, with a clockwork motor that drove the prop and underwing bomb releases; suspended on thread from the ceiling it would fly in circles, progressively dropping four little lead bombs (with percussion caps) in pairs. Alas, it needed parental assistance to get it suspended so it flew on only a few occasions, on the last of which the thread broke with obvious results. It was painted in all-over light grey with insignia somewhat like the Jugoslav markings, and I have since identified it as a very good scale model of the Polish PZL P8/11. Who made it and where it came from I shall probably never know. Another thread-suspended model was an accurate Dinky Toy scale model of the Cierva C.30 autogyro of about, I would guess, 1/36th scale, in blue with white trim. From a cord suspended at one end higher than the other, it would trundle down rotating the rotor slowly and airscrew rapidly, both being gear-driven by a pulley wheel, hidden in the rotor head, on which it sat on the cord. There were of course other Dinky Toy aircraft of which I can recall only an AW Ensign (or it may have been an Atlanta!).

I never got into aircraft modelling in any big way until after I was evacuated with my school in 1939. A cousin showed me how to make folded paper aeroplanes and airships, from which I learned a little about the importance of getting the balance right and the effects of tabs on wing and tail trailing edges. My *"Wonderland of Knowledge"* books had several plans for making small models from card, which flew after a fashion. I made up several solid models from wood, which I wasn't very good at, having neither the tools, skill or the right material to do it properly: a Percival Gull painted in the blue and white scheme depicted on a cigarette card was one. Much better results were obtained with

Plasticine, using pins for wing and undercarriage struts. The one flying model with which I had any success was the little rubber-powered Frog 'Imp,' with its balsa wings, pressed paper fuselage, black plastic prop and red plastic wheels, which could be bought for sixpence from Woolworths, and I had several of these. Nothing my grandchildren can buy today represents such good value and flies as well! But then Frog were so unbeatable at flying models, from the Interceptor to the fabulous Hawker Hart. The Interceptor at 5/- was out of my reach, and the Hart, at 42/-, represented a week's wages for some adults! I can recall vividly watching a boy a little younger than myself, out in Gladstone Park with his Nanny, attempting to fly a Hart. Neither she nor he had the faintest idea of how to launch it into the air and I felt like crying when after several futile attempts they finally got it up at too steep an angle, only to have it stall straight back in and disintegrate into crumpled pieces.

Evacuation in September 1939 was something of a turning point in my life. I was at Kilburn Grammar School, having won a scholarship at 'eleven-plus' time (it didn't work out as I lost the first six weeks of the very first term due to bronchitis, and never caught back up!). At the evacuation station the school party was split into two groups, my group boarding the wrong train and finishing up at Market Harborough, whereas the main group went correctly to Northampton. There they started school on a half-day basis, sharing with an equivalent Grammar School. My party however, was virtually 'lost' to the authorities and attempts to have us similarly share with our local Grammar School came to nothing. We were eventually 'discovered' and left for Northampton on a black day in November. In the meantime however we were having a whale of a time for two glorious months in a golden Indian Summer – no school, no parental restrictions, in the course of which I made two major discoveries. One was how the rest of the school lived, four of us being billeted with the family of the General Manager of Symington's Soups (the major employer in Market Harborough at that time); this was a real eye-opener for me, an entirely different standard of life with gentle people (in the real meaning of the word), way beyond anything I had experienced before. The other was an exciting introduction to building flying model aircraft, which opened up a whole new world.

At home, pocket money had been almost non-existent and there were no opportunities to earn money for youngsters such as myself. With the onset of war, employment had been picking up and both my parents were now working so that when I was evacuated, I was given a sum of money to buy necessities and started receiving occasional further payments in the form of Postal Orders for one or two shillings at a time. These were princely sums indeed, not to be squandered on sweets etc. Instead, I and one or two of my classmates discovered a toyshop in town which had seemingly inexhaustible stocks of model aircraft kits. The cheapest of these were American Guillows and Megows; ninepence would buy a 16 in-span kit of a whole range of WW1 biplanes, Camels, SE.5As, Nieuports, Spads, Fokkers etc., mostly complete with everything needed to build the model except shrinking dope. Some even included little tubes of balsa cement. The only sombre note about this perfect new world I had been thrust into was when the shopkeeper told us one day: "Make the most of it boys, you'll never see the like of this again." How right he was. When questioned he explained that when his present stocks had gone he would not be able to order any more, coming as they did from the USA. And we did run him out of stock; by the time we moved on there were no more cheap kits to be had in the town, and the last few we bought had suddenly increased in price to a shilling! It didn't matter that the models flew badly or not at all. Gradually we learned how best to build them and eventually how to get them to fly, culminating for me in a Fokker D.VII whose movable, horn-balanced control surfaces enabled it to be trimmed properly. Launched from my upstairs bedroom window it was finally persuaded to make long straight flights before coming to earth in a flat glide.

Returning home in February 1940, when everyone was beginning to think nothing dangerous was actually going to happen, it took a while to get me into Willesden County School, the only remaining Secondary School in my area. Schooling was not exactly well-organised and by the time the headmaster had got things running on a reasonable basis the Battle of Britain had started and we spent endless days in the shelters where, if nothing else, I learnt how to play solo whist! By August my mother and I had moved to Horsham, returning in November for the London Blitz! At Horsham I had a golden opportunity to watch the sky-borne comings and goings with the contrails weaving overhead, and being shot at by a low-flying (200 ft?) Dornier Do.17Z chased by a Hurricane (whose guns could be heard when it despatched the Dornier a few minutes later). We survived the blitz, the nearest bomb falling in my road about twelve houses away. Each morning my friends and I would be out searching the road for shrapnel, some of these being terrifying shards of jagged metal up to four inches long. Back at school, I realised there was no way that I could catch up with the subjects being taught sufficiently to pass the Matriculation exams the following year, and eventually I persuaded my mother that I should leave school and learn a trade. And so, eventually, to Park Royal Coachworks as an Apprentice Pattern-Maker, where I learnt how to read manufacturing drawings, handle wood- and metal-working tools, and operate machine tools such as lathes and grinders. At last I got close to some real aircraft, as we were building Halifax outer wings as part of the London Aircraft Production Group.

Around 1941 I got back into building flying models again, starting with an *"Aeromodeller"* design, the Air Cadet, which must have served as an introduction to countless thousands of lads like me. By now, materials were in very short supply, though the situation improved slightly as the war went on, and it was mainly a question of hunting out those shops which still had small stocks of balsa, tissue and rubber. With some of my friends we started up again the old Willesden & District Model Flying Club, hiring again the old prewar basement clubroom which had been closed in September '39. It was like digging back into the past: the room had not been entered since then and a number of flying models hung from the ceiling, just as they had been left at the last meeting. We wondered then how many of those modellers had survived that far into the war, and how different it would be for them if they ever returned.

In 1943 at 17¼ I was finally old enough to volunteer for aircrew duties with the RAF. Two disappointments awaited me here: because I had not matriculated I could not be considered for Pilot/Navigator/-Bomb-Aimer duties and had to be content with Wireless Op/AG. And because I was employed in building aircraft I was in a reserved occupation and could not be called up for Service – ouch! But I was advised that I was expected to join the ATC, 'benefiting' from the semi-Service atmosphere and drilling, Morse Code and aircraft recognition instruction; the latter I liked, the former I did not, and it and the thought of giving up Sunday mornings to church and drill parades was what had put me off joining before. At least in return we all got an occasional chance to fly; such chances were extremely rare however, as all the London ATC Squadrons had just a few local airfields for such visits, ours being Hendon which we shared with probably 20 other Squadrons. Whenever we were scheduled to go there the weather seemed to be at its worst, but here I finally got my first flight, ten minutes in a Dominie. Before the flight I feared the worst, that I would not like it or that I would be airsick, an all-to-common experience amongst the lads (who were always expected to clean up the mess after landing!). But once strapped in, the tremor felt through the seat and the floor as the engines were opened up, the slightly bouncy take-off from the grass, and the thrill on looking out along the wings as we banked steeply, seemingly pirouetting around the slender wingtip, all this was sheer magic, all I had ever dreamed it would be.

I only got three flights from Hendon – another Dominie where I made sure that I sat in the seat behind the pilot where the view out was not blanketed by the wings, and in the co-pilot's seat of a USAAF Norseman going to Northolt and back. This was the only flight in which we were going 'cross-country' (in this case 'cross-urban') and I marvelled that the pilot could pick out the destination airfield or keep track of where he was going. He said that it soon became second nature but that at first he had difficulty because of the closeness of the airfields compared with back home in the USA, where the fields were all spaced well apart. There were annual weekend camps where one was almost guaranteed to get in a number of flights in operational-type aircraft, but the only one I attended was to RAF Wing, a Wellington OTU. Would you believe that the weekend we were there all the aircraft were on standby for operational flying on a 1,000-bomber raid. Because they were all tanked-up and armed with ammunition and bombs, we weren't even allowed to visit the aircraft in their dispersal bays!

Another 'nearly' flight was on a free-lance visit to USAAF Bovingdon just after D-Day. We had found that our ATC uniforms would get us past the gate guards at Bovingdon with no questions asked. Once in we could roam freely round the field and climb aboard any of the aircraft, which were almost all transport and communications machines. Whilst looking at a Cessna Bobcat the pilot turned up and climbed in; I asked him if there was any chance of a flight and he said: "Sure, climb aboard." I thought I had better check where he was going and he told me Cherbourg. Wow, over into France, an unrepeatable opportunity to see the beaches and landing ships from the air. When was he returning, I asked, and he replied, not for some days. My heart sank when I realised that I had told no one where I was going, with no way of getting a message home to tell them not to worry if I failed to turn up that night. Reluctantly I had to turn away, and ever since have regretted doing so and wondered whether everything would have turned out OK if I had gone.

But there was one prize flight that came my way and even now I find it hard to believe my luck. We were invited to visit de Havilland's at Leavesden, where they repaired Mosquitoes: there was one Mosquito that had to be flight-tested while we were there, with an opportunity for one cadet to go up in it. Somehow I made sure it was me and that was one unforgettable flight, the only time (other than on Concorde) I have seen over 400 mph indicated; I was inadvertently re-enacting photographs I had seen of aircrew suffering facial distortion under high-'g' turns – as we pulled out of high-speed dives I could feel myself being forced uncontrollably down into the seat, arms pinned down each side and my jaw, lips and eyelids sagging. Gee (or 'g'), that was great!

With the war nearing its end Halifax production was terminated, and in March I found myself looking for a job. Following up an advert in *"Flight"* I landed one with Woodason Aircraft Models at Heston Airport, making non-flying scale models for a variety of purposes. The biggest was a six-foot long, battle-damaged Lancaster fuselage for the film *"A Matter of Life and Death,"* but mostly at that time they were recognition models of Japanese and Russian aircraft for the Air Ministry and museum models for Blackburn Aircraft and the Science Museum.

Heston was an interesting place, with Spitfires being test-flown from one side of the airfield and Fairey Fireflies and the ungainly prototype Spearfish from the other. There were always USAAF visitors, including a damaged B-17G which I found jacked up in a hangar one day. I simply could not resist climbing into the ball turret with my knees round my ears and marvelling both at the design ingenuity and engineering skill that could produce such a weapon, and the gunners who would go to war in them. It easily accommodated my 5 ft 9 in and was surprisingly comfortable for the few minutes that I was in there, and the view through the oval sighting window much better than I expected. But I was soon routed out by the foreman in the hangar who blasted me off for the danger he felt I was in – if the aircraft had fallen off its jacks I would have been in compressed trouble with the whole weight descending on the turret, but to me it was inconceivable that the fitters would have made that bad a job of jacking and securing it!

For years I had been expectantly waiting for the day when, after the war was won (and I never had any doubts that we would win it), there would be some sort of public exhibition of captured enemy aircraft, on the lines of that held at Olympia after the first World War. I simply could not believe my atrocious bad luck to be called up for service with the RAF in September 1945, after the end of hostilities, and to be on a square-bashing course at Greenham Common when the expected display of German aircraft was held at Farnborough. There was no way I could get to that fabulous one-off display: all I could do was to glower at the few poor-quality black & white pictures that appeared in *"Aeroplane"* and *"Flight"* when reporting on it. For such as I there was no more aircrew training at that time and, faced with the standard choice of batman, cook, general duties erk, RAF Regiment or Accounts Clerk (or radar fitter if I signed on for umpteen years) I chose Equipment Accounts Clerk – well, what would you have done?

On the Trade Course, for the only occasion in the 30 months I spent in the RAF, I was actually on a Unit which had an aircraft in its grounds – a tidy Mustang Mk. 1, a remnant from the days when they ran fitters' courses there. We passed it most mornings on the way to the classrooms but I was never actually able to get close enough to examine it. For the rest of my Service career I was on Personnel Dispersal Units in the UK and, fortunately for my sanity, with an Airfield Construction Unit at St. Hubertus in Germany from Xmas '46. At least at the latter I was able to get into RAF Blankensee (Lubeck) airfield (not past the gate guards but unofficially through a hole in the fence – the RAF still didn't want me anywhere near their aircraft!! – and wander round the aircraft dump). This contained wrecked German and RAF aircraft, including Me.109s (yes, I know about Bf.109s!), Me.110s, Ju.88s, Ju.188s, He.177s and even a couple of Arado Ar.234s, together with Meteors from recent RAF exercises. In the woods surrounding the airfield were many dispersal areas containing dozens of Fw.190 wrecks, still there when I left for demob in February '48.

Returning to Woodason's I found things had changed almost out of recognition. Work became scarce and eventually I had to leave. Fortunately another modelling company had gained some new contracts and was expanding, which saw me arrive at the Eaton Bray Model Sportsdrome to work for Dagra Models (<u>D.A.</u> & <u>Gra</u>ce Russell) under Eddie Riding. The significant thing here was that Eddie was organising a series of Air Displays, among the first postwar events. Here I met up with Dominies again, used for joyriding, and such aircraft as Tiger Moths, Magisters, Messengers, Proctors and Austers, and learned how to swing a propeller. Eddie occasionally hired a Piper Cub (G-AKAA) and took me up several times, and for the first time ever I was able to handle the controls – I was hooked, but Eddie's unfortunate death when a passenger in an Auster Autocar put a stop to that and it took me another fourteen years before I could do anything more. Now married and struggling in buying, first a caravan to live in and, later, a house, followed by a larger one, with a family expanding to three sons and a daughter, I was 37 before being able to fulfil my earliest ambition in life – to be a pilot.

M.J.BRETT '82

CHAPTER 2
GAINING WINGS

Put it down to one of those peculiar quirks of fate that I ever managed to get a pilot's licence at all. After leaving the RAF in 1948 I worked at home as a sub-contractor for a while, in the course of which I allowed our insurance agent to talk me into taking out an insurance policy for £100, the weekly payments being very small, spread as they were over 15 years. At that time, things were barely moving in the direction of a return to prewar conditions, but in my ignorance I thought they would eventually get back to them. Then it had been possible to buy a new car for £105 (the 8 hp Ford Popular) and I thought that if nothing else, when the policy matured in 1964 I could use it for that! With hindsight, how could I have been that stupid?

I more or less forgot all about it as the years passed and it came as quite a surprise when I was informed that it was about to mature, and with bonuses would be worth £125. This caused a certain amount of consternation at home as my wife and I went through all the possible uses to which we should put this manna from Heaven – it would obviously be insufficient to use even as a deposit on a new car, not that we could have afforded the subsequent monthly payments. It had to be something worthwhile and of lasting effect and in the end, after I had discovered that the sum was sufficient to buy a full PPL course at Luton Flying Club, we settled on that – my eternal gratitude goes to my wife for giving up all the necessities and niceties she could have spent it on! What follows is an hour-by-hour outline of my experiences, from detailed notes I made at the time.

Preparatory steps were to obtain copies of *"Flight Briefing for Pilots Vol. 1"* by Alan Bramson (from the library) and *"The Student and Private Pilot's Handbook"* by H.Edwards, the latter proving of lasting benefit as an *aide memoire* right through my flying life. In those days the pilot's medical could be carried out by one's GP and optician, using a form obtained from the Ministry of Aviation at Shell Mex House, and I seem to recall my doctor (an ex-RFC pilot) waiving his usual charge of 5/- for a private examination just because it was a pilot's medical! A Student Pilot's Licence valid for one year was duly obtained from the Ministry and I was all set to go.

At that time, and for some years beyond, MoA-approved Flying Schools were able to offer 30-hour courses provided they were completed in six months, otherwise a minimum of 40 hours was required if spread over a longer period or taken with a non-approved organisation such as a private-membership Group. The costs either way were roughly the same, Group rates being generally proportionally less. But, everyone I asked said the same, a professional School or Club could get the job done in the six months but it would be more likely to take a couple of years to get in 40 hours of instruction with a Group and the longer the elapsed time the more certain it was that it would take more than 40 hours to get the licence! The other factor to be determined was what sort of aircraft to train on. I had set my heart on learning to fly on Tiger Moths, but I soon found that it was going to cost significantly more to do so locally. The reason for this was the higher operating and maintenance costs of the Tiger – whilst the purchase price of a Tiger at that time was considerably less than say an Auster J/1N (typically £600 against £1,200) Tigers were often grounded by weather conditions which the Austers could take in their stride (principally limiting wind conditions – 15 kt and 25 kt respectively); Tigers were reputedly more prone to damage (due to lack of wheel brakes?) and certainly out of action more frequently than Austers. This proved to be the case at Luton Flying Club (LFC) where I eventually chose to take my course.

There was little choice of Flying School where I lived. Luton Flying Club, 16 miles away, operated a number of aircraft ranging from Austers, Chipmunks, a solitary Tiger Moth, Tri-pacers and several other exotic but expensive American aircraft. Of these, only the Austers at £4.12.6 an hour or the Tiger at £5 per hour came within my bracket. However, buying 30 hours in advance reduced the Auster rate to £4.2.6 per hour. The other choice was Cambridge Flying Club (20 miles distant) who operated Tigers at £4.15.0 per hour. Elstree was further away, their rates were somewhat higher, and it was also a much busier airfield. So Luton it was, especially as I would frequently go flying straight from work at Stevenage, when the distances became very much more favourable to Luton (10 miles against 25!).

I still hankered after the Tiger Moth, but when on Saturday 6th June, 1964, I met Dave Campbell (the CFI) he pointed out that I would need to purchase protective clothing, helmet and goggles: instructors could find all sorts of reasons for not using the uncomfortable and cold, open-cockpit Tiger if the weather was at all 'iffy': the Gosport tube intercom used on the Tiger made communication that much more difficult. Their sole Tiger was, not unusually, out of action at that time, whereas their three Austers were rarely unserviceable for more than a day: on the Auster I would learn to use flaps and brakes. The general feeling was that if I learnt on Austers and could cope with their built-in 'bounce' (on landing) I would be better equipped to fly anything else. Besides which, they would probably sell the Tiger as soon as they could find a buyer! Did I get the impression he was trying to tell me something?

Once I had impressed on Dave that I really wanted to go ahead, had a rough inkling of what was involved and that I had flown in light aircraft before, he suggested I take a 20-minute trial lesson there and then. He wanted to satisfy himself that I was not too ham-fisted and that I would want to continue beyond a trial lesson before I signed up for the full 30 hours. He also intimated that at 37 I was getting just a little long in the tooth and that it might take somewhat more than 30 hours to get my licence! It needed no 20-minute test to confirm my intent, but I had gone there about learning to fly and then was as good a time as any other to start. My second son Terry (then nine) was with me and I asked if it was OK for him to accompany us; Dave agreed to that but indicated it was a pity that he wouldn't be able to demonstrate a spin with Terry aboard. If anything was likely to show any hesitation on my part there was nothing better than a spin to do that!

Initiation

Sitting close by on the tarmac was G-AGXH, an Auster J/1N Alpha (J/1 Autocrat modified by having the 100 hp Cirrus Minor replaced by a 130 hp Gipsy Major 1, and fitted with a taller, horn-balanced rudder). LFC had two others, 'IGT and 'IJI, identical in all respects except that 'IJI had aerobatically-stressed seats, a comparatively vast and uncomfortable rubber grip on the control column and an inverted compass mounted up on the cabane struts instead of the more usual P11 compass mounted centrally on the floor. All were finished in aluminium dope with red upper nose cowl, cheat lines, and registration letters.

The instructor took me through the simple pre-flight checks, so simple as to look positively primitive. Flap the control surfaces up and down, checking for full and free movement, heave on the wingtips looking for no movement at the wingroot or strut attachments (mentioning that two weeks earlier that had revealed a loose wing-root bolt), repeat on the tailplane, listening for a dull bass note when the bracing wires were twanged with the finger tips. Finally, having satisfied himself that everything that should move did, and nothing that shouldn't didn't, we climbed aboard (with me in the right-hand seat) and strapped ourselves in. Dave went quickly through the cockpit and starting drills, the prop was swung by an engineer, and after a very brief warm-up, we moved off. I was asked to place my feet lightly on the rudder pedals during taxying but to remove them during take-off. We waited on the grass for a green light from the Tower, then taxied to the downwind end of the field, with a running commentary from Dave on the use of the heel brakes, rudder bar and throttle. One notch of flap, throttle to fully open, and with that old familiar engine roar and vibration (which I hadn't experienced for some 13 years) we bumped across the grass, rapidly gathering speed until, with a quick bound, our nose was pointing skyward, the roughness stopped and the ground was falling away beneath us.

We climbed out at full revs with 60-70 mph showing on the A.S.I., until Dave levelled off at 2,000 ft. Then he went through the operation of the controls with me resting hands and feet on them lightly, and finally allowed me to take over, sitting there with his arms visibly folded. So this was it – I had waited a long time for this. Gingerly I did as instructed, pulled the stick back and watched the horizon drop away beneath the nose. I remembered what I had read so many times and glanced at the A.S.I. which looked reassuring enough, but I wasn't sorry when told to ease the stick forward and saw the horizon come climbing back up the windscreen: the revs increased and the airspeed went up accordingly. All very reassuring – exactly as the books had said. Back to straight and level, bank to the left, bank to the right, rudder to the left, then to the right. I had flown several times as a passenger but apart from a very brief few minutes with Eddie Riding at the controls of his Cub (merely attempting then to keep it straight and level), this was the first time I had the controls to myself. I was allowed to experiment a little, swinging the nose left or right, up or down and finding it much easier than my memories of the Cub.

As expected, the controlling of an aircraft provided a sensation quite unlike anything I had tried previously – there is simply nothing to compare with it. The nearest other thing experienced before was riding speedway bikes on cinder tracks in Germany, drifting round corners using the handlebars to control the front wheel and the throttle to swing the rear wheel out, whilst maintaining vertical balance with the steel-shod left foot and right leg 'hook' and footrest. But that is like comparing two-dimensional with three-dimensional – it simply cannot be done. Even flying a radio-control model aircraft or computer simulator does not provide the sensory feedback you get from the movement of the aircraft.

After what seemed far too brief a period, I was told to head back to the airport which, somewhat to my surprise, had suddenly appeared in the lower left corner of the windscreen. Previous air experience had shown that airfields come and go mysteriously – I never could locate my position when in the air and how that airport had appeared in front of us I could not imagine. From the air, landmarks familiar on the ground may become lost in the general flatness of the terrain when viewed from above; other features not obvious on the ground become all-important – the shape of the sprawl of a town, the pattern of roads, railways, rivers, lakes and woods – a whole new 'language' to learn!

Dave took control and we were soon back on the ground. After parking the Auster we went into Dave's office to discuss the routine. We agreed that I should carry on with the course and that I would pay for the lot in advance to take advantage of the contract rate (£123.15.0) and this would include the 20-minute trial flight just completed, which was logged as 'Effects of Controls.' I joined LFC as a Club Member (£3 per annum) and bought a pilot's kit – the basic essentials including MoA booklet CAP46 (Radio-Telephony procedure), CAP53 (The Student Pilot's and Private Pilot's Licences), CAP85 (Aviation Law), a copy of

"Flight Briefing for Pilots Vol. 1," a local 1:250,000 flying map, sundry Shell BP booklets, a rule giving miles and nautical miles in all the major map scales, an Airnava 360 deg protractor and, most prized of all, my first Pilot's Flying Logbook, all in a smart, zipped Flightcase, the whole lot costing the princely total of £3 and most of them still in use today!

Another small but rather necessary expense was insurance. Ordinary Life Insurance does not cover flying except at a handsome premium; through the Club it was possible to insure life and limb against flying accidents to the extent of £1 for £1,000 up to a maximum of £3,000 cover. Such figures seem almost meaningless these days, but then they gave a certain peace of mind – £2,000 would have paid off my mortgage!

With the preliminaries completed I booked two hours that weekend, one for that evening and the other on Sunday afternoon. The weather had been reasonable that morning but by the evening a stiff wind was blowing and low clouds had reduced visibility to the extent that when I rang the Flight Office I was told that flying was washed out. This was repeated on Sunday, the first two of many frustrating cancellations which came my way! Not an auspicious start but I booked a further four hours during the following week and kept my fingers crossed!

Effects of controls, power & trim

My boss (an ex-RAF prewar pilot who had flown Hawker Furies with 1 Sqdn.) had agreed that, providing I made sure there was no real inter-ruption with my work schedules, I could take time off on a half-day basis as required. The first hour was on a beautiful sunny Tuesday morning, a clear blue sky with just a light breeze, giving conditions which could not have been more ideal – the excitement of actually learning to fly was even further enhanced by a feeling of truancy. What a day and for what a reason to be off work!

I was introduced to my instructor, Elizabeth Overbury, and to our aeroplane – Alpha 'IGT. Elizabeth had a Commercial ticket, and I believe later became the first woman First Pilot to fly with a scheduled airline (I forget which). I had no qualms about women instructors, and she turned out to be the best of the bunch, with a gentle but firm and reassuring manner which brought out the best in me.

First step was to inspect the aircraft and ensure it was correctly positioned for starting. Commencing at the wing-root trailing edge on the port (pilot's) side we walked slowly right round the aircraft, checking flaps, ailerons, wing struts, engine cowlings, oil level, propeller, under-carriage, tail unit for security and, where appropriate, operation – also looking out for obvious damage or wrinkled fabric on all surfaces and, before climbing aboard, checking for loose objects in the cabin.

With me in the pilot's seat we strapped in and carried out the cockpit checks. Operation of the elevator trim (to all intents and purposes a car window winder set in the roof above the throttle quadrant), control column and rudder pedals (producing the correct movements of ailerons, elevators and rudder), and flap lever above and behind the pilot's left shoulder (locked by a sleeve that had to be pushed forward to unlock, up or down to raise or lower the flaps, then pulled back to lock in the correct position, a very awkward control to operate initially and always ten times more so in the air than on the ground!): setting of the twin magneto switches (DOWN for OFF), throttle closed (fully rearward) and friction nut slack, petrol ON, altimeter reading (zero feet), handbrake ON: check sufficient fuel for the flight, all instrument glasses in place. Phew! I would never remember that lot.

Then came the starting procedure: "Check and repeat the instructions called out by the flight mechanic." "Switches OFF – petrol ON – throttle closed – suck in," and the mechanic turned the propeller through four revolutions to prime each cylinder. "Throttle SET" (and Elizabeth cracked the throttle open perhaps one quarter inch), "contact" (and she pushed the starboard switch knob up), the mechanic swung the propeller blade sharply down and the engine fired immediately. The instructor pushed the second switch up and blipped the engine revs up briefly before allowing it to tick over at 800 rpm, at the same time checking the oil pressure. The engine had already been warmed up and run up to check max. revs at the start of the day's operations, so Elizabeth waved the chocks away and taxied clear of the line, asking me to try the heel-brakes (two little pedals on the floor in front of the rudder pedals, fitted on the port (pilot's) side only; "gently or we may tip on our nose."

When we got to the end of the runway we stopped, facing any approaching aircraft and carried out our pre-take-off checks. Engine at 800 rpm; check the elevator Trim is at neutral; tighten the Throttle friction nut; check that the Mixture control is at fully rich; set the Flaps down 15 deg (the first of three notches on the quadrant); check Fuel ON; Harnesses tight; and Hatches closed (mnemonic "TTMFFHH"); check oil pressure is between 30 and 60 psi and oil temperature 15 to 80 deg C; pull the stick fully back whilst pressing both heel brakes fully on and run up the engine to 1,800 rpm, switching off each magneto in turn and noting that the resulting revs drop is less than 100 rpm in each case, then back to tickover; check the altimeter still at zero feet (airfield surfaces can be quite undulating); check the controls again; and, finally, check there are no aircraft on their final approach for landing.

We turned, watching the Control Tower for a continuous green, then, when it came, Elizabeth opened the throttle fully, held the Auster down until the A.S.I. showed above 40 mph and then eased back on the stick – and up we went. At 300 ft with 60-70 mph on the A.S.I. I was told to raise the flaps and we sailed on up to our operating height of 1,500 ft. First we repeated the exercises of my initial flight, checking the effects of the controls, both primary and secondary. The latter were demonstrated by banking first with ailerons alone, noting that the nose dropped slightly and that the aircraft turned in the direction of the bank, then by yawing with rudder alone, the aircraft dropping a wing in the direction of the yaw and losing height. This was followed by straight and level flying at cruising revs, medium (Rate 1) turns, and the effects of increasing and decreasing power and adjusting the trim for the changes. The latter brought in my second mnemonic, APT – Attitude, Power and Trim. All too soon I was told to fly straight and level, maintaining 2,000 ft and 1,900 rpm, back to the airport; this I did, with considerable satisfaction at being able to do just that. I lowered the flaps, not without a struggle (trying each hand), and Elizabeth landed the aircraft.

With this and all subsequent lessons, there followed a debriefing back in the Clubhouse, going over what had been covered, and points to watch out for. It should be noted that the Austers were not equipped with radio, control being effected by Aldis Lamp signals from the Tower. We had no intercom, communication being by raised voice over the engine roar, any points that the instructor felt were essential to be made clearly being preceded by throttling back to a more comfortable level. I learnt to fly without a helmet or headphones and never felt comfortable with head-phones on when subsequently accompanying friends whose aircraft was equipped with radio. I never missed the radio and cannot remember any occasion on which I regretted not having one! Perhaps because I could never unravel the gobbledygook that came over? – or more likely I enjoyed the freedom of the air and making my own decisions (whilst observing flying's "ten commandments").

Turns, climbing, level, taxying

My second hour was at 6.30 in the evening two days later, with a stiffish breeze and stacks of cumulus – the big, fluffy, friendly grey and white clouds. This time we were in 'IJI but with the same instructor. We took off as before with the instructor pointing out the attitude of climb, the revs and the airspeed during the climb; at about 1,500 ft I was told to take over and hold her in the climb, levelling out at 2,000 ft. I found that 'IJI might have been a different type of aeroplane for all the similarity of feel: the joystick had a seemingly vast rubber grip, the instrument panel was slightly different, the elevator trim felt completely different and the plane wanted to fly in left-hand circles – or so it seemed. On top of that there was a small hole in my perspex side window and all the air in the sky came rushing in at me. My confidence of two days earlier ebbed slowly away, helped on by the fact that the horizon was lost in a general haze and when flying straight and level could not be 'placed' on the windscreen.

Still, I gradually settled down to a program of climbing, gliding, with and without flap (the aircraft, not me), straight and level, and medium turns under all three conditions. APT took on a new meaning when levelling out from full climb or steep glide – in either condition the level attitude was to be attained first, followed by throttle adjustment to cruising revs, finally adjusting the trimmer for 'hands off' straight and level flight. For descending turns we needed to increase speed by 5 mph, by increasing power or dropping the nose further if gliding. Just when I thought I had mastered the turns – apply bank then a little bottom rudder to match, holding the nose on the horizon with a little up elevator, then holding off the bank (with a little opposite stick if climbing, or retaining bank if descending), contentedly watching the world slide from the top corner of the screen to somewhere behind the nose – I was reminded that the slip indicator should be nicely centred even during turns. That ruined my day, as for the rest of the turns on this flight I tried miserably to meet both requirements – smooth turn in the correct attitude and slip needle central – and never really quite managed both simultaneously!

But Elizabeth seemed reasonably satisfied with my progress to the point of allowing me to fly round the circuit for landing back at Luton, taking over the controls to land only after I had put on full flap on the final approach. My struggle to get the flaps down boded ill for the future when I had both to lower them and land!

The next two hours booked were scrubbed through bad weather and frustration was mounting, but I got a compensating hour on the following Sunday evening, booking a further hour on four of the following five evenings.

Turns, climbing, level, taxying (second)

This time I was back in 'IGT but with a new instructor, Howard Brunt. I had spent my previous hour getting used to 'IJI and now it all seemed different again – but we had a friendly horizon this time which helped no end. I was told to taxy out to the runway in use, which meant nearly half a mile of crosswind taxying. What an awkward beast a taildragger is in a crosswind! While I was trying to cope with the heel brakes – which seemed void of all 'feel' – 'IGT revealed that she could have a not inconsiderable mind of her own when on the ground. I made a miserable hash of taxying, nearly got tangled with an inconvenient Tiger Moth which fortunately was keeping a better lookout than I was, and finally nearly ran into the 'rough' at one point. Howard showed how easy it really was by putting us straight using rudder and power alone and eventually we reached the end of the runway.

This time on take-off I was told to take over the rudder controls and the instructor would do the rest. I swallowed hard, not through changes of altitude, and nodded dumbly, thinking of all the horrible things that could happen if I failed to keep it straight. It was the untidiest take-off to date as Howard juggled the throttle during the run and every time this happened we swung one way or the other – this way we learn! We got off and, incredibly, the instructor said encouragingly: "That was quite good." I thought it was awful, but realised later that he was deliberately swinging it about to see how well I could correct it.

The routine was much as before; to start with I was trying to fly 'IJI and 'IGT responded by persistently flying right wing low. I was convinced we were straight and level until Howard observed that the right wing was down on the horizon while the left wing was noticeably above it. This time I remembered to watch the slip indicator and it plagued me for the rest of the flight, though I think I was beating it towards the end. On my first turns I was too eager and turned without checking the sky was clear before doing so, being audibly reminded to do so without fail in future. This time we carried out Rate 4 turns, which at first convinced me we were about to pull the wings off. The drill was to bank to about 60-70 degrees whilst opening the throttle wide, pulling the stick back to turn and maintaining the nose on the horizon using a little top (opposite) rudder. It was exciting stuff but felt all wrong and after umpteen hundred degrees of turn I wasn't sorry to straighten out.

I was beginning to look at the Auster in a different light; it was a willing little beast with plenty of power when I knew what to do. I was also discovering that flying straight and level was no longer quite the tight-rope balancing act it had seemed at first. Flying back to the airport was a pleasant relaxation after our manoeuvring and I was now having time to look around and enjoy my flying. Howard took over when we were nearly back at the field and demonstrated the approach, circling to look at the ground signals area and noting the direction of the landing Tee, before letting down to 800 ft to the right of the runway (the 'dead side') to join the circuit.

Stalls and spins

The next evening the sky was cloudy at first, with a stiffish breeze. This time in 'GXH, I made a much better job of taxying out and the cockpit checks were coming a little more naturally. We faced into wind and Howard said: "Right, you take her off, you know what to do." Which was perfectly correct – I knew what should be done but the thought of actually putting it into practice was a little overwhelming. But there was no turning back, we had been given a 'green' and almost without thinking I had the throttle wide open and was frantically trying to counteract the swing to the right and keep the nose at the right attitude. Everything seemed to be happening at once and my hands (of which I seemingly had only half the required number) were suddenly very full of bumping, roaring, bouncing, kicking aeroplane. Miraculously, while I was still sorting out what to do next, the bumping stopped and I snatched a quick glance at the A.S.I. to see it registering 40 mph: we were flying and from then on control became normal again. Life was very sweet at that moment; what a docile pet the aircraft suddenly seemed when in its own element and how reassuringly it answered the controls.

I glanced at Howard who was sitting with his arms folded, grinning like an ape. I was convinced he must have helped us off but, when I reached 1,500 ft and throttled back so that we could talk, he assured me that he had his arms folded all the time and his feet clear of the rudder pedals. We climbed on up to 4,500 ft, just under the cloudbase, and the instructor then took over and flew up through a partial rift in the clouds, with the sun just visible through the dense white 'fog.' We emerged into a breathtaking, glistening white Arctic snowscape at 5,500 ft, skimming over the top of the undulating cloud mass, chasing our rainbow-haloed shadow up hill and down dale for several glorious minutes before climbing on up to 6,500 ft. This was the first time I had flown above the clouds and, no matter how much other aspects of flying may have become 'old hat,' it is something magic that has never lost its fascination – if ever I had to explain why I loved flying so much this would be the first reason!

Glimpses of shadowed countryside showed through breaks in the cloud, and we selected one such over which to practise stalls. I was shown what to do: sky and cockpit check, power off, nose up, stick well back and wait for it, stick forward slightly after the nose dropped to build up airspeed and then back, to regain altitude, opening the throttle whilst doing so. It all looked very easy, but I needed three attempts before I could get her stalled properly: I instinctively wanted to push the stick forward before she had fully stalled. Recovery was simple but I was far from being as 'clean' as the instructor.

The next exercise was spinning and for this we needed to go back below the cloud in order to have plenty of clear airspace below. Our original break in the clouds had closed up so we selected another, a long narrow canyon which took us halfway through the depth of the cloud before closing in around us and enshrouding us in a London-smog-like gloom. I was glad I had not got the controls as there was nothing to steer by except the instruments. When we emerged below the cloud, Howard demonstrated the spin: "Conditions as before for stalling but give it hard right (or left) rudder and pull the stick right back just before it stalls," and the bottom fell out of my world; we seemed to cartwheel over on to our back before going down vertically and rotating rapidly. "Opposite rudder to stop the turn, centralise all controls to convert into a dive, ease back on the stick and when the airspeed drops to 100 mph, full throttle"; and there we were in a reassuring climb again. After several attempts I managed what passed as a spin and recovery. Then followed a spiral dive and a stall recovery using power, after which I was quite happy to fly in a sane manner back to the airport.

"Do a circuit and approach as I did last night," from Howard, who then lapsed into silence, broken only when I confessed unhappily that I had forgotten to keep to the right of the Tower when descending to circuit height, or look at the signals square. But the circuit passed off well enough though I was still having difficulty in getting the flaps down. Howard landed, and when we stopped I remarked that I thought I would never be able to get the plane back on the ground; during the approach I had wanted more height and would have pulled the nose up more, and held it down on the 'sink' onto the ground. He grinned and said: "We'll have a ten-minute break and do another hour, and then you'll see." Well, I suppose I had asked for it.

Circuits

'IJI was standing by the tarmac, ready and refuelled. I checked her out, started up and taxied out to the end of the runway. The convection clouds had almost disappeared and the wind had dropped considerably by now, making taxying a relatively simple matter. Amazingly, 'IJI's brakes had more 'feel' in them – or was it me?

The instructor said he would take off, do a normal circuit and landing and then, having followed him on the controls, I should repeat it for him. Oh dear! He made it look incredibly easy and I thought I knew *what* to do and *when*, but when it came to my turn I made all sorts of hashes. For one thing I had just been introduced to the compass, and attempted to make use of it on my downwind leg to check that I was running parallel to the runway. This was a major error because by the time I had it lined up, my turning point for base leg was far behind; I had not done my downwind checks either and I remarked that we seemed to have gone too far. "I thought you were doing a cross-country," said the sphinx at my side. I retrieved this one by rejoining the circuit halfway down the base leg – highly undesirable but it was now late in the evening and there was nothing else in the sky. Having rejoined I left closing the throttle for too long, forgot to trim for the glide and wrestled with that wretched flap lever for so long that by the time I got the flaps down we had passed our turning point and were several hundred feet too high! I finally got roughly onto the correct line of approach but now failed to correctly pick out the landing area which was at an angle to the trimmed grass area. I suppose I would have finished up in one of the hangars had I carried on but Harold made an overshoot correction and pulled round for another circuit.

I went round again, much more tidily this time but again started my downwind checks too late. "Never mind those now, that farm sliding beneath us is your turning point and we don't want another cross-country on this circuit!" from Howard. Again on the base leg I forgot the trim and struggled too long with the flap lever, but we eventually got onto the correct line of approach and very quickly I was committed to going in.

A little throttle to save an undershoot, and we seemed to be spot on, glide path correct, speed OK, attitude just about right. But when to level out? The ground seemed to rush up at us and I pulled back on the stick far too hard whilst still a little too high and we ballooned away from the ground. Howard gave a burst of throttle and told me to get on with the landing. Unfortunately I put the stick a little forward to level out when I should have kept it hard back and again the instructor had to retrieve the situation. While we were running along at 20 mph he said to take her off again and away we went.

After several more equally calamitous tries I finally managed to get it on the ground but not without banging and bouncing about all over the place. On one of the take-offs, Howard demonstrated the approved 'power failure on take-off' procedure, which was good fun. Subsequent landing attempts produced no better results and I was beginning to get ragged all round so we called it a day after 65 minutes. I felt a little disappointed for myself that I hadn't done better and rather sorry that I hadn't been able to reward my instructor's patience and persistence with at least one passable landing. That night at home I went through the process mentally dozens of times, trying to analyse my mistakes. I read up all the learned advice in my manuals and memorized the circuit plan so that I wouldn't forget the trim and the correct checks etc. At least flap lever handling had suddenly become more manageable in the process of repeated circuits, but this was little compensation for my miserable attempts to get the aircraft down satisfactorily.

Circuits (second)

The next evening I had another hour booked and despite a stiff breeze we carried on with the circuits and bumps. If ever an exercise was aptly named this was it, with the accent on the bumps! I profited from my reading the night before as my first circuit went off beautifully – I remembered everything at the right time, positioned the plane correctly on the approach, came in at the right speed – then did everything wrong again. I checked the descent too soon, then kept the nose too low and bounced, soaring back into the air, remembering this time however to open the throttle at mid-bounce. Round we went again and the same thing happened. What Howard was calling me under his breath I didn't know, but he took over, and I followed on the controls again. I knew what should be done but was experiencing extreme difficulty in judging just when to level out and how much to move the stick back; I also produced an instinctive forward movement of the stick once we had touched the ground which was all wrong for a glide approach. Anyway, round we went again on a 'short' circuit which the instructor was adopting in order to save time, and this time I got it in with a reasonable minimum of bounce or bump. Much cheering and clapping from Howard who said: "Right – now take it round on a full circuit and do it again."

Which I did – or nearly so. Flying round the circuit was very pleasant, control now seeming to come more naturally, and as we came back onto the approach I allowed the plane to settle down at what seemed the right attitude and speed; she touched down lightly and I congratulated myself on what seemed a perfect touchdown when I suddenly realised that the instructor had banged the throttle wide open and was yelling at me to keep the wings level. I looked over the side and we appeared to be about 30 ft up with the nose way up high and just above stalling speed. This was just about the rudest shock I had received; how I came to think we were on the ground when there was no bumping or banging from the undercarriage I cannot now imagine, but I soon woke up. Howard put it back on the ground in a powered descent and we stopped for breath.

Anyway, it seemed I was beginning to get the right idea because at this stage Howard asked what I would do in the case of engine failure on take-off. My answer was that I would 'stuff' the nose down straight away which seemed to be on the right lines, because I was reminded of the procedure the previous evening when he had carried out a dummy engine cut on the climb out. He told me to take off again and I was wondering how he was going to arrange an engine cut without me seeing what he was doing, but didn't notice the sleight of hand by which he closed the fuel cock.

Suddenly, at 400 ft, just as I had raised the flaps, the motor coughed and died. I did as I had said and 'stuffed' the nose down, picking up speed to some 80 mph, which of course was higher than needed. I flattened out, allowing the speed to fall off to 60 mph, closed the throttle, lowered the flaps one notch and headed for the nearest green field. Only then did I check the switches and fuel cock, finding the latter closed! After putting the fuel 'on' and what seemed an eternity, just when I was beginning to think I was really going to have to get into the field, the engine picked up, I slammed the throttle open wide and climbed thankfully back into the circuit. In those days we almost did it for real! And only later did I learn the error of my ways in 'slamming' open the throttle; progressive and smooth operation is advisable to avoid the possibility of a 'rich' cut or of damaging the engine!

We carried on circuiting and bumping for an hour and 25 minutes and I lost count of how many times we went round. Out of all of them, and it seemed like a dozen or so, I only managed to get the plane down three times, and only one of those was a passable, unaided landing. But strangely, I had no feeling of despair. It seemed that it would only be a matter of time before I saw the light, and apart from learning a lot of things not to do on a glide approach, normal handling now seemed quite routine. Admittedly, it still required a fair amount of concentration to keep the slip needle vertical, but flap operation and trimming were becoming a lot easier and these two had caused me a certain amount of trouble on earlier flights. On counting up my total flying time at this stage I found it almost unbelievable that it amounted to no more than 6 hrs 45 mins – it seemed so much longer!

Circuits (third)

The following two hours booked were washed out by weather, a thunderstorm breaking out just as I was starting up on the second of these. I was anxious to get cracking again while everything was still fresh in my mind, and the delay was most frustrating but I managed to book an hour the following morning, a Saturday. In the meantime I discussed with my boss the problems I was having, and mentioned that I had been advised to look at the grass and when I could pick out individual blades that would be the correct height to flatten out – but it hadn't worked for me at all. He suggested that I should think of the height to level out as being like sitting on the top deck of a bus, and to look ahead and not at the grass! I likened the top deck height of a bus as being about the same as my upstairs windows at home, and spent time getting accustomed to recognising what the lawn looked like from that height.

The wind had changed and we were using a different runway which had a much more straightforward approach. I was back with Elizabeth in 'IGT, and she did a circuit to show me the different turning points and approach, and I felt happier with the new approach path. On my first circuit everything clicked quite nicely and on the approach I remembered to look further ahead than I had before. Checking the descent a little higher (from upstairs window height at home!), we levelled out at – I would guess – about 12 ft and, as the speed and height fell off, I eased the stick gently back and we settled down with only a minor bounce. It worked!! Suddenly I felt I knew what I was doing and what had been wrong on previous attempts; this was important as earlier I had seemed to be getting on the ground more by good luck than judgement and hadn't really appreciated why some landings were no worse than bad and some impossible.

My next attempt would show whether I was right or not and to my immense relief and intense satisfaction the next landing was also a good one. We carried on for a total of 75 minutes and all the landings were happy ones. I had a satisfied feeling that on my next hour, booked for the following evening, I would go solo. That night I went over the landings in my mind and began to wonder whether or not I should be able to repeat them the following day, and almost convinced myself that I would not!

Circuits (fourth)

Sunday started out as a rather miserable-looking day but by the evening had cleared sufficiently to suggest that flying might be possible. My wife and children came along to watch and, if I did go solo, to take some pictures. We were using yet another runway so again Elizabeth (once more in 'IGT) did the first circuit to show me the layout. I took over and on my first approach felt that I was undershooting a little and corrected with power during the glide, making a reasonable landing. That my fears of the previous evening were unjustified was shown by the next three or four landings. Now I knew that I had the bogey beaten and was really enjoying the circuits; I found that a good landing gave immeasurable satisfaction and one that remained very clear in my mind was when the tailwheel touched just before the main wheels and the aircraft seemed to run a few feet on the tailwheel alone before the main wheels settled with scarcely a bump.

And then came the big moment when Elizabeth asked if I felt like doing one on my own. With a reminder of all the things I was not to forget and an encouraging "Good luck – but don't forget to pick me up," she climbed out and left me to it. I taxied up to the end of the runway and sat facing downwind while I went through my checks at least three times over, carefully searched the sky and turned into wind. I received a green from the Tower, put my hand on the throttle and momentarily paused as a chill of doubt struck me. Could I really do it on my own? Had I really checked everything? Before I went over it all again, the throttle was somehow wide open and I was checking the swing and lifting the tail automatically. Without really being fully aware that the seat beside me was empty I noticed how much more quickly the Auster climbed away and how more skittishly she bucked the turbulence over the buildings at the edge of the airport. Then out of the corner of my eye I noticed the second stick moving slightly in sympathy with my own and turned and looked at the empty seat: this was really it – my first solo! But there was a slight feeling of anti-climax; there was plenty to keep me occupied, I knew I would cope alright, and before I had time to marvel at this flight which I had waited for so long and dreamed about so many times, I was on the approach and all attention was focused on the landing. It just had to be a good one – I felt I owed that much to my instructors and to myself – and the critical gazes of at least the two eldest of my four children would be directed at me.

Fortunately the landing was a reasonable one but I had little time to reflect on that at the end of the landing run as I found myself directly in the path of an aircraft on the approach. I rushed over to the left-hand side of the runway and picked up Elizabeth, who congratulated me and told me to taxy back to the hangars. Only then did I begin to really enjoy my solo but even so it seemed such a normal part of what I had been doing up to then that it still seemed a little flat. But I felt I could now count myself as a pilot, albeit very much a fledgling. It had taken just over two weeks and 8 hrs 45 mins air time – beyond my wildest dreams!

Circuits (fifth)

The next evening I had booked another hour and started on the next stage, five hours of solo circuits interleaved with circuit checks with an

31

instructor. Once again with Elizabeth and 'IGT we used one of the long runways but this time I did the first circuit and perhaps due to over-confidence made a terrible hash of it. The next two were not a lot better and then it was pointed out to me that with a lighter wind I had to allow the plane to float a little longer. The next landing was a little better, sufficiently so to encourage Elizabeth to get out and leave me to a solid hour of solo circuits.

This time the full impact of being on my own bit a little harder and my first solo landing was as bad as any I had made before. I bounced badly, and soared back possibly 50 ft into the air, slamming open the throttle at mid-bounce and frantically trying to remember everything about overshoots: "Remember I have full flap on. Open the throttle w-i-i-i-de, it's only three-quarters open! What's the height? Are we clear of the hangars? Look at the speed! Are we . . .? Look at the speed! It's only 40 mph at 100 ft up! Hold the nose down and get the flaps up one notch – hold it, something's not right." But then the speed built up, I suddenly realised I was needing a lot more pressure on the stick because I had forgotten to retrim, but after retrimming things settled down a bit; I was up to 200 ft, put up more flap, and settled into a normal climb away. "Phew! I really am alone now; no one to put the trim back on the overshoot, to remind me of the speed, or what to do with the flaps, or keep an eye open for other aircraft."

The next circuit I spent getting my breath back and remembering to let it float longer before pulling the stick right back. The landing was disappointing; I got down alright but bumped quite a bit. And the same thing happened on the next one; but after that they went off very smoothly and several seemed to be almost perfect three-pointers. Ah! the joy of a really good landing! The hour went all too quickly but I had time to really enjoy flying on my own and making my own decisions. This was more like how I had imagined that first solo would be!

Circuits (sixth)

The following evening I had a preliminary 25 minutes dual with Elizabeth in 'GXH in which, using yet another runway, the instructor did the first circuit and I did another three. Visibility was quite poor, the ground being hidden in haze in the middle distance. I was very anxious to learn the turning points so that I wouldn't get lost, as the only thing I could yet recognise from the air was the main runway at Luton; if I had lost sight of that I *would* have been in trouble!

The 25 minutes of dual were followed by 40 minutes solo and gradually my landings were improving. I seemed to be able to get down far more smoothly on my own; whether this was psychological or not I never knew!

Circuits (seventh)

I missed the next evening and then put in another hour. This was a calamitous session, back with Howard and 'IJI (by now, 'IGT was emerging as my favourite and 'IJI as a distinct enemy). Howard was seemingly not in a good mood that evening, and developed a habit of yanking at the controls if I wasn't on the ball and found an unhappy knack of pointing out my errors just as I noticed them myself, before I had a chance to put them right.

I started off badly on the wrong foot by taxying towards the wrong runway and then on changing direction finding myself receiving a flashing red from the Tower: 'clear the landing area.' From then on everything went wrong: my flying became ragged, my landings got worse; the more mistakes I made the more I was corrected and the more I was corrected the more I made mistakes. By the time 50 minutes was up we had only one gallon of fuel showing on the gauge and both of us had had enough. Not one decent landing and no solo: I felt as if I had gone back about five hours in time. Possibly I was tired, possibly it was the weather (it was humid and muggy), possibly it was because I was concentrating too hard on on not making fool mistakes for my instructor to seize upon, possibly because I had a row with someone that afternoon that I should not have had; whatever it was I knew I could do very much better and this only made matters worse. Still it was a sobering thought that I had been unable to fly to the instructor's satisfaction!

Circuits (eighth)

Saturday morning, two days on from that disastrous session with Howard, I was back with Elizabeth and 'IGT, 25 minutes dual and 65 minutes solo, which passed off happily enough. The only incident of note was when another Auster on the ground was given a green for take-off whilst I was on a landing approach and also given a green. Whether he had hung about unduly was not clear but at about 50 ft up on my glide approach I decided there was a good chance he would still be on that piece of runway I was about to land on, so I carried out an overshoot, opening the throttle and climbing clear of the plane on the ground. Only, to my horror, he was only just on the ground, having started his take-off run, so that as I passed overhead I was able to look straight down into his cabin, with an upturned face alongside the pilot. I had an uneasy feeling that if he hadn't seen me he might start climbing and come uncomfortably close; as it was we were separated by about 40 ft. I should of course have banked away to the right but I was still green enough to be worried about spinning or stalling at low speed near the ground, not realising I had sufficient speed to take quite rapid evasive action.

I had noticed the other Auster circuiting with me most of the time and when we both got down I discovered that Howard was the instructor in it. He merely remarked that it had been quite exciting for a while. It seemed

I had done the right thing by overshooting but I felt my copybook would have been cleaner had I banked away from his line of take-off.

Circuits (ninth)

The following period of instruction saw the last of my circuits with instructor checks: 25 minutes dual and one hour solo. Despite being back with Howard, this time in 'IGT, it all passed off uneventfully though my landings were still not as good as those I managed before my first solo.

Circuits (tenth)

My final hour of circuit work was a true solo, in that I had no instructor checks beforehand. I was told to check out with the Tower and obtain from them the runway in current use and the wind strength. The latter was 10-15 kt gusting to 20, although from the attitude of the windsock I would have thought it was a little above this. I identified the runway from the airport layout plan and was horrified to find that the wind appeared to be roughly 45 deg to the runway. Howard laughed this one off by observing that it was a reflection of how much confidence they had in my piloting that they would risk one of their precious aircraft with me in such conditions.

At least I had my favourite 'IGT to do it in. Taxying out to the end of the runway, not without some misgivings, I lined up as much into wind as possible on runway 27 and took off. With such a crosswind I found the Auster quite a handful but was thankful that Howard was not with me to criticise my crabwise progress. Even so, I was more than a little apprehensive at the thought of having to get it down again unaided in a crosswind which was much worse, both in direction and strength, than anything I had previously tackled. First time round I was not consoled by the amount of drift on each of the four legs and when letting down on the approach had to use a long burst of power to save undershooting. Again I angled across the runway as much as possible into wind and felt like a bronco-buster whilst waiting for the Auster to stop bouncing after touchdown. It not only swung wildly when the wheels touched with something like 30 deg of drift, but hopped up and down in the process. This was a ghastly landing and the next attempt was even worse.

This time we bounced badly whilst trying to kick off the drift at the point of touchdown, and ballooned back into the air, the tail weathercocking so that I was facing about 60 deg across the runway, and heading towards a 15 ft sloping rise in the ground to the right marking the edge of the local rubbish tip. Slamming open the throttle I gave up any hope of completing the landing, skimming over the rising, rough ground at just above stalling speed. The plane staggered back up to a safer height and speed, and somewhat breathlessly I let her head into wind. I was determined to get the thing down again and managed it next time round, though it was still a rough ride. The following time around, a Piper Colt was sitting innocently enough in the usual position, waiting for me to land, but with my angling so much into wind, he was exactly where I had finished my landing run the time before. Overshoot procedure again!

I got it down on the next occasion in a much better landing, right wing low and kicking off the drift just before touchdown, but on the following one I managed my first and only (still!) groundloop. By now the wind was at right angles to the runway and I was offsetting about 30 deg by landing obliquely. As I came in there was a fair amount of turbulence over the boundary and what with this and a further 30 deg of drift I had my hands full. The touchdown was a reasonable one at first, as before kicking off drift just at the right moment, but as we rolled past the end of that rubbish dump on the right, now much closer than usual due to the angled line I was taking, a gust hit the aircraft and swung the tail through 180 deg. I was certain the wing was going to dig in but fortunately it did not. That, I decided, was quite enough of that; I looked at my watch and by the time I had taxied back the hour would be up. Never had I been more thankful for the hour to pass and never, whilst flying, as frightened. When I mentioned to Howard how much of a crosswind there now was, he laughed and said: "The Tower must have been watching your antics because they've just changed the runway!" One point he did make was that, as the pilot, it was always up to me what runway to use and if I thought the one the Tower was suggesting was not right for me I should choose another more suitable – a valuable point.

Forced landings and sideslipping

Still in 'IGT, but now with Elizabeth aboard, the next session covered forced landings and sideslipping. We went up to 2,000 ft and flew south alongside the M1 Motorway (the area the Club used for sideslipping practice), and I was reminded that on the climb I should waggle the nose every 500 ft to make sure that nothing was lurking in my blind spot under the nose. Sideslipping sounded easy enough: bank in the direction of slip (usually left) and counter it with opposite ('top') rudder to hold the required direction, and stick back to slow the descent. But again I found it one of those manoeuvres that seem fundamentally wrong; I had to exert full pressure on the rudder to hold the nose 30 deg right with about 30 deg of left bank. However I soon got the feel of it but wasn't sorry when told not to sideslip when less than 300 ft from the ground until I had a lot more experience. With the Auster, equipped with flaps, there was rarely need for sideslipping, but all the aircraft I owned subsequently were flapless, and sideslipping is as much part of the landing routine as lowering flaps would be, and right down to the ground at that if required!

For forced landings we regained the usual cross-country height of 2,000 ft and the instructor turned off the fuel to simulate power failure. The routine was to have already noted a field to land in (normal practice for cross-country flying), choosing first one suitable field within gliding distance, then another as we passed out of range of the first, and to be aware of the wind direction. Unfortunately, the forced landing practice field was unavailable and all the practising had to be done at Luton airport. This at one and the same time both simplified and complicated things; simplified because by now I knew the shape and approaches of the airport, but complicated because we had to keep a special lookout for traffic about its normal business which would not necessarily realise what we were up to.

When the engine cut, the throttle was immediately closed, the nose held up to convert our cruising speed of 80 mph into height whilst dropping to best gliding speed of 60 mph, and the position of the field and wind direction verified. We turned across the downwind end of the field and chose a marker, in line with the approach boundary, at which it was estimated we should be down to 1,000 ft and turning onto the base leg. Then followed a check to see if the power failure could be rectified easily, e.g. petrol cock CLOSED or switches OFF, finally, if not able to restart, closing the petrol cock and switching off to prevent a possible fire on landing. As in the case of a real forced landing we checked brakes off, harnesses tight, any jettisonable hatch seals broken or hatches open, then, as this was a practice, setting petrol and switches back on and doing normal downwind checks for our simulated forced landing. Once we reached our marker, the landing was virtually routine, the only difference being that we still blipped the throttle every 500 ft to prevent the plugs oiling up and keep the engine warm, the engine now having restarted. An essential check was to confirm there were no electricity poles or cables now visible from this lower height, and to keep the field in sight and ensure height was not lost unnecessarily until certain of getting in.

Having done this once to show me how, Elizabeth reset the altimeter so that I couldn't use it directly to judge our height above the ground, then handed over to me, allowing me to do it on my own with promptings, and then doing it once more giving a running commentary on what I was doing (the only really difficult part). It seemed strange, not using the altimeter to measure height, but the approaches were by now fairly familiar and I found that I could manage quite well without it providing I didn't look at it at all. One more practice landing completed the hour, to be followed by two hours solo forced landing and side-slipping practice.

The first of these passed off with three good landings and one over-shoot, perhaps because it was my birthday! This was most encouraging as, in the case of an emergency with too much height in hand, it would be possible to adopt corrective measures not allowed on the Luton approach i.e. making S-turns in front of the runway or sideslipping to less than 300 ft.

There followed a long break of nine days before flying the third hour which was also largely uneventful. I practised sideslipping near the M1 which I had come to regard as a friendly landmark. This time however I discovered that other people felt the same way, as I encountered a Chipmunk flying in the opposite direction at the same height on the other side of the Motorway, both of us correctly keeping this important navigation feature on our left. I banked slightly to the right keeping an eye on him as I did so and noticed him do the same moments later; it was nice to know that I instinctively banked the right way without thinking about it. However, minutes later I received a ruder shock. Having made a mental note to keep a better look out for others "flying by Bradshaw" (a term loosely applied to navigation by following railway lines or trunk roads), I diverted from the practice area and flew over a house I had lived in some years earlier, not strictly speaking within my remit. Circling at 2,000 ft I unintentionally gained 400 ft in the process then headed back to cross the M1, thinking to sideslip it off. There I encountered my "Bradshawing" Chipmunk again, flying back along the M1 directly towards me, almost too close to take any avoiding action. To my immense relief I saw him slide away directly underneath some 100 ft below. This was a rude awakening indeed, with me definitely in the wrong.

The rest of the hour passed off happily enough, making four practice forced landings and one mock approach down to 800 ft at an innocent cornfield several miles from the airport. When I got back and related my tale of jousting with the Chipmunk I was told I shouldn't have been off the circuit anyway but at least it would teach me to keep my eyes open!

Compass courses

A week later, after two more cancelled bookings, I was due to do 'precautionaries,' i.e. emergency landings with power, but the wind was too strong, so Elizabeth decided we should do compass flying instead, fortunately in 'GXH with its 'normal' compass. Having car-rallied count-less times as a navigator I was looking forward to aerial navigation, regarding the business of sorting out courses to fly and times of arrival as something of an interesting challenge. What I never really thought much about was the additional complications of flying by compass. Put a magnetic compass in an aeroplane and it immediately develops nasty little habits, and these introduced a new factor of complication to my life.

I discovered that apart from the well-known fact that the compass spins madly when the aircraft is in a high-rate turn it will also swing, albeit mildly, when the aircraft is accelerating, decelerating or banking under certain conditions. Flying north or south the needle will swing towards the lowered wing when banking, but ignores changes in acceleration or deceleration. Flying east or west, banking has no effect but acceleration will swing the needle northward and deceleration will swing it south. Flying on intermediate headings produces a combination of the two! Put it down to 'dip,' which also causes the needle to lag by 25 or so degrees when turning onto north or similarly lead when turning south. Hey ho, as if life isn't complicated enough! In practice only the latter effects were of any great importance, the rule being to straighten out 25-30 deg before reaching the desired heading when turning north, and similarly past the heading when turning southerly.

These effects were demonstrated to me in the air and then I was told to take over and fly a number of different courses. The air was particularly turbulent and it seemed that every correcting action taken threw the idiot compass off course so that I had great difficulty in deciding just what heading it was indicating. One is supposed to allow the compass to settle when coming out of a turn but the aeroplane was bucking about so much that the instrument rarely got a chance. At one point I suffered an embarrassing mental aberration; flying on 300 degrees I was told to turn onto 170 degrees. I turned through 230 degrees in a series of erratic Rate 1 turns in order to get there – I had made a right-handed turn instead of a left. Eventually I made some sort of order out of it all although it was still difficult in the conditions to fly straight by compass alone. I still preferred to turn by eye onto some previously selected line and correct by compass afterwards, or to fly by a landmark ahead with only occasional glances at the compass for confirmation.

Elizabeth also got me used to flying with the altimeter set to height above sea level (QNH) instead of height above the airfield (QFE). Unlike the forced landing practice where I was not to use the altimeter, I now had to fly circuits using the QNH setting, and circuiting at 1,300 ft and landing at an indicated 520 ft seemed all wrong. My approach height went haywire on my first landing and I had to overshoot from halfway down the short runway. Going round again I was a lot happier but it still seemed very odd coming in at an indicated 800 ft over the aerodrome boundary where I would normally have seen 300 ft on the clock.

Precautionaries

The following evening the wind had dropped so we did an hour on 'precautionaries.' This involved flying at 400 ft to simulate flying below a cloudbase of 500 ft, which would necessitate an emergency landing to stay legal. Once again I was with Elizabeth in 'GXH and she took over to show how it was done. Our circuit took us over the outskirts of Luton and the houses looked awfully close from 400 ft.

Having 'selected' our emergency landing field (back on Luton airport) we did an initial inspection run at 200 ft, flying to the right of the selected landing run, inspecting first the approaches for tall trees or power cables and then the surface of the field for slope, ditches, or major obstructions. After the first inspection run we did a second circuit at 400 ft, keeping the landing run in constant view, followed by another with 15 deg of flap at 60 mph and 40-50 ft, having a good look at the approach and the surface of the field. For the landing we did another circuit at 400 ft, this time carrying out landing checks on the downwind leg, and on the base leg dropping engine revs and speed, so that when we turned onto the approach we were down to 250 ft at an airspeed of 60 mph and with two notches of flap. After the final turn I put the flaps down fully and trimmed nose-up and, using elevator and throttle Elizabeth let our height and speed fall off together so that we crossed the end of the runway at about 10-15 ft in a three-point attitude with 35 mph on the clock. Closing the throttle allowed the plane to sink rapidly but gently onto the grass in a three-pointer, stopping with a minimum of run. Fantastic!

However, the A.S.I. reading and the attitude and height of the aeroplane on the approach looked all wrong, and it didn't seem possible that it wouldn't stall or that we would even reach the end of the runway. But I was getting used to the idea of the apparent wrongness of the feel of the aeroplane under certain extreme conditions and I knew it would fly happily at about 40 mph with flaps fully down, having flown over the rubbish dump under those conditions on my earlier crosswind landing excursion.

We did two more landings with Elizabeth keeping a watchful eye and hand on the controls, then two more on my own. I really quite enjoyed this session once I had got used to the lower altitudes, and in fact the approach seemed to make more sense, coming in with power on. Only later did I come to fully appreciate the glide approaches we were taught then, based as they were on the ability to glide in to make a good landing from anywhere on the 800 ft circuit in the event of power failure. I was told that I shouldn't practise this solo but that during revision I might be asked to do a short-field landing; this would entail a similar power-on approach but off an 800 ft circuit with a long downwind leg, settling well over the boundary with a short landing run.

Local flying

The following two hours were to be spent getting myself orientated in the local flying area. By now I had begun to recognise local features and was looking forward to being let loose on my own with no mission other than to wander round and become thoroughly acquainted with the area. On the west the area is bounded by the M1 and on the east by the A1: south by the M10, and Radlett and Hatfield aerodromes (then still busy factory airfields used by Handley Page and de Havillands respectively). The only side of the area having few easily recognisable features was to the north, but I had no difficulty in locating myself with the aid of the local 1:250,000 map. I looked up some of my friends from a safe height of 2,000 ft and 'buzzed' my home from a 'reckless' 1,500 ft! I had heard too many tales of inexperienced idiots who had crashed whilst low-flying and showing off to friends to want to do the same. I found that looking over the side whilst circling usually led to a nose-up attitude and on one occasion I was very glad indeed that I had 1,700ft below me when doing that! I was trying to locate a friend's house near a village and went too long without glancing back at the horizon or instruments. Suddenly I was aware that the normal flight noises of revs and windroar had changed; looking ahead I found the nose well up and the airspeed well down. Hastily I banked level, opened the throttle wide and pushed the nose down and, suitably chastened and red about the ears, left the area as inconspicuously as possible, feeling that all eyes on the ground were on me, including my friend of some six years experience as a pilot.

One thing I did notice was that, after a break of just three weeks due to bad weather and holidays, I had already half-forgotten things which had been becoming second nature, and resolved not to let that long elapse between flights until I had a lot more hours in my Log Book.

Cross-country

I was now due to do my first cross-country flight, something I had been looking forward to with perhaps even greater anticipation then my first solo. I had booked a two-hour dual session and Elizabeth and I were to fly to Stapleford Tawney by way of Chelmsford, using 'GXH. First thing was to obtain, from the Tower, wind speed and direction at surface and 2,000 ft, and the general weather conditions. Problem number one was how to extract this information from the mass of hieroglyphics on the met. sheet, which I did with the aid of a helpful official. At 2,000 ft, wind speed and direction were 15 kt at 260 deg, and the outlook showery and thundery!

Back at the Clubhouse the instructor and I plotted the course on the local 1:250,000 air map measuring track bearings and distances, then added the magnetic variation quoted on the map. I had by now purchased an ex-RAF Dalton computer (7/6d) and, using this, converted wind speed into mph and calculated true course and drift for each leg from our track, using the wind data and planned airspeed, entering the figures on a Flight Planning Log. Elizabeth obtained clearance by phone for us to land at Stapleford, cleared the flight with Luton Tower, and away we went.

Our first leg gave several good pinpoints after about five minutes flying which enabled us to check our track. These revealed us as being a little south of track and we altered course by five degrees to offset this. The next checkpoint at nearly halfway showed that we were still a little south of track and I altered course by another five degrees. I was flying this leg with the instructor assisting with the map-reading. I had the map on my knees with the log card on the coaming, and found it quite simple to check the points on the ground with those on the map. Fortunately in this corner of England there was no lack of railways, trunk roads, rivers, towns and airfields to aid the intrepid navigator, which was just as well as I found that with the turbulence we were encountering it was most difficult to get the compass to make up its mind. Every time I looked away it seemed to automatically move off course by anything up to 20 deg!

Elizabeth flew the next leg, Chelmsford to Stapleford, leaving me to concentrate on the map-reading and make suggestions regarding course corrections. Despite this, we arrived at Stapleford and I took over for the landing, my first away. Here I had to make allowances for the different altitude of the airfield. Stapleford is at 150 ft a.s.l. (350 ft below Luton) so we dropped down to 1,650 ft indicated to check the landing direction and then to 950 ft for a left-handed circuit. No problems with turning points or approach and we made a smooth landing. Our stay was a short one, just long enough to report to control, pay a five shilling landing fee (extortionate!), have a quick glance at the interesting collection of aircraft in the hangar (Jungmeister, Bolkow Junior, Aircoupes, etc.) and then we were away again.

I was to fly the last leg on my own, with comment from the instructor only if I got obviously and hopelessly lost. Which I didn't, though I had to alter my course by a total of 15 degs to offset an increasing drift southwards. It was most satisfying to find Luton airport, with its familiar pattern of runways and taxy strips, dead ahead albeit a few minutes earlier than estimated. However it seemed I still had to gen up on circuit rejoining procedure as I would have sailed round a full circuit, whereas I was firmly told to cut the downwind leg by 1/3rd to keep out of the way of aircraft already on the circuit or taking off. Again, the standard altimeter setting (QNH) fooled me and I had to use a good burst of power on the final approach in order to get in.

Two days later I did the same cross-country flight solo, but doing only a touch-and-go at Stapleford. It seemed there would be no one available to swing the prop for me, but at least it saved the landing fee! Again I had to make a fair amount of correction for change in wind speed and direction, not helped by the fact that the first one I made was in the wrong direction! Fortunately I quickly discovered the error before any harm was done, but even so had corrections totalling over 20 degs for the two main legs. There were no real difficulties, my worst fears of not being able to pick out the small grass field at Stapleford Tawney not being realised.

The third and final cross-country was to Ipswich, returning via Stapleford Tawney. I was to land at Ipswich for refuelling but, as before, only a touch-and-go at Stapleford. Twice the flight was cancelled for bad weather but eventually a fine summery day coincided with my booking. I plotted course and track as before for the three legs, this time also getting a check from further east as to actual conditions. The Tower tried to get an 'actual' from Ipswich but the best they could manage was from Weathersfield which was about halfway on the first leg. There was no significant difference at this point so no further corrections were necessary. I checked the MCA Air Pilot Danger Areas map to see if there was anything I should avoid: lo and behold, near Ipswich there was one within a few miles of track on the outward leg. I marked this on my map and firmly resolved not to be lost at that point. Finally I checked the descriptions in the Air Pilot for the airfield at Ipswich, finding this had two grass runways and there were no special remarks about it.

This time I checked out myself with the Tower, who liked to know where one is going so that in a case of non-appearance at the destination a timely search can be instituted. I climbed into 'GXH and settled myself and my gear so that everything would be within easy reach during the flight, at the same time ensuring nothing was likely to fall where it could jam the controls. As with every other flight, starting up, taxying out and taking off were still carried out with a sense of eager anticipation, the actions now semi-automatic and familiar yet still strangely unfamiliar – could this really be happening to me? This time there was a new spirit of adventure about it. Old hands may smile at such a description of a 60-70-mile cross-country flight but to me it was venturing out into the unknown. No guiding hand from an instructor on this flight – they had not even checked my flight plan and I had never previously flown to this part of East Anglia.

I set course over Luton as planned, allowing two degrees on my True course for compass deviation (marked on a card near the compass) and settled down to enjoy the flight. It occurred to me that there were two reasons for circling over the airfield before setting out: one to ensure that the aircraft was still within gliding distance before a safe height was gained and departing from the circuit, the other being to ensure the course was set as drawn on the map, i.e. directly over the airfield.

I searched around the sky to check nothing was about and idly glanced ahead to pick out the chalk pits at Codicote, which should have appeared to my right. No sign of them and the compass was indicating some 30 deg off course. I quickly brought the plane back onto course and looked over the side to see where I was, and recognised nothing! Surely I couldn't be lost already, after only three minutes or so? After a transient moment of near panic when I realised just how easy it would be to get lost I reasoned that I must cross the A1 shortly and then could easily establish where I was. As it was, within a minute I recognised the 'skyscrapers' of Stevenage New Town, which was slightly to my right and as I had to pass over the town flew directly towards it. No correction to track was required as the error was mine – I had flown too long off course, letting my attention wander on to other things.

After this every landmark came up almost spot on, flying the calculated course with no corrections. It seemed almost uncanny the way each point swam into view almost as I was thinking to myself that I should soon see it. At first, though, I had to continually correct my direction; as soon as I took my eyes off the compass it got up to its old tricks again and went meandering off on its own. Experimenting with the controls eventually showed me where the trouble lay; one wing very slightly down produced a gradual and almost unnoticeable turn which, however, the compass unerringly and faithfully picked up. Flying feet off confirmed this and I resolved to concentrate more on this aspect; I had previously thought I was more leaden in one foot than the other but now it appeared more likely that I 'leaned' more one way than the other. Things certainly seemed a little easier after this.

Eventually, and several minutes before my ETA, Ipswich, with the airfield on the eastern outskirts, lay before me and I dropped down to 1,650 ft to check the wind direction and the Landing Tee. This time I remembered my approach sequence and landed correctly albeit bouncily, with a 30 deg or so crosswind. Taxying past the air traffic control office up to the hangar I was waved onto the refuelling apron, the first time I had been on the receiving end of handwagging marshalling signals, which proved easy to interpret. I had five gallons put in the tank, making a total of 13 gallons, ample for the return flight, and after signing the fuel chit, wandered off to the control office to check in and pay my 3/- landing fee. I booked out again *en route* for Stapleford Tawney after finding that the refreshments room had closed 45 minutes earlier.

The return flight was also uneventful though, now that I was flying into the setting sun, I was painfully aware of a ground haze which cut forward visibility considerably so that I could more readily see where I had been than where I was going! Stapleford Tawney turned up precisely where expected and again I did a touch-and-go, landing without stopping. Strangely, on the last leg back to Luton, I had to correct considerable drift which was not apparent on the other legs. All in all it was a thoroughly enjoyable trip, rendered all the more so by the manner in which the landmarks turned up when and where they should.

Revision

My hours by now totalled 28½ and I was to do revision until the instructors considered I would be ready to pass the flying test. I booked two hours of dual and in the first, with Howard in 'GXH, we went over straight and level flying, compass courses and Rate 1 turns, followed by Rate 4 turns and stalls with and without power. I found that in the 24 flying hours that had passed since doing Rate 4 turns I had forgotten how to do them! Amazing! We spent five minutes on these until I got it right. At least my stalls were much sharper than before though at first, when recovering with power, I neglected to push the stick forward initially, losing some hundreds of feet in the process as we mushed soggily down whilst the airspeed built up. Also I forgot to check below before stalling, and later to scan through 360 deg before spinning. After successfully spinning and recovering, whilst well and truly disoriented, Howard told me to fly back to the airport and carry out a rejoining procedure. Fortunately I fairly quickly located Henlow behind us, but I had no map with me and tried desperately to visualize the map and the course to fly to get back to Luton. It would have needed a round tour of the area before I got it right, but the lesson was sharply learned. Never fly without a map although I wouldn't normally have done so unless flying with an instructor – an obvious point but it had never arisen before! Apart from the flying aspects, my knowledge of air law was tested in subtle ways such as being told to turn right and fly along the M1 after we had crossed it; this entailed recrossing it so that it lay on my left!

We finished up by heading straight back to the airport, the location of which I now knew, the M1 being familiar territory. I gained height to cross the airfield at 2,000 ft and after looking at the signals square let down to lose height on the dead side of the circuit. Here Howard took over to land on the 'near' 06 runway, the one right in front of the terminal buildings on which only instructors were allowed to land; it seemed he was in a hurry to get away and couldn't wait for me to go trundling round the circuit. Anyway, it seemed my general flying was OK but I needed to brush up more on steep turns.

The second hour of revision covered forced landings and precautionaries, once again in 'GXH but with Elizabeth. After leaving the airfield and setting course as requested by the instructor, I was told to fly straight and level at 60 mph IAS maintaining height. This foxed me a little at first but I soon caught on, throttling back and holding the nose higher. Apparently I could expect to be told to fly at anything down to 40 mph on the test! After several turns we arrived back over the airfield and without warning the engine cut – forced landing procedure! I closed the throttle, held the nose up to convert speed into height, and searched for confirmation of the wind direction. We settled down into a 70 mph glide, and after trimming for the glide I looked around for a suitable 1,000 ft turning point. I was reminded to check for the cause of the failure, but as I was just about to do this I wasn't too much worried.

What did worry me was when I remembered on the approach that the altimeter was on a QNH setting and not QFE, and that I was down to just over 500 ft and not over 1,000 ft! However due to the fact that there were two parallel runways in use and I had aimed for the furthest, we managed to get down on the nearest, but only just! I carried out an overshoot and was reminded in no uncertain terms not to use the altimeter on a forced landing approach.

After this we practised short field landings. My first attempt was made off a 400 ft-high base leg and I landed a little to one side of the runway; also an old habit of cutting corners on the last turn crept back in. We did several of these landings, the last advice being to treat a request for a short field landing as requiring a normal circuit with a slightly longer downwind leg and final approach, the main idea being to not be too low and depending on the engine when outside the aerodrome boundary!

Ground test

That same evening I took the Air Law exam, a 30-question 'which of the following is correct?-type paper. A 70% pass was necessary and I got 80% so I was reasonably happy. This despite the fact that six of the questions involved knowledge of aircraft and airfield lighting and other aspects of night-flying which I hadn't bothered to review. I am still at a loss to understand why a knowledge of night-flying was necessary for a licence which enabled its holder to fly only under VMC conditions; night-flying required an instrument rating which involves far more stringent exams! The best thing that came out of this was when I mentioned to Elizabeth that I could never remember which colours were port and starboard, she merely replied: "Port wine." Brilliant, why hadn't I thought of that before?

Air test

I booked another hour for solo revision and confirmed that I should take my air test two days later. Unfortunately my revision hour was scrubbed as some vile creature had bent 'IGT and to my horror I was unable to book another period before my test. I had planned out a flight programme covering all the aspects on which I felt a little woolly and the loss of this hour was certainly a cruel blow. Despite my instructor's apparent confidence in me I wasn't as happy about the forthcoming test as I should have been! They suggested that at the stage I had reached one more hour wouldn't make much difference; technically they were probably right but that did nothing to improve my morale at that point!

When the time came for the test I embarked on 'GXH with Dave Campbell; I now saw the CFI in a totally different light to when I had flown with him at the start. Now he was to be regarded as next to God, with the power of life or death over my chances of obtaining my licence, and this may well have been my undoing!

I did no end of things wrong. To start with I forgot that I and not the CFI was expected to check runway in use with the Tower and did not book out. I took off into wind alright but on the wrong runway, as the Tower had not changed the runway to suit the wind direction. During the 'engine-out on take-off' test I put the nose down too sharply and allowed the speed to build up too high. Climbing to 1,500 ft I forgot to weave, looking out for traffic in the blind spot under the nose. I was instructed to fly at 40-45 mph without using flaps and without loss or gain of height. Stalling speed on the Auster was 42 mph 'clean' and we were flying in very turbulent conditions. At first I couldn't get the speed much below 50 mph whilst maintaining height, but eventually I got it down to 43-45 mph, engine full-bore, stick well back, right on the sloppy edge of a stall.

If this was a demonstration for short-field landings I reckon I would have overshot long before I got the speed down had I actually been preparing to land.

I gained more black marks on my forced-landing attempts. I was supposed to be giving a running commentary on everything I did, but when the engine cut my repartee quickly dried up while I concentrated on getting into the field with a dead engine. I didn't trim for the glide, didn't open the throttle every 500 ft, put the flaps down too soon and on overshoot let the speed build up to 80 mph with the flaps still down.

On a second forced landing attempt I made a classic schoolboy howler. "Take your time and pick a field you would land in," said Dave, "and show me how you would do it." Which I did, happily observing a long plume of smoke from a factory chimney which gave very clearly the wind direction. I chose a field, cut the throttle and carried out my approach. When I was down to 500 ft, feeling very comfortable and virtually committed, I suddenly realised that I had completely misread the wind direction and was about to land with it instead of into it! I fiddled about so that I could have got in OK but it was patently obvious to the wily old bird sitting next to me that I had swung through 180 deg at a late stage in the approach!

Then a major black when I rejoined the circuit. Cloudbase was down to 1,650 ft so that I could not cross the airfield at 2,000 ft to check the signals square; this was a factor I had not encountered before. At the last moment I turned right to join the left-hand circuit – clang! What I should have done was to go round not across, before letting down at the start of the dead side and not near the end! To round it all off I taxied too fast!

At least Dave commiserated with me and suggested we should enter the flight not as an air test but as revision. It was another 18 days before I could do another revision flight and I booked another air test for the same day. I drew up a list of all the things that had gone wrong and detailed what I would do on the revision flight. That was a glorious sunny day at the end of September and in the morning I thoroughly enjoyed 85 minutes going through all the points I had been unhappy about, so that when I took the test in the afternoon I felt very relaxed. The cornfields had all been harvested and the hay gathered in (in those far-off days farmers had not got round to the black art of stubble-burning so for several months every cornfield was a golden invitation for a forced-landing).

This time I made no mistakes on the air test: I even finished off with a near-perfect three-pointer and both the Chief Instructor and I thoroughly enjoyed the flight. The dreaded CFI suddenly became very human again and made me feel very much one of the fraternity of the air when he told me I had passed.

Two weeks later I went to the Club in the evening to take the written Navigation and Meteorology exam and the final oral exam with the CFI, both of which I passed. Dave had booked to do some night-flight testing in a new Piper Apache and invited me to go along for the ride. What a day! I had never flown at night before and was fascinated throughout the flight, at the end of which Dave signed up my logbook, now bearing the magic stamp of approval. 14 hours solo, 19 hours dual, 4½ months elapsed; now I was a certified PPL and could fly the Club Austers with one passenger. Seventh heaven!

H. J. BRETT '82

CHAPTER 3
OWNING OUR OWN

Before I had finished my PPL course at Luton I knew I was going to have to find a cheaper and better way of flying than with the Luton Club; already replacement of the Austers by Cessna 150s was on the books, with an hourly rate of £6 to match! Talking with another student I found that he felt very much the same as me. Apart from the hourly rates there was another drawback in depending solely on using the Club aircraft. Because their main business came from the School side, it was not on to take the Austers away for weekend, all-day visits to Fly-Ins or Displays. In hiring the aircraft for, say, a 60-mile-distant venue such as Ipswich, total flying time might amount to no more than two hours, whereas on training duties on a Saturday or Sunday the Club could expect to hire it out for 8 or 9 hours. The best we could look for was a morning or afternoon session, with the aircraft on the ground for no more than two hours at most.

Bob Oates, a Lloyds Bank employee in Stevenage, agreed to investigate the financial aspects of running a group, and wrote to the PFA for guidance. They offered advice on setting up a group and also obtaining an interest-free loan through the Shell-BP/Kemsley Trust Private Flying Loan Fund (ex-Nuffield), in which we would have to put up 25% of the purchase price and make three annual repayments of 25%.

I was working for the British Aircraft Corporation at the time in their GW Division which, unlike the aircraft divisions, did not encourage the running of an aircraft group for their employees; understandably perhaps because there were no airfield or hangarage facilities at Stevenage such as existed at Hatfield or Bristol. In any case the management could see no point in encouraging their employees to risk their necks in flying when none would gain in their work aspects from the experience. However an article in the company newspaper at the end of July produced a few enquiries which showed there would be some interest locally. An ad in the local newspaper in August brought forth a number of replies and a meeting, at the home of one enquirer in Stevenage, with four student pilots and two others, laid the grounds for proceeding further. We arranged to hold monthly meetings in a pub in Stevenage New Town Centre, the first in September, followed by another at a local airstrip a week later.

By now we had been in contact with the Cambridge Private Flying Group, who operated two Tiger Moths from Cambridge Airport, and they gave us a very detailed breakdown of their running costs. The owner of the airstrip, a farmer who leased a Tri-pacer for varying periods throughout the year, was interested in Group operation, but it was evident he was looking for a much more sophisticated machine than we could contemplate. However, he did agree to us operating from his strip and using his barn as a hangar when it was not filled with grain, which was a useful start.

Costings from two other groups were 3 guineas p.a. and £3/hr for the Cambridge Group, and £1 per week for one hour per month and £2.5s per hour for further hours with the Hornet Group at Luton for their Hornet Moth, which new members had to buy into. It was obvious from the figures quoted by the Cambridge Group and the PFA that most groups derived their main income from the hourly rates charged for flying, the minimum annual rate being a target of 200 hours per aircraft. I was not keen on this approach. It meant that if the aircraft was grounded for any reason, income stopped there and then. Whilst this was a great incentive for keeping the aircraft flying at all costs I felt that with loan repayments over three years this could be asking for trouble. Instead, I thought that we should ensure that all fixed outgoings were covered by members' subscriptions, and income from hourly rates restricted to actual hourly expenditure such as fuel, oil, and any replacements related to hourly running, such as engine overhauls. This would entail a high subscription but minimal hourly rates – a great encouragement instead of deterrent for members to put in as many hours as possible.

A further meeting at the airstrip saw us consolidate the figures we were aiming at. By now we knew that for a 3- or 4-seater we would be looking at a Private 3-year C. of A., with 50-hour or quarterly minor checks and an annual major check. Much of the work involved was of a nature that we could do ourselves if we could find a friendly engineer to oversee what we were doing and sign it out for us. Insurance figures would be based on 10-15% of aircraft value for comprehensive cover. We saw no difficulty in finding an hours-hungry instructor who would take on pilot training in return for low-cost hours-building, there being then no restriction with training from unlicensed airfields for owner pilots. The basis for membership was that all current paid-up members would be equal part-owners, their part-ownership being non-transferable and ceasing if they stopped paying subs.

Finally, at a meeting in October we agreed on the official formation of the group, to be known as the Stevenage Flying Club (a title chosen in the hope of obtaining contributions from local businessmen, which in fact brought forth just a few). A set of Rules was drawn up and agreed, based loosely on sample Rules issued by the PFA and modified to suit our proposed ways of running the group. Copies of those and membership entry forms were printed shortly afterwards. The basis for operating at that point was that members would pay a nominal subscription of 2/6d per week simply to cover printing and postage etc., but that as soon as an aircraft was located that would suit our purposes, this would be raised to

10/- a week. Also at that point, we would need members to raise the deposit required to purchase the aircraft through the Private Flying Loan Fund. Not unexpectedly, as soon as a weekly sub was required, even as low as 2/6d, we lost four of the 17 prospective members. We lost another four when later we needed to raise the initial deposit and increased the subs to 10/- per week!

At that stage we thought we should be aiming at something like an Auster Autocrat, a 3-seat, 100 hp, high-wing monoplane, the market value being of the order of £750. At that time, W.S. Shackleton was advertising a Tipsy B Trainer (a 2-seater) for £300, a low-hours Miles Messenger (four-seater) for £800 or a thirsty Percival Proctor (also a four-seater) for £650. We were not keen on buying an all-wooden-construction aircraft, which all these were, because the first hints of dubious glue joints were coming to everyone's notice. The Autocrat had a welded steel tube fuselage and wooden-sparred wings with metal ribs, a much safer bet. However, an even better bet was thought to be the Thruxton Jackaroo, a 4-seat cabin conversion of the Tiger Moth. Apart from the attraction of being a biplane, this also offered a steel-tube fuselage with extra seating and the reliable Gipsy Major engine, zero-timed examples of which were then still available for £295! The normal overhaul life of the Gipsy was 1,500 hrs, with 600 hrs between top overhauls, unmatched at that time by any other engine. When a one-owner example was found to be for sale at £775 we felt this had to be the one for us!

I was fairly *au fait* with the Jackaroo. When details were announced in *"The Aeroplane"* in the late fifties I had been impressed by what it could do, but like most Tiger fans felt that they had merely ruined a good Tiger Moth, the resulting tadpole-shaped fuselage doing nothing to enhance its appearance. It had been designed to provide a more effective crop-sprayer than the Tiger Moth, with a larger hopper in the fuselage. Taking advantage of the abundance of Tiger Moth airframes and spares, and a similarly seemingly endless supply of Gipsy Majors it was a cheap and variable alternative to anything else on the market. When not spraying, it was easily possible to remove the tank and change the top decking to create a cabin-covered four-seater using modified Proctor cabin doors: same fuel tank and engine as a Tiger but with a wider undercarriage which gave it better crosswind capability. Aimed principally at the Antipodean market it was given the name used in Australia for a general 'jack-of-all-trades' on the farms, but it took the ARB so long to grant it a C. of A. that the market was lost to American cropdusters by the time it was ready for export. Around 22 were built, mostly as 4-seaters, a few for private owners in the UK, where it sold complete for £1,100.

Capt. Chas Watson, a farmer at Winkfield near Windsor, bought G-APAL from new and kept it on his farm, using it for – among other things – flying to various Rallies on the Continent. He weighed 16 stones and took his mother (who weighed the same), his daughter Alison and boyfriend, and suitable luggage for a week across to Berck and Deauville every year. When the Heathrow Control Zone expanded sufficiently to include his farm and close down his airstrip he moved it to Thruxton and finally, reluctantly, decided to sell it. As a measure of his reluctance, he agreed to join our Group on the understanding that he or his daughter could have the use of it for a week occasionally, based then at Thruxton. To which we joyfully agreed, the number of members who were prepared to put up £20 for the purchase deposit now having dropped to nine, despite the £20 being in the form of a loan to the Club and repayable at the earliest opportunity. Not only did Chas join us, he stood as one of two Guarantors for the loan repayment, and we duly paid £190 as initial payment.

Accordingly on March 31st 1965 I drove to White Waltham to meet his agent, D. Rimmer, and fly down to Thruxton in Dave's Tri-pacer to collect the Jackaroo. There, as related elsewhere ("Check Pilot"), I was given one brief conversion circuit and then flew it to Fairoaks with Chas, where a 50 hr check was to be carried out. Three days later, joy of joys, Chas, Bob Oates (by now the Club Treasurer) and I, accompanied by my eldest son Alan (then 12) took delivery of 'PAL and flew it over to our new home at Baldock. One look at the 400 yd strip from the air, with the sock indicating a vigorous crosswind, was enough to send me scurrying over to Old Warden as a safer haven; even that, after the wide open spaces of Luton, and before the runways were extended to their present lengths, looked postage stamp-sized! We had by then met Malcolm Frazer, Works Manager of Warden Aviation, the commercial arm of the Shuttleworth Collection, who had agreed to help with the servicing of the Jackaroo, so knew it was OK to divert to Old Warden if in any difficulty.

Also at Baldock I had met Ed Ferguson, who acted as personal pilot to the American Ambassador at that time, and was a regular at Baldock, keeping his Messenger G-AJYZ there when there was room; he was quite a character who was reputed to have done a touch-and-go at Baldock with the Ambassador's Dakota, and swore he could have got it in but could not have guaranteed to fly it out again! When I explained to Ed my fears about getting the Jackaroo safely down on the strip, he offered to pick it up for us and deliver it there the next evening, which he did, with four of us aboard. Even that was quite something, because Ed was about 6 ft 3 in tall and big-built with it; if we had any doubts about Chas' stories of his four-up trips to France that flight certainly allayed them. When I mentioned to Ed my concern about our converted Tiger taking such a load and flying safely at approach speed without stalling, he threw it around over the strip at about 100 ft up with 40 kt on the A.S.I. just to show how controllable she was when fully loaded. That did a lot for my confidence from then on and I never again had any doubts of how well she handled. After that I did 20 minutes of circuits with him and found how easily she could be put down, even with a healthy crosswind. To my great surprise, Ed suggested I should fly his Messenger, which handled superbly and could be put down in almost the length of the barn, and I clocked up another 20 minutes with a really delightful flying machine. Thanks again, Ed.

The first time I went to fly the Jackaroo at Baldock I learned another valuable lesson, in the process narrowly averting disaster by the quick thinking of the farmer. We had positioned the aircraft so that nothing would be damaged by the slipstream, chocked the wheels and started the engine, with me sitting in the front seat, and the stick held right back, as I had been taught at Luton. After warming up the engine, I opened the throttle to check for maximum revs, concentrating on the rev counter, when there was a great shout from outside to close the throttle immediately. Startled, I did so and looked round to find the cause. It seemed that with no one holding down the tail, and with me in the front seat, the tail had started to rise as the revs rose, and only the farmer's quick action in jumping to the tail and pulling it down had avoided the propeller contacting the stony ground; the cost of repairing or replacing the Fairey-Reed propeller and carrying out a crankshaft check on the engine didn't bear thinking about! On all future occasions we made sure there was always someone holding down the tail: it wouldn't have been so bad had I been in the rear seat, behind the CG.

For just a few delightful weeks, we had our own aeroplane, in my case almost on my doorstep. We had settled the hourly rate at £3 (with the removal by the Government of the petrol tax relief of 10/- per hour our original aim of £2.10.0 could not be met) but this also hit the other organisations as well, so we were not alone. The only snag with our stay at the farm strip was that the owner, who would take no rent for our stay there, would not allow us to have a key to the barn, and was very difficult to contact. Thus we could only get the aircraft out if he was there, and we had no means of finding out for sure when he would be. There was also no fuel available at the strip, and we didn't know at that time about using car fuel. So refuelling had to be done at Rush Green, near Hitchin, the home of Farm Aviation. This was run by Bill Bowker and in him we found another helpful individual and an organisation dedicated to light aviation; Bill was always helpful (and still is) and knew all about Tiger Moths, Farm Aviation using Tigers for cropdusting at that time.

But then, towards the end of May, disaster struck. One of our most experienced members wanted to fly into Silverstone for the British Grand Prix but found that they would only accept those involved with the racing. He knew of a farmer who had a field next to Silverstone, which had been successfully used by aircraft, and was quite prepared for him to land there at his own risk. Mike duly went off, found the field and landed in it. Unfortunately, because he was late, he had not done a precautionary fly-by and thus did not realise that the field sloped down to a hedge and ditch; he only found this out when the Jackaroo failed to stop as usual, and in fact trundled right down to where it buried its nose in the hedge and dropped its wheels into the ditch, bending the centre-section and undercarriage struts. Because of the resulting damage, it was not going to be flown out. In fact, we went to the field and removed the wings and with the help of the farmer and his tractor, hoisted up the fuselage in order to remove the now somewhat bent undercarriage. Fortunately, the prop had stopped horizontally when Mike switched off and was undamaged, which also meant that the engine did not need a crankshaft check. At least, Mike got to see the Grand Prix! We got the aircraft moved to Brooklands Aviation at Sywell, and left it with them to put right. As it was going to take them several weeks, Frank (their Engineer) suggested we have them renew the C. of A. at the same time, which should have reduced the cost of that to about £65, as much of the work would be covered by the damage repair (paid for by the insurance).

As so often happens, things didn't quite work out like that. It was soon discovered that the glue joints in the tailplane ribs had given up the ghost and it would be cheaper to fit a new one from stock than to repair the old one. At least, one could buy a brand new tailplane then for £10, which justified our original arguments that a Jackaroo would be a good thing because of the cheap availability of Tiger spares. But it didn't stop there. With the fuselage fabric opened up Frank discovered considerable corrosion in the bottom longerons of the fuselage side frames, as half a ton of seaside sand cascaded over the floor of the hangar! Then we discovered that the Jackaroo had been hired out to Giro Aviation for joyriding off Southport Sands for several summer seasons – one careful owner indeed! As if that was not enough, there was more yet to come!

When the ARB Man searched diligently through the Log Books he discovered that the Fairey-Reed propeller fitted originally had been adapted for the Jackaroo by having the pitch angle changed by a few fractions of a degree; this is a normal procedure, but this time the work had been done in the BEA workshops at Heathrow, and somewhere along the line someone had signed out the work who may not have been qualified to do so, which could have meant us having to have the prop reworked or, worse still, finding a replacement. So, much time was spent by persons unknown chasing through all the appropriate records, both at Heathrow and at the ARB, which finally resulted in us having the prop refitted, unchanged, but with another entry in the logbook – now all *kosher* but having delayed the return to 'serviceable' by several costly weeks! Then, when test-flown, the pilot reported that the Turn and Bank instrument was not working properly, this eventually being rectified by relocating the venturi from the top decking to the starboard diagonal centre-section strut – the only Jackaroo so fitted! We finally got the aircraft back at the end of August, but more significantly, were presented with a bill for £240 over and above the insurance-funded work! A bitter lesson learned.

Yet another blow awaited us when we came to fly the plane back to our base at Baldock. It was now harvest time and the barn was full of grain, with no room for aeroplanes. We were welcome to tie the Jackaroo down in the open, but even in 1965 in a quiet little market town like Baldock, that was asking for trouble from local vandals (already aircraft had suffered minor damage when left tied down there). Neither Rush Green nor Old Warden had any spare hangarage and it was suggested that our best bet would be Panshanger. We got permission to house it there in an open blister hangar, where airfield security was sufficient to have a reasonable chance of safe keeping. But this in turn brought a new monthly charge (£12 per month) to dent our severely-damaged finances. At that point our chances of survival looked very bleak indeed.

Meanwhile, we collected the Jackaroo from Sywell, visibly little different than before the accident, and arrived at the vast open spaces of Panshanger, then a large, delightful and apparently informal grass air-field, formerly the home of 1 EFTS and its Tigers from when it left Hatfield in September 1942 until, after renaming as 1 RFS, it disbanded in 1953. Amazingly, there were several Nissen huts still containing the bulk of the stock of Tiger spares; these ultimately found their way to Old Warden and for many years helped keep the Jackaroos and later, my Tiger Moth, flying.

More articles in the local paper brought forth several new members and an instructor, so that we increased our membership to around 16, subscriptions now fixed at £2 per month and the flying hour rate at £3.10.0 (a temporary surcharge of 10/- per hour being added to help cover the cost of the C. of A.). New members now also brought with them a deposit of 3 months' subscription, returnable on leaving if 3 months' notice was given (we had already suffered several members departing without settling their bills). We were hanging on in there by the skin of our teeth!

Meanwhile we were approached by one introducing himself as the Count de Serigny who, seemingly with the blessings of the airfield owner, Matt Summers, had established himself as a sort of father figure to the several groups operating from Panshangar. He had an Instructor's rating and ran the Wasp Flying Group, operating an Autocrat G-AIBX, notable for its unusual colour scheme – orange wings and black fuselage with orange trim. Thirty years later I came across this same aeroplane, in the same colour scheme, still operating as the Wasp group, in the hangar I was using for my Taylorcraft at Little Gransden; at the time of writing it is still there, now recovered and bearing a more usual colour scheme for the first time in some 40 years, though Serigny alas is no longer with us! The Count's idea was that we should all get together to form a bigger organisation to be known as the Panshanger Flying Club with more aircraft available to us all. I can no longer recall why we did not want to go along with this scheme, but we certainly saw considerable drawbacks for us, in effect handing over our aeroplane to him. He offered to provide instruction for our members if we went along with him, and talked us into letting him fly the Jackaroo. If nothing else, he demonstrated that, although not cleared for aerobatics, the Jackaroo was quite capable of being looped and spun!

The next blow came shortly after. On returning from our first day out trip, to a Fly-In at Swanton Morley (see Chapter 4, "Hot and Bothered"), just two weeks after our arrival at Panshanger, we were met by the airfield manager and told that we had to leave the airfield straight away. It appeared that we had obtained hangarage under false pretences; had he known that we were operating as a Flying Club we would not have been allowed in, as they did not want competition for members. In vain did we point out that we were not operating as a normal Club, our members being all part-owners. At least we got permission to stay for the following week. An approach was made during that week to Matt Summers to see if there was some way we could stay: "Yes," said Mr Summers, "if you pay me £1,000 per year." When I protested that we could not possibly afford that he implied that in that case we were not the sort of people he wanted on his airfield anyway. Again he relented to the extent of allowing us to stay for a further four weeks to enable us to find another home.

We eventually came to a compromise which would allow us to stay another three months until we could find somewhere else, but we were not to do any training at Panshanger. Again Bill Bowker came to our aid, allowing us to carry out training flights from Rush Green, and in the spring of '66 we moved there, tying the aircraft down in the open. One day, someone left open the gate leading into the field and the cattle got in amongst the aircraft. They were soon shooed out but not before one of them had licked her way through the leading edge of the lower starboard wing: it's amazing how much damage a cow's tongue can do to fabric and spruce! When our first instructor left us (a charming lady from the Civil Service Flying Club) we soon found a replacement in Phil Marlowe, a training captain from one of the airlines operating out of Luton, and he actually got one of our student pilots solo from Rush Green, quite an achievement. Eventually we had to give up training as we were told that it was no longer possible to train from an unlicensed airfield.

From our earliest days at Panshanger we had looked for a farmer's field that might be suitable. The one we favoured most was earmarked for future development by the Stevenage New Town Council. We persuaded them that the New Town really ought to keep abreast of developments elsewhere, and that a Municipal airstrip complete with a local Flying Club (ours) would be a boost in their drive to encourage more businesses into the area. It all went very favourably at first, especially after paying a visit to Cumbernauld New Town who had their own airfield. Not to be outdone, Stevenage looked to be well on the way to drawing up proposals for an airfield, but then we all fell foul of Luton Airport's planned growth, with their flightpath almost overhead our field. Finally the whole scheme was replaced by a plan for a helipad: such is progress!

Members were always asked to keep an eye open for an alternative home and at last an opportunity to move presented itself. Phil Marlowe was an ex-test pilot with Martin Baker and through his good offices we were offered a Quonset building on Chalgrove aerodrome that was due to be demolished. If we cared to dismantle and remove it we could have it free. The Quonset was a sort of oversized Nissen hut, some 30 ft wide and 96 ft long, with thirteen semi-circular arches, formed from four flanged-end, curved steel tubular sections, bolted together. It was covered by curved corrugated iron sheets attached to 8 ft-long, 2-inch angle iron sections bolted to the arches. We thought it could accommodate five light aircraft, though the Jackaroo, with its high top wing, would have to be at one end and turned diagonally across the width. As is so often the case, what looks to be a straightforward job turns out to be a little more difficult than imagined. On initial inspection it was found that many of the covering sheets were rusted through, allowing the weather full access to the interior. Consequently, everything was rusted and bolts that had been in place for over 25 years were sometimes reluctant to be undone. One of the arches had rusted through at the bottom, and the ends were infilled with brickwork, which meant we would have to design and build full-width opening doors.

Nevertheless, such a gift horse could not be looked in the mouth, and at weekends through the winter of '67/8, whenever the weather permitted, a few of us would be there, dismantling and cleaning the structure. The tops of the arches were 16 ft above the concrete floor (which can look terrifyingly high for those not trained as steeplejacks), but we managed to get the lot down without a crane and without any accidents. I simply cannot remember ever being involved in a filthier operation – one only had to touch the inside of the covering to be showered with flaking rust. I do recall though the perilous drives back home with the 12 foot-long curved sections of the arches sticking out of the back of my Ford Thames 12 cwt van, with the springs bottoming at every bump in the road. Logistics showed that it could take us a year to transport the parts in my van, assuming it would stand up to such treatment, and in the end a local truck owner moved it all in one go for the princely sum of £12.

Acquisition of the Quonset coincided with the demise of the plan for an airstrip at Stevenage, but through Malcolm Frazer an approach was made to David Ogilvy, manager of the Shuttleworth Collection. He was quite happy for us to operate from Old Warden, thinking that our aeroplane flying at weekends would be an attraction to visitors, but could not offer any hangarage other than a temporary stay in their big open blister hangar while some of their aircraft were away at Henlow. It was suggested that we could erect the Quonset at Old Warden and rent out space to several other private owners interested in being based there. Shuttleworths were so desperate for more covered accommodation at that time that the arrangement proposed by them was that in return for us giving them space in the building, we could erect it rent-free on the opposite side of the airfield to their main site. This soon turned into their proposal that we give them the building in return for free accommodation in their new No. 5 hangar for as long as we operated the Jackaroo. The upshot of that was that our Quonset, split lengthwise into two sections erected side-by-side, provided the workshop accommodation for airframe woodworking and erection until 1984 (nowadays used to house the Carriage Collection). In practice we never moved out of the blister but at last it seemed we had a permanent home and on what to me was the most glorious grass airfield anywhere.

Meanwhile, in August 1966 we had carried out our first Annual Check under the watchful and sometimes belligerent eye of Harold Best-Devereux. I knew "Dev" from my days in 406 Sqdn. ATC, where he had been at first our Aircraft Recognition Instructor and then, postwar, our OC. When I left the RAF I had returned as a civilian Aircraft Recognition Instructor for a year, so thought I knew "Dev" quite well. He had always been very keen on light aircraft and I knew he had been employed from 1936 by Luton Aircraft at Barton, Beds. However, by 1966 he had risen considerably in the world of light aviation, and was now a Consultant and 'B'-licensed Engineer, with a reputation for getting things done. When I approached him for assistance he agreed unhesitatingly to do what he could to help and arranged to come and do a pre-inspection survey and tell us what we had to do to get it signed out. "Dev" felt he had a reputation to maintain, and as a 'B'-man was a different kettle of fish altogether to the person I had known in the ATC. I got a real blasting-off when he came to look at the Jackaroo: in effect, how dare I present him with such a filthy aeroplane to look at – if this was our idea of presenting an aircraft for inspection we had better think again. I still don't believe it was that bad, but he made his point and on the odd occasions when he had to look it over later on, such as the next Annual, I made sure that it was spotless. He relented sufficiently to enable us to complete the Annual to his satisfaction, and in the process taught us quite a bit about the work that had to be carried out. I never looked at him as other than a good friend but, as with my favourite ginger tomcat, I learned to handle him with care.

Just as things were settling down in our new home at Old Warden, with the right quota of Flying Members and a whole load of Social Members (who at 30/- p.a. were delighted to help with cleaning etc.. in return for a little flying), with the final loan instalment of £195 paid off, things suddenly went very wrong again. We wrote off 'PAL in a stupid accident (see Chapter 8, "Flash, Bang, Wallop") and remained grounded for over 18 months. With the Insurance payment of £750, less £100 paid to the Insurance Company for the wrecked 'PAL, we looked around for a replacement. At first we could not locate another Jackaroo, which by now we all loved, and tried an Auster Autocrat G-APUK, again through Rimmer Aviation, at Fairoaks. It performed quite nicely two up, flown by D. Rimmer, but when asked to demonstrate its performance three-up, he suggested I fly it. With two other well-built chaps aboard it frightened the life out of me. At that time Fairoaks' main runway was faced by a row of poplar trees bordering the adjacent field. We got airborne in ground effect, but it didn't want to climb and, as with the Jackaroo at Swanton Morley, made its way across the rest of the airfield at less than 20 ft, with insufficient room to put down before we crossed the airfield boundary. Now faced with a field edged on all sides by trees, I really had severe doubts about what would happen next. We just cleared the poplars, making a very close inspection of the tops as we did so, and decided unanimously that this Autocrat was not for us.

Later that week we heard of another Jackaroo, G-AOIR, for sale at Blackpool, out of C. of A., but dispensation could be arranged for a positioning flight for renewal. At £450 we thought we could get the C. of A. done at Warden Aviation for the remaining £200, having now learnt how to do most jobs, including rebuilding wooden structures and recovering. What I had not reckoned on was that, having started helping with the rebuild of Shuttleworth's LVG C.VI, there would be pressure on us to get that done as quickly as possible, to the extent of having Warden Aviation do the C. of A. on the Jackaroo so that we could finish dying the lozenge fabric for the LVG, a time-consuming job that took us 1,100 hours before we had finished it.

We flew 'OIR down from Blackpool, getting slightly lost when almost home (see Chapter 9, "Lost"). When we finally had a chance to have a good look at what we had bought, some extreme doubts were expressed as to whether it had been a good buy or not. It was indeed the tattiest Jackaroo I have ever set eyes on and we determined to fit the better, undamaged bits of 'PAL wherever possible. It still retained the last paint scheme used by Wiltshire School of Flying before they went into liquidation in 1967, black fuselage and tail with aluminium-doped wings. Unvarnished aluminium dope has a habit of turning a scruffy shade of grey when it ages. The black was dull and sundry red-doped patches applied liberally here and there on both black and aluminium did nothing to enhance the general scheme. The rudder and elevators had decidedly un-Tigerlike kinks in the tubular trailing edges and the cowlings looked as if they had been used as a goal in a game of ice-hockey. I knew we could have done something with it, but alas some newly-recruited Warden Aviation staff seemed considerably less experienced and able than we now were, and the job stretched on and on, gathering a considerably greater number of booked hours than did our LVG fabric work.

I had done a lot of research on the colours and history of the LVG, and at that time probably knew as much about the lozenge camouflage patterns as anyone else in the country; what was more I had undertaken to mix the dyes and establish a way of applying them in the correct repetitive pattern to the fabric, and once started on the very messy task, no one else wanted to take it on. A small team of Club members beavered away on dying the fabric, sometimes working to as late as 1.00 am. The LVG has a wingspan of 45 ft, and both surfaces of wings and tailplane are covered with dyed fabric, using five colours on top and five different colours underneath. Five galvanised steel sheet templates were made, one for each colour; each colour dye, mixed from the three basic hues, had to be sprayed separately, drying the wet fabric with a hair dryer immediately after spraying, so that the colours would not run into the adjacent lozenges. A forever, very mucky, job, but one that gave immense satisfaction when it was completed, and probably for the first time in the UK in 50 years it became possible to view a full-size, authentic, lozenge-camouflaged WW1 German aircraft.

Finally the work was finished and the Jackaroo emerged in a more normal colour scheme of all-aluminium with red top-decking, fin and registration letters. With 'PAL's undamaged cowlings, rudder and elevators it looked even tidier than 'PAL had done. Unfortunately, we had already discovered another hitch in the proceedings, in that the previous owner had not settled his debts with the maintenance organisation at Blackpool who had signed out the positioning flight. They had retained the Log Books and threatened to hold them until he had paid them what he owed them, and this dragged on for many more months. Not until April 1970 did we finally have 'OIR returned to us for test-flying, and another six weeks before the C. of A. air test was completed by Desmond Penrose and we were clear to use it again. It took many months to pay off the cost of the C. of A., aided by David Ogilvy's agreement to offset the

1,100 hours we had spent on the LVG fabric against those booked on the "Jack" by Warden Aviation.

By now we were down to 8 members and relieved we were not dependent on annual utilisation to maintain our income. Before the accident we had recouped enough to remove the temporary surcharge of 10/- per hour that had helped cover the first high C. of A. costs, but now had to put it back up to £3.60 for the same reason plus an increase in fuel costs. In 1971, our insurance cost £89, covering £1,000 hull and £50,000 Third Party and pilot indemnity, including ". . . whilst officially practising for and competing in Air Displays, Competitions"! £50 excesses, pilots' experience 70 hrs minimum and a 15% No Claims Bonus! Ah! Happy days.

But we were not out of the woods yet, as the ARB advised at the next Annual that the fabric on the wings and the rear fuselage was now so old (under the aluminium dope could be found the wartime camouflage applied when they were Tiger Moth components!) that it would have to be replaced on at least the lower wings before the next Annual. The plan to get round this problem was to repair and recover all four wings from 'PAL so that they would be ready to fit when the second Annual was due, leaving only the rear fuselage to deal with at the next C. of A.

The best laid plans don't always work out and a couple of months before the Annual was due we had finished only one wing, with the second ready for recovering. Dave Elphick had by now been a member of the Club for a year or more and like me was interested in obtaining a Tiger Moth. We had done most of the work on the lower wings and offered to pay Malcolm Frazer to do the upper wings (Farm Aviation had just billed another owner £360 for recovering two upper wings) in return for the acquisition of the remains of 'PAL and the wings from 'OIR. In fact, the uncovered but reworked lower wing was found to have a cracked front spar on inspection, and that set the whole job back again while the spar was changed. Fortunately we obtained dispensation to continue with the existing wings, replacing the fabric at the next C. of A. Eventually all the wings were repaired and recovered, the rear fuselage stripped, decorroded and recovered, and the opportunity taken to remove the unsightly strakes. The Jackaroo finally emerged from the '73 C. of A. better than when it left the Thruxton workshops, now with new fabric throughout, new perspex, a new lighter aluminium cabin floor in place of the oily Tiger original ply, and in the smart new colour scheme which it still carries, though now the original red has been replaced by blue.

During the rebuild we finally found an explanation of why the Jackaroo was so much easier to land than a Tiger, and lent itself so well to crosswind landings. We had always put it down to the extra width of the undercarriage, which it largely was, but another factor was the angle of incidence of the tailplane: whereas the Tiger's tailplane had an

TOP: Eddie Riding gave me my first "hands on" in Piper Cub G-AKAA.
Photo: G.A. Cull.
MIDDLE: Best of the bunch! Auster J/1N Alpha G-AIGT of the Luton Flying Club.
Colour was all-silver with red trim and registration letters. Photo: The author.
BOTTOM: 'IGT just after my first solo, the 21st June 1964.
Photo: Alan Brett.

TOP: Delivery flight 1 – Thruxton Jackaroo G-APAL and myself on arrival at Old Warden, 4th April 1965. Photo: The author's collection.
BOTTOM: 'PAL somewhere over Bedfordshire in 1967.
Photo: D. Wright.

TOP: 'PAL after removal from the hedge near Silverstone, May 1965 – note the downhill slope! The friendly farmer hoisted 'PAL up from the ditch with a tractor, and perched it on a haybale, with another to hold the tail down. Photo: The author.

BOTTOM: Wings and prop removed in preparation for transport to Sywell. This shot shows well the shape of the Jackaroo cabin and the amount by which the engine was moved forward on conversion from a Tiger Moth. Photo: The author.

TOP: Hauling away the sad wreck of 'PAL at Duckend Farm, Wilstead on the 6th July 1968. The tailskid was broken off by Electricity Board engineers when pulling down the tail. Note the twisted top wings, which sprang straight when removed!
Photo: Alan Brett.
BOTTOM: The nose of 'PAL after arguing with cables at Duckend Farm, Wilstead. The upper cable creased the spinner and the lower rear cut into the front cowl and engine. The rear c/s struts buckled, allowing the petrol tank to drop at the rear.
Photo: Alan Brett.

incidence angle of 0 deg, that on the "Jack" was decreased to −3 deg to partially offset the moment of the engine, located 6 inches further forward than the Tiger. This gave better penetration in turbulent conditions and noticeably more stable flight, but the really beneficial effect was that the stick could be hauled fully back just before touchdown and held there, and the Jackaroo would obediently stay on the ground without any suggestion of a bounce. Most of those who derided the "Jack" never discovered just how much more delightful she was to fly than a Tiger Moth.

In the course of the C. of A. rework, another shock awaited us. It seemed that though civilian Gipsy Majors were cleared for 1,500 hours between major overhauls, ex-military engines had only 1,200 hours unless they had the infamous crankshaft Mod. 2495 incorporated, which seemingly ours had not. Suddenly, from 550 hours remaining engine life we were down to 250 hours, which would keep us flying for less than three years before some expensive expenditure would be required in the engine department! Zero-time Gipsies were no longer available for £295 as they had been when we started: by then one could expect to pay £2,000 or more!

Apart from the Sword of Damocles hanging over us engine-wise, the next three years passed largely without incident, although by the winter of '72 we had been threatened with eviction from Old Warden; this was averted by reminding David Ogilvy of the letter he had sent us promising rent-free accommodation for as long as we kept the Jackaroo. Shuttleworth's were always short of accommodation, so we agreed to pay a hangarage rent of £8 per month to help with the costs of building a new hangar. To offset this, the subs were raised to £3 per month and new members were to pay a non-returnable joining fee of £30. At the same time the hourly rate was increased to £4.80 to provide a contribution towards the cost of engine life extension, with advance payment for hours in 10-hour blocks giving a 10% reduction. This was indeed a period of 'high' national inflation!

1976 started with an unfortunate minor accident at Rush Green. I flew the Jackaroo there as previously arranged for signing out a 50 hr check; with Malcolm Frazer now departed from Old Warden for New Zealand, Farm Aviation had agreed to continue with the arrangements whereby we did the work and their engineers checked it out. On taxying up to the hardstanding in front of the hangars, I was waved on by a man in white overalls, who I expected to haul on the wingtip to swing the Jackaroo to a stop in front of the hangar. There was a very slight downslope, and when it became clear that the aircraft, now moving at about 1-2 mph was not going to stop of its own accord, I could scarcely believe my eyes when the marshaller turned and ran, leaving me to trickle into a Pawnee parked on the apron. Although I switched off as soon as I realised the overalled figure, having got me into this situation, was not staying to help, the metal prop continued to rotate, biting into the Pawnee's aileron. The Jackaroo's starboard wing nudged into the Pawnee's rudder, causing no damage to that but snapping the wing leading edge. It appeared that the chap in overalls was not a member of the groundstaff and had no right to be emulating one! Very embarrassing all round, and the last person I wanted to upset in this way was Bill Bowker.

The solution to our engine hours problem presented itself in a way we would not really have wished for. The summer of 1976 was a very hot dry one and the mown grass surface at Old Warden hardened like concrete, offering no bite to the steerable tailskid and little rolling resistance to the wheels. One of our newer members, though with plenty of hours on taildraggers, had perhaps not at that time cottoned on to how necessary it was to taxy slow enough to be able to steer out of trouble with a goodly blast of slipstream over the rudder. Taxying over to the fuelling bowser, the customary slowing when the throttle was closed just did not happen, and faced with an oncoming wire fence, and a skid that was definitely not steering, it would have taken a great deal more nerve than he was willing to expend to open the throttle fully and hope that the rudder would respond. Consequently, once again the"'Jack" trickled into an immovable object, this time with the prop rotating sufficiently fast to damage itself and require a crankshaft check. The fence was damaged and pieces of broken wire hurled themselves at the windows of the Control Van sufficiently hard to break several. Fortunately there were no spectators close by, but we had put up a big 'black' in the eyes of the management.

With the crankshaft needing to be removed and refitted in order to be crack-tested, much of the cost of incorporating crankshaft Mod. 2495 and 2690 (which gave a further extension to 1,800 hrs) was to be borne by the insurance, and Hants & Sussex Engineering who did the work were only too pleased to modify the crankshaft at our expense at the same time. Needless to say, the crankshaft was not cracked! Thus we retrieved our 300 hrs and gained an extra 300 hrs for an outlay of less than £200, but at quite a cost to our reputation at Old Warden. Whilst the engine was away we carried out the Annual, and the happenings during the subsequent air test can be read about in Chapter 15, "Things That Go Bump in the Night."

Meanwhile, national inflation was still galloping away, and we increased our monthly subs to £5, joining fee to £40, and hourly rate to £7.80. 1978 and '79 passed quietly enough, perhaps the most notable event in which we took part being the DH Moth Club's "'Famous Grouse' Rally" from Hatfield to Strathallan and back. We had joined the Moth Club as Founder Members and had taken part in most of the events they held, most important being the annual Woburn Abbey Meetings. We made the "Famous Grouse" by the skin of our teeth, picking up our C. of A. renewal documents from the CAA office at Hatfield on the morning of the event! What a fantastic outing that was, at that time seeing probably the biggest assemblage of Tiger Moths on one airfield since the war, some 45 or so being present (one day I will count them again, having photographed all the entrants). This has probably been surpassed on subsequent Woburn meetings.

1979 also produced a real windfall at the end of the year, when the late-lamented John Crewdson approached us with the offer of some film work. This was no ordinary scene-shooting, the flying needing to take place in Egypt for filming *"The Curse of King Tut"* for ITV. There had been thoughts of flying the aircraft out there, something I would have given my eye teeth to do, but there was insufficient time to do that and it was dismantled and flown out in a Tradewinds CL-44. We were extremely worried about the possibility of the engine imbibing desert sand, and wanted an air filter fitted. Although assured this would be looked after, it did not happen, but the Gipsy appeared to have suffered no harm. The film, perhaps deservedly, was only given one showing; unfortunately I did not then possess a video recorder so have only watched it once. It was amazing how much the aircraft's appearance was changed for the film, especially when in some interior shots it appeared to have grown to the size of a Dakota! The original arrangements had been for one month's hire, but by the time we got it back it was just over two months, and our bank balance had increased by £4,500! There was no evidence of any damage and the paintwork looked as good as when it left us.

By now 80-octane lead-free petrol had gone, to be replaced by 2-star car fuel, both the latter and the aviation spirit substitute 100LL burning at too hot a temperature for the aluminium-bronze heads fitted to the Gipsy Major 1. Consequently, the bronze heads suffered burnt valve seats and the valves were also prone to burning, so that the heads needed to be removed every 40 hours for reseating and checking. As it took us approximately 40 hours to do this, it meant that for every hour spent in the air we had to spend at least one hour working on the engine! The answer was either to fit aluminium heads and high-compression pistons (converting the engine to a Major 1C with a higher horsepower rating and fuel consumption) or to fit steel inserts for the valve seats, an approved mod that originated in Australia. We had succeeded in sourcing the required steel and having the mod carried out on the heads so that we could get back to a more normal life between head overhauls. The lead content in the fuel however continued to give us problems in the way of lead deposits on the plugs; on the last check before take-off one of the plugs would foul up and the resulting mag-drop would see us all climbing out and repairing to the workshops to clean and retest the plugs. A real pain in the neck! Eventually it was found that modern car or motor-cycle plugs would get round this problem and give a much more reliable life than the ancient approved plugs we were using.

Another change that came about was that it was no longer possible to ask passengers to sign away their dependent's indemnity before a flight (that they flew at their own risk), much to their disgust. The consequences for all members if one had an accident in which a passenger was killed was too frightening to contemplate. It meant that we had to take out cover for the passengers and, what with this and the astronomical indemnities asked for by the Crown and others for flying into their airfields, our insurance costs were soaring. Another change that caused us a headache was the requirement for seats to be fitted with shoulder harnesses. Whilst this made sense, it was finally recognised that in some aircraft this simply could not be done, there being nowhere strong enough to take the strain, in which case the aircraft owner had to apply for dispensation. We did both, in that we got our dispensation, and fitted shoulder straps to the backs of the front seats (the rear seats were always so fitted). The reason we applied for dispensation was that we could not see a way in which to ensure that the extra harness could apply more than token restraint, fitted as they were to the seats themselves – even so they were better than nothing.

By 1980, subs were increased again, to £7.50 per month, the joining fee to £60 and flying hour rate to £10.80. With our new-found wealth, the value of which was ebbing away rapidly due to inflation, we looked around to decide what best to use it for. The prime requirement was for a replacement engine, preferably zero-houred, but we also needed some new boots, the tyre wear indicators now so shallow that something would need to be done soon. The other item, almost falling into the class of a luxury, was to replace the steel bracing wires and end fittings with stainless steel ones, saving the continuing, time-consuming and hated chore of decorroding and reprotecting the surfaces. The original wires were protected with a form of cadmium plating when new, some 40 years previously, but this had long been weathered away on the edges so that rust was continually bubbling through the protective paint, no matter what we did with them. The DH Moth Club obtained for us both tyres and a set of bracing wires and fittings, but as an example of the inflation we were then suffering the costs had increased from £291 when ordered to £413 by the time they were delivered, and any new sets ordered were over £600!

Meanwhile, the late Peter Franklin had offered us a zero-timed engine, a frustrated export order to Brazil some 20 years previously, which he had acquired then and sat on ever since, inhibited and in its original packing. That cost us £2,250 and took almost a year actually to extract from him, finally being fitted in 1982. This resulted in halving the oil consumption from 2 pints/hr to one! We had also acquired a metal cabin top from a Mk. 3 Jackaroo (G-APAO) which had been stood on its nose in N. Ireland and converted back to a Tiger. This was a desirable replacement for the earlier wooden version fitted to 'OIR, the wood now showing its age and the glue joints becoming very suspect. This and the new bracing wires were to be fitted at the next C. of A. due in '85. By 1984, subs had risen to £10 p.m., entry fee to £75 and hourly rates to £12!

From 1973 on, we were under continuing pressure to move out of the blister hangar at Old Warden, for a whole variety of reasons, but mostly put down to insurance requirements and the need to be able to quickly evacuate, from the main hangar behind the blister, any Collection aircraft housed there. Financial problems for Shuttleworths came and went, and the upshot of this was that the blister was rarely left entirely devoid of private aircraft, always a vital source of income. We had abandoned our rent-free status but had continually to remind the new management that we were there because they had our Quonset as their main workshops and had written assurance from them of our stay as long as we had the Jackaroo. Hangarage charges, like everything else, had continually risen but a crunch point came in '84 when we were asked to pay £20 per week, still for an open blister, thought by the management to be the going rate. We finally convinced them otherwise by producing a receipt for lock-up hangarage at Cambridge for £10.59 and had ours retained at £10.

But the writing was on the wall. Our C. of A. renewal, started early in '85 at Andy Brinkley's airfield at Meppershall (Andy having been a member for several years), proved too ambitious and too much for a new generation of members to cope with in a reasonable space of time, and by now my son and I had our own Tiger Moth to look after as well (based at Gransden from mid-'84). Another time-consuming activity I became deeply involved with from early '85 was a proposal to ship the Tiger and the "Jack" over to the States for a double coast-to-coast flight, following the Oregon Trail on the westbound flight. This finally came to fruition with the Club winning the Canadian Club "Club Challenge" competition that year, in which most of the flying members would take part, flying the Jackaroo over various stages of the flight in the summer of 1986. The C. of A. work dragged on right through to the end of the year, but not before we celebrated both the Club's 21st anniversary and our winning the "Club Challenge." We had continued paying our hangarage rental at Old Warden whilst the aircraft was away at Meppershall, and we were pleased to move back there in January.

The first half of 1986 was spent feverishly preparing for the American trip, everyone involved being tasked with some part of the extensive preparation work (see Chapter 21, "Pinpoint Navigation" and Chapter 22, "Offa's Dyke"). Alas it all came to nought when Canadian Club's PR

Agency (believed to have overspent the funds allotted for the Competition) successfully cancelled the flight, leaving three of the members and their wives to carry on alone, mostly at their own expense, using an Aeronca Champion bought for the flight (see the book *"Flying the Oregon Trail"*). The damage had been done though, morale bottomed, serviceability suffered, members left and when the Club was finally forced to leave Old Warden in April 1988, steps were soon taken to wind up, the Jackaroo and its spare engine etc. being sold to one of the members, Les Smith (still at the time of writing a part owner). One problem was that by then the older members (including the writer) were finding difficulty in ground-handling the Jackaroo, and wanted to opt for something lighter and cheaper to operate such as a Piper Cub, subs by then having increased to £26 p.m. and hourly rate to £15.

So, after 24 years, in July 1988 the Stevenage Flying Club finally came to an end, unique in having exclusively operated a Jackaroo throughout its active life, 21 of those years flying from Old Warden. It is fair to say that a great many people enjoyed many hours of grass-roots, vintage flying, either as a pilot or a passenger, which otherwise they would not have done; especially in conjunction with the Vintage Aircraft Group from Finmere but particularly at Old Warden, with David Ogilvy's continual encouragement and support during his time as General Manager with the Shuttleworth Collection. The Club was always a hungry, 'hands-on' organisation, and those of the members who wished to gained very useful experience in servicing and rebuilding not readily available elsewhere. I have no regrets about my time with the Club and I know that most other members feel the same way: when we were up, we topped the clouds, and with one last exception, when we were down (and we often were) we found ways to survive.

CHAPTER 4

HOT AND BOTHERED

Nowadays, the private pilot is served very well by articles in magazines and textbooks etc., stressing the points to watch, whether obvious or obscure, to ensure that all flying is safe flying. All the more surprising perhaps that each issue of the quarterly Safety Bulletin of the General Aviation Safety Committee (GASCO) bears a distressingly long list of accidents of all types, that have occurred to all sorts of people, in all kinds of aeroplanes, operating under all manner of conditions. Why should this be? I suppose in the end it depends on the extent to which each individual reads, learns and inwardly digests all the welter of facts and fancies thrown at him, together with the experiences he undergoes and how much he feels "it won't happen to me." Those lessons that are learnt best tend to be the ones where it did happen just like the books say; fortunately, the average pilot has it happen to him under conditions in which he gets away with it, others are unlucky and are the subject of entries in the GASCO Bulletin. If he is very lucky, he gets quite a fright but nothing worse, and this drives the lesson home swift and sure. In my ramblings about flying, inevitably some frights show through; although at the time I may not have been at all appreciative of the future benefits, in retrospect I feel that it was fortunate that they happened under the conditions in which they did, so that they were no more serious than a fright.

Like the first time we went to Swanton Morley. A Breakfast Patrol was organised by the local Flying Club and we had received an invitation. It all sounded very exciting – defending aircraft would be circulating within a 5-mile radius of the airfield and would attempt to read the registration letters of any visiting aircraft entering this circle, and before they reached an inner zone, corresponding to the airfield circuit. Visiting aircraft were restricted to flying above 1,500 ft altitude but otherwise could take whatever evasive action they desired short of actually ramming the defenders. Any crew landing between 09.00 and 10.30 without having their registration taken would be entitled to a free breakfast in the Clubhouse.

At this time we had just had our Jackaroo, G-APAL, returned from an extensive and protracted C. of A. which had occupied all but six weeks of the time since we had acquired her, and very smart and clean she looked. We had no trouble in mustering a full crew of four; apart from myself there was Bob, about the same build as myself, i.e. about 11½ stones in weight, Sid with a solid, stocky 15 stones and Ken, a lanky Australian who came along with Sid and who probably turned the scales at about 14 stones: i.e. about 730 lbs total.

Comparing earlier notes with the findings of 'PAL's previous owner, we saw no problem with getting airborne off the 3,000 ft of grass available both at Panshanger (where we were then based) and Swanton Morley.

Penetrating the defence zone on this, our first Breakfast Patrol, obviously called for devious tactics. If we had been defending, where would we concentrate our resources? Maps of the area showed very few airfields and little else other than the North Sea to the north-east, so that might be expected to be the most lightly-defended quarter. Should we come in high or low? One line of argument followed the "Hun in the Sun" approach; with the sun still in the east this would be from the right direction, but how high should we be for this to be effective and how would we get down within the inner zone? Would a fully-laden Jackaroo aspire to great enough heights for that to be practical? Second thoughts on this one indicated not. So, we would come in as low as possible on the basis that aircraft flying below one's own level are the most difficult to spot against the background of the earth below. Well then, how about the detour so that we can approach from the north-east instead of straight in from the south-west? To be worthwhile we would need to skirt round the defence zone well out of sight, which implied probably not nearer than 10 miles to it. Calculations indicated that this would add some 27 miles to our direct route. Further, more urgent, calculations, with an eye on the time, showed that if we deviated that much we would arrive after the defending aircraft had all gone home and wouldn't qualify. In fact if we didn't soon get under way we wouldn't have enough time for even a straight-in approach; which settled all arguments without further ado.

Swanton seemed a long way away, further than I had flown before in one hop, and with a chance of getting lost it seemed desirable to have the tank filled to its full 19 gallons capacity; so it was. There was just a hint remaining of that light early morning mist that portrays a fine summer's day in the making, but the air was still cool and calm, with barely enough movement to stir the leaves on the trees. Thus, at the hour of 9.15 on a mild sunny morning in early September, the Jackaroo lifted easily and comfortably off the long, smooth grass runway.

We had stowed ourselves and our belongings aboard, with no more difficulty than is usually involved in getting four large adults settled into the cabin, in the best compromise between having room to operate controls, spread maps and not suffering too much from cramp or creature discomfort. Bob, as a student pilot just approaching the end of his training, was in the rear pilot's seat so that he could put in some dual time (not loggable as such but good practice) and the lanky Australian sat in the front passenger's seat where his nether appendages could find maximum stowage space, accompanied by stern warnings to keep his oversize feet out of my rudder pedals. This left Sid in the rear passenger seat surrounded by cameras and bags and maps, with the rear parcel shelf piled high with coats and other paraphernalia.

The flight up to Swanton Morley proceeded smoothly enough; the air was as calm as a millpond and 'PAL, proud of her smart new appearance, positively purred, performing impeccably. In fact so smoothly did things go that four pairs of eyes, swivelling constantly round all four quarters above, below and at our own level, saw no sign of any other aircraft at all until we were on the circuit and safely inside the inner zone, comfortably within the time limit (well, a few minutes within). We concluded that the defending aircraft were all swarming at the north-eastern side of the airfield, guarding against the "smart Alecs" coming in from the sun. Smugly we wandered into the Clubhouse to book in but sadly could find no one who professed to know about free breakfasts. By the time we had actually got ourselves booked in it was well beyond 10.30 and if we didn't hurry up and place an order soon, breakfast would be finished. Inner men being what they are, first consideration was to actually feed the brutes, pay for the meal and try and sort it out later. Much later we discovered a list of aircraft reported by the defenders, plus those miserable few which had both got in undetected and, more difficult, had unearthed someone to report this fact to. In the latter activity we had failed dismally and were not even recognised as being there at all. We were convinced that the Club had an invisible man on their books because we never saw anyone actually pin the list to the wall despite constant surveillance.

But a good time was had by all and we enjoyed browsing round the parked aircraft and the hangars which, at a place like Swanton Morley, always had something of interest lurking in dark corners at the back. It was also interesting to listen to, and occasionally join in, odd snatches of conversation in the crowded Clubhouse, in those days more of the form: ". . . and just as I had given up all hope of locating where we were, we flew over a road junction which had the road numbers painted on it; we were 10 miles off track and 5 miles ahead of where we expected to be . . ." Nowadays of course such conversations tend to be more of the form: ". . . and our VOR packed up and I couldn't find the frequency of . . ." which by comparison leaves me a little cold.

We had arranged to be back by lunch, and after taking our place in the refuelling queue and booking out we reckoned to be off by 12.00. By now the sun was high in the heavens and the temperature was climbing rapidly. Already the tarmac in front of the hangars was noticeably hot through the thin soles of my sandals, and the early morning mist was replaced by a shimmering haze. It was well on the way to being a real scorcher and we could hardly believe our luck in getting such beautiful weather. We planned to fly north up to the coast and follow the coastline round to Kings Lynn and then go up to 3,000 ft over the top of a military zone that lay on our direct route back to Panshanger. Hence with this added distance, again it seemed wise to top the tank up to the full mark when we refuelled.

Having crammed everyone in, somewhat bloated by the generous breakfast they had partaken of, together with our assorted paraphernalia, we taxied out for take-off, the long expanse of grass stretching out clear before us. Receiving a 'green' from the tower I opened up and started to roll. We gained speed quickly enough but there seemed some slight reluctance on the part of the aeroplane to leave the ground. When we seemed to have reached normal flying speed I hauled her off thinking it would be better once we had got into the air. Again, there was a hesitance about wanting to fly, and she touched down again, lightly and briefly several times, before finally becoming positively airborne. The controls felt strangely soggy so initially I stayed level to let the speed build up before climbing away. Any peculiarity in the feel I put down to my inexperience with what was then still a new machine to me, but I was still concerned that by the time we reached the edge of the airfield we had little more than 50 ft or so of altitude. Our Jackaroo wasn't feeling so good!

Ahead, the open greensward was now replaced by parkland, with some big old trees looming menacingly here and there. "Come on, old girl, what is the matter with you?" The engine was giving its normal maximum of some 2,150 rpm indicated, but the A.S.I. seemed reluctant to move off the 50 knots mark while the altimeter was positively glued below the first 100 ft division. Any attempt to pull the nose up was accompanied by a downward movement of the A.S.I. needle, that soggy feeling back in the controls and no marked change on the altimeter. I tried it a couple of times before I accepted that that was not the way out of this situation. On top of that, to add to my troubles, we were encountering a lot of thermal turbulence in flying so low and the aircraft was lurching and wallowing about, so that I was continually wrestling with the controls.

Fortunately the ground fell away slightly to our left, with fewer trees, and thankfully we turned, albeit a flat, cautious turn, seeking out the lower ground. We gained perhaps another 50 ft or so ground clearance this way and gave ourselves breathing space to try and think the thing through in a logical manner.

Normally, I prefer to gaze on hilly scenery and for this reason very rarely visit Norfolk, but now I blessed the flat terrain. I can think of several places I have flown out of where this performance would have had us touching down outside the airfield!

There seemed no immediate explanation for the loss of performance; the engine sounded smooth and sweet enough and the revs, with the throttle lever hard up against its stop, were as to be expected. Although the turn and bank needles were jumping about in sympathy with the bucking and swaying, they were more or less centred, showing no extra drag through holding yaw or slip. There didn't really seem to be anything else I could do to improve things. In a car for example, one may be suffering clutch slip or binding brakes etc., if the engine is running satisfactorily while the car is not, but here there seemed no obvious reason why we were not flying normally!

It was hot in the cabin, with the sun beating down through the orange-tinted perspex roof panels although, in my case at least, that was not the only reason for the beads of perspiration on my forehead. Suddenly I realised that all the sliding windows were fully open and that this would create some degree of increased drag. By now I was clutching at any straw and at least in getting them closed I was doing something positive, but any difference was not immediately noticeable except that the pleasant cooling draught was no longer blowing through the cabin and hot became hotter.

Hot? . . . Hot!!! Of course, that was the explanation! What was I thinking about to have overlooked the adverse effect a rise in temperature has on the lifting ability of an aeroplane? Oh! yes, I had read often enough of aircraft not being able to lift off high-altitude airfields in the tropics, but this was near sea level, in England, in late summer! Nobody had rammed this possibility home to me and I had not experienced these conditions during my recent training, but it was suddenly obvious that there could be no other explanation. There was no way to check there and then just what effect the heat was having but at least there was a plausible reason for the loss of performance.

So what to do? Continue on round the circuit and land back on, or carry on and hope? In the latter case it was not just hope, as every minute flying at full throttle lightened our load by nearly a pound of weight of fuel burnt. In the five minutes it would take us to complete a circuit we would be 5 lb lighter. We were also almost imperceptibly gaining height and by now had probably 150 ft clearance whilst all around us the land was flat. The higher we went the cooler it would become and this would ease the problem; all these factors were cumulative and all in our favour. By the time we had completed the third side of the circuit my mind was made up. With some 200 ft of altitude and feeling better every minute, we kept on going, heading north to the coast.

When we reached the coast the altimeter was showing 900 ft, and the aircraft was behaving more normally though still slow to climb. We ambled along the coast from Brancaster Bay well into the Wash, now enjoying the sunshine and the scenery, and then started to climb to gain the regulation 1,500 ft altitude over Kings Lynn. From there, things settled down to normality and we had no further difficulty in attaining the required 3,000 ft clearance over the MATZ (Military Air Traffic

Zones) that we would pass over on our return to Panshanger. After we landed I talked over what had happened with Bob, who up till then had merely thought I had been indulging in some unorthodox low-flying. At least he also would now be aware of the dangers of the situation if it ever repeated itself, but I didn't mention it to the other two: "where ignorance is bliss 'tis folly to be wise"!

Later on we obtained a copy of the Flight Manual (which the previous owner should have had but did not). From this we discovered that the official maximum fuel load for a Jackaroo, as quoted in the Operating Instructions, was limited to 14 gallons when carrying four 160 lb-weight occupants, i.e. 5 gallons of fuel less than we were carrying, and with about 90 lb less passenger weight. But as we had no Operating Instructions or Flight Manual we didn't know that we were considerably overweight and, as with the bee which can be scientifically proved to be incapable of flight, nobody had thought to tell the Jackaroo that she couldn't fly with that much weight; so she did – easily and comfortably in the cool morning air, despite being something like 125 lb overweight on take off, with the C.G. position behind the rear limit (i.e. tail-heavy, though I had not noticed that).

At 80 deg Fahrenheit and normal maximum load, the theoretical ceiling was 750 ft maximum and an extra 400 ft was required for take-off, although with the length of run available the latter was not a problem. No wonder then, that with that excess 125 lb she had to be coaxed into the air! With a less forgiving aeroplane the other factors could well have been disastrous. It was not possible to establish from the Manual what the theoretical climb rate would be as there was no way to extrapolate for overweight conditions – that however was something we found out the hard way and I would guess was less than 50 ft per minute. If there was one thing I gained from this trip, in addition to the overall enjoyment and a rather worrying 30 seconds or so after take-off from Swanton Morley, it was an unforgettable meaning for the phrase "hot and bothered"!

CHAPTER 5
IF YOU'VE TIME TO SPARE GO BY AIR

The words of the title are reputed to have been originated by BEA passengers marooned by fog at London Airport, as was so often the case before the successful 'no smoking' (as in chimneys) laws took effect. As a jet sardine I have very rarely had to spend more then the customary hour or so waiting at an airport but, in terms of flying myself anywhere, the title is very appropriate. Oh, I know that, as a means of getting to and from the sort of large-scale national air displays that are attended by the public in their tens of thousands, one saves all that tiresome queuing to get in and queuing to get out, but otherwise there are very few occasions on which I would choose deliberately to fly by ancient biplane purely to save time.

There was just one occasion when I naively thought I could more successfully keep a business appointment, some 125 miles away, by flying rather than taking the alternative surface travel. It was actually a job interview, about which I was fairly lukewarm, and the company involved fixed the time as 10.30 on a Monday morning in April. They offered a first-class train ticket with overnight accommodation but the thought of setting off from home in the opposite direction, for Sunday night in a hotel in London, did not appeal to me at all. The alternative was to travel by car, involving rather a lot of mileage on the old A5 road; this was mostly two-lane single carriageway at that time, still carrying the bulk of the heavy goods traffic to and from the industrial north-west and the corresponding ports. In the days before the motorways reached that far, this was not an appealing option either.

To ensure a timely and calm arrival meant leaving home at around 06.30 – ugh! At this time I had not long had my pilot's licence and was longing to make some practical use of it; apart from that, the travel expenses I could claim would cover the cost of the equivalent flying time if only I could find some way of flying. Out came the air charts and although there was no immediately adjacent aerodrome, a disused airfield was marked at Meir some 14 miles away. That 14 miles really should have warned me off but I wasn't going to give up that easily. According to the Air Touring Guide, Meir was listed as a disused wartime airfield operated PPO by the local council of Stoke-on-Trent. The Town clerk confirmed over the 'phone that it was available for use and promised to send me some literature.

Flying time would probably be around 1½ hours and allowing an hour at each end would still demand an early start from home, though 07.20 sounded nearly an hour better than 06.30. If the weather forecast on Sunday evening was bad, then it would be a last-minute change to go by car. Accordingly, when I wrote accepting the interview I mentioned that, rather than travel by train or car, I would fly into Meir and make my way from there. They agreed that this was OK and enquired solicitously whether I would like a car to meet me at Meir. This immediately put me on the spot. Of course I would prefer to be met, but it meant giving them a time of arrival with no easy way of informing them if I decided at the last minute to go by road. Regretfully I declined their car, 'regretting' being the operational word; I regretted it much more later on!

True to his word, the Town Clerk sent me a folder of bumf about Stoke-on-Trent, outlining how attractive the area was from the business point of view. To my relief there was a little map showing the location of Meir relative to the town; his letter explained that the airfield was also open to the public as common land, that I could land anywhere an the open spaces but that it was up to me to ensure that I didn't damage any of the local human or canine population that might be wandering at large. There were no security arrangements for visiting aircraft but he suggested that I park adjacent to a hangar on the north-west edge of the area. There was a bus service on the main road into Stoke and taxis could come out from the town centre if I telephoned them.

It was obvious that I would need someone with me to help manhandle the aeroplane for parking and swinging the propeller etc., so I contacted Julian, an old colleague who I knew would be dead keen to help. Sure enough, Julian leapt at the opportunity and we arranged to meet at the airfield at 07.45 for an 08.00 take-off. Providing the aircraft was left fully fuelled and oiled, a quarter of an hour would be ample. Accordingly, I filled the tanks late Sunday afternoon and, knowing that nobody else had booked to fly the aircraft, went home leaving it ready to go. The Met man was quite hopeful about the weather for Monday, so the final act was to ring Julian and confirm that it was on.

We met as planned at around 07.40, but that was about the only one of the day's actions that went according to plan. The first thing that I found was that the fuel tank was no longer full – a glance at the flight log confirmed my worst fears. One of our Group members, notorious for flying without booking, had nipped in after I had left on Sunday and had flown for an hour without refuelling afterwards. He was not to know how vital a part of my careful planning he had disrupted and I am sure that had he known, he would not have done so. What to do? There was no fuel available at Meir and I could not afford the time it would take to divert to another airfield in the morning in order to fill up. Equally there was no certainty that I could get away from Meir in time to divert to an airfield that would still be open on the return journey, as I had anticipated doing if necessary. It was essential to have a full tank for the round trip and even that could, if the wind proved unfavourable for the return journey, be barely sufficient.

At least the engineering staff at Old Warden started work at 08.00, so we might still get away no later than, say 08.15. We could do little until they turned up. As the fuel pumps at that time were at the entrance to our hangar we could not even save time by pushing the aircraft out onto the field.

The minutes ticked frustratingly by until, at some time after 08.00, the first of the staff arrived. Now perhaps we could get on with refuelling and still retrieve the situation. But we were not yet finished with the hitches at Old Warden. The vital fuel pump and oil store keys were not in their usual place and more time was lost tracking them down. It seemed that someone who was working in a store shed over the other side of the airfield was the last known person to use the keys and it was thought that he had gone straight over there. So, off we went to seek out the elusive keys, fortunately, with some degree of success. However, by the time we had retrieved the keys, fuelled and oiled the aircraft, returned the keys to their rightful place, moved the aeroplane onto the airfield and started the engine, most of another precious hour had trickled away.

At last, we were airborne at 08.55. The wind was, if anything, slightly favourable and by running at maximum revs I managed to pull back 20 minutes, completing the flight in 1 hr 10 mins instead of the planned 1½ hours. We had no trouble either with navigation or in finding and identifying the old airfield. There were no runways, just a very large, rather irregular-shaped expanse of grass with slight undulations and more young trees scattered about than I had expected. Identification was rendered positive by the presence of a large black hangar as noted by the Town Clerk, and a main road and adjacent railway running past the north-eastern boundary. Circling round to pick out the best landing run, I was vastly relieved to find only one man and his dog on the field, and then nowhere near where I wanted to land. We touched down at 10.05 and the landing was smooth enough, but it did seem strange to be alighting on what was now, to all intents and purposes, a Public Park.

The next problem was where to leave the aeroplane. From the air there had seemed nowhere obviously better than anywhere else. The hangar was locked with no enclosure around it, though a public path ran along one side of it. Wherever we left the machine, it could be seen from a distance; in the end I taxied some 100 yards from the path so that casual passers-by would have to divert to get close to it. Julian, having seen how far we were from the town centre, elected to stay near it, having armed himself with plenty of reading matter, a flask and some sandwiches, and seemed quite happy to act as a guard.

All this had consumed more time and after I had climbed out of my flight overalls, found my brief case and made final, rather open-ended arrangements with Julian about our return, another 15 minutes had ticked by. This left me an impossible ten minutes to do 14 miles. It took most of that time to get down to the main road! When circling over it on arrival, this road had been full of buses (or were they trolley-buses?), lorries, cars etc., but now it was deserted. What was more, there was no sign of either a bus stop or a telephone kiosk in either direction. There was not even a pedestrian in sight to ask which way lay the nearest. Turning towards the town centre, I resolved to take whatever came first – telephone kiosk or bus stop. As it happened, neither appeared before the first bus bore in sight which fortunately stopped in answer to my frantic waving. That took twenty minutes to get me to the city centre where at last I found a telephone.

It was past eleven o'clock by the time I got through and made my apologies and the chap at the other end was understandably just a trifle put out. He suggested that I should walk round to the railway station and a car would meet me there. And so it went on – by the time the car turned up and delivered me to the reception area, and I had been met and conducted to the department where I was to be interviewed, it was so late that the man had gone to lunch!

I don't remember a great deal about the job interviews as such; the people I saw had presumably already written me off and were far more interested in the flying aspects, about which we had successive but, for me, rather repetitive conversations. Eventually, all the interviews had ground their way through and the last person I saw had the task of settling up my expenses and arranging for a car to take me back to Meir. Expenses were no problem, even taking the full hourly rate for the three hours flying time (then £9 total!), it came to less than what first-class rail fare and overnight accommodation would have been, so they were quite happy on that score. But now, I was becoming a trifle concerned over the time; there was no car immediately available and I was hoping to have time to top up with 80-octane if possible somewhere *en route*. As the minutes ticked by the possibility of so doing became progressively more remote.

Two cups of coffee and 20 minutes later the car returned and we were all relieved to see me on my way. I had time whilst waiting to reflect on what could have been happening at Meir in my absence; one could hardly expect Julian to have stayed in attendance all the time and the thought of leaving an old, fabric-covered biplane unguarded for any length of time in what was in effect a Public Park was something that had concerned me all day.

The chauffeur couldn't wait to get first-hand knowledge of all the details. He knew of Meir being used for occasional flying visits and that there were several resident aircraft, but he had never had occasion to visit the place, let alone pick up or deliver a pilot. His interest was even greater when be found out what type of aircraft it was! With his having more than a passing interest in old aeroplanes at least the drive back to

Meir gave little opportunity to brood further on what might await me there! When we got to the airfield he insisted on driving his large, plush, Armstrong Siddeley limousine over the grass to where the aircraft was parked, in case we needed his help.

To my relief the aircraft sat unconcernedly as I had left it, without sign of visible damage, but the fuel gauge float seemed even lower in the sight glass than when I had last looked at it. It was not that I thought that any fuel had been taken, simply that in the rush after our morning arrival, I had not looked at the gauge after parking. The next problem was fortunately soon resolved, this being that Julian was noticeably absent when we arrived. By the time I had walked round checking for damage and had discussed his absence with the chauffeur (who offered to drive me around to look for him), Julian could be seen approaching from the direction of the hangar.

Julian's story was soon told. He had stayed at or within sight of the aeroplane all day, having no great desire to walk any distance to anywhere else. He had caught up with some of his reading and had enjoyed a quiet picnic lunch in the sun. There had been very few people about, only one or two had come over to find out what the aeroplane was and what it was doing there, and his main preoccupation with animate objects had been in preventing the local canine population from watering the wheels. Bored? No, he had enjoyed the peace and quiet and his book. What more could I have asked in the circumstances?

Looking at the wind (which was now on our nose) the maps and the fuel gauge, confirmed that it would be advisable to try and find some fuel. Leicester would be closed, so too probably would Sywell, but Husbands Bosworth just might be open. They professed to be PPO but I already knew there was no phone near and this might soon be, if not already, an emergency landing, so I planned to fly over and have a look at them. Such airfields tended to be friendly havens in those days, PPO or not, and so it turned out.

Husbands Bosworth (there were actually two different airfields so-called, both I believe being separate remaining parts of one wartime aerodrome) was then, as now, a major gliding centre. Although powered aircraft are sometimes not over-welcome at such centres (like when arriving unannounced at the height of gliding activity with tow ropes and winches and tug-aircraft and, not least, gliders, in all directions), by the time we arrived at 5 minutes past 6 on a weekday evening, all the gliders had been tucked up for the night. At that time they were using two Tiger Moths as tug aircraft and the Jackaroo was recognisably one of the family – the fact that it was, as they said, a pregnant Tiger with four seats instead of two made it all the more interesting to them.

They knew all about administering to the needs of thirsty Tigers and quickly produced the necessary chamois leather-lined funnel, gallon measure and 45-gallon drum of 80-octane fuel. My request for a quart of "Straight 100 oil" (as opposed to detergent oil) was met by a blank stare and I was directed to another drum prominently marked "Tiger oil." The interest in Tigers and near-Tigers was mutual. I was invited to look at their Tiger standing out on the flight line and to commiserate with them over the state of its stable mate, which sat forlornly in the hangar with wings and tail unit removed. They mourned the temporary loss of the services of this machine and muttered about an unwelcome move afoot to replace the Tigers with something "more modern, like Piper Super Cubs"(!) which hopefully would spend less time in bits in the hangar.

Wandering out to the one standing outside I was amused to note that the registration letters on the fuselage were noticeably different to those on the rudder. Not altogether unheard of; their tongue-in-cheek reply to my facetious question about the identity of the aircraft was to the effect that they weren't certain whether to paint out the letters on the fuselage or those on the rudder: it didn't make much difference to them what this highly interchangeable set of parts was called today as it would probably all be changed round again next week.

We did not hang around too long; I had not looked up sunset times and in thinking about times of lighting-up over recent weeks it seemed that if we were still flying at 19.30 I might be getting worried. It was 18.30 when we bade farewell to our new-found friends and we were safely back on the ground by 19.15, well ahead of dusk as it turned out.

It had been an interesting day to say the least, but I resolved never again to attempt to fly in the Jackaroo to attend a business appointment in such circumstances. Certainly I had picked up another three hours of very enjoyable flying at no cost to myself at a time when for me this was an almost overriding consideration; we had visited two new airfields, but without Julian's help, it would have been even more impractical.

It is perhaps a reflection of the quality of life in those now far-off days to think that one could contemplate such a flight in such a carefree manner, be invited by the Town Council to land on their local parkland and leave an aeroplane unattended there for at least some of the time; one has to remember that in those days virtually all youngsters were either employed or at school during weekdays, so that one rarely found gangs of hooligans or school truants roaming around in the daytime looking for trouble.

The job interview? Well, what do *you* think?

CHAPTER 6

DAWN-TO-DUSK

It was in 1966 that the Tiger Club's annual Dawn-to-Dusk competition first came to my notice when, as Group Secretary, I received a poster and a sheet outlining the rules. Basically, the rules were simple: fly as far as possible between dawn (04.30) and dusk (21.30) on any one day in the Midsummer fortnight, June 14th to 28th. Distance was defined as straight-line tracks between start and finish points of every leg flown – dogleg tracks were allowed using observed turning points but tracks would only count in one direction. No other limit on flying time, but each time a landing was made, the aircraft had to stay on the ground a minimum of thirty minutes. Start, turning and refuelling points had to be aerodromes marked on a current half-million map, and were all decided by the entrant, but all competitors had to finish at Redhill, the home base of the Tiger Club. The competition was to be judged on written logs to be submitted within seven days of the flight and on information entered on the entry form. Entry was open to all with no restrictions on the type of aircraft.

As a flying and navigation competition it was to me the most appealing that I had come across. Unfortunately a few simple calculations showed that 14 flying hours' costs would be incurred by the entrant (solo crews only in 1966) and with my cost-imposed ration of hours per year this was more than I cared to invest in one event.

However, the following year, one of our Group members splashed out and bought himself a Tiger Moth, which he seemed keen to enter in all sorts of events. He was quickly made aware both about the 1967 Dawn-to-Dusk (which was now opened to 2-man crews) and the fact that I was ready, willing and, to a certain extent, able to crew with him if he were interested. The bait worked. Wally and his Tiger 'LTW were duly entered with me as co-pilot, on the understanding that I would look after all the organising and paperwork. Any expenditure would be split 50/50, but this would be significantly less than a solo entry at Group rates. Wally would also arrange for me to have some dual for conversion to the Tiger.

One thing was obvious from the start, the winner would have put in a lot of planning, preparation and careful thought beforehand, and I was going to be busy for the next few weeks. Neither Wally nor I was expecting to win, not having tackled anything like this before, but we were determined to enjoy an interesting and valuable experience in trying.

Early discussions revealed a prime problem straight away. Wally had not flown his Tiger long enough to have much idea of its fuel consumption or best cruising conditions, and until we knew range and airspeed we could only make half guesses at a route. Wally suggested we should spend a couple of weekends finding out, flying on some longish hops under differing cruising conditions, to establish optimum range and speed. If speed and range were not inversely proportional we could cruise too fast, incur additional 30-minute periods on the ground and cover a shorter distance overall – conversely one could cruise too slowly, spend more time in the air but cover less ground.

Initially, we had thought of trotting round the Continent, but the more we looked at the details, the more we began to realise that this was not going to be just a question of climbing into an aeroplane and flying all day long. We had no radio (which reduced the number of airfields that would accept us) and the Tiger lapped up only 80-octane unleaded fuel (which further reduced the number of airfields that we could use). We could only plan on being able to stay up for something like 2¼ hours (assuming a 30-minute contingency period) and in this time might fly between 150 and 250 miles depending on the wind. Furthermore, to achieve a 30-minute turnaround on the ground would virtually exclude Customs clearance or making ourselves understood in a foreign language (neither of us were linguists).

So ideas of going to the Continent began to fade; when we looked at the difficulty of flying differing tracks in and out we finally accepted, if reluctantly, abandoning the thought of crossing the Channel (as it happened, the second-place man started on the Continent and flew via Norway). Then we considered the idea of flying all round the coast but again all sorts of drawbacks presented themselves. Airfields were persistently not the right distance apart, or involved much crossing of long stretches of water or very high ground. Again, if the wind changed after flying up to, say, the North of Scotland on a tight schedule, it could prevent us getting back to Redhill before 9.30 in the evening.

So we dropped the more exotic routes and decided to work on the basis of one that took us on long straight legs initially, followed by many shorter dog-leg sections which we could cut if necessary, if and when time became tight. We assumed a prevailing south-westerly wind of 15 mph as that most likely to be encountered during the competitive fortnight, and then aimed to get as far upwind as possible, so that when heading back to Redhill on the later stages the wind would be on our tail.

However, we were stumped for really detailed planning until we knew 'LTW's optimum cruising conditions. Here we ran into the first of a series of snags which beset us till the start of the competition, some due to our lack of experience, some due to unforeseen circumstances, others due perhaps to shortsightedness on our parts. We had about ten weeks in which to prepare; this seemed ample and probably would have been but for two factors. One was that a C. of A. was shortly due on the Tiger and the other was that Wally was liable to hop off overseas on business at very short notice.

"DAWN to DUSK"

The
TIGER CLUB
ANNUAL   NAVIGATION   and
PILOTAGE ENDURANCE   Competition

is now open to all comers

The Competition will be held annually during the weeks of

JUNE 14—28

PRIZES :—The Duke of Edinburgh Trophy.   replica & £100
2nd : £50.   3rd : £25

In addition, signed Certificates designed by Chris Wren will be
awarded to entrants who perform well

The
Tiger Club

Send now for Regulations and Entry Forms to :
THE TIGER CLUB
REDHILL AERODROME,
REDHILL, SURREY

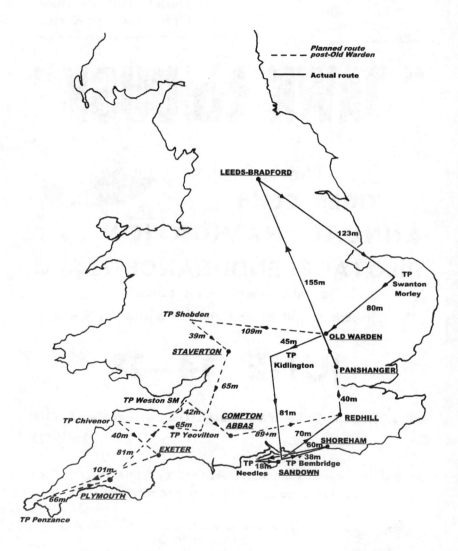

Planned route
post-Old Warden

Actual route

LEEDS-BRADFORD

123m

TP
Swanton
Morley

155m

80m

TP Shobdon

39m   109m

45m   OLD WARDEN

STAVERTON   TP
Kidlington   PANSHANGER

65m

TP Weston SM

42m   40m

TP Chivenor   COMPTON   81m   REDHILL
         ABBAS

40m   65m

81m   TP Yeovilton   89+m   70m   SHOREHAM

EXETER   60m

38m

101m   TP 18m   TP Bembridge
         Needles   SANDOWN

66m   PLYMOUTH

TP Penzance

82

The opportunity to check the fuel consumption properly just did not arise before we lost 'LTW for its C. of A. although a very rough check gave me a shock. Wally estimated that, on the basis of a one-hour flight, having filled the tank before and after, the consumption was of the order of 8 gallons per hour at normal cruising. This seemed rather high and caused some frantic reassessment. We simply had to do a more thorough check at the very first opportunity.

Meanwhile another and really inexcusable delay resulted while we obtained an Air Touring Guide for airfield information. Wally had one somewhere but he and it never seemed to come together, and neither of us managed to get to an airfield where they were on sale, until I made a determined and sizeable detour to get one myself. Table-top planning at home proved completely abortive, without some guide as to when airfields were open, and whether or not they had 80-octane fuel.

Our main hurdle however, was that of deciding where the first leg would finish. We needed an airfield which was open at 06.30; would accept non-radio aircraft; had 80-octane petrol; lay between 160-200 miles away, preferably north of Panshanger, so that we could build up distance early on before getting down to the West Country. Eventually we settled on Leeds-Bradford airport at Yeadon. This was not quite as far away as we would have liked (156 miles) but we could plot a straight track to it, with only a small vertical diversion over RAE Thurleigh, and still achieve a respectable stage length. It was indeed the only airfield we could find that even nearly met our requirements.

Assuming a westerly wind of some 15 mph, our first stage would take just under two hours, giving us an earliest arrival time of 06.25. Leeds opened at 05.45 so we would be alright for time, or so we thought. Unfortunately, as we discovered later, their times were in GMT which meant that they would not be open until 06.45 local time, twenty minutes later than our ETA!

Stage 2 was not quite so awkward to plan, because there would be more airfields open, both for landing at, and as observed turning points. As we had to stay on the ground for 30 minutes, the earliest we could take-off would be 7.15 and by 8.30 there would be a very wide choice. We opted finally for a dog-leg track, turning over Swanton Morley in Norfolk and landing at Old Warden, where my old friend Malcolm Frazer would minister to the Tiger's thirst. This stage was 203 miles, and before deciding if it was on, we just had to know our fuel consumption and best cruising speed. With a tank of 19 gallons capacity, 8 gallons per hour would last for just about 2¼ hours – at 90 mph this would give an absolute maximum range of 203 miles with no reserves. We did not fancy pushing the Tiger from one end of the airfield to the other if the engine ran dry on the landing run. However, with the dog-leg it would be possible to turn at other airfields than Swanton Morley if it proved necessary to shorten the Stage length.

From Old Warden we reckoned to fly west as far as possible in long hops and then wiggle back in many shorter legs, keeping ourselves within easy reach of Redhill in the latter stages.

We eventually got 'LTW back from its C. of A. on June 8th, and with only six days to the start of the competition, it seemed much too late. We still had to check the fuel consumption, and finalise both the route and the Stage alternatives, before we could get our letters off to the airfields we wished to use in all but the first two Stages.

I had yet to convert to Tiger Moths; although my logbook showed some 50 hours on our group Jackaroo, the latter was not a Tiger and is easier to land and handle on the ground. In fact, one hour of circuits and bumps on the 9th of June had me wondering whether the Jackaroo and Tiger had anything in common when in contact with the ground. Landing in a Tiger seemed a very much more touchy affair than in a Jackaroo – if the latter was a lady, whose feet stayed delicately on the ground when put there, the Tiger lived up to Walt Disney's Tigger image of "bouncy, bouncy, bouncy." Tigers may be wonderful things but, though bouncy they are not made of rubber, and I needed to get the hang of putting 'LTW down as smoothly and certainly as I could the Jackaroo (then 'PAL).

Our first opportunity to get a good check on fuel consumption did not occur until the following Sunday, when we took 'PAL and 'LTW to the East Anglia Flying Club's International Rally at Ipswich. We filled 'LTW's tank to the brim and persuaded Wally to throttle back to 'PAL's cruising speed (75 mph) for the trip to Ipswich. But Wally's natural exuberance could not be contained entirely to that extent and I got the impression at one time that he intended to keep down to my cruising speed, not by throttling back, but by looping all the way. At Ipswich we topped up the tank again and on the return, Wally cruised at his usual 90 mph, topping up again at Panshanger. At least this trip, though nothing like as comprehensive as the three we had hoped to carry out, indicated that the higher speed would be more economical in terms of mpg (ignoring the looping factor). Even so, I was still not really convinced that the resulting figure of 7¼ gallons per hour was accurate but in the absence of anything more positive we decided to work on this basis. Any improvement would be a bonus.

At 7¼ gallons per hour, Panshanger to Leeds-Bradford would be definitely 'on' in any conditions in which we could fly. Our next stage, Old Warden via Swanton Morley, could be achieved with a safety margin of at least 30 minutes, providing we had a head wind of no more than 15 mph on either leg.

We then planned to go:

1. Via Shobdon to Cheltenham (Staverton).
2. Via Yeovilton and Chivenor to Exeter.
3. Various shuttling to and fro between Exeter, Plymouth and Chivenor, settling at Compton Abbas.
4. From Compton Abbas to Redhill, the exact route depending on the amount of time left at departure from Compton.

Meanwhile, having sorted out a rough route, I ran off a duplicated letter to send to various airfields we thought we might visit, leaving spaces for anticipated time of arrival and whether we would be landing or just turning. These were sent with a s.a.e. for reply.

We ran into a snag when writing to RAF Chivenor, asking somewhat naively if we could use the airfield as an observed turning point. The CO politely left us in no doubt that a civilian, non-radio Tiger would be liable to get more than its whiskers singed if it poked its nose anywhere near his airfield, where numerous Hunters were usually to be found orbiting at high speed. Hunters and Tigers are not good mixers. Point taken – back to the map. This served to make us appreciate all the more the interest and help offered by the Leeds-Bradford Airport Commandant, who allowed us to intrude on his busy airspace. Similarly, BEA at Penzance gave us precise instructions on how to get ourselves noticed in turning there, with a timetable to ensure that we didn't get chopped up by one of their helicopters. Shaftesbury Flying Club even took the bother to telephone me from Compton Abbas to say that we would be very welcome to use their facilities and to wish us good luck.

All too soon June 13th was on us, and several replies to letters were still outstanding – until these arrived we were unable to finalise our route. As it happened, neither Wally nor I were free for the 14th but by that evening our route planning was completed and a pattern set for the following fortnight.

First ring the Met. Office at Uxbridge: "Can you tell me if I can expect VMC (Visual Meteorological Conditions) for a flight, Panshanger to Leeds-Bradford, at 04.30 tomorrow morning?"

"*What* time???"

"04.30, dawn."

"Visual to Leeds?"

"That's right."

Noises off while the resident expert is called to deal with this idiot who wants to fly Visual to Leeds at DAWN. The weather man was very helpful; having looked at all his pieces of seaweed he thought he had clear skies, reasonable wind conditions etc., during the day but, no matter which way he assembled the pieces, he could not oblige with guaranteed Visual conditions for the early morning. His gloomy forecast was one of ground mist and restricted visibility until around 08.00 or

09.00, and after 18.00 or 19.00, especially in the Midlands and West – not only for the morrow but for some days hence. The call to Uxbridge was followed by one to Wally at Hertford who agreed that in the circumstances it would be better to wait in the hope of an improved forecast.

This performance was repeated with variations due to Wally's unexpected absences on several evenings when I called. Some days were out because Wally could not make it, others because 'business called' for me, and the remainder due to the gloomy forebodings of the men who made the weather down at Uxbridge. Until eventually, we had in one way or another used up the whole fortnight but for the last day!

We were determined to go, and fortunately the weather conditions relaxed to be just sufficiently acceptable to make it worth trying, though we were still faced with the prospect of a late start due to early morning ground mist.

Wally's initial reaction to my first announcements about start time had been one of amusement: "Now pull the other one". For Wally, 04.30 was a time that simply did not exist and he took a lot of convincing that I was being serious in announcing a take-off at that time. In the end I could get no more than a smiling agreement that he would at least try and be at Panshanger by 04.00 for an 04.30 take-off. Nevertheless I pressed on with my plans with a touching faith in humanity.

Mr Met. Man had not been overly hopeful the night before about the general conditions, forecasting a belt of low cloud spreading from the west during the course of the day, though he reckoned the day would start well enough, but with a risk of early morning fog.

Accordingly, I set my alarm clock for a totally impossible hour and, more asleep than awake, drove over dark, deserted roads to Panshanger, contriving to arrive only ten minutes after our pre-arranged time!

The prospects were not all that inviting. Visibility and cloudbase were both below limits, dawn's thin cold light being held back by low cloud, with the far end of the airfield hidden in ground mist. After about 15 minutes the cloud started breaking up, revealing patches of lighter sky overhead, and the ground mist was dispersing to show the distant trees beyond the western end of the airfield; by which time also, realization of how cold it can be at dawn, even in late June, was upon me. Wally was joking about going back to bed but that was the last thing I wanted, having come this far in arranging things.

Stage 1

We got the Tiger out of the hangar (already previously fuelled and oiled), put on our ex-RAF sheepskin jackets, leather helmets and Mk. VIII goggles, gathered together all the paperwork, maps etc., and then took another look at the weather. Wally was to fly the first leg and felt that it was just about on for him. Certainly it would be well worth going up to have a look at things from the air.

Timewise we could just about make it to Leeds – it was now 04.55 and with any luck we could be on our way by 05.00. Wind was forecast as 15 mph at 245 deg, very much as planned. This gave us only ten degrees of drift and a groundspeed of 84 mph against true airspeed of 85 mph. Cruising height to be 2,000 ft except where we crossed the Thurleigh high-speed flying zone where we would go up to 3,000 ft.

Whether it was the cold, or the fact that I still had not got used to the Tiger's funny little wooden propeller (compared to the larger and heavier metal Fairey-Reed fitted to the Jackaroo, which required far less follow-through once it was swinging) I know not, but it took several minutes of energetic twirling before the Gipsy caught on to the fact that it was expected to fire. So, in a way, I started off very much warmer than Wally and probably stayed so throughout the flight, the front cockpit being that much closer to the warm air blowing back from the engine.

We got off the ground at 05.05, with the day well under way and the last shreds of mist gone. Not at all like the dawn take-off I had pictured; I suspect that one has to be at the airfield on quite a number of occasions before being able to make a take-off such as that described so pictur-esquely by Victor Yeates in his *"Winged Victory"* (that doesn't mean I have given up such notions completely, even now).

Having given Wally his course (335M) which would take us all the way to Leeds, there was little for me to do except fill in times and observations on my Flight Log, and keep an eye on our track. Initial enthusiasm for the latter quickly waned as head-over-the-side indicated just how chilling the slipstream was at that time of day. We were due at Henlow after 11 minutes' flying and this came up spot on, but in another 11 minutes Thurleigh was off on the right and I yelled a course change to 340 into the mouthpiece of the Gosport Tube. I was never very certain how well Wally heard me through this fiendish arrangement – certainly with my wearing spectacles I could never get my helmet to fit closely, and consequently got a lot more engine noise intruding than might be expected. It must have worked though, as coincident with "OK" from Wally, our nose turned slightly to the right. This correction took us right through to Leeds without further change. The wind must have swung behind us as our groundspeed went up to 89 mph.

By halfway the wind had obviously been doing funny things because we were still two miles left of track but our groundspeed had dropped to 84. Up till then we had enjoyed fairly clear skies with a high thin overcast which had not been unpleasant but now, ahead of us, a solid-looking bank of lowish cloud stretched from east to west. Wally pressed on to have a closer look but, as so often happens, the nearer one got the more open the clouds became. There was just a single, solid band beyond which we could see that the cloud was generally about 5/8 cover. This persisted so that visual navigation was by snapshots through the breaks until it abruptly cleared near the Sheffield area.

We were then confronted by an absolute maze of new motorways, rivers, canals, railways, open-cast mine workings, industrial swamps, tips and, on all sides, smoking chimneys, steaming cooling towers, gasholders and a scattering of factories. We could have been anywhere and there were so many navigational features jumbled in together that I could not match them with the patterns on my chart. Wally had been flying an accurate heading and I knew that we could not be too far adrift, but nevertheless I was inexperienced enough to be a little put out by my inability to pinpoint our position. Shortly afterwards, a shadowy line of eight cooling towers emerged from the up-sun haze on our right, to identify Doncaster and confirm our position and track. Some 20 minutes later, Wally picked out the Leeds-Bradford airport at Yeadon and settled into a long circuit round the deserted-looking airfield. Air Traffic Control were wide awake, giving us a steady green light and we touched down at 07.02 on a long wide concrete runway. It took a further five minutes taxying to get to the refuelling point and we climbed out stiff and cold but vastly relieved to be there.

Stage 1 log

Straight line track: 135 n.m.
Block speed: 65 knots.
Fuel uplift: 13 gallons.
Av. fuel consumption: 6.295 gal/hr.
Chock-to-chock time: 2 hrs 4 mins.
Weather conditions *en route*: Fine, little cloud, light ground mist in low-lying hollows. Encountered 25-mile belt of low, broken stratus at 1,500 ft and later 1,000 over South Midlands. Wind forecast 245 deg, 5 kt at surface, becoming 15 kt at 2,000 ft.

There was no immediate sign of life, so while Wally went to book in and fill the fuel tank, I looked round for somewhere that might be dispensing hot liquid refreshment and anything resembling breakfast. Eventually, we found what passed for what we were looking for, though we had to wait for the man in charge of the fuel to come on duty. Over a nearly hot coffee we discussed the vital question of fuel consumption – our first real check under actual conditions. Wally had squeezed 13 gallons in and this gave a much more realistic figure of less than 6.3 gallons per hour. We breathed again – at least I would not have to trim stage lengths on that count!

But timewise we had a problem: it had become obvious that 30 minutes was inadequate for what we had to do. In fact, after we had thawed out, drunk, eaten, emptied, refuelled the aircraft, booked out and got started it was almost 08.00, nearly an hour after touchdown, but worse was to come.

Stage 2

Wally and I switched seats at this stage, he acting as navigator with me peering out of the rear cockpit on a seat cushion designed for Wally's rather larger frame, which did not help much in taxying. We had to taxy what seemed like miles round the perimeter track (always a slow, painful task in a non-braked tailskid aircraft) and then hold, miles out in the country, to wait for the 08.00 (roughly) Viscount to somewhere-or-other take off and for its wake turbulence to clear (yes, we knew a little about such horrors even in those days). The Viscount sat at the end of the runway, and sat, and sat, and sat. I had visions of the air hostess walking up and down the aisle counting passengers and getting a different number each time. After what seemed an absolute age, it trundled off, gathered up its skirts and got airborne, leaving us apparently the sole occupants of the deserted field. Still the necessary signal from the tower did not appear, the reason becoming obvious when a second Viscount sneaked up from behind some trees on the other side of the runway and also sat waiting clearance. His wait was due to yet a third Viscount on finals. Eventually, both were despatched, one to the terminal area and the other one airborne and after a further, respectful period a green light replaced the red from the tower and at 08.15 we were off.

Now, the wind had swung to 260 deg at 12 mph and was forecast to increase to 270 deg and 15 mph by 10.00, so the first leg of 133 miles to Swanton Morley was calculated on the former and the second leg to Old Warden on the latter. Ground speed on the first leg worked out at just under 95 mph and, as our track took us straight across the widest part of the Wash (some 15 miles over water), this was just as well. It meant that we were only over the sea for some ten minutes but this seemed long enough at the time, ears tuned for every little unusual noise (and they all seem different over the water!). At least by now, the sun was well up and visibility was good although there was a fair amount of air turbulence even at our 2,000 ft cruise altitude.

After crossing the Wash, the flat, featureless expanse of Lincolnshire was replaced by that of Norfolk, but we had no trouble picking out Swanton Morley, though whether anyone was sufficiently awake thereat to record our passing at 09.35 was another matter.

We swung hopefully round the control tower at above circuit height and then did a low pass up the grass runway but saw insufficient sign of any activity to have much hope that anyone actually observed us doing so. Time was pressing so, without further ado, we set course for Biggles-wade and Old Warden.

With a favourable tail wind we had made good time and, with the fuel tank float bobbing about the halfway mark, knew that we need have no concern about fuel consumption for the next leg of roughly 60 minutes. No problems with navigation on this leg though the wind was not quite as strong as forecast. I noted a 1-degree change of course after four minutes, with another of 8 degrees after 40 minutes, with flight time three minutes less than estimated: my reply to Wally's 1-degree course change is lost in the mists of time but it probably would not have been printable!

No trouble finding Old Warden aerodrome as our track lay straight over Biggleswade, and on down the Old Warden road for two miles, to position us nicely over the airfield.

Stage 2 log

Straight line track: 176 n.m.
Block speed: 76 knots.
Fuel uplift: 17 gallons.
Av. fuel consumption: 6.375 gal/hr.
Chock to chock time: 2 hrs 40 mins.
Weather conditions *en route*: light ground haze initially. High cloud banks to the east. Wind light on surface but much turbulence at 2,000 ft altitude over East Anglia.

When we landed at 10.35 there was no sign of life, and the slick sort of activity required to achieve a turnaround time of 30 minutes was noticeably absent. Even when we found Malcolm Frazer (then Works Manager), the key to the fuel store was not in its place and further time was lost in tracking down Wally (Berry) who was thought to have it in his pocket. Hardly surprising that this state of affairs existed as they were not in the business of selling aviation fuel (and were in fact doing us a favour by letting us use the facilities) but that did not preclude a certain feeling of exasperated frustration as our planned timing melted away!

When we had eventually completed our refuelling (which had to be by hand as the pump had blown a fuse) we hit a real snag. It had proved difficult to get through to Staverton Air Traffic Control on the phone but when I did they informed me that they would not accept us as the weather was forecast to be outside the minima for VFR at our estimated time of arrival. This was very difficult to swallow, as cloud cover and wind were better than they had been all morning and there had been no noticeable front passing through. Their refusal and general disinterest were in line with the reply we had received to my letter and we reluctantly abandoned the leg. We did try the weather men again, who confirmed that conditions were expected to deteriorate from the west but not until mid- to late- afternoon. We tossed around the idea of going up to Shobdon and then south-west, but if Staverton were right then we could have been stranded the wrong side of the line of the front. Wally was understandably not keen so we looked for a more southerly route.

Our best bet perhaps would be to edge westward along the south coast until forced to turn back, and then make a run for Redhill. Accordingly, a zigzag route was planned to Shoreham via Oxford and Bembridge on the Isle of Wight. How different was our reception from Shoreham when I phoned for acceptance – they obviously liked aeroplanes using their aerodrome!

Stage 3

Wind forecast was now 17 mph at 270 deg. Visibility was still good but we elected to fly at 2,000 ft to try and get over the worst of the turbulence, though in fact this made little difference. Wally was flying this stage and he got us airborne at 12.25, nearly two hours after landing – we had lost 1 hr 20 minutes on the ground and never recovered this time. From this point on the result was a foregone conclusion, but we pressed on for the experience.

Our first leg to Oxford was almost straight into wind, which proved stronger and much more turbulent than anticipated, and it veered a further 10 degrees which caused me to change heading by 13 degrees before we got it right. No problems with navigation but our ETA was out by 6 minutes on this 46-mile leg. Wally turned onto our new course high over Kidlington – we had now lost so much time that the question of ground confirmation of turning points was purely academic.

The second leg was Oxford–Bembridge and on this one we made up a few minutes, but more important to creature comfort was the fact that the turbulence decreased significantly as we approached the coast. When we crossed the narrow waters of the Solent, between Gosport and Ryde, conditions were very pleasant, and stayed this way as we turned over Bembridge to head east to Shoreham. With the wind behind us, the 12-mile crossing to Selsey Bill took only 7 minutes, and 12 minutes later we were overhead Shoreham, this leg being perhaps the most enjoyable of the day. At 14.23 we landed, having put another 165 miles behind us. As we taxied back a Hornet Moth took off and we learned later that he was also a competitor, the only one we encountered.

Stage 3 log

Straight line track: 142 n.m.
Block speed: 72 knots.
Fuel uplift: 13 gallons.
Av. fuel consumption: 6.5 gal/hr.
Chock-to-chock time: 2 hours.
Weather conditions *en route*: Good visibility but much turbulence encountered on legs Old Warden–Oxford–Bembridge.

Wally's inner man now needed feeding (again) and we took a leisurely lunch – we were so far behind schedule that there was now no possibility of getting in amongst the awards. We decided to fly down the coast to Portland, up to Yeovil and back to Compton Abbas, giving a stage length of 146 miles. This would make for an interesting flight along the coast, and by turning north at Portland we would fly along the line of the front, and if it became at all threatening would simply turn east and run before it. The Met. man gave us two hours before the front reached Yeovil which, if he was right, would be enough. We had already put in another 13 gallons of fuel and at 15.52 I took off and set course at 268 deg straight into a 20-knot wind.

Stage 4

Our progress back up the coast was somewhat slower than the flight into Shoreham, and crossing the Solent took twice as long: I climbed to 2,500 ft and ahead stretched the Isle of Wight, with the Needles dead on our nose. The sun was still shining and visibility was first-class but I noted that it was not possible to define the horizon ahead of us. By the time we had crossed the island, at just over halfway along the first leg and something like five minutes behind schedule, due to a freshening wind, the lack of horizon had resolved itself into a continuous bank of stratus stretching from somewhere ahead, northward across the mainland coast.

Diving off height to try and get under the cloudbase gave us a closer look at Alum Bay and the famous chalky outcrop of the Needles, but also indicated that the cloud extended from about 500 ft to 1,000 ft. I pointed the Tiger's inquisitive nose forward on course at about 300 ft, out over the empty expanse of cold-looking, slate-grey sea, and thought about it. But not for long. Ahead lay a 16-mile crossing over Swanage Bay, with a further similar crossing from Purbeck to Portland. At worst we would be six miles off the nearest coast but already the shore at Milford, three miles to our right, was disappearing in the mist. Ahead was nothing but water without even the benefit of a decent horizon and the cloudbase was getting noticeably closer. It required little imagination to visualise what could happen in even the next few minutes and we quickly beat a hasty retreat, circling north to maintain visual contact with the mainland coast.

We decided to land at Sandown and get a weather report on how things were going inland before deciding what to do next. In any case it would be wise to fill up as we would have been airborne for 1 hr 20 minutes by the time we got to Sandown. Once we had left the cloud behind us we were able to climb to 1,500 ft and visibility was again very good ahead of the front.

At ten minutes past five we landed at Sandown in bright sunshine.

Stage 4 log

Straight line track: 35 n.m. (Shoreham to Sandown).
Block speed: 25 knots.
Fuel uplift: nil.
Av. fuel consumption: n/a.
Chock-to-chock time: 1 hr 23 min.
Weather conditions: Good visibility and conditions initially but after one hour encountered continuous bank of unbroken stratus at 500-1,000 ft altitude, lying approx. north-south and extending inland to horizon.

We wasted little time at Sandown, but even with the added urgency of the impending weather change, and scalding ourselves gulping down hot coffee to boot, we still needed that 30 minutes on the ground before take-off. By the time we had established that Redhill was clear, and expected to remain so for at least another hour, and had plotted our course back to Redhill it became obvious that we had enough fuel to get there but precious little spare time to get airborne from Sandown, so we didn't stay to refuel.

Stage 5

The weather was catching up fast and as we taxied out to the north-easterly end of the airfield, cloud mist was spilling rapidly down the slopes of the hills at the opposite end. How long the South Downs would stay clear was uncertain – at a little over 1,000 ft high, they stretched eastwards across our direct route to Redhill. It seemed a good idea to dog-leg west of the straight-line crossing on the basis that we would get to the Downs more quickly that way; if the cloudbase had beaten us to it, we could run along the southern face of the Downs until we got in front of the cloud, failing which we could land at Lydd if necessary. A dog-leg also gave us a few more route miles, so we set course to Wisley for the first leg.

Wally was flying this stage and, after the scramble of getting off the ground before the cloud closed us in completely, things went pretty well according to plan. Wind was forecast as 20 mph at 260 deg but it must have increased a little in strength, because on both legs I had to change course, from 040 to 035 to Wisley and from 130 to 140 to Redhill. Once airborne we found clear air and good visibility still to the east but that persistent bank of low cloud to the west, extending northwards as far as we could see. By the time we got to the high ground around Haslemere we found the cloud stretching probing tendrils amongst the treetops in the wooded ridges just to the west of our track.

At Wisley we had gained a couple of minutes, having achieved our highest ground speed of the day of 110 mph, and turned across the wind towards Redhill. By 18.25 we had landed and were hoping once again for a quick turnaround in order to beat the weather back to Panshanger (whereas we had looked forward instead to a leisurely and cosy chat in the bar).

Stage 5 log

Straight line track: 61 n.m.
Block speed: 78 knots.
*Fuel uplift: 13 gallons.
*Av. fuel consumption: 6 gals/hr.
Chock-to-chock time: 47 mins.
Weather conditions: Visibility good to the east, unbroken cloud bank to the west at time of take-off, forecast as reaching Redhill one to two hours later.
*Stages 4 & 5 combined.

Our arrival at Redhill proved to be something of an anticlimax. We hadn't known quite what to expect but I suppose we had thought to find one or two other competitors and at least some of the organising officials, but the place was pretty dead. We booked in and the Air Traffic Controller was mildly interested but had little to tell us, and we left feeling just a little deflated. With hindsight there was no reason why anyone should have been there to see us in – had we arrived at the planned time of dusk it might have been a different matter, both in respect of other competitors and Club officials. As it was, at 18.30 on a Thursday evening on the last day of the competition, in weather that still looked good locally it was, perhaps, hardly surprising.

At 19.00 we were airborne again on the short hop back to Panshanger where we landed 35 minutes later, with no further problems from the weather. One could only assume that, having inched us back from the west, that bank of low cloud had given up for the night.

What had we achieved during the day? We were back at Panshanger 14½ hours after leaving and in that time had flown a total of 9½ hours in six stages (counting the return to base). Our average ground speed during the competition stages was 71.5 mph and, having used 56 gallons over 636 competitive miles (as distinct from true distance flown), we had on this basis averaged 11.35 miles per gallon and 6.29 gallons per hour. The joys of calculating the latter figures were yet to come, as I still had some work to do in making up the Competition Log and submitting this, and copies of the Flight Logs, to the Secretary of the Tiger Club.

We never heard any more from the Club so we never knew whether we counted as one of the seven finishers reported in the Sept. '67 issue of *"British Light Aviation."* A few statistics from the Tiger Club report in that issue follow. There were 19 entries, including three ladies and one foreign entrant, average age 47 and average experience 370 hours. The seven finishers flew seven different aircraft types, only one of which was a single-seater, five carried VHF and full panels and three had radio navaids. Four competitors exceeded 1,000 miles, and three exceeded 15 hours (which says something of the ranges of the aircraft concerned). The winner (Paul Herring) in a single-seat Fournier RF.4 flew 1,159 miles in 14 hrs 58 mins, averaging 77 mph and 2.09 gals/hr. Second was Hubert Schnabel in a Jodel DR.1050, covering 1,361 miles in 15 hours 4 minutes at 90 mph and 4.25 gals/hr. A Twin Comanche flown by John Welch managed 1,941 miles in 15 hrs 11 mins at 128 mph and 12.6 gal/hr. Faced with that sort of opposition plus the vagaries of the weather we felt that our honour was reasonably satisfied. With a little help from the weather our original planned route length of 1,250 miles would have been more nearly achievable and our final figures would probably have looked very much more respectable.

It had been every bit as enjoyable as expected; more frustrations than hoped for and a few more disappointments maybe, what with the weather and the occasional awkward, pompous official, but nevertheless an exercise I would have loved to have repeated. Perhaps I could never have taken it seriously enough to have done more than made up the number but I would have enjoyed trying again. Wally unfortunately sold his Tiger and I never came across anyone else with all the essential ingredients of an aircraft, the time, the cash and the interest, who needed a co-pilot/navigator. The nearest I got to entering again was in helping out another Tiger Moth entrant in 1982 (see Chapter 18), itself a very enjoyable exercise.

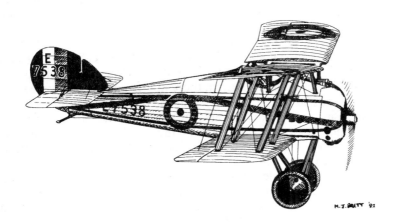

CHAPTER 7
CHECK FLIGHT

'Check flight' probably means many different things to different pilots, but for me it refers to a flight carried out by a licensed pilot under the watchful eye of either an instructor or another pilot. The check may be that after having not flown for some time he needs to get his hand and eye in, either because he feels it preferable for his own peace of mind or because the rules of his Club or Group require it. Or it may be a question of 'showing him the ropes' of a type of aircraft he has not flown before or perhaps the way round the circuit if he is new to the base airfield.

My earliest experience of such a check flight was on the receiving end when I first sat in a Jackaroo with the express intention of flying it myself. This was at the old Wiltshire School of Flying at Thruxton, from where I was to collect the Stevenage Flying Club's newly-acquired Jackaroo, G-APAL, and deliver it to Fairoaks for servicing. Nothing very much in that you might say, but, to misquote Einstein – it's all a matter of relativity.

In the sheltered cloisters of Luton Flying Club, having just acquired my brand-new PPL I was not allowed to take more than one passenger in their 3-seat J/1N Austers nor to fly in winds of more than 20-25 mph. Now I was to take 3 passengers in a strange aeroplane with a wind strength of 30 mph, gusting to 40, and I wasn't at all sure that I ought to even consider it. Knowing that, at Luton under such conditions, I certainly would not have been allowed anywhere near any aeroplane, not even the familiar Austers, I could hardly believe my ears when the CFI at Thruxton turned not a hair (not that he had many) requesting only that he be allowed to finish his beer.

The alacrity with which he took up the suggestion that he check me out on 'PAL was soon explained – at that time selected flying clubs trained ATC cadets to PPL standard under a Government scheme and Wilts. S. of F. had a number of them there at Thruxton. They were sitting around in various stages of dejection and the School Jackaroos (all six of them) were sitting in the hangars eating holes in the club finances without earning their keep. All due to the wind, whose low moaning outside was more than matched by that inside. Thus if I, with my miserably small total of hours, was willing to act as a guinea pig on a private Jackaroo, he would soon find out at no cost and little risk whether it was safe to let the cadets fly the club machines. So excited at the prospect was he that he elected to do the check flight without payment, which I thought unusual to say the least.

There was no shortage of volunteers to help get the aircraft out of the hangar, or for wingmen to hold on at the wingtips. As I had never taxied a machine without brakes, or with nothing more steerable than a pivoted tailskid, the instructor condescended to manoeuvre us from the low-lying area, in which the hangars were situated, up to the upper part of the aerodrome where the control tower and runways were. I suppose it was a measure of the awe with which the cadets quite rightly regarded the CFI that, despite the speed at which he taxied, there was always someone on each wingtip, although I had a vision of us leaving a long trail of exhausted cadets sprawled panting on the grass behind us.

At the top of the airfield I was relieved to find little of the gusting which had been evident down in the dip by the hangars, the windsock staying fairly steady even though nearly horizontal. Whilst taxying we had been going through the few instructions necessary for flying a Jackaroo. "Slats locked, *there,* for taxying; unlocked for take-off; throttle lever friction nut, *there and there,* tighten one for take-off, both slack for taxying; elevator trim lever, *there,* about halfway through the quadrant; remember the "Jack" is a 50-50 aeroplane – 50 kt climb and 50 kt approach: the engine is the same as in a J/1N, no flaps, no brakes and that's all there is to it: what's *what* lever? – oh! that's the rudder trim, you don't want to worry about *that.*"

By this time he, occupying the rear seat, had turned us into wind at one side of the tarmac runway and at 90 degrees to it. "You'll find she will lift off before you get to the other side in this wind: let's go."

I swallowed hard and enquired in a faint voice whether the great man was not going to fly the first circuit to show me how. The answer I got indicated that if I had a valid license and had trained on Austers then there was little he needed to do: all that was required of me was to fly it like an Auster without flaps and we would be alright.

Which surprisingly enough was borne out in practice. True, throttle and stick were reverse-handed: Austers are flown with the left hand on the control column and right hand on the central throttle, but that proved surprisingly unimportant, perhaps because my method of getting the flaps down in the Auster was to change hands on the stick and attack the flap lever with my left hand.

Opening the throttle fully, we were off the ground before reaching the far side of the runway, before I really knew what was happening, and then we went up like a lift. This was something completely new to me! And of course the Jackaroo is such a forgiving old lady in comparison with the Auster when it comes to landing that, once I had lined up and shut the throttle, it all happened without much assistance from me; she just gathered up her skirts and sat sedately down almost before I realised it. I heaved a sigh of relief, and turned to the instructor, sitting behind, intending to ask if we should take off again from where we were, only to find him undoing his straps.

"Yes," he said: " I reckon the cadets will cope with this wind." And that was my check flight!

Within the group formed to operate the Jackaroo, I was, as of that moment, the resident "expert," whose job it was to check out the other members!

Applying the same tactics worked amazingly well, and without incident, perhaps because in those days nearly everyone with a licence had learned to fly on Tigers, Austers, Miles Hawk Trainers (Magisters) or, if they were very lucky, Chipmunks, which meant that they were used to handling tailskid or tailwheel aircraft fitted with Gipsy Major or Cirrus engines.

Apart from checking out the Group members, occasionally there were prospective new members to show the Jackaroo. One such flight in particular stands out as a measure of how the blind led the not-so-blind. A Tiger Moth is noticeably faster than a Jackaroo when the latter is fitted with its standard fine-pitch prop (there is little difference when both are fitted with similar pitch propellers and flown at the same all-up weight – if anything the "Jack" is then slightly faster due to the streamlining effect of the cabin compared with the open cockpits of the Tiger). Thus while the Jackaroo, fully loaded, cruises at around 65 knots, a typical Tiger at the same revs flies at about 85 mph (I have deliberately left these figures in different speed units).

One Tiger pilot with 'n' thousand hours to his credit, unable to find a Tiger Group to join, came along to see what a Jackaroo could do, bringing his son who also had a PPL. I took them up with a fourth occupant and a full load of fuel and, after a demonstration circuit, let him have a go, swapping seats with his son so that he could also try it. Although I had shown him that the Jackaroo could climb quite easily at full power and then maintain height at cruising revs (1,950 rpm), he complained that it would not maintain height at those revs. He and his son were in the front and rear pilot's seats respectively, with me beside him and so unable to handle the controls to find out what he was doing. Reading the A.S.I. as if it were mph instead of knots he felt that at cruising revs he had to fly at a minimum of 70 indicated for comfort. In an attempt to keep the needle showing this figure (forgetting knots-to-mph) he had trimmed out to a nose-down attitude more in keeping with the Tiger flight characteristics than those of a fully-laden Jackaroo, and was thus steadily losing height.

Anyway, before I could sort it out, he had opened up to full throttle, completed the circuit and made a perfect landing, but he went away muttering about underpowered aeroplanes and we lost a couple of would-be members. This at a time when the next loan repayment on our aircraft was looming large. As a comparative novice I simply had not enough experience to assess quickly what was wrong and be able to put him right. I guess I was also too much in awe of his enormous number of hours to suspect that I could teach him anything. Since then I have had it demonstrated to me, several times over, that five-figure hours of experience doesn't help an airline captain to land a Jackaroo on a small grass strip at 65 knots, and that if he tries and fails he is glad of a word of advice even if it comes from a tyro such as me.

Within the Jackaroo group, for insurance purposes, new members were required to have a minimum of 15 hours on type before taking it solo, so that the final check flight should normally have been no problem. However, I remember one such final check where the pilot concerned had been waiting for some time for weather or perhaps completion of a major service on the aircraft, and in the meantime had flown a fair number of hours on a Cessna 150, the aircraft he was most familiar with. As with most light American aircraft the propeller rotates the opposite way to that of a British engine, and any slight swing on take-off as the throttle is opened is also the opposite way. The more experienced a pilot is, the more likely he is to counteract swing automatically.

Sure enough he subconsciously corrected the slight swing with, as was his wont, a light application of right rudder. As the swing, which was already to the right, then worsened, he wrongly applied more right rudder in an attempt to correct it. This resulted in us veering rapidly to the right under full throttle, at which point I decided to take some more positive action and applied left rudder from the rear dual controls, tapping him on the left shoulder and yelling suitable abuse as well. Simultaneously he realised what he was doing wrong and hastily changed feet, as it were, and also applied left rudder. The resulting full left rudder suddenly bit, stopped the swing to the right and started an equally ferocious one to the left.

I am told that the ensuing waltzing as he over-corrected right, then left and right again, would have gladdened a Strauss, and certainly onlookers alleged that nothing had been seen quite like it before: they said they had been taking bets as to whether the undercarriage would fail *before* we dug a wingtip in or *after*! This perhaps serves to highlight the difference between a relatively inexperienced pilot such as I was, and a competent instructor; the latter would have left corrective action far longer, realising that the pilot would sort out his problems on his own, far quicker and more effectively.

Once again the old Jackaroo showed her qualities by finally taking matters into her own hands in mid-swing, leaping desperately into the air and staggering sideways across the field with only a foot or so of daylight under her wheels, until we all got our breath back and resumed a more normal manner of progression. Actually he was a very good pilot and this was the only error I ever knew him to make either before or after that time.

Later on, as more and more pilots learned to fly on modern School aircraft with nosewheel undercarriages, the Club check pilots had more work to do in converting new Group members from nosewheel to tailskid techniques, and in operating from wide-open paved runways to the confines of a small grass airfield. There was nothing really new in all this: our predecessors had all flown like this from the early days, but now new pilots were rarely taught this way.

Perhaps one should explain that the landing flare and hold-off for an aircraft with a nosewheel undercarriage is markedly different to that for a 'taildragger,' i.e. an aeroplane with a tailwheel or skid. The main wheels on the former are positioned behind the CG whereas on the latter they are just forward. This means that on touchdown, the nosewheel aircraft pivots forward about the main wheels until the nosewheel touches, automatically reducing the angle of incidence of the wing and thus the lift, so that the aircraft has a natural tendency to stay on the ground.

This is just the reverse on a taildragger, where after the wheels contact the ground, pivotal movement is tail-down, increasing the incidence angle and, if still above stalling speed, lift from the wings, so that there can be a tendency to bounce back into the air. With a tricycle undercarriage, the aircraft can be flown onto the ground with little likelihood of bouncing, whereas the taildragger has either to be stalled just before touching down in a three-point attitude, or wheeled onto the ground with sufficient speed to maintain elevator control to hold the tail up until flying speed is lost.

Another often-overlooked factor is that when the tail is down and with minimal slipstream blast over it due to the engine being at tick-over, the rudder no longer gives the same degree of control, and if the wheels are unbraked (with consequently a skid in place of a steerable tailwheel), there is another whole world for the tricycle-trained pilot to discover! Brakes are not required for landing a skid-equipped taildragger, but a tricycle pilot used to relying on brakes to slow him if he lands long can also find himself in difficulties if he doesn't get down somewhere near the threshold of a short grass runway.

For a good three-pointer therefore, it is much more important to judge the flare height, airspeed and nose-up attitude accurately so that the wheels are not allowed to touch the ground until flying speed is lost. Flaring too high will cause the aircraft to stall onto the ground and perhaps damage the undercarriage, while too low will cause it to touch down too fast and balloon back into the air. Generally, a 'wheelie' has to be even more finely judged. A broad comparison of the degree of difficulty of landing a taildragger as against a tricycle can perhaps be drawn with learning to drive on a car with a manual, unsynchronised gearbox as against one with 'automatic' transmission.

So we come to another member of the Group who also had been taught on Cessnas and, with some 60 hours to his credit, had never flown in any other type of light aircraft. He was a solid, 'mechanical' pilot who reacted to known recognisable 'book' type situations with model answers, but somehow failed to recognise danger, even when it came and stared him in the face, if it was outside his range of learning and experience. Over some hours, of what progressed backwards from check-out procedure to the nearest I have been to instructing, we came time and time again to situations which left me like a wobbly jelly and him as calm and collected as if nothing had happened.

He also suffered from swing on take off; but in his case, even when I left the swing to develop so much that even he could recognise it, and then still had to take the corrective action myself, he would turn and ask blandly if that was better. He would flare out 10 feet too high (this was after he eventually got the idea that you don't land a tailskid aircraft by flying it straight onto the ground) and porpoise across the field on circuit after circuit and act as if nothing was wrong.

One beautiful June evening in particular stands out, when the wind was westerly, forcing us to land into the sun. Initially, the sun was high enough not to concern us too much, but as the evening wore on, it sank lower and lower so that throughout the vital transition between flying and landing it was shining straight into our eyes. Moreover, as the throttle was closed on the approach, the propeller would slow and set up a stroboscopic, mesmeric flickering of the dazzling golden glare, which dominated one's senses no matter in which direction one looked.

We bounced and swung and cavorted in coarse mockery of more conventional-style landings, and although the Jackaroo patiently accepted all this in her normal good-natured manner, my voice grew steadily hoarser with my many pleadings, cajolings and imprecations. It was with relief that, after the inevitable near-perfect landing eventually happened, I suggested in a croaking voice that perhaps we should now call it a day. No, he felt that perhaps he ought to consolidate it with one more, and so round we went again – and again – and again . . . But, sooner or later, all things, good or bad, come to an end and persistence won through, with him eventually mastering his problems, although the coward in me was relieved that it was someone else who finally sent him off on his own.

Apart from the mechanics of flying a particular aeroplane, there was also a need, especially with newly-qualified pilots, to show new members the techniques for operating from small grass airfields. Not that 'small' and 'grass' makes for a bad airfield in any way, but simply that pilots trained to fly from the vast, open concrete plains such as Luton later became, or Cranfield, can be a little disconcerted when faced with the confines of a grass airfield having closely adjacent woods and buildings. In fact at almost any small grass airfield or strip, the locals expect to be entertained with some interesting diversions when visiting aircraft are in the circuit, especially if there is some local feature notorious for its special effects. This may be a wood or lake or cornfield on the approach, known to create unusual thermal effects on a hot day (nowadays in accident reports universally classified as 'wind shear') or perhaps a hump or gradient on the grass runway which can throw the unsuspecting pilot back in the air if contact is made at the wrong point and speed.

Again, the methods taught for landing modern tricycle aircraft, on tarmac runways stretching some 3,000 or more feet, with clear approaches which allow the aircraft to be flown onto the runway from a long, flat, powered run-in, have to be forgotten when using a small airstrip. With no flaps to slow him down, the Tiger pilot has to adopt a steep, slow approach when dropping into short fields or in over trees, side-slipping being the nearest equivalent to flaps; again that is something that tends to he dismissed as quickly as possible or ignored altogether by some modern training schools.

So part of the check flight consisted of going round the circuit pointing out landmarks and turning points and any habitations housing trigger-happy or otherwise unfriendly natives which had to be avoided.

Old Warden for instance, was typical of many small grass airfields (before the marked runways were extended), in that at many times of the year the cut grass runways do not stand out in the way that tarmac runways do and, nestled as it is amongst the trees, some positive landmarks are needed in order to pick out the airfield from the surrounding, somewhat similar-looking fields. A small lake to the south-west of the airfield is perhaps the most infallible guide, together with the A1 trunk road at Biggleswade, some 2 miles to the east. Similarly, at Rush Green, near Hitchin, an adjacent scrap yard is a very prominent local feature.

At Old Warden, the most troublesome line of approach was that over the hangars. This could be quite a problem in the early days when we were first based there, before an approach lane was cut through the trees over the road from the runway threshold and before the opposite end of the runway was extended. There has always been a high spot on this runway, some 100 yds from the westerly end, the ground falling away deceptively, and this has caught out many a pilot new to the field. We quickly learnt that unless the wheels were in firm contact with the ground at the time you reached this high spot, the aeroplane would float on down the hill, finally touching down near the intersection with the crossing runway, and the original shorter end of the runway then looked menacingly close at this point.

The best approach over the trees to ensure the desired early touchdown was a slow, steep sideslip, but this had to be watched very carefully if the wind was gusty as the trees added considerably to the turbulence. Similarly, if it was a warm day, the cold air over the trees could produce a sudden and unexpectedly high rate of sink, so that one could find the aeroplane dropping far more rapidly than intended, just at the worst moment. In a side-slipping approach the throttle is closed and the controls are crossed, e.g. rudder hard right and stick hard left, controlling the speed, *and* the angle and rate of descent, solely by the degree to which the stick is pulled back; pilots not used to this could find it all rather unnerving the first few times. Thus it was necessary to demonstrate this to them, and have them show that they could handle the aeroplane in such conditions, as part of their check flights.

I remember in particular watching a Tiger Moth on the approach, the pilot of which obviously knew about side-slipping as an aid to short slow landings. As he neared the airfield boundary at a height of about 300 feet, he banked and yawed as in a side-slip but put the nose down; this steepened the glide well enough but also added considerably to the speed (in a full side-slip the excessive yaw induces a low reading on the A.S.I., and the natural tendency then is to want to hold a normal indicated speed by lowering the nose). The dive got him down to flare height successfully enough but with perhaps some 30 mph excess speed so that as he straightened out, the aircraft went skimming on down the hill, necessitating an overshoot. With controls fully crossed it needs a little determination to pull the nose up to drop the indicated speed to 45 mph or so, but with practice this can be safely maintained almost down to the ground, kicking level and straight at the last moment, with no excess speed.

On one occasion watching a Rallye Club, which is reputedly one of the simplest and most docile STOL trainers to land, make three abortive and badly misjudged passes at this runway (this even after the trees were cut back and the runway extended) and then give up and go away, brought home just how unprepared modern training, on modern aircraft, using lengthy tarmac runways, leaves the newly-qualified pilot for this sort of flying. I should add that this comment about the Rallye's pilot is not made in a derogatory sense, in fact more the reverse; better to go away and try again in safer surroundings than make a mess of it in a marginal situation. Other visiting pilots were sometimes not so wise and it was not unknown for Cherokees and the like to be fished out of the ditch at the north end of the runway, having not finally touched down until well over two-thirds of the way along, the brakes then not helping after locking the wheels on the grass.

One last experience perhaps falling under the heading of check flight was again with me on the receiving end, but this time in a single-seater where the owner could give only a pre-flight briefing on the ground.

Most pilots enjoy flying different aeroplanes and I had always wanted to fly an open-cockpit single-seater. Consequently when, quite early on, whilst flying a new type was still something of a challenge, the oppor-tunity to fly a Turbulent was offered, I had no hesitation in accepting. John, a fellow member of the Jackaroo group, was now the proud possessor of a very smart little Turbulent which he had built himself. I had watched this little bird grow over a period of time and knew what hours of loving care and attention it had demanded of him. So although I was both delighted to have the opportunity and flattered to think that he would entrust his baby to me, I was not without some qualms at the thought of a possibility that I might damage it. He soon put my fears at rest: "You bend it, you mend it!"

John had been flying for an hour or so one evening when the opportunity came. The engine was still ticking over and without further ado I climbed in at John's invitation, not without some difficulty, being slightly taller than John. Although the windscreen was quite a large one, the top was at eye level for me and it was obvious that I would need goggles. John's simply would not fit over my spectacles, but we eventually unearthed a pair that nearly did. Never again will I fly with 'nearly'-fitting goggles. These were the old RAF Mk. VIII pattern with angled lenses which rested on my spectacle frames and left a ¼-inch gap between the lower padded edges and my cheeks.

John's instructions were to fly it like a Jackaroo for landing (speeds and attitude) but that the main differences that I would notice would be much lighter and more responsive controls and a reluctance to slow down when the throttle was closed. On enquiring about fuel John said in effect that there was more than enough to keep going until it was dark and if I wasn't down by then, fuel would be the least of my problems.

Looking at the evening sky I could see what he meant as it was rather later than I had thought! There was obviously not going to be time for much more than a couple of circuits.

He was right about the lightness of the controls, especially the rudder, which became effective immediately the throttle was opened. I pedalled the rudder very early so that I could tell when it started to bite, but I was already too late as I found out when the tail wagged quickly and excessively in response. The slightest amount of pedal pressure seemed to cause an over-correction and we eventually became airborne with me still trying to get the rudder and tail properly centralised. Once off the ground, of course, we settled down straight away but John must have had a few anxious moments watching.

As the airspeed started to build up so did my problems with the goggles. Air streamed up through the gap at the bottom and out somewhere at the top, and the air pressure forced the goggles hard down on my spectacles and thus the latter hard down on the bridge of my nose, both combining to bring tears to my eyes. As I turned my head to look out sideways only a frantic grab prevented the slipstream whipping off both goggles and glasses. An interesting period followed as I endeavoured to hold reasonable control with one hand whilst reassembling glasses and goggles into a barely acceptable state of alignment with each other and my eyes; from this point I had to content myself with facing only to the front to avoid a repeat performance. But then my sideways vision was very severely restricted because the lenses of the goggles were so much further forward that I got the impression almost of looking down a tunnel. Added to that I had not bothered to put a helmet on and my hair was blowing about all over the place – decidedly uncomfortable.

I glanced at the A.S.I. and was surprised to find that whilst all this had been going on the airspeed had built up to over 100 mph despite the fact that we were already up to 1,000 feet. My one thought was now to get back on the ground as quickly and safely as possible although the aeroplane was performing beautifully and was a delight to handle.

I throttled back and held my height expecting to see the A.S.I. needle unwind significantly but to all intents and purposes nothing happened – we seemed to carry on at virtually the same speed. We pressed on round the circuit losing very little height or speed; what did I have to do to this little aeroplane to make it slow down? Attempting to effect an arrival back on the ground did not appear to be a good idea until I felt I had some better degree of control over its forward rate of progression.

On the other hand I had such a pressing problem with my goggles that there was really little alternative other than to land as quickly as possible. It says a lot for the handling characteristics of the Turbulent that it got me down in a fairly respectable manner – it certainly received precious little assistance from me other than to point it in the right direction, as I was too concerned with goggles and eyes and hair to do much else. Another little lesson learned and all that suffered was my ego and the full enjoyment of the flight.

CHAPTER 8

FLASH, BANG, WALLOP

It was the day after my birthday, a beautiful golden July evening that I was to remember long after I had forgotten which birthday it was. Not a cloud in the sky and the air calm and still like a millpond. One of our Group's earliest members, who had joined us when we had been training at Panshanger and Rush Green, rang me to fix up a final check-out, having completed the necessary number of hours and acquired the required degree of expertise, and I had no qualms about agreeing to do it with him.

When, earlier on, we had to call a halt to *ab initio* training due to restrictions imposed in the late sixties, he had amassed quite a few hours on Jackaroo G-APAL but had not at that time gone solo. He subsequently finished his training and took his licence on Cessna 150s, coming back confidently expecting to step straight into the Jackaroo and go off on his own. It took a little longer than he anticipated to get out of his newly-acquired 'tricycle' habits, but now one more flight should do it. He flew 3 or 4 circuits including a practice forced landing in which I chickened out and opened the throttle on the approach when I felt he was going to undershoot. He was probably right in arguing that he wouldn't have done so, but in my judgement it looked too tight for creature comfort! He followed this with another, nicely judged over the hedge, after which I pronounced myself satisfied on behalf of the Group, and that he was cleared to go ahead from then on as P1 solo.

Anyway, it was such a beautiful evening that he wanted to do another circuit as P1 and I agreed to go along for the ride. Once up, I suggested he might like to have a look at a local strip some five miles distant which the Group had been using recently, although personally I had not flown from there before, having seen it only from the ground. On the downwind leg we could see some haybales on the field, so a landing was out of the question, but the pilot said he would carry out a dummy approach, there being sufficient room for a touch and go if necessary.

The approach was over a small wood and he made a long flat run in with just a trickle of power. Looking over the side all I could see were treetops getting uncomfortably closer, whilst ahead his bulk in the front seat, combined with the slightly nose-up attitude due to our slow speed, prevented me seeing anything.

Remembering my *faux pas* on one of the circuits at Old Warden I hesitated longer than perhaps I should have done, with my hand hovering over the throttle lever, desperately wanting to ram it wide open and climb away from the menacing trees. This time however I was not acting as a check pilot, being merely the passenger, and with no right whatsoever to interfere with what the pilot-in-charge was doing, however

106

much my self-preservation instincts might persuade me otherwise! As it turned out, on this occasion my hesitation possibly saved my life.

At the same time that I spotted the edge of the trees just ahead of the lower wing there was a vague impression of a blue flash together with a barely audible crack, and the aircraft slowed slightly and dropped its nose. Looking ahead past the pilot's shoulder I could now see that we were in a shallow but low-speed dive towards the open ground and that the prop was still rotating. I wasn't absolutely certain whether I had seen or imagined the flash and could only think that something outside, perhaps a camera flashgun, had caused it and had made the pilot jerk the controls and nose in. Then, as all this was registering, the prop stopped in a horizontal attitude, and although we both hauled back on the stick, we were by now at too low an airspeed and height to have any effect. 'PAL slammed heavily down on the undercarriage, jerking forward onto her nose, but then immediately settled back and ran along in a tail-high attitude.

Just as I was thinking that we were going to get away with it, with very little damage, there was another almighty bang and all hell seemed to be let loose as I was jerked violently forward against my shoulder harness. Something seemed to grab the nose, shake us like a terrier shaking a rat, and spin us violently through 180 degrees. Our forward motion abruptly became a sideways one at right angles to our original path. Then things really started happening. As if in slow motion I watched the cabin door on my side swing open, bang round against the centre-section struts and disintegrate. With a sideways lurch the under-carriage partially collapsed in a shower of dust and earth and the centre-section struts buckled sideways with the weight of the fuel tank. Finally she stopped this mad sideways movement and came to rest, now tipped up on her nose, wings all askew and twisted to unbelievable angles!

In the sudden, silent, stillness, in which I could clearly hear a blackbird singing, I remembered too late to knock off the ignition switches, but the action at least reminded me of what we must do. Quickly establishing that we were both (a) still alive and (b) relatively undamaged, I yelled to the pilot to get out as fast as he could, undid my straps and leapt over the side, expecting any moment to have the whole thing go up in flames. An ominous crackling that I had heard came from a small fire, just starting to establish itself amongst the straw some 20 feet beyond the port wingtip, but there were no other signs of fire, and we quickly stamped it out.

Having done this we had time to regain our breath, take stock of the situation and try to sort out what had happened. Disconsolately wandering round the wreck revealed only too well the extent of the more obvious damage, and it seemed unlikely that our dear old 'PAL would ever fly again – I really felt like crying. But what had done this to us?

There was *nothing* on the field. There was *nothing* on the approach other than the trees we had just cleared when disaster struck. Whatever could have caused us to violently spin half round and change our forward movement of perhaps 20 mph to a sideways one? No laws of motion that I could think of could do that to nearly a ton of aeroplane, moving with the momentum that we had, other than some hefty outside force. Yet there was nothing to be seen. Then again, what had started the fire some 20 feet beyond where we stopped? I was reasonably certain that there had been no fire or smoke when we flew past the strip on the downwind leg! There was nothing at all to show what had started the fire, just the blackened straw stubble and ash.

I was intrigued by the fact that the propeller, still horizontal, appeared undamaged, but why was there a dent in the spinner and – wait a moment – what was that cable coiled round the rear of the spinner and trapped between the hub and the engine? Suddenly all became clear. A glance back to the edge of the field showed the culprits, a line of low-tension electricity supply cables, nestling up to the edge of the trees, with an ominous gap on the line of our approach. The dented spinner showed where it had contacted the upper one of three cables, the lower pair being in line with the centre of the engine cooling air intake. Because we had hit the cables fairly squarely on the engine thrust line the propeller had cut through them and little tipping effect had been felt. Had I opened the throttle earlier on and stopped our descent we almost certainly would have hit one or more cables with the undercarriage and this would probably have flipped the aircraft over on her back – doesn't bear thinking about. Who says he who hesitates is lost?

The rest of the details then fitted neatly into place. One of the cables had wrapped a broken end round the prop shaft, jammed between the hub and the crankcase and stopped the engine. Meanwhile we continued more or less in the same direction, but hooked like a fish on an angler's line! When the aircraft had taken up all the elastic slack in the cable, first of all she was spun through 180 deg round her now tethered nose and continued moving in the only direction open to her, i.e. on an arc round the pole to which the cable was still attached – hence the sideways movement. The fire on the field was started either by a flying spark as the cables shorted together, or perhaps by the hot end of a shorted cable.

At least we had established the cause of our misery and at this point a Land Rover hurtled onto the scene, with two agitated and worried-looking gents, who had seen it all happen and were convinced they would find us somewhat the worse for wear.

"Keep away from that aircraft," they yelled. "Don't touch it, there are 11,500 volts going through it! Where are the crew? Keep away from it! Who are you? Don't touch it! What are you doing here?"

The questions and directives came tumbling in a frantic mixed-up stream. If anything they were far more shaken by it all than we were, understandable perhaps, as they had the long minutes, between seeing it happen and arriving on the scene, to have their imaginations run wild. Their problems of how to handle some feebly-twitching bodies strapped in an untouchable wreck were only compounded by finding two idiots walking unconcernedly round it and close enough to touch it, who, they were convinced, were merely inquisitive ghouls come to pick over the remains.

We calmed them down by pointing out that we were the sole occupants and were still alive and kicking, which they found very difficult to believe. Why weren't we fired to a cinder, they demanded to know, there being 11,500 volts through the lines to be explained away somehow, and that blinding blue flash which they had seen more clearly than we had. In my ignorance I had assumed that shorting the lines together had opened the overload trips, but there appeared to be a more ominous explanation than that. It seemed that, only the evening before, a thunderstorm had tripped the circuit breakers either side of our line and, as an expediency, only one side had been reset in order to quickly restore the supply to RAF Cardington. The circuit breakers on the cable which had wrapped itself round our prop shaft were still open, so that when we made contact with the ground the line was already dead, otherwise . . .?

Meanwhile, Cardington was off the air again and we were probably the most unpopular people in the area. We were almost certainly the luckiest!

CHAPTER 9
LOST

"Lost: one Jackaroo, silver wings, black fuselage and tail with sundry red patches, registration G-AOIR, last known position somewhere south of Bedford. Anyone seeing this aircraft please inform the pilot of his precise location."

How nice to have been able to get an instant response to such an advertisement; I would even have used the radio lying uselessly on the rear shelf had it been connected and working, such was the predicament in which I found myself one Saturday evening in September 1968. For me to admit that a radio just might be worth its weight to carry around is unusual to say the least, but that could lead to a considerable digression.

"Lost" is a relative term; the Concise Oxford English Dictionary defines it as: "become unable to find, fail to keep in sight or follow, e.g. one's way." This, as you would expect from such a source, is a very good definition. For instance, being lost is not necessarily to do with knowing the precise location of whatever you happen to be flying over: if you can see your destination ahead, it may not matter at all. If you know you have been consistently on track for the last 10 minutes the fact that some unidentified object turns up below, or one that you are looking for fails to materialise, need not be cause for panic; man is an industrious animal and builds or removes things sometimes much faster than the cartographer can record. Even if you are blown off track over featureless countryside it is usually not long before some positive landmark will appear ahead, to tell you whether you are left or right of track and by how much, long before you need really believe you are lost.

"Lost" always follows some carelessness and is often linked with time, the latter related perhaps to the amount of fuel left, and thus flying time, or perhaps the amount of daylight left. The less time there is available the more seriously lost you are. By this definition, I have been totally lost perhaps three times, on each occasion in similar circumstances, in which, had time and low visibility not been factors, I would not have considered myself lost at all but merely off-track. On two of these occasions, by the time I admitted to myself that I had failed either to keep in sight or to follow my way, and that I was unable to find it having lost it, I knew I was within 10 miles of my own home airfield, which made it all the more frustrating and inexcusable.

The first occasion was when flying Jackaroo 'OIR on a ferry flight from Blackpool to Old Warden, having just bought it to replace our wrecked 'PAL. Sid, another member of our Group, and I had gone up to the resort, travelling over Friday night. We had thought that to go by coach from Dunstable would deposit us at Blackpool, bright and early, refreshed from an overnight sleep on the journey in comfortable semi-reclining seats. What was more it was very much cheaper by coach than by train (the only other practical alternative), and our finances, both personal and of the Group, were in a state whereby this was an important factor. An early breakfast, followed by an invigorating stroll along the near-deserted beach to the airport at Squires Gate, would see us arriving pretty well on time to meet the chap selling the aeroplane, at the appointed hour of nine o'clock. There might even be time to look around the airfield at all the interesting aircraft that would almost certainly be based there. With any luck we should be away by 10.00 and home in time for lunch!

As so often happens, theory is one thing, practice is another, and the eventuality bore little semblance to the plan. The coach turned out to be a double-decker bus with non-reclining, anything-but-comfortable seats! It would perhaps be an exaggeration to say that it was the most uncomfortable ride I have ever taken; I can remember worse journeys in the swaying backs of RAF lorries, but I was younger then and they were never over as great a distance, nor did they go all through the night! Also, this was early September, which until then I had always regarded as a mild month, but on this occasion, following a beautiful sunny day and during a sharp, clear night, the weather was getting in some training sessions for a cruel 'ard winter.

In short, we were delivered bright and early (the wretched bus even contrived to be about half an hour early), bleary-eyed, with aches and pains in every joint, and shivering with cold, to an uncaring and unsympathetic Blackpool at something like 5.45 in the morning. Our visions of a nice, warm café with a well-rounded, buxom Lancashire lass cheerily dispensing hot breakfast and steaming cups of tea were sadly shattered. There was nothing open and no one in sight except a stray black cat that refused to cross our path.

The sun had just got up as we wandered down to the sea front; we couldn't stroll along the beach as the tide was in (why is the tide always in when I want to walk on the beach?). It was too chilly to sit and contemplate the grey sea so, like Felix, we kept on walking in the general direction of the airport, in the expectation of finding something open somewhere on the route.

By 7.00 we had reached the deserted entrance to the airfield and had seen nothing open anywhere. Blackpool dies sometime during the night and is extremely reluctant to get up in the morning; it could not have been more deserted if it had been suffering the aftermath of an atomic fall-out. At 8.00 we finally found a café that was open, but which had only British Rail-type sandwiches and what passes for coffee in that area, and at 9.00 sharp we were back on the airfield.

Unfortunately, no one had any idea where the Jackaroo was kept ("a what?") much less where its owner might be, until we had walked from

111

one end of the airfield to the other. There, skulking in the furthest, darkest corner of the very last hangar in the line were the unmistakable outlines of a Jackaroo. On closer inspection it hardly seemed possible that we were going to fly it anywhere that day and we would certainly not get away in it by 10.00. Various panels were off, the seats were out, there were radio "black boxes" lying around loose and, quite apart from that, it was the untidiest looking "airworthy" aeroplane I had ever come across.

We had previously seen some of the old Wiltshire School of Flying Jackaroos at Thruxton after that unfortunate outfit had closed down, lying in the old School hangar, covered with dust and bird droppings and many with parts missing; this machine looked as if it had been transported direct from there, complete with dust and dirt and, if I can put it that way, missing parts. The whole was now very scruffy; the cowlings looked as if they had been vandalized and there were sundry fabric patches, still in red/brown shrinking dope, liberally scattered around on wings, fuselage and tail. Unkempt, uncared-for and unloved!

We hung around miserably for about half an hour before anybody appeared; the new arrival turned out to be the engineer who apparently was signing it out for the ferry flight to Old Warden for C. of A. renewal, the latter having expired shortly before. He was even more gloomy than we were, his general impression being that we would be lucky if anybody could be found who would agree to it ever being flown again – ever; certainly not him, certainly not this morning. However, the thought that just by putting his name on the relevant piece of paper would ensure its removal that very day, thereby eliminating, hopefully forever, one of the major blights of his life (he was sure it would never arrive safely any-where), provoked a gleam in his eyes and encouraged him to actually start work on it (egged on also by the threat of us doing the job ourselves).

Having got things moving again we turned our attention to the task of tracking down the owner. Somewhat belatedly, another character arrived, who was a friend of the owner and had been despatched by him to look after things until he arrived. Meanwhile the engineer was muttering about not having the Log Books, and we "wouldn't get nowhere without them." The morning and early afternoon wore on with us alternately chasing the owner and keeping the engineer moving on the task of getting the aircraft signed out and ready to fly. And as for interesting aircraft to look at while we were waiting, if there had been any they had all arranged to be absent – we saw none at all!

Eventually, the owner did deign to arrive, the Log Books were produced and duly signed up and by about 15.00 the engineer finally washed his hands of it though he refused to allow the radio to be installed. We made then the biggest mistake of all in arranging for the Log Books to be sent through the post as we thought we were not allowed to take them in the air, but that is another story. Without radio we had another problem, in that Blackpool ATC would not handle non-radio traffic, so off we rushed to the Control Tower to sort that one out and also to find out what was happening to the weather which, while we had been otherwise engaged, had more than somewhat deteriorated. The hard bright sunny morning had been replaced by a sullen overcast and the distant hills were lost in a dirty haze.

Our radio problems vanished the instant we told ATC that we were planning to take the Jackaroo away and not bring it back. Where they had been totally disinterested and inclined not to let us out anyway because of the poor vis. reported on the edge of the Liverpool zone, suddenly they could not do enough for us. They even got their Aldis lamp out and blew the dust off it so that they could clear us visually for take-off, and as for the weather, that was suddenly going to improve in time for us to take off in about 30 minutes' time, i.e. about 15.30.

On the way back from the tower, the owner's friend explained with an amused grin. It seems that the Jackaroo radio never kept going for very long and the aircraft was always coming back with it totally unreadable, causing ATC to tear their hair out with rage especially as it rarely came back at its declared ETA. They had been threatening eviction for a long time and obviously were now going to let nothing stand in the way of its promised departure.

We had to skirt round the edge of the Liverpool zone so we decided not to take any chances with an unknown range factor, planning to land at Wolverhampton for fuel. Wind was light and variable and once up we could see what they had meant about poor visibility, as we had little more than a couple of miles. There was no real problem with navigation as we planned to fly down the coast, across the Ribble estuary, through the gap between the Liverpool and Manchester Control Zones and then south along the western edge of the Pennines, cloudbase dictating the need to look for low ground rather than take a chance of crossing the hills.

All went well with the first leg, and about two hours after leaving Blackpool we touched down at Wolverhampton, then a pleasant grass Club field (it was closed soon after our visit). The visibility had improved as we flew south-east, once we cleared the hills to the north of the Liverpool zone, but there was a perplexing tendency to drift to left of track despite meticulously flying on the required compass heading, constantly adjusted for drift. We eventually discovered that the compass rim clamp was so worn that the lock failed to stop it imperceptibly rotating in sympathy with the engine vibration. Once we had established that that was the reason why, like an oozlum bird, I seemed to be flying in an ever-decreasing circle, I relied on Sid reading corrections from the compass in the back.

Wolverhampton was an interesting place and we spent far too long wandering round the hangars and discovering amongst other things a Chrislea Ace, a Magister and several Nissen huts full of derelict Tigers. Suddenly it was getting late and to make matters worse they were short of fuel and would only let us have 10 gallons. A quick calculation on what we had used and how much flying we still had to do indicated that this should be ample, so we set off once more, the time now being 18.20 with a weak sun hovering above the haze to the west.

Once up, to our horror we found that what had earlier looked to be clear visibility to the north-east now bore a distant line of haze, and the light evening suddenly seemed to have become dull again, making us conscious of how foolish we had been in spending so much time on the ground with still a fair way to go.

But I was still not really bothered at that stage. That came later when I discovered that the variable winds had developed into a stronger south-westerly, pulling our ground speed back to less than 50 mph. We got a little off course with the vagaries of the compass but were able to get back onto what I thought to be our track without any bother except that it cost us extra time. After that I got into the habit of clamping the compass ring with my fingers, or if necessary, remembering to reset it every time I took a reading.

To add to the niggling concern at the back of my mind about time were, first, the fact that the haze was definitely thickening, and second, that the contents indicator float in the petrol tank seemed to be disappearing faster than it should. Being a strange aircraft I knew not how accurate the float reading was or whether there might be a leak somewhere in the system. By the time we should have got to the outskirts of Bedford, the haze had become a thin fog of evening mist aided by smoke from the stubble-burning activities of the Bedfordshire farmers, and the city refused to materialize out of the murk. I was aware now that we had no time to spare running round looking for familiar landmarks, both on the score of daylight – which was ebbing away fast – and fuel, the gauge float giving only spasmodic jerks off the empty mark.

Suddenly, way off to our left, I spotted a double row of amber lights glowing through the haze, roughly parallel with our track, with more lights dimly perceptible beyond them in no recognisable pattern. These had to be street lighting on the outskirts of Bedford but, if so, we were west of track, and I altered course some 15 degs east to bring us back in line. At least now we knew where we were, and within 10 minutes we should be safely back on the ground at Old Warden – and none too soon as the fuel gauge indicator had now sunk to EMPTY (though I knew we ought not to be desperately short of fuel yet). The minutes ticked by and despite my change of course the expected urban sprawl of Bedford had not appeared; were we even further west than I had thought so that we had missed the town altogether? Just as I was deciding to alter course another 15 deg easterly, the open countryside below was indeed replaced by the scattered outskirts of a large town.

Looking back, the vague glow of amber lights could still be seen behind us marking what I had taken to be Bedford, and yet unmistakeably, Bedford was unfolding below and ahead. It was now obvious that those amber lights were too bright for street lights. Of course! They had to be the runway lights at RAE Thurleigh(!); had we just missed the arrival of one of their research aircraft which then usually took the form of big, fast and jet-powered? On the other hand, possibly having spotted us on their radar screens, perhaps they had helpfully switched on the lights to guide us in to an emergency landing in the worsening conditions. No use dwelling on what might have been, here at least was what we were looking for: the worst aspect now was that we still had ten minutes to go. We had actually been pretty well on track before my earlier 15 deg course alteration as we now flew over the western outskirts of the city. Ahead and to the right I could see the dark blocks of the Cardington airship sheds looming out of the mist and I turned towards them to pick up the railway line which would position us nicely for the run in to Old Warden.

Putting the maps away and now letting the compass top wind its unlocked way round the bowl, I concentrated on picking out the railway line. I knew all I had to do was follow it until it entered a tunnel and then turn left and fly due east, when the airfield would quickly swim obligingly into sight. Sure enough, there was the railway, and I turned to follow it, thankful now for this friendly guide in the half light of dusk. We had about four minutes flying at most before the tunnel appeared, then a further two to the airfield. At that time I was not all that familiar with the geography of the Bedford end of the line, so I had nothing to check until the tunnel appeared. However, when after five minutes flying, there was not only no tunnel, but a whole grouping of unfamiliar terrain, buildings and water, including a great spread of glasshouses, I became aware of only one fact – I was lost!

At first I could not believe that I could possibly have been following the wrong railway line. As far as I knew there was only one line passing Cardington; that was the one going through the tunnel and I had been following it. I wasted precious moments wondering how I could possibly have gone wrong, before reaching once more for the map.

That also was a waste of time as it was now too dim in the cabin to read it! This was ridiculous – six miles from home and I was lost! It is difficult for me to remember a time when I felt more frustrated, more inadequate or more frightened. For a moment I was as near panic as I have ever been; I had been sustained through the now rapidly failing light and low fuel situation by the certainty that safety was only a few minutes away, and that sheet anchor had been rudely snatched from me. It was not only that suddenly I was lost, nor that I could not think what to do next; there was the fear that if I did not find somewhere to land in the next few minutes it would either be too dark to do so or we could run out of fuel. As at that time I had never attempted an emergency landing, even in daylight, the possibility of picking out a good enough field in this half-light and pulling off a safe landing seemed remote. My instructor's advice about a slow pass at 400 ft looking for obvious obstructions on the approach, followed by a low pass at 50 ft looking for ditches, or uneven surfaces, or wire fences, across the selected field rang in my ears and I could only think miserably that there could simply not be enough time for that even if I could find a suitable field.

After what seemed an interminable period but which was literally only seconds I decided that before looking for a field I would have another attempt at locating where we might be. The first thing was to establish on what heading the railway lay. If it was roughly south-east, then somehow I had to be on the right line and had probably overshot my tunnel in the gloom.

Checking that I was still heading along the railway I swung the compass rim round until the lubber line aligned with the north marker – it was difficult to see what the exact heading was but even so it was obvious that we were flying north of east instead of south-east. That meant absolutely nothing to me, so that was that; it would be a question of finding a good big open space, but quick! Swinging round into a right-hand circling turn, suddenly ahead through the murk appeared four bright red lights, one above the other. I had seen those before! Where? Where?? Of course! The low aerial mast at Moggerhanger which could be seen from the ground at Old Warden. An agonising few seconds followed, while I tried unsuccessfully to place Moggerhanger on a mental map in relation to Old Warden, before I realised that the most certain way now to find the aerodrome was to fly due east till I came to the A1. Hopefully I could recognise whether to turn left or right towards Biggleswade, and then follow the road to Old Warden which passed one side of the airfield.

This proved to be the case. Before reaching the A1 I could see it ahead from a steady stream of headlights of traffic running north/south. A small town to the right could only be Sandy or Biggleswade, so that was it – turn right and look for the Old Warden roundabout. The town turned out to be Sandy, with the lights of Biggleswade dimly seen beyond it.

Was it imagination through relief of knowing where we were or was it getting brighter ahead? Certainly I picked out the roundabout quite readily as we passed at 500 ft over the Caldecote turning, roughly half a mile from it, and cut the corner in a wide turn. Now we were flying west again, losing height steadily, and a minute later I could pick out the sheds and hangars on the airfield, with friendly lights showing through the hangar roof. No time to waste on a formal circuit; there would be nobody flying from Old Warden in this light, so it was simply a matter of a 180 deg turn, swinging off to the right towards the village of Ickwell before dropping in over the trees on the approach to the long runway. Looking down at the ground it was now difficult to pick out the contours, or to judge our height for the landing flare, and I blessed the safe handling characteristics of the aircraft which allowed one to virtually let it land itself!

Once down on the ground the sky looked much lighter and good for another ten minutes flying, but this was the difference between looking down into the shadows or up into the evening sky. Certainly, by the time I had taxied back up to the hangars and switched off, even the sky looked too dark to be flying in. I remembered being caught by that difference once before, circling like a moth round a candle at 1,500 ft over the lights of Welwyn Garden City, still in daylight under a glorious sunset sky, only to find how difficult it was to pick out the grass for landing at the adjacent airfield of Panshanger where, back on the ground, the sun had long since set.

We had been completely lost for probably no more than three or four minutes at most, but even now I can recall those minutes as seeming like an eternity, and the misery of uncertainty in a situation which called for instant, correct decisions is still with me. Certainly I have never been so relieved to be back on the ground, and some very sharp lessons were learned, although even so there were other occasions (as I mentioned earlier) that were still to come.

One final thought: it has been said this was a situation in which, had we had radio fitted, and used it, we need have had no problems at all. While this may arguably be true I also recall that, on that same day, the pilot of a Cessna 172 planned to fly up to Liverpool from, I believe, Luton. Equipped with radio he had felt it safer to go above the clouds we had stayed beneath; not realising he was a long way off course, and no doubt lulled into a sense of false security by his radio contacts, he let down blind through the clouds, flying into the top of a mountain in the Snowdon range! Safer?

CHAPTER 10

ONE DARK AND DIRTY NIGHT

Annual checks on aircraft, like MOT tests on cars, are necessary evils that come round far too often and always when you have forgotten all about them. So it was no surprise when John, an old friend of mine, mentioned that the Annual was due on his Jodel and he needed to get it over to Shipdham in a hurry while it was still legal to fly it. He had been experiencing some difficulty in finding an organisation prepared to do the job at short notice and, when told by one at Shipdham to bring it in straight away, promptly arranged with me to ferry him back the next evening (a Tuesday). It had sounded quite feasible though I neglected to check the distance on a map personally – John would fly the Jodel out in the late afternoon and I would rush straight from work to the airfield and follow him.

On Tuesdays I finished work at 17.00 and reckoned to get out early enough to be over at Old Warden by 17.20. If John had, as promised, already got the Jackaroo out onto the flight line and fuelled up, it should be possible to be off the ground by 17.30. Shipdham was 66 miles to the north-east, about 55 minutes flying time, so ETA would be 18.25 and return by, say, 19.30. It was early April, and on the previous evening, when we made the arrangements, it had become dark at about 20.00 (sunset was around 19.40) so we had a little leeway though, even so, we would have to be slick. On that Monday night we had a nice clear sunset with light winds and there seemed no reason to believe that the weather would be much different the next day. If John felt it was too bad to leave he was to ring me before 16.45.

As one might guess, the weather was decidedly different the next day, with a low cloudbase, a light drizzle giving visibility of about four miles and a strengthening northerly wind – setback No.1! By 16.45 there had been no word from John so, not without some misgivings, I left work a little early and ran straight into a traffic jam on a road normally clear at that time. By some divine chance, the local Council had got wind of my plans and thought to upset them by digging a hole in the road! So the second setback was my arrival at Old Warden some 15 minutes late, to find that although John had left in the Jodel as arranged, the Jackaroo was still in the hangar. That took more time to find a willing pair of hands to help get it up the incline to the airfield so that, by the time I was finally ready to go, it was some 25 minutes later than planned.

Subconsciously, I had been putting off the decision to actually go until ready to leave, perhaps in the hope that John might either return or phone through to change the plans. In the end, with engine warmed up and chocks away, the fact that John had gone and would have no ready way of getting back left little alternative; having made the arrangements I would have to stick to them.

Flight planning had been minimal but sufficient for the outward trip. I had a course but only a rough approximation of the wind, though this was no problem as drift could be corrected *en route*. A heading for the return journey would be worked out taking the outward drift into account. The outward flight caused no real concern although the mist had, if anything, thickened and the wind, now on my port quarter, had stiffened. Because of the latter, little time was made up on the journey, as it was 18.45 when Shipdham's old wartime hangars loomed darkly out of the mist ahead. Circling round the black hangars, shining wet in the drizzle, looking in vain for the Jodel or John, the only sign of life to be seen was one damp-looking figure, unrecognisable to me, waving like mad. "Jolly nice of him," I thought and waved back before returning to the far end of the runway.

The runway was longer than expected and having landed short it took ages to taxy on the tarmac to the other end. There I was met by the solitary figure I had seen earlier, who came running along the runway to meet me. In between his gasps for breath I gathered he was telling me to go away at once – turn round straight away and get back as fast as possible. At first this did not make sense but eventually the message came through. John had dropped in, they could not do the job at such short notice, so he had gone back to Old Warden, and he had left a message for me to go straight back. The urgency was due to it now being fairly late and if I did not hurry, I would not get back before dark.

Looking around, the truth of what he was saying suddenly struck home. It was in fact much darker tonight than at this time the previous evening, due to the thick blanket of cloud above and the general mist, and it was probably going to be too dark to fly long before 20.00! Without wasting any more time, I turned round, going only a hundred yards or so back down the runway. Take-off in this distance was no problem, the Jackaroo having climbed to 50 ft by the time we crossed the perimeter track, and I quickly turned for home.

In the excitement, I had not worked out the course and, with the quartering wind, a straight reciprocal was no use. By the time I had remembered what my previous heading was, added 180 deg, doubled and subtracted the corrections for drift, then allowed for the difference between my new course and the straight reciprocal I had initially set off on, and recalculated because I did not believe the answer, I was some five miles from Shipdham with not a navigational feature in sight. We crossed open fields and dykes, an occasional deserted road or grey, wet hamlet, but nothing with which I could check my position. I had been well and truly caught out, doing all the things I prided myself on not doing.

It was noticeably darkening, the mist if anything was thicker, but at least the tailwind component was going to significantly shorten the return; nevertheless I pushed the throttle fully open. That was not without some concern as John had not topped up the fuel tank and neither had I before leaving, thinking that if necessary it would be easier to put in a few gallons at Shipdham where refuelling would be faster.

This, of course, had not been done and now the float was bobbing near the bottom mark. When that sank, I would have about five gallons left, enough for nearly an hour's flying at cruising revs, but an unknown amount at full throttle, perhaps 40 minutes.

The flight back was a most miserable one. Sticking religiously to my compass heading brought no confirmation at all of my track. Expected features did not materialise and by flying at 500 ft due to the low cloud-base, I could see very little distance on either side. The only comfort was that I could not be very far off course and that sooner or later on my present heading I was bound to cross the A1 trunk road unless the wind had swung through more than say 60 degs. The only question was how late was 'later' – would daylight and fuel last long enough? Because I could not fix my position there was no telling. Time and distance passed, the former rapidly and the latter woefully slowly, but still no fix came up and it was getting steadily darker. As in my previous 'lost' situation the moment of truth was rapidly approaching when I should have to take the unpalatable decision to land somewhere other than my intended destination. The frustrating thing was that there were plenty of both disused and active airfields about in the area but, without knowing my own position, there was no point in leaving my present heading to go looking for them. At least by sticking to this course, I was going in the right general direction and there was as much chance of finding one on this heading as on any other – the thought of stumbling about East Anglia, in failing light, with low fuel and with no idea where I was going did not appeal to me at all.

Faced with the prospect of landing in an unknown field, which would have had more daunting subsequent side effects (like getting it out again and back to base) than the actual landing as long as I did not leave it too late, I kept putting off the decision. The twin syndromes of "something is bound to turn up" and "it can't happen to me" are very powerful at a time like this. Ahead now I could pick out nothing beyond perhaps a mile – just a succession of woods and fields and hedges with an occasional minor road or farm – I could have been anywhere. For all I knew the A1 trunk road might be no more than one minute away in flying time, or it could be 10 or 15 minutes away. Now there was another problem: even if the A1 suddenly appeared out of the gloom ahead it could still prove difficult to recognise the point of crossing quickly unless I flew over or in sight of Biggleswade or Langford water tower. "Put it down now, while

TOP: Delivery flight 2 – Jackaroo 'OIR at Old Warden as bought from Piers Martin at Blackpool (7th September 1968). Still in late Wiltshire School of Flying colours of black fuselage & tail with aluminium wings & trim, plus sundry red patches. Note stub exhausts. Photo: Alan Brett.
BOTTOM: 'OIR undergoing its second C. of A. at Old Warden, with rear top decking and original fabric removed, showing standard Tiger Moth rear fuselage and warped stringers. The hideous anti-spin strakes were removed at this time. Photo: The author.

TOP: Wally Calway and Tiger Moth 'LTW at Redhill at the conclusion of our "Dawn-to-Dusk" flight on the 27th June 1967. Photo: The author.

MIDDLE: Neil Williams took me aloft in the gunner's cockpit of the LVG CVI at a Cranfield display in September 1973 for a dogfight with the Bristol Fighter. Photo: The author's collection.

BOTTOM: Dave Elphick's Piper L-4H Cub in its original all-yellow colours. This was a delightful aircraft to fly. Photo: Clive Norman.

TOP: Jackaroo 'OIR and myself with tent at Bodmin on the 18th September 1971. As near to "sleeping under the wing" as we cared to manage in England.
Photo: D. Elphick.
BOTTOM: Another camping exercise, this time at Welshpool on the VAC Annual Camp (26th August 1973). The "Jack's" ample cabin made for easy stowage of tents etc. Photo: D. Elphick.

TOP: Forerunners of the Diamond Nine? Not as immaculate a formation as those worthies fly but good fun behind the Navy's Swordfish. Halfpenny Green, 29th August 1977. Photo: Arthur Mason.

BOTTOM: Tony Harold in 'NFM formates on 'OIR over Finmere. A regular occurrence in the seventies, often with several other Tigers.
Photo: By courtesy of the Vintage Aircraft Club.

you can – OK but hold it just a few seconds longer." "No, put it down now – yes, in a minute." "No, now!"

At that point my Guardian Angel took pity on me (again) and ahead and to the left appeared red and green horizontal bars of light glowing through the mist. For a moment, nothing registered except a feeling of familiarity with that particular pattern of lighting. Like a moth round a candle flame I headed towards it while I tried to remember where I had seen it. The only things that came to mind were the neon signs over "The Plough" public house at Topler's Hill on the A1. It just had to be that, and with that realisation, there could be seen car headlights on the A1 itself. What fantastic luck! It meant that I had been only about two miles south of track!

It was now a definite race against the light, as I really ought to have landed before. Had I been forced to put down in a strange field it could have been very worrying indeed as it was too dark to pick out cables or potholes around or in the field or, indeed, to assess field length and gradient with any certainty! Neither were the instruments easily readable, their vertical faces under the coaming picking up virtually no illumination from the remaining daylight, only the horizontal face of the compass conveying any useful information. As it was, I followed the A1 almost round to Biggleswade, with street lights and signs etc., now well lit, and then across to the Old Warden road, down to the airfield, still readily discernible. On the airfield was a car with its headlights on but it was not yet dark enough for these to serve any purpose other than as a homing beacon for lost aviators!

A quick turn by the side of the hangars brought me floating down above the line of the main grass runway. Now it was a question of depending on 'feel' to gauge flying speed; losing height with the stick back and a trickle of power as the speed fell away, holding it at a reasonable rate of sink. Missing the flattish ground at the top end of the runway, we sailed on down the slope, it now being impossible to estimate height accurately, hoping that I had not flattened out too early so that the Jackaroo would still be flying by the time we got to the end of the field. At times like this the downward slope on that runway seemed awfully long and the light weight of the aircraft, with only myself on board and low on fuel, merely prolonged the agony. After what seemed far too long we bumped down more heavily than usual and quickly stopped.

This time there were no illusions about how much longer it would have been safe to keep on flying. I really ought to have landed minutes before spotting the pub's lights, but how frustrating it would have been to then discover subsequently how close I was to track and literally only a few minutes from base.

Back in the warm glow of the hangar, having been helped to put the aircraft away by John and Keith, the latter having gone along with John for the ride, John's side of the story quickly unfolded. Shipdham had not been able to do the work straight away after all and he confirmed the message I had been given there, adding that he had waited as long as seemed prudent before departing, hoping that I had not left because of the deteriorating visibility. On the return journey he and Keith had been only too aware that if they and I were both on track, they would encounter me flying towards them, with me not expecting to meet anybody on my reciprocal. They kept their eyes skinned the whole way, consoling themselves as they neared home without having seen me, with the thought that I probably had not left. Then, of course, when back on the ground, they had seen the empty hangar and knew that I had gone after all.

Although they were somewhat faster than the Jackaroo, it was already depressingly murky when they got back, so that they spent a miserable 20 minutes or so with ears straining to catch the first sound of the returning aircraft. As it got darker, they drove their cars onto the field, facing the direction from which I was due, with headlights on. Eventually, just when they had got to the point of certainty that I would not return that evening, they heard the sound of a Gipsy Major running full out, though they could not pick out the aircraft until I dropped in by the hangars. They were as relieved as I that we had all got safely back.

Afterwards, looking at the map, it seemed almost impossible for me to have threaded a way between the bigger towns and villages that were dotted about between Shipdham and Old Warden without having seen one. This despite my track lying within two miles of the City of Cambridge, not to mention the airfields of Feltwell, Lakenheath, Mildenhall, Waterbeach, Oakington, Bourn and Gransden, all less than three miles from track!

My journeys by road to Old Warden always take me past "The Plough" at Topler's Hill and if I were asked to name the most regular reminder of past follies this surely must be the prime contender.

CHAPTER 11
LAND'S END AND BUST

It was a glorious Indian Summer, when Jackaroos were young, only the snootiest of airfields demanded payment of landing fees with PPO (Prior Permission Only), and avionics were barely thought of.

The occasion was an invitation to a flying weekend at the then newly-opened Bodmin airfield, with the promise of camping facilities on the field. Having read avidly in the past of the exploits of 1920s barnstormers in the United States, it seemed that here was a chance to at least partly emulate their activities in bedding down under the wing, at the same time (and perhaps more importantly) keeping the costs down. Accordingly Dave Elphick (whose essential ingredients amongst others was a lightweight two-man tent) was sought out as sharing crew member and the aircraft was filled with overnight camping gear.

As Bodmin, and hopefully Land's End, was farther away than either of us had flown the aircraft before, and because the Cornish coastline was an area that I wanted to fly round more than any other, the whole thing took on an air of adventure which subsequent trips have rarely matched.

Refuelling in distant places can often be problematical and we knew that Bodmin had no 80-octane petrol, so planning had to take into account the need to be able to get back to the last known source. In this case we could refuel at Compton Abbas and try Roborough (Plymouth) for a final top-up as being the nearest airfield to Bodmin with fuel. Distance out on Saturday (Old Warden–Bodmin) was around 230 miles, say three to four hours' flying depending on headwinds. With two stops and an ETA of say 16.00 we should aim at take-off around 10.00 for a leisurely and unhurried flight. For the return on Sunday, any wind should be behind us, needing only one stop, so we should be able to leave after the small air display planned for the afternoon (in which we were to participate) by, say, 16.30.

Saturday morning was bright and clear, and with light hearts and a full load of camping gear and fuel we set off to the golden west at 11.00. This was a good start – for me to be only one hour late was something of an encouraging sign. David had only recently converted to the Jackaroo and was happy to exercise his navigation to pastures new, leaving me to do most of the flying (an admirable arrangement). We headed for Compton Abbas, which I had visited once before, remembering it as unusual in its location along a high east-west ridge, being a long, narrow, undulating strip of grass with the Clubhouse and hangars at the western end. It had been a friendly, informal, run-down sort of place before, with the sort of hangar that has interesting aircraft lurking in the darker corners. David had rung control and established that they were open and had fuel and we found a friendly welcome (no landing fees!) when we landed at 12.40. Due to David's impeccable navigation we had no trouble locating the field and the wind was behaving itself for a change, though visibility, as so often seems to be the case in this part of the world, was hazy under a clear blue sky.

The Clubhouse was dispensing light snacks, so the inner men were suitably refuelled, as was the Jackaroo, and we set off again for Roborough two hours later. Our route took us down to the South Coast at Lyme Bay and I had no qualms about flying along the coast just offshore. We even paid a visit to a group of yachts milling around in a seemingly aimless fashion a mile or so out to sea off Seaton. We dropped down to masthead height to give them an encouraging wave, but their reactions left us wondering whether they were waving back or shaking their fists at us, so we quickly left them to their own devices. They made a striking picture as we approached, with the bright sun back-lighting their sails to a brilliant white, leavened by odd splashes of colour from spinnakers worn by some of them, all set amidst the silvery golden reflections twinkling back from a comparatively calm sea.

Rejoining the coast we flew along at perhaps 20-30 ft, with the cliffs of Beer Head towering above us, until we reached Sidmouth, where we transferred to above the cliffs. Perhaps it was the advancing years or a memory of what happened during this trip that caused me to fly above the cliffs most of the way when I retraced the route ten years later! Certainly, with the red sandstone cliffs stretching up for several hundred feet above us and for several miles in front of us, the thought did cross my mind even then that engine failure could lead only to a very wet end. At that time I had never suffered any form of loss of power, nor knew anyone else who had, from a Gipsy Major, so the thought was instantly dismissed.

We flew a direct route to Plymouth, leaving the coast at Budleigh Salterton and overflying the wild and rugged desolation of Dartmoor. At 1,500 ft a.s.l. the ground often came up to meet us but we saw very little sign of any life that might be concerned at our low flying over the higher ridges. Halfway across, we spotted the grim, grey buildings of Dartmoor prison off to the north of our track, and realised how ideally located it was for its purpose.

At Roborough we found no activity at all, getting a green from the tower as soon as we joined circuit. Landing short on the into-wind grass runway we discovered just how undulating the field was – as I flared for touchdown I seemed to be flying into the side of a hill and even whilst still airborne the airport buildings had disappeared from view. We soon had the Jackaroo refuelled and after a quick look round the hangars (containing, as almost inevitably in those days, a Tiger Moth plus a dozen or so Tiger wings suspended on the beams) left on our final leg to Bodmin.

This stage saw us heading out due west, with Brunel's Tamar Bridge at Saltash on our left, to follow roughly the route of the railway via Liskeard to the wastelands of Bodmin Moor. Visibility was a little hazy flying straight into the sun and we were grateful for the shining rails to follow.

Bodmin I knew well, and had no difficulty in identifying the little grey town nestling in a steep-sided valley. During a wide turn over the town, it was easy to pick out the A30 trunk road descending steeply from the north-east and I followed its line back up over the edge of the escarpment. The airstrip lay above the town, one field to the east of the A30, and we found the yellow windsock, black and white chequered control van and mown grass runways without difficulty.

There was little sign of life other than a cream-coloured Auster waddling off to the end of the into-wind runway and we waited until he had taken off before lining up for landing. Circling round, we realised how easy it was to locate the field – just as well as it turned out later. After landing we taxied towards the control van and were met by a solitary but welcoming individual, who showed us where to park and where we could pitch our tent.

Neither of us were particularly hungry and I was longing to fly over to the northern coast to view familiar landmarks from the air. We were a little restricted by the fuel situation but a plan resolved itself. We would fly down to Land's End early next morning and refuel there, with enough to get us back via Bodmin direct to Compton Abbas, assuming a following wind. If the wind veered before our return we would leave earlier and call in at Roborough. Meanwhile we had enough petrol to fly out that evening to Wadebridge, then round the coast to Tintagel, before returning to Bodmin, a distance of approx. 50 miles. This would leave us ample fuel to fly the 60 or 70 miles down the coast to Land's End the next morning. The 50 miles would take us about 45 minutes and with sunset at around 7 o'clock we should aim to be off not later than 18.00.

That still left us about an hour, so we unpacked our gear, erected the tent and unrolled our sleeping bags. There was time to boil a kettle for coffee but we didn't bother with eating – the local map was far more interesting, though barely necessary for me. Having spent three or four weekly or weekend holidays at Perranporth every year over a 12-year period, I reckoned to know the countryside pretty well. And so it turned out.

We got off just after six and, without its load of camping gear, the Jackaroo eagerly leapt into the air. There was now no wind, it was still pleasantly warm and the earlier haze had all but disappeared, leaving a golden sky to the west, with the lowering sun promising a fine sunset and a good day on the morrow. Climbing out of Bodmin and pointing our nose north-west, we headed for Wadebridge and Padstow and almost immediately could see the sun reflecting off the burnished waters of Padstow Bay and the Camel estuary.

There was no need to hurry and no point in gaining more than the minimum 500 ft above ground, so we ambled leisurely along the course of the River Camel and followed the winding north shore of the estuary out to Polzeath. It was a most enjoyable flight, with the sun brightening the yellow sands of the foreshore, picking out every detail with needle-sharp clarity and casting long dark shadows of hedgerows, trees and ridges of undulating ground over the emerald green grass, but what followed was an all-too-brief 15 or so minutes of sheer bliss. If asked what was the most pleasurable flight I have ever undertaken it would unhesitatingly be this; nothing since has surpassed it. For one thing, caution steps in too assuredly with age to repeat what I now recognise were the risks so lightheartedly taken then.

In my opinion the northern coast of Cornwall, with its towering, rugged, grass-topped cliffs, sandy coves and beaches, blue sea with white breakers, and isolated 'olde worlde' fishing villages, is a stretch of wild beauty unequalled anywhere. Consider then the other ingredients: late evening with very few people to upset by low-flying; no wind to cause cliff-top eddies or turbulence; an obedient, well-mannered and manoeu-vrable biplane; and a golden sunset as offered only in Cornwall.

The 15-mile stretch of coast from Pentire Point to Tintagel takes in the cluster of tiny harbours of Port Quin, Port Isaac and Port Gaverne and precious little else in the way of human habitation. Typically, we would follow the coastline exactly for a short spell at perhaps ten feet or so above the waves, banking sharply to left or right, out round the head-lands and tight-turning into and out of small bays and coves with the roar of the engine echoing back when we closed the throttle; now flying straight towards the base of a promontory and competing with the wheeling seagulls, zooming up at the last minute to clear the top of the cliff by what seemed like feet, with a momentary, pin-sharp glimpse of a middle-aged couple, with upturned faces and open mouths, walking their bounding white and brown fox terrier along the cliff-top path; following the winding path as it descended towards the cove on the other side of the point, now throttled well back so that the engine roar had died to a subdued tickover; sideslipping down to sea level again as we chased the surf towards a deserted beach, then opening up to hedge-hop over the next headland. We skirted seaward of the villages, remaining close enough to return the waves of the few people who noticed our brief passage and hopefully disturbed no one with the possible exception of the couple on the cliff path (who must have been somewhat startled to find an old biplane suddenly roaring just over their heads from below the cliff edge).

At Tintagel we circled the legendary site of King Arthur's Castle and peered at Merlin's Cave from the seaward aspect (from where it looks even more impressive than from the ground). But all good things have to come to an end; it called for a great mental effort to leave this Utopian coastline and, with great reluctance, turn inland to return to Bodmin before dusk.

Back on the ground at Bodmin we found the field deserted and with no transport available decided to have a light supper and retire early. Having no form of lighting other than a small torch considerably eased the decision-making process! We both got to sleep fairly early but woke around dawn to find that this barnstorming business can be cold, wet and uncomfortable at that time of day. Dave's nylon tent had not seen any waterproofing for many a long year and a fairly heavy dew was dripping noticeably through. A hearty camp breakfast sizzling in the frying pan soon cheered things up and we had plenty of time to formulate our plans for the day before anyone arrived.

We decided to fly down to St. Just, the little cliff-top airfield near Land's End, if they could supply us with any fuel (of which there was little doubt) and then return in time for the air display after lunch. By the time we had phoned St. Just and established that they would accept us and had fuel, the first spectator had arrived. Noel introduced himself, expressed interest in the Jackaroo and eagerly accepted an invitation to join us.

So at 10.45 we found ourselves airborne, now three-up, aiming to skirt south of the control zone around St. Mawgan and follow the coast from Newquay. It was already a fine, warm summer's day, with a distant blue haze that I associate in these islands only with the north Cornish coast, where the intense ultramarine of the sea merges with the pale blue sky.

Visibility seemed limitless and from our initial cruising height of 1,000 ft we could see both north and south coasts, with the conical, gleaming white 'mountains' of the St. Austell china clay pits in the distance off our port lower wingtip. There was no sign of life from the great sprawl of RAF St. Mawgan but we kept well clear, crossing the coast just west of Newquay. Swinging wide of the resort, we flew over the cliffs at West Pentire and Holywell Bay and then let down to beach level for an exhilarating long, low run up the near-deserted, two-mile stretch of Perran Sands. This was a beach I knew well and the temptation to land on that flat golden expanse was great, but time was just a little pressing and there were stretches where the apparently firm surface could be treacherously soft. From the south end of the beach stretched a forbidding line of high cliffs, on top of which lay the old wartime fighter airfield of Perranporth, still in use by a gliding club. Thermalling above the cliffs a pair of sailplanes indicated probable activity at the airfield so we swung off seaward to follow the base of St. Agnes Head.

With never more than 10 to 15 ft of air beneath our wings any significant power loss would have entailed a certain wet conclusion to our trip – but Gipsy Majors never let you down. Beyond St. Agnes lay the prohibited danger zone of Portreath and we lifted briefly up over the cliffs to detour inland, wide of the area, before rejoining the coast opposite Camborne. Inland, the stark, featureless moorland with its isolated, grey, tin-mining villages held little attraction while the lure of the golden beaches was ever-present.

Ahead now lay the great sweeping bay of St. Ives with the inner scoop of Carbis Bay. Following the curve would have entailed a considerable detour so we took a straight line to St. Ives, three miles across the water, prudence suggesting a gradual climb from masthead height to the necessary clearance over the port. Beyond St. Ives we had a further 15 miles of starkly beautiful rocky coastline, past Gurnards Head to Cape Cornwall, before turning in to land at the idyllic grass airfield of St. Just, situated almost on the cliff edge.

St. Just at that time, even before the late Viv Bellamy moved in with his exciting replica construction and vintage rebuilding activities, was an interesting place to visit. A Dragon Rapide still carried out joyriding trips round the coast and out to the Longships lighthouse, and it was here that I saw a Lake Skimmer amphibian for the first time (or was it a Teal?). Here we met, among others, John Isaacs of 'Fury' fame, "just out for a ride." But here also we encountered a snag. Although the chap I spoke to on the phone that morning had said fuel would be available, it transpired that they were very low and were most reluctant to let us have any on two counts: one that they needed fuel for the Rapide joyriding but, perhaps more to the point, the fuel was in a tank suspected of having water contamination when at low level, and filtering manually was a lengthy job. We were fairly desperate, knowing that we had to get back to Roborough at least, and in the end they let us have 10 gallons, checking the delivery sight glass very carefully for any signs of water. After completing fuelling we drained off a little into a clean rag to check again for water but it appeared to be clear.

After a coffee we quickly got airborne again for the return to Bodmin, planning to fly up the south coast from Falmouth to St. Austell. First though, we had to visit Land's End, *en route* to which we could see the two-mile-distant Longships lighthouse and were sorely tempted to detour out to take a closer look. Fortunately, we decided it wasn't worth the extra 10 minutes that would take and contented ourselves with circling over the cliffs at Land's End, returning the waves of many of the groundborne visitors.

The direct route to Falmouth took us over the incredibly tiny fishing harbour of Mousehole (pronounced "Muzzle") and five miles across Mount's Bay to Praa Sands.

However, St. Michael's Mount was slightly to the north and the cross-water distance from Mousehole was only three miles, so it needed little self-argument to detour to take a closer look from the air at that unusual conical island and the nearby remains of the old battleship HMS Warspite, which sank there in a gale when on its way to the scrapyards.

Any extensive water crossing in an old, slow aeroplane is a time for extra-finely tuned ears listening for unusual engine noises; distances seem much greater than shown on the map and cowardly fellows (like me, nowadays) tend to climb to sufficient height to allow for gliding to the nearest shore. On this occasion, having spent so much time just above sea level and/or below cliff-top height with little cause for concern, there seemed no reason to suppose that anything could go wrong in the next three minutes or so. Nevertheless, after circling Mousehole at around 500 ft I stayed at that height initially though found myself climbing subconsciously as we progressed further out over the fairly extensive stretch of sea in Mount's Bay.

In front of us now lay St. Michael's Mount and when more than halfway across the Bay we already felt we were as good as home and dry. Which is when the gremlins struck (n.b. 'gremlins' – wartime RAF slang for nasty bug-like creatures that put spanners in the works and sand in the wheels). Just as I was about to throttle back for a slow descent toward the half-mile-distant Mount, there was a single loud, explosive report from the engine. We were cruising at about 1,900 rpm and at that point I had not changed the throttle setting for several minutes so there ought not to have been any cause for blowback in the carburettor or backfire in the exhaust. A glance at the altimeter showed us to be about 950 ft above the sea and, with three of us aboard and a fair load of fuel there was little certainty of gliding the mile or so that separated us from the broad flat sands of the mainland beach. With the tide well in, the tidal causeway to the Mount was covered and there were no alternatives for a safe dry landing.

The engine continued running as before and as yet there was little cause for alarm, but even so it seemed a good idea to gain height just in case we lost power later. Pushing the throttle evenly forward to initiate the climb brought an immediate howl of anguish from the engine, setting up a vibration that threatened to shake loose my last remaining teeth.

Waiting a few seconds to see if it would clear itself, it soon became evident that it would not, so there was nothing for it but to ease the throttle back to a point where the engine would resume its previous reasonably even tenor, which proved now to be lower than before, at about 1,800 rpm. In this brief exchange we had gained perhaps a hundred feet in height though our speed had dropped from 60 knots to 55 knots.

The vibration had been such that it was obvious to Dave and our passenger, Noel, that something was seriously amiss. Dave as navigator had the maps in front of him and quickly located the nearest airfield at Culdrose and estimated the distance as being about 10 miles on a heading slightly south of east – would the engine keep going for 10 minutes?

At this point, because the engine was still running perfectly at just short of 1,800 rpm there was no reason to suppose the fault was mechanical. It could have been magneto trouble but that would be unlikely to affect both mags together. Knowing that the fuel was suspect left us thinking that, in some way, at higher throttle openings, something was getting through to cause misfiring, without our really being convinced that this was the answer.

Having got our breath back, on course to a nearby airfield and with the engine still running, even if it was not entirely capable of holding altitude, any thought of sitting back to relax was rudely shattered by the realisation that the engine was starting to run roughly again. Within a few seconds it was again threatening to vibrate itself out of its mountings and could only be placated by closing the throttle slightly. Revs now down to 1,780, altitude back to 950 ft, speed still 55 knots, St. Michael's Mount now beneath us and still half a mile to shore.

At least we would certainly make it to the beach, even if the engine stopped now, but thoughts running through my mind were concerned with the practical difficulties after landing with engine trouble on the beach. Was the tide coming in or going out? Would the sand be firm or soft? If we got it down what could we do about the engine? We had no tools or spares with us. The nearest engineers would be those at Land's End who, even if present at the airfield on a Sunday, would be extremely unlikely to be able to get out to us until next day at the earliest. And what would we do with it overnight – leave it on the beach? Even then, with the group's finances as usual very thinly stretched, could we afford to run up an enormous bill or would we attempt to get it back home to sort it out? Take the wings off and trail it some 325 miles over one of the busiest trunk roads in southern England? The answer to all these questions was "no" – not if there was any alternative.

Well, what were the alternatives? Running parallel with the coast was a ridge which earlier had looked of little significance but now seemed to be looming up menacingly. It ran all along the coast and would obviously have to be crossed at some point if we were to get into Culdrose. Turning to Dave, I asked for the heights of the ridge and the airfield and, while he was sorting that out, enquired how Noel was faring. He seemed to be entirely unconcerned, adding that this was more exciting than being on the ground at Bodmin – undoubtedly true but I knew where I would rather have been at that instant!

Dave's answer was that the ridge height appeared to be about 600 ft and that the airfield was 268 ft. It would have been best to follow the coast past Praa sands to Porthleven, with the certainty of somewhere safe to put down, but we might then not have had sufficient altitude to cross the ridge. In fact, it was beginning to look touch and go as to whether we would get across even by the most direct route. The revs at which the engine would run smoothly were gradually dropping and our rate of descent increasing correspondingly.

Some quick calculations showed that if the engine did not dramatically increase its rate of reduction in revolutions we would make it with sufficient height to spare providing we could get across the ridge. Dave suggested that we should go direct to Culdrose so we let the inviting flat expanse of sand slide rearward under our wings. Revs 1,750, speed holding at 55 knots, altitude just over 800 ft.

All attention now was on the 'mountain range' lying across our path. From the seaward side it had a fairly shallow gradient to the top, and we watched anxiously as the ground slowly came up to meet us. In fact the top of the ridge slid past below with little more than fifty feet to spare but we all breathed a sigh of relief as the ground dropped away rapidly once we were over. Until, that is, it became apparent that the grass was not greener on the other side! Although on the seaward side the ground was fairly open, we were now faced with an unending vista of the tiny fields so typical of this part of Cornwall. Separation of the fields was by high, very solid dry-stone walls and the best we could hope for, in the event of having to put down, was a steep side-slipping approach; even if we managed to avoid damaging the aircraft on arrival, there would be little possibility of taking off again!

Turning south-east onto course for Culdrose we tried to pick out the airfield but it was some minutes before we were able to do so. At the same time it became evident that just short of the airfield was a belt of trees which on closer examination were partially shielding a valley. Revs now 1,730, height 450 ft and falling off quickly enough to make the valley crossing look by no means certain. Faced with these options, three occupants sweating it out in a Jackaroo obviously generate enough lift to counteract such loss of power, because we still had 150 ft in hand as we cleared the valley.

There was no time, or rather, height, for any fancy circuit work. Ahead now was a vast open expanse of grass and concrete. A large runway lay on our right, besides which was a small knot of people, Land Rovers, several gliders and a power winch. There were no gliders in the air or being launched, so I went straight in, to land close to the group on the ground, engine now throttled right back. As we slowed to a walking pace the engine was ticking over evenly and smoothly as if nothing was wrong. Neither did a short burst of power, to perhaps 1,500 revs, to swing round and taxy up to the gliders, bring forth any protest from the engine. So it was hardly surprising that the reception given to David (who had quickly unstrapped and jumped to the turf) by the rather irate-looking individual who detached himself to enquire what the hell were we doing there, was frosty and disbelieving – he had heard all there was to hear about mysterious engine ailments many times before! All quickly changed when, at Dave's shouted request, my brief opening of the throttle to 1,750 rpm produced very obvious rough and noisy running and about 12 inches of flame from the exhaust.

Now they could not do enough for us. When I explained my theory about water in the petrol only getting through at high throttle openings they quickly produced a kit for checking fuel contamination. We ran off some petrol from the carburettor into a beaker and were almost sorry to find that it was clear of water. After much head-scratching and investigation no one could think of anything that would produce our symptoms, so it was suggested that we walk the aircraft over to the hangars where they had plenty of tools, engine fitters and possibly some Gipsy Major spares retained for their glider-towing Tiger.

It was by now just past midday and the sun was beating down from a cloudless sky. We started out on the long trek to the hangar (at almost the opposite end of the airfield) trundling round the perimeter track fairly jauntily initially, but by the time we arrived we were hot and sticky and very tired. Two of us on the tail and one on each lower wing makes light work of moving ¾ of a ton of aeroplane a short distance, but a mile or so round an undulating perimeter track on a hot day is a different kettle of fish. We took turns on the tail not so much because of the weight but because it is very awkward for two people to get the balance right; one may want the weight a little higher and be pushing up and the other may feel it going and pull it down so that it gets heavier and heavier! We had plenty of opportunity to observe all the evidence of a glorious English summer day: the distant heat haze, the shimmering glare from the concrete, the chirruping of grasshoppers from the grass and the soaring notes of the skylarks mocking our painful progress on the ground.

When we got to the hangars the attention we received was quite fantastic. Obviously, though some of the mechanics would have been quite keen to get actively involved, they were not allowed to work on the engine, but they helped in every other way possible. The hangar doors were rolled back for us to get into the shade, the most comprehensive tool kit I have ever seen was put at our disposal, and people were constantly in attendance for anything we required. Trouble was, neither Dave nor I had much idea where to start. Oh! we did the obvious things like checking the plugs and contacts, cleaned out the fuel lines and carburettor, listened intently to the Gipsy's clatter as we slowly turned the prop. But by three o'clock, when we tried another engine run, we were not unduly surprised that, at just over 1,700 rpm, the engine complained loudly and we hastily shut down.

We had not replaced the cowlings or cooling air duct so the push rod tubes were exposed to view. Whilst despondently chewing the matter over and idly eyeing the port side of the engine, the inspiration we were seeking suddenly came. David noticed that the exhaust and inlet push rod cover tubes (which are in two telescopic parts to allow for fitting) on No. 4 cylinder had a 3/32-inch band polished round the sliding joint of the two halves, whereas all the others had not. Why had these push rod tubes expanded and been moving? The only reason Dave could see was if the gap between the crankcase and the rocker cover was varying in some way. The halves of the tube are spring-loaded so that they bed on oil seals in the crankcase and rocker box and normally, once sprung into place, no further movement occurs.

At this point, I didn't see how movement could occur. If, as mooted, the cylinder head was broken, the engine would hardly tick over as smoothly and quietly as it did. Dave ended all argument by seizing the rocker box and managing to waggle it visibly up and down. It just didn't seem possible that the head could be split to such an extent but there was undeniably movement. After some discussion we decided to remove the head and see what other damage may have been sustained with a view to obtaining replacements and returning at some later date to fit them. Despair loomed large as we would have to return home via Bodmin by surface transport (next train was 16.30), then arrange another weekend in conjunction with a licensed engineer to sign the job out, plus hangarage to pay at Culdrose.

Fortunately, as soon as we removed the rocker box cover, we saw what had happened. A mounting bracket for the valve rocker arms is secured through the rocker box to the cylinder head by three bolts and nuts, and the head had broken off the bolt at the exhaust valve side of the bracket. This must have been the report we heard over St. Mount's Bay. With one bolt effectively gone, the nut on the centre bolt quickly vibrated loose and continued to slowly unscrew. As it slackened, the bracket (and rocker box) was increasingly free to move at the exhaust valve side, the effect of this being for the rocker arm to move the bracket rather than the exhaust valve, thus reducing the opening of the latter. This was a lesson in engine valve design and operation – if the inlet valve lets more mixture in than can escape past the exhaust valve the engine will run roughly! All the time that the mixture passing the throttle could be scavenged by the exhaust valve the engine would run satisfactorily but, with the valve opening becoming progressively smaller, the throttle had to be similarly closed manually to match.

From despair we saw a glimmer of hope. Perhaps if we could find a replacement bolt we could yet get going. The Navy, urged on by the thought that if we could get away before dark they would have no troublesome paperwork or enquiry to handle, searched for their supply of Gipsy spares, but the fitter who normally serviced the Tiger was away. They did produce several similar-sized but different-threaded high tensile bolts and nuts and we selected the most suitable. Meanwhile, David phoned his wife and got the message to mine to say that we would not be back until the next day (again?). Now it was a race against time.

We had about 35 miles to fly back to Bodmin, say 35 minutes take-off to landing, so we needed to taxy out by 45 minutes before dusk. Sunset was about 18.45, allow 30 minutes to lighting-up time, so we solemnly agreed that our latest time of departure was 18.30. This gave us by now about 1¼ hours (it had taken ages to find the bolts) to remove the cooling duct mounting plate, remove the push rods and rocker box to check for any further damage, fit the new bolt, reassemble everything and set the valve clearances etc. Then carry out an engine run, replace all the cowlings and go. It was going to be very tight!

Progress against the clock was painfully slow. By 17.45 Noel decided to cut his losses and return to his home at Sidmouth by British Rail as there was no certainty that we would finish in time. He departed, sorrowing, with needless apologies for 'deserting' us, declaring that this was a day he would long remember and had enjoyed despite all the problems – or perhaps because of them.

By 18.30, our "latest" time for departure, we were nearly ready but reckoned we still had about 15 minutes work ahead of us. At 18.40 we were ready to run but decided to press on and put the cowlings back; if the engine ran OK we would go straight away; if it still ran rough then we would not have time to sort it out anyway. It needed a further 10 minutes to get the cowlings back, everything stowed or returned to the Navy, and me back in the pilot's seat ready to go.

Dave swung the prop and the engine fired straight away; with a line of matelots on each wing leading edge holding us back (the chocks could not be relied on to hold on the tarmac), I held my breath and, with fingers crossed, opened the throttle gingerly. At 1,750 rpm the thin blue line was just able to hold the aircraft back and the engine was running smoothly. On up briefly to 1,900 for a dead-cut check on the mags and still smooth; but then I throttled back intending to do a final full-throttle check as we taxied out, not trusting the line of helpers to be able to hold the aircraft on the tarmac.

Just then, the new Duty Officer came along and, apparently previously briefed, enquired how things were going; were we planning to leave that night? When we replied: "Yes, if we could get straight off," he said not to worry about booking out at the Control Tower, he would see that that was done. Flying had officially finished for the day so it would be OK for us just to taxy out onto the east-west runway and go. How far was the end of the runway, I asked, to be told that it was about half a mile. That would take nearly 10 minutes taxying on concrete or tarmac, with the necessary manoeuvring round the hangars!

Ten minutes that could kill us! Looking desperately in turn at the evening mist which had crept up on us and the red sun just about to sink into it, and my watch which said "you should be in the air by now," I asked the officer who had been with us most of the time whether the grass beyond the perimeter track was clear or whether there were any hidden obstacles in it. He thought that there were only the taxyway lights to worry about.

Turning back to the Duty Officer, I explained our predicament and suggested that we be allowed to take off from where we were between the hangars, as I thought we would be off before we got to the grass. Duty Officer, drawing himself up to his full height, said he could not possibly give permission for us to do that, but – he was just about to depart the scene and what he didn't see would not concern him. With that he turned and walked away!

We had filled up with fuel during the afternoon so all that was left to do was to make a final arrangement for a carrier-type take-off, using all the available 'bods' to hold us back in lieu of brakes until we had full revs and then when I dropped my arm to all let go and drop flat if in the way. For an unrehearsed, co-ordinated action it worked like a dream. With hurried, profuse thanks for all their help, I opened the throttle fully and at 2,050 revs waved them away. The tail came up immediately and we surged forward in an entirely uncharacteristic manner. First bounce was just short of the grass, a distance of less than 200 feet, and we touched briefly once before climbing away at three minutes past 7 o'clock. Banking over sharply, just enough to clear the hangars, we did a quick thank-you circuit before waggling our wings and departing, shouting unheard to those on the ground: "Fly Navy!"

In the continuing excitement, both David and I had overlooked one vital thing. Neither of us knew what course to fly! A quick mental calculation (the map, naturally, had buried itself under our gear) suggested 050 deg and whilst Dave dug out maps I swung onto that heading. Once up I quickly realised how tight everything still was. The sun by now had sunk behind the gathering mists, the latter reducing visibility to perhaps less than two miles.

Fortunately the engine was back on song at nearly 2,200 revs with the throttle hard against the stop. There was little wind so our airspeed of nearly 80 knots was also our groundspeed. Within about five minutes of setting course the mists ahead rolled back a little to reveal an open expanse of sea, which stretched away into the distance.

"Hey Dave, check the course, we're flying out over the Channel – we'll finish up in France at this rate."

While Dave checked and pinpointed our position on the map, I circled over the coast – suddenly I had no desire for long or even short sea crossings.

Reassurance came quickly from Dave; we were heading out across the broad estuary of the River Fal, north of Falmouth, and several miles south of track, needing some 15 degs of adjustment from the initial guessed heading. Even so it took a definite mental effort to fly out over the water with nothing but mist and sea visible ahead!

Within perhaps half a minute the far shore of the estuary swam into view and we were climbing slightly to stay clear of the rising ground ahead. Twenty miles to go, less than 15 minutes flying time, but now I could not believe it would stay light for that long. After another five minutes we could pick out the huge conical chalk tips of the St. Austell china clay diggings and were soon flying over the open pits. In the half-light conditions now prevailing these presented a most awesome and eerie sight.

It took little imagination to believe we were flying over the cratered landscape of the moon, except for the colours – luminous white tips and slimy green, water-filled craters with all shades of grey between the two, the pits themselves having a repellent, unnatural appearance. This lunar landscape, viewed from a height of several hundred feet, stretched away into the dim distance – I suddenly realised that I was listening even more intently than usual to the sound of the engine.

Eventually, the clay workings and the evil-looking green brew came to an end and we were back over featureless open country again. It was impossible to determine where we were – all my faith was pinned on the compass and Dave's course. We could now be no more than five minutes flying time from Bodmin, but would we recognise it if we saw it, and how would we find the field?

Ridiculously, a half-remembered quotation came to mind, something like: "When the world ends it will be with a whimper, not a bang." Grimly I reflected that I felt like whimpering just then and our world would end with a bang if we could not find the field. As on several other occasions, at the very instant of making the decision to effect an emergency landing, I was saved by a sudden stab of recognition of the scene unrolling before us.

We were flying over high undulating moorland that dropped into a steep valley ahead, in the bottom of which night's shadows had already fallen. A few lights were showing dully through the gathering autumnal mist but, other than that it was a town or village down there, they meant nothing to us. Until that is, a straight row of lights stood out, strung at an angle of about 15 degs from the town to the crest of the far ridge; they were car headlights marking a major road which just had to be the A30 where it descends into Bodmin, and Dave's navigation was spot on again.

Abandoning the idea of an emergency landing, and throwing away any last chance of picking a spot if it proved not to be Bodmin down there, we set out across the valley towards the lights at the top of the ridge. After what seemed an age we crossed the ridge, flying parallel with the road and half a field's width to the right. This way we could see both the road and the adjacent fields from which hopefully would materialise the one we were looking for. Thankfully the hangar and the chequered control caravan stood out in the gloom and from a height of about 100 ft I closed the throttle, crossed my fingers and side-slipped into a controlled arrival, at 19.35, 20 minutes later than our "latest" time!

Taxying back to the control van we were surprised to be met by a small knot of people who were almost as relieved to see us as we were them. It seemed that Noel had thoughtfully phoned to tell them what was happening and they had stayed on after everyone else had gone in case we came in. They had just decided that it had become too dark for us to arrive and were in the act of leaving when we hopped over the hedge. They had even saved a Cornish pastie for each of us, followed by strawberries and Cornish cream!

We chatted for perhaps half an hour over the events of the day before the last of them left, but not before making arrangements to sleep in the control caravan rather than our damp tent. We declined the offer of a local bed as we hoped to get away early in the morning. There were no problems with waking as a wind sprang up during the night, and the noisy, unoiled squeaking of the weathervane mounted on the roof of the caravan, as it swung backwards and forwards, made for an efficient if uncontrolled alarm clock.

Homeward-bound the next day, the journey was completely uneventful, this time carried out from a safe altitude of 2,000 feet to ensure that the Gipsy would perform in its usual, unfaltering manner. The wind was behind us and we were able to fly straight to Compton Abbas as originally planned; by mid-afternoon we were home.

Since then I have occasionally wondered why that bolt broke. No one else seems to have heard of such a thing happening to a Gipsy before or since, although there had in the distant past been problems with the rocker brackets before a modification was introduced to substitute these larger-diameter bolts. As for why it broke when it did I regard as clear evidence of the perverse nature of things – with all the trouble-free hundreds of hours that the engine performed it is doubtful if as much as a tenth as many minutes were spent over open water. Which is why on the "Famous Grouse" Moth Rally in 1979, I crossed the 10-mile width of the Firth of Forth at 5,000 ft to be sure of gliding to the shore if another one of those wretched bolts broke!

As a postscript I would mention that two days after we returned I had a letter from Noel to say that on his way to lunch at around 12.30 on Monday he had heard the familiar sound of a Gipsy Major. Looking up he saw the Jackaroo sail straight overhead at a very respectable altitude and thus knew that we had sorted things out. He again said how much he had appreciated flying with us and how exciting and in retrospect how enjoyable, the whole thing had been. From this distance in time I can only agree with him.

M.J. BRETT '82

CHAPTER 12

VINTAGE WEEKEND – WELSHPOOL

It had been a good day for flying – a high, thin overcast that had kept temperatures comfortable, whilst the sun was bright enough to cheer, visibility was fair with haze on the far hills, and enough breeze was blowing down the strip to make take-offs and landings easy, despite the loads we had been carrying and the uphill gradient of the grass runway. But with dusk gathering in the remaining daylight we finally called a halt.

All was comparatively quiet now that I had switched off and, with the aircraft stopped just off the end of the runway awaiting my turn for refuelling, I sat in the cockpit for a few moments longer, taking in the peaceful scene around me and aware of the feeling of easy tiredness that is pleasurable when associated with a period of enjoyable activity.

This, I reflected, was what my type of flying was all about, although there has been no shortage of other occasions in quite different circumstances when the same thought had occurred. As on most such occasions it all seemed almost too good to be true, and I found myself making a careful mental note so that clear memories could be stored and trotted out to savour again and again in less fortunate times (like when the aircraft was unserviceable or the weather had clamped in).

This was the occasion of my second visit to the friendly little strip at Long Mountain, high and remote on a ridge that overlooked the quiet country town of Welshpool which, despite its name, lies on the English side of the Welsh border. The strip was the home of a cheerful bunch of amateurs (only in the sense of not getting paid for it), the Montgomery-shire Ultra Light Flying Club (MULFC) who, by dint of sheer determination and hard work, largely on the part of Claude Millington, the Club Chairman and CFI, had survived some 15 years of trials and tribulations, operated a single Tiger Moth at probably the lowest rates in the world, trained budding pilots from scratch and ran a successful social side to boot. They had persuaded a local farmer to lay down the strip, had built with their own hands a corrugated-iron hangar for their Tiger and a little Clubhouse for their members, and maintained a convivial atmosphere congenial to the very best in grass-roots flying, quite unlike the plate glass and chromium outlook of the professional Clubs (who after all have to make their livings out of it).

Every year the Welshpool boys (and girls) organised an invitation weekend Fly-In and barbecue, and those who had savoured the proceedings thereat acclaimed them as second to none. The Clubhouse became the centre of operations for the barbecue and with the Tiger unceremoniously bundled outside (albeit carefully covered and picketed down for the night) the hangar took on the setting of a hill-billy barn dance. A bar was erected at the back of the hangar, forms and haybales were placed around the sides and the MULFC ensemble provided an excellent musical background to those wishing to drink, natter or jig around (or all three). This particular year the Vintage Aircraft Club had combined their summer weekend camp with the Welshpool Fly-in, which was how I came to be there.

Dave Elphick, who at that time was a comparatively new member of the group, had agreed to come with me for the weekend and the two of us filled the Jackaroo with camping gear and set off bright but not too early on the Saturday morning. Low cloud and mist induced a short detour and unplanned stay at Finmere *en route*, but after this cleared Dave navigated us impeccably to Long Mountain, so much so that we had flown smack over the top of the strip without seeing it. This was partly because I was looking for a more obvious hangar and grass runway but also because in the Jackaroo, any point on the ground to which one is directly heading lies on a blind arc to the aircraft occupants.

It is usual to have any wind to one side or the other, the resulting drift angle ensuring that no point remains completely blind, but on this occasion the wind was dead on our nose. I was just a little bit lax in not weaving on the approach because, having visited the field before, I expected to find it easily once we were in the right area. Also, we sighted the resident Tiger circling a little further on, and followed him hoping to be led into the strip, but he suddenly dived down into the valley over Welshpool, disappearing from our view and we didn't see him again until we had landed. Needless to say we did eventually find the strip and, as is usual in such cases, failed to understand how we could possibly have missed it first time. Our mystification was the source of great amusement to those on the ground, who had seen us fly straight overhead and to whom we had been visible most of the time we were searching.

Once down, we erected our tent and ran across a major snag – my memories of my first visit were that meals were available from the Clubhouse, so when David had suggested taking cooking and eating gear and food, I had said not to bother with cooking our own as we would get all we wanted from the Clubhouse-cum-café. First subsequent fears that we would spend the weekend living on cups of tea and scones, which was all that proved available from the club, were soon allayed by the generosity of various fellow Vintage Club members whose planning had been that much more thorough than mine in the food department.

There were not many visiting aircraft unfortunately and the Vintage Club's aim of getting all its attending ground members airborne was suffering somewhat. So the arrival of the Jackaroo with its capability of carrying three passengers was more than usually welcome. We worked out an arrangement whereby one Club member would collect names of the ground members who wanted to fly and organise them into groups of three, whilst another would organise a supply of petrol and refuelling. It

140

was thought that approximately 15 minutes should be allowed for each group including time for loading, unloading and taxying, giving approximately 10 minutes or so in the air, and this would mean dealing with 12 or so people an hour. In practice of course it worked out more like 9 an hour as 10 minutes in the air invariably stretched to 15. Initially, we thought that perhaps 1½ hours would see everybody up and away, in conjunction with the resident Tiger and some of the other visiting aircraft, there being (we thought) some 30-35 people who wanted to fly. What went wrong with our calculations I do not know, perhaps it was because, being unlicensed for carriage for hire or reward, there was no charge as such, a collection being made to cover fuel costs etc., but we went on joyriding for far longer than 1½ hours. I strongly suspect that I was flying as many non-members as members!

Anyway, Carl Butler, the Vintage Club Chairman, and Joe Pallett, who always seemed to be lending a hand at almost every form of activity the Club got involved in, were prominent in the passenger-organising department. It was simply left to them to wheel up new passengers, help unload those already in and strap in the new ones, and organise the supply of fuel and oil. As on other such occasions, the names and faces of the passengers tended to merge into a stream, but the procedure on each flight was much the same. We tried to ensure that at least one of the three passengers was a youngster (to help keep the load down) and that there was always at least one adult or responsible older sister or brother if there were any very small children. We seemed to have gathered a complete cross-section, from apprehensive small children, some putting on a brave face and others not, to apprehensive old ladies, determined to accept a sudden opportunity; from keen youngsters, anxious not to miss a chance to fly in a biplane, to old men hoping to recapture, however fleetingly, some of the magic remembered from earlier Service flying days.

Sometimes it was only necessary to look at their faces to decide that we would take it very gently, and other times their questions like "Can you loop-the-loop?" saved asking what they wanted. "No – we can't do aerobatics but we can do tight turns and wingovers if you like." My stock question was always "Have you flown before?" and I tried to fly accordingly, and this seems to have worked as I believe no one has ever actually been airsick on these occasions.

I am not sure who gets the most satisfaction out of this sort of flying – the pilot or the passengers. Certainly I felt very privileged to be able to offer the opportunity to do something different to so many people: whether it was to those flying for the first time; or flying other than straight and level in an airliner; or a quick up-and-down on commercial joyriding; or first-time flying over the clouds; or in a "stick-and-string" biplane; or even those old hands who wished to sample a Jackaroo only out of disbelief that a Tiger Moth could fly with four people on board. Not forgetting either the old faithfuls who came up on every opportunity to share the fun. My outlook on this aspect of flying was very simple. If the aeroplane was serviceable, if the weather was OK, if there was fuel available, and there were people who wanted to fly, then it was all wrong for that aeroplane to be sitting on the ground. Flying in a small plane, in which one can feel a participant rather than a spectator, is such a wonderful experience that people who can fly can have no moral right in not wanting to share it, at every possible opportunity, with those who cannot. There are too few aeroplanes, too few pilots, too few occasions when conditions are right, and too many people who want to fly for it to be otherwise! Perhaps I remember only too well, when I was young, how desperately I wanted to fly and how infrequently I got that chance!

But enough of philosophising. Suffice it to say a lot of people went flying. The drill was to load up at the end of the landing run and taxy to the opposite end of the strip for take-off. Here I should explain that the airfield is located at 900 ft or so above sea level and runs along the top of a ridge with two grass runways in the form of a tee. The longer runway, forming the upright of the tee, is approximately 2,000 ft long and lies in the direction of the prevailing wind, whilst the short crossing runway is about 900 ft in length, one end finishing with a very steep drop into the valley. The theory is that you only need to use the short runway when there is a very strong wind across the main runway – with a strong wind the short runway is amply long enough for any aircraft likely to use the airfield.

The long runway is even more interesting, as it runs down a 1 in 10 slope from the intersection to about halfway, where it flattens out. On more than one occasion I have seen underpowered or overloaded aircraft take off from the flat part and climb at a rate which matched the slope, still being at an altitude of some 3 feet or so above the rising runway when they reached the end. Although they were then faced with a 3 ft fence, the ground fell away quite sharply and they were able to pull up over the fence and waffle down the slope the other side in a semi-stalled attitude until they had picked up sufficient speed to climb away.

As the prevailing wind blew down the slope, taxying a tailskid aircraft to the take-off point could also become quite interesting for a pilot un-wise enough to try it without someone on the wingtip. Without wheel brakes, steering can only be controlled by use of the rudder, and on the ground, that is only effective when the propeller creates a strong blast of air (slipstream) over it (so-called steerable tailskids provide a very lim-ited degree of control). In creating a powerful slipstream, the propeller also moves the aircraft forward. This is acceptable when the aircraft is stationary or only just moving, as the rudder responds faster than the aircraft accelerates, so that a quick burst of throttle can be used to swing the tail round without having too great an effect on its forward speed.

Unfortunately, a strong following wind reduces this control, by itself trying to blow the tail round so that the aircraft faces into wind, rather like a weathercock, calling for more prolonged throttle work to keep the aeroplane moving in the direction required. This in turn increases the speed and, if allowed to build too high, control is virtually lost and the only recourse then is to shut the throttle completely, let the aircraft stop where it will, and start again.

Add then to this tailwind a downhill slope, and the pilot's troubles really start, because the aircraft doesn't slow down when the throttle is closed. The final ingredient at Welshpool is the narrowness of the strip in that the aeroplane cannot safely be left to stop of its own accord once it has started an uncontrolled swing. I discovered all this for myself on my first visit to Welshpool: the further I progressed downhill, downwind, the faster my speed built up in my efforts to keep the aircraft heading straight down the strip. Eventually, the tailwind turned us through almost 90 degrees across the strip and we were heading towards some tents and interested bystanders; it took all the courage of my convictions to ram the throttle wide open in order to regain rudder control and head downhill again away from the tents. Fortunately for me, by the time the aircraft was running straight again, we had reached the bottom of the slope and started slowing down. One more burst of throttle may well have seen us taking off downwind towards the trees at the end of the strip!

However, having learnt the hard way, we had no untoward incidents this time, but taxying became a prolonged business, usually leaving some very breathless wingtip men at the bottom of the slope. Later in the evening, the wind dropped sufficiently to enable us to take off down the slope and land up it, a practice normally frowned upon even at remote spots like Welshpool, although it was safe enough on this occasion with very little activity going on, and under ground control (visual signals, naturally). By the time we called a halt, the barbecue was well under way, and left me feeling more than ready for it, and perhaps part of the enjoyment of the evening scene was the thought of wrapping myself round a tasty portion of barbecued chicken.

This was about the time that the infamous withdrawal of lead-free 80-octane petrol was part of the magnificent service provided by the major oil companies (one of their unhappier advertisements proclaiming the quality of their service to aviation is "lying" on my desk right now). It was typical of the warm-hearted generosity of the MULFC that they willingly filled us up with 80-octane fuel from their precious but dwindling stocks, rather than insist on us drawing the dreaded, leaded 1OOLL from their latest consignment.

The evening passed all too quickly if somewhat noisily, the local folk-music group occasionally making themselves heard and the bar going great guns, whilst the couples jigging around in what passed as dancing were usually outnumbered by the little groups of hangar flyers. All great stuff and it was just as well that so many of those present were camping overnight, judging by the hangovers the following morning.

It would be nice to record that the next day dawned bright and sunny, but if it did there was no one sufficiently awake to see it. Certainly the scene that met the bleary-eyed gaze of the earliest risers was one to send them scurrying back to their tents, with cloudbase indistinguishable from the thick mist that filled the valley below and spilled over into the field. Whatever it might promise later, flying was definitely not on then. In fact it remained "not on," certainly for cross-country flying through the hills, with the limited experience that Dave and I mustered between us, for the rest of the day. Now and again the mist cleared sufficiently to raise our hopes but this was short-lived and, even before our latest time of departure arrived, it was obvious we were not flying back that night. This is a hazard facing anyone flying any distance, under visual flight rules, over a weekend, in these islands of ours.

We had on the previous day been generously looked after in the way of solid and liquid sustenance and entertainment, firstly by Carl Butler and his friends and later by Joe Pallett and his family, who seemed to be anxious not to have to take any food back with them! We reckoned we would have to leave by 17.00 to be comfortably sure of getting back before the light faded. By 16.00 most of the Vintage Club ground members had departed for their long drive home, and we were faced with the decision as to whether or not to take down and pack our wet tent, and load up the aeroplane. It didn't look very promising at that point and we decided to call it a day.

Claude Millington fixed up transport to the nearest telephone, so that we could let our wives know, and then insisted on us spending the evening with him. Naturally this included a visit to the Club's then-current building project, an Evans VP-1, and what with this and that the evening passed all too quickly and we were on our way back to the field to spend the night, not in our little tent, but bedded down in the Clubhouse. Transport to and from remote fields is always a problem when flying, and if we were to be away early in the morning, weather permitting, then we needed to be on the spot, all our MULFC friends having to be at work the next day, and thus unable to drive us out there. The drive back to the field, up the winding and hilly country lanes in the wee small hours, behind an ex-Rally driver, was not to be forgotten either, and took me back to my own rallying days in no uncertain way!

As is so often the case, after laying on the most miserable weather he can find for a Sunday, the weather man relents for Monday, so that people can go back to work in the sunshine, and the resulting flight home was an uneventful if enjoyable one.

144

CHAPTER 13
CUB ANTICS

Apart from jogging around in the Jackaroo I managed to put in a number of hours in a very nice Piper L-4H Cub belonging at that time to Dave Elphick. This was normally fitted with with a 65 hp Continental A65 which, in combination with a fairly fine-pitch wooden prop, endowed it with a cruising speed even lower than that of the Jackaroo – as I said many times to whoever would listen, I had at last discovered an aeroplane that the "Jack" could literally fly rings round. Which perhaps helped convince Dave to take up with some alacrity the offer of the loan of a 90 hp Continental for the Cub, to see what difference that would make, the engines being fully interchangeable. The 90 hp engine had a standard-pitch metal propeller to go with it, the thinner blades of which made it more efficient than the wooden one. Perhaps more importantly, the maximum rpm was increased by 300 rpm to 2,600 rpm, and cruising from 2,150 to 2,450, so it was not surprising that the cruising speed went up by some 15 mph and the increased rate of climb (despite the slightly coarser-pitch propeller) produced more noticeable changes in altitude, even with two people on board, even on a hot day.

All this sudden new abundance of power and performance could not however be achieved without some sacrifice, and retribution was exacted, not unexpectedly, in the way of an increase in fuel consumption of something over one gallon per hour. There were other side effects, due for instance to the increased weight of that metal prop at the foremost moment point, and the very slightly greater weight of the 90 hp engine, which I felt degraded the almost perfect balance of the standard L-4H Cub and rendered my three-pointers correspondingly less precise. But, back to the increased fuel consumption. This was in itself little more than a trifle irritating but, apart from its minor affect on one's pocket, it did eat into the miserable range of 155 miles (with 30 minutes reserve) offered by the Cub's standard 10 gallon (Imp.) fuel tank; to make matters worse it had proved difficult to establish exactly what the new fuel consumption was.

It had taken Dave a considerable time to define what the original fuel consumption was, largely because of a combination of unfortunate circumstances. Like the fact that the tank contents are shown by a type of indicator which dates back design-wise to early Roman times; this entirely unsophisticated device consists of a cork, bobbing on top of the petrol, with a length of wire through its middle which protrudes up through the filler cap. The most ingenious part of the design is that the upper end of the wire is bent over at right angles to prevent it falling out of the filler cap when either the tank is empty or the cap is removed. As the tank empties, the float drops and the length of wire remaining visible gives some indication of the contents until, at some undefined point, the bent end of the wire comes to rest on the filler cap. At this point all is not lost as there is some fuel remaining in the tank and when flying this will cause the wire to make erratic upward leaps – it is only when all signs of life cease that disaster is felt to be imminent if one is still airborne.

Furthermore, Mr Piper elected not to mark his bent wire with contents indications such as coloured paint, or if he had it had long since washed off (indeed it would not have been visible from the rear seat, which the pilot is advised to occupy when flying solo). When you consider that the tank is roughly elliptical in cross-section and the bottom slants down to the fuel exit point it becomes evident that the rate at which the wire sinks is not constant: halfway down does not indicate half empty! Thus while it may be reasonable, with all three wheels planted statically on *terra firma*, to imagine that with experience one could form a rough estimate of how much fuel there is in the tank, doing so whilst *en route* to some distant point was more than my feeble mind could calculate. The rate of sink during the first hour seems encouragingly low, and goads one on to greater things than changing course to an alternate, closer destination. Having got one firmly committed, the wire then proceeds to disappear into its hole at a totally disproportionate rate as the petrol level drops to ever narrower sections of the tank. When the tank is full and the wire fully extended, it is easy to see in one's mind's eye how much wire represents 'half full'; after about an hour of watching the barely descending and erratically bobbing wire it becomes difficult to remember how long it was when it started. As for determining what length of wire represents ¼-full, I couldn't even sort that out on the ground!

Which brings me to another of those unfortunate circumstances mentioned earlier. Full tank implies the maximum amount of fuel in the tank, the operative words being 'maximum' and 'in.' In order to achieve this absolutely one has to pour petrol in until it starts coming 'out.' If one is very cunning and uses artificial artifacts like dipsticks, one can cause the filling to stop at the neck (have you ever tried peering round the side of a chamois leather-covered funnel to see where the level has got to?); even this has a sting in its tail unless you remembered that the not inconsiderable bulk of the cork float is removed with the filler cap, and on refitting when the tank is full to the brim will raise the fuel level over the rim of the filler! "Ah!" you say, "but what's a little drop of fuel wasted if it enables you to ensure that the tank is FULL?" Well, Mr Piper looked after this one by mounting the fuel tank in the fuselage in front of the pilot, with a gap cunningly contrived between the filler neck and the fuselage coaming so that any overflow runs down the neck, round the tank and onto the floor (or the pilot's feet if he is foolish enough to sit in while the tank is being filled). And if you think that petrol evaporates very quickly I can assure you that it doesn't when deposited in any quantity on the cockpit floor of a Cub! I have seen half a pint or so swilling around as a tribute to someone's enthusiasm and it takes a long, long time for the cockpit to become safely tenable again. So – there is always a tendency to underfill the tank to 'nearly full.'

One tended to always top up to 'nearly full' after flying, using gallon containers or jerricans, filling then resulting in so many gallons plus odd fractions of gallons being added; the flight time would also have been in hours and minutes, so calculation of consumption could become quite complex. I mention filler cans because one doesn't lightly take a modern high pressure hose to a Cub: an enquiring squeeze of the trigger can convert the empty dark cavern seen dimly through the filler neck into a raging torrent of overflowing fuel!

So, when I flew the Cub with this big new powerplant up front, its thirst had not been established beyond "around just over four gallons per hour." *Ergo*, less than two and a half hours max. endurance, somewhat less than two hours max. safe range. Cruising speed was thought to be about 80 mph, so the range would be much as before, i.e. about 160 miles.

Now, it so happened that an Air Display down in the West Country at Dunkeswell that I particularly wanted to go to coincided with the Jackaroo being grounded but the Cub being available, as Dave was on family duty that day. When I suggested that a good, long-distance flight might helpfully establish the fuel consumption with some degree of accuracy, Dave agreed to my using it but not without some reservations about its capability of flying that far in one hop. Dunkeswell was an ex-US Navy WW2 operational airfield, from which VPB103 flew PB4Y-1 Liberators on anti-submarine patrols, and I had not flown into it before.

Armed with the then usual paraphernalia of air navigation, to whit the 500,000 Southern England air chart and appropriate scale, we established the point-to-point distance of Old Warden to Dunkeswell (dog-legging slightly via Keevil to avoid the Lyneham Special Rules Zone) as being 150 miles. "Just right," you may say, "even includes a half-hour reserve." But what about headwinds? Prevailing wind is south-westerly and at 15 mph would reduce our ground speed to, say, 65 mph and now the flight time becomes 2¼ hours and there is no reserve. If we get lost and spend 10 minutes getting back onto course we won't make it! Still, we don't usually get lost and if the headwind component is significantly less than 15 mph it might be worth considering; the important thing is to have an alternate destination, open and with fuel. It is a very comforting thought that the Cub can be put down on a football pitch and its thirst satisfied by 2-star petrol in an emergency.

So it seemed to be on, although with the very variable weather that we experience in these islands of ours you never can tell until the last minute and sometimes, as we shall see, not even then! It seemed a pity not to fill the passenger seat, even though leaving it empty would significantly improve the range. Accordingly I arranged with Alan, an old work colleague, to share the flight and the fuel costs. Alan had flown with me on a number of occasions in the Jackaroo so I knew that I wouldn't have to worry about airsickness or an attack of the jitters with him. Just as well, as it turned out!

A weather forecast obtained the night before wasn't too hopeful but suggested a fine morning with showers spreading from the west with light westerly winds. Definitely worth proceeding with and Alan agreed to meet me at Old Warden at 9.00 next morning. Arrangements had been made for the fuel tank to be filled so that an immediate start would be possible. One great thing about flying from East Anglia is that one usually departs to the west, with the sun behind, and into the prevailing wind and whatever rubbishy weather conditions the Met. man cooks up. If conditions worsen one turns round and high-tails it back home or, if on the ground, departs in front of it. In theory!

Somehow, though disappointed, I was not too surprised to find that although there was a healthy-looking length of wire bobbing around from the filler cap, removal of the latter showed no sign of the petrol level. On enquiry, 'filling' had been done by putting in 6 gallons, which was the last of any readily available low-octane stuff, the remainder being inaccessible in a padlocked drum. By the time I had elicited this much information, time was marching on and I didn't fancy my chances of getting into Dunkeswell on time if I had to first go through the rigmarole of filling from Old Warden's bowser (there was never anyone handy with the key on a Sunday morning and experience told me one could while away a whole morning finding somebody). Dipsticks and earnest verbal assurances indicated that it must be nearly full and so I let it go at that especially as, even with a known full tank, range was questionable on the 'out' journey and I would probably have to find somewhere *en route* to top up.

Alternates were sadly lacking but I decided that, if deemed necessary, I would detour to Chris Lovell's strip near Newbury, where I knew that a warm welcome awaited any forlorn aviator whose Cub developed an unexpected thirst, even if his arrival was without 'prior permission' (most airfields and airstrips in the UK, then as now, offer their facilities to non-radio aircraft on a PPO (Prior Permission Only) basis, which implies a whacking great phone bill!).

The Met. man had little different to say about the weather in the morning except that, having deteriorated during the day, it was expected to clear by the evening, and that the wind would be about 10 kt, confirmed by the feeble flapping of the windsock. The sky was clear, the sun was shining, visibility was good, and anyone could see that no self-respecting aeroplane had any right to be sitting in its hangar!

Dave kept his Cub in prime order and she looked nice and clean sitting in the sun. A quick D.I. (Daily Inspection) revealed that all the obvious bits were nailed on in the right places, everything that should move did, and nothing moved that shouldn't; even the tyres looked to have about the right amount of air in them (it doesn't really do any good kicking them even though this seems to be a standard method of inspection carried out by most pilots to most aircraft!).

Alan (an ex-RAF mechanic) was an old hand at swinging props, so after priming (four strokes on the throttle lever), I left him to it. "Throttle closed, switches off, suck in four," and he pulled the prop through four turns. "Throttle set, brakes on, contact," and, ever a willing starter, the engine fired first swing. Oil pressure responded almost immediately, the needle swinging up to 35 psi, and by the time he had pulled away the chocks, climbed in and strapped in, the needle on the oil temperature gauge was registering. Running up to 1,000 rpm against the brakes, I switched each mag. off in turn to check the other mag. was working, then ran her up to full throttle, the rev counter showing the expected 2,550 rpm. No significant mag. drop from either when switched off in turn at 1,600 rpm, but with carburettor heat ON the requisite immediate drop of 100 rpm showed, followed by a return to 1,600 when I selected carb. heat off some 20 seconds later.

Taxying down to the far end of the east/west grass runway, I set the altimeter to 110 ft (Old Warden aerodrome height above sea level), trim to neutral, checked fuel ON, carb. heat OFF, hatches closed and harnesses tight, to complete the very simple cockpit checks. Nothing seen in the circuit or on the approach and runway clear so we taxied out, turned into wind and opened the throttle wide.

With a short run and a light bound we were airborne by 9.15. With its new zest the Cub bore us readily to 3,000 ft, which was at or below the bottom levels of Airways Amber 1, 1 East, 2 and Green at the points under which we had to pass, at which height we also had the necessary clearance above the MATZ (Military Air Traffic Zone) around the RAF complex of Abingdon and Benson.

At 3,000 ft the air was calm and smooth like a millpond, the sky above was a deepish blue, and we were above the thin brown layer of ground haze (topped at 1,500 ft) so that visibility was around 20 miles; the engine purred contentedly and the Cub trimmed out nicely for hands-off control – yea, verily, all was right with the world! Even that wretched length of bent wire bobbing peacefully in front of my nose seemed not to be descending at all. Indeed the only fly in the ointment was a layer of cloud forming slowly out of the haze on the horizon in front of us.

By the time we got to the Oxford area we were flying over scattered cumulus and, now clear of the lower Airways Restrictions, had gone up to 4,000 ft to stay clear of the tops. Cloud-flying, and by that I mean over and around, forms one of the greatest attractions for me and I determined to stay above the clouds whilst there were still breaks through which the ground could be seen. This kept me legal, on track and safe whilst enjoying the sun, the blue sky and the everchanging cloudscapes. As we progressed westward, the clouds became bigger, topping out way above us at about 7,000 ft, and the breaks, in what was now becoming a more continuous cloud layer below, got smaller and less frequent, until eventually we were forced to come down below the clouds as we approached the main east/west M4 Motorway. It had become increasingly difficult to pinpoint our position exactly and it was obvious that the wind was veering somewhat erratically.

I chose what threatened to be the last break in the layer, and pirouetting the Cub on its left wingtip, closed the throttle, selected carb. heat ON and concentrated on getting down through the hole as quickly as possible without exceeding some 75 mph. We started off in bright golden sunshine, surrounded by the brilliant whiteness of the clouds but, as we tipped down into the funnel formed by the hole in the cloud, the cloud walls became greyer with the disappearance of the sun. At first, there was ample room in our cloud cavern to lose height by side-slipping. With full right rudder and the stick held well back and fully over to the left we slipped off several thousands of feet with the A.S.I. hovering around 55 mph, straightening out only when it became necessary to backtrack to avoid entering the cloud. The last 500 ft or so was completed in a spiral dive when the hole threatened to fill in, and as we emerged from the cloud there was no sign of sunlight anywhere – we had probably chosen the very last hole! We could have been in a different world, so great was the contrast.

The combination of the sudden, chill gloom below the cloudbase at around 1,500 ft, and the uncertainty of whether we were NW or SE of track as we crossed the motorway, was disconcerting to say the least, and on top of that, that wretched piece of wire that passed as a fuel level indicator had taken the opportunity, while I was not watching it, to slink away almost out of sight.

I had confidently expected to find what remained of the old wartime airfield of Membury, and the modern motorway service sation built on what was left of it, if not to my left, at least in sight, and as I reckoned I could see some five miles of mtorway either side of us I just knew it had to be down there somewhere. Faced with the prospect of flying the wrong way up or down the mtorway looking for it I decided to carry on in the expectation of finding a large enough town to recognise and thus fix our position. Meanwhile, cloudbase had dropped to around 1,300 ft and the visibility was gradually shortening due to thickening haze and hilly terrain. Study of the map indicated two courses of action open once I had established my exact location: if east of a line running due south of

Membury I would fly east and land at Chris Lovell's strip at Hannington (just SSE of Newbury), and would then have to abandon Dunkeswell on the score of time if nothing else. If west of Membury then I would go into Keevil, an old RAF airfield now used only for gliding but one almost certain to be operating at least one tug aircraft and thus able to accommodate a thirsty Cub. Whilst one steers clear of gliding sites like the plague (because tangling with cables is highly undesirable) I was certain there would be no gliders up in such conditions.

Normally, the English countryside in the South is dotted with villages and towns such that, when motoring and looking for a quiet secluded spot to stop, you can't get away from them. But I've noticed that the aeroplanes I fly have a remarkable tendency to nose out large tracts of uninhabited land, especially if they sense that I'm not exactly certain where I am: I expect they notice this weaving sort of course I then follow and the upset balance due to my agitated peering over the side. Whatever the reason we flew and flew and flew, without so much as a village or hamlet in sight, and as for railway tracks one would have thought British Rail had never existed at all (actually, it was only about 7 or 8 minutes but seemed much, much longer).

Just as I was beginning to wonder if the compass was on the blink causing me to fly, like the legendary oozlum bird, in ever-decreasing circles, a large town swam into view about one mile to the left and two miles ahead. This was quickly identified as Marlborough and any further decision-making was saved, as the combination of Keevil's presence just 18 miles away, together with that wretched level indicator giving only spasmodic jerks, meant that I had no real alternative but to keep going!

Even if my ETA for Dunkeswell was looking a little suspect due to the unexpected headwind component, at least I was still on track, and I was grateful for that owing to the nearing proximity of the MATZ complexes around Lyneham and Boscombe Down. Fortunately, the RAF at that time mostly shut itself down at weekends, but of course that did not apply to Lyneham, then as now a major Transport Command base. To stray into Lyneham's Zone I would first have to cross a prominent railway for which I had been keeping open a wary eye, so I wasn't too worried on that score.

There was no problem in locating Keevil and a cautious probing approach revealed no airborne gliders, closer inspection indicating that for some reason they were only just preparing for the day's gliding. Opening the side window so that I could get my arm out, and throttling back, I did a close circuit over the gliders at about 30 ft, vigorously pointing downwards and shouting "OK to land?" as I passed over to indicate that I was landing and give them a chance to wave me off if there was some reason they knew, that I didn't, why I should not put down just there. They merely waved cheerily back so I landed in close on the runway, finishing my landing run conveniently near to an attractive young girl who showed us where to go for fuel.

This, naturally, was at the other end of the airfield near the Clubhouse, and on the way we passed the grass strip where we could have landed had we known it was OK to do so. People sometimes get very cross about unannounced and uninvited aircraft landing on their grass (especially if it is waterlogged and they have to get their crash wagon out to dig it out) and the gliding fraternity are no exception. They tend to be an untidy lot and often leave lengths of steel towing cable lying about in the most unlikely places (like on the greenest, smoothest, closest-cropped stretch of grass on the field). So, if in doubt, I don't unless I have to.

But there was nothing unfriendly about the reception we got when we taxied up and switched off by the clubhouse. A little knot of people soon gathered round – who, what, why, where, can we help? It quickly transpired that we had come in the RIGHT SORT of aeroplane. After all, the Piper Cub, through Taylor, Taylorcraft and thence Auster, was a blood relation of the faithful Austers they used for tugging, and anyway was evidently regarded as little more than a powered glider!

They couldn't have been more helpful, even to letting us have some of their precious tug fuel, precious because it was kept in drums which had to be manhandled about and hand-pumped for refuelling. The custodian of the fuel store key was unearthed, not without some difficulty, as they were not expecting to do any tugging that day; willing hands pushed the Cub several hundreds of yards to and from the fuelling point. Everything was delightfully informal, even when it came to paying for the fuel. It had been difficult to establish just how much we had put in as the pump had no measure on it, and when asked how much I reckoned we had had, they rounded the figure down to give us the benefit of the doubt. "Our pleasure," they said, "its not every day we get a Cub visiting us," and we felt honoured indeed. Is it any wonder that owners and pilots of vintage aircraft often feel that they are only the temporary custodians of something of much greater importance than themselves?

What with this and that and chatting about the other, time passed all too quickly and we had to be on our way if we were to get to Dunkeswell at an acceptable time. Down on the ground, the weather looked quite reasonable now that we had become re-accustomed to the dullness of a sunless day and, as we had seen the RAF's Memorial Flight Lancaster with its Spitfire and Hurricane escort heading westward, it seemed a fair bet that the weather was not going to deteriorate much more. Such precious aircraft, flying VMC, are not encouraged to fly into bad weather conditions!

This time we used the grass strip to save a long trek down to the end of the runway (gliding had still not commenced owing to problems with the winch), so we were soon airborne again and, with an interchange of much arm-waving, circled the Clubhouse and set course. Once up, we could see the odd rain cloud about dropping its nastiness, with very limited visibility in its immediate vicinity but, these apart, the weather was quite acceptable. Cloudbase over Keevil (airfield level 200 ft) was about 1,500 ft a.g.l. so had improved slightly; there was about the same clearance above the Mendips and as we passed beyond the edge of the hills near Shepton Mallet we gained another 700 ft clearance between cloud and ground.

Crossing the wide flat plain between the Mendips and the Blackdown Hills we could see the large Naval Air Station at Yeovilton, six miles to our left, with a shiny glint from the runway indicating that rain was falling or had fallen there recently. Our track took us across the edge of Yeovilton's MATZ so we dropped down to the 1,000 ft mark to be well clear of any military aircraft, possibly on long finals, and were thankful for the standard Cub high-visibility colour scheme of all-over chrome yellow that G-AXHR then sported.

We soon had to climb again to 1,500 ft to fly over the 1,000 ft-high range of the Blackdown Hills, on top of which lay Dunkeswell, the hills happily still enjoying an acceptable cloudbase for adequate terrain clearance. At 500 ft a.g.l. there is usually much of interest to see on the ground, and this time was no exception. In particular, a large gathering of cars a little to the right of track near the disused airfield of Culmhead caught my eye, and we ambled off to see what the attraction might be so far out in the wilds. We soon found out as we passed over a glorious splash of colour in the beautifully kept grounds of a large country house (the Bird Gardens near Blagdon Hill). There were masses of what appeared to be rhododendrons and other shrubs and trees in full bloom, and an attractive string of ponds and paths, well-groomed box hedges, streams and miniature stone bridges. We circled several times, drinking in the the scene, and then, like guilty truant schoolboys, remembering our lateness for arrival at Dunkeswell, hared off onto track again. We were close enough to our destination now to need to get up to circuit height and I pushed the throttle wide open to gain height and speed quickly.

Once off the plain, the countryside was quite undulating, typical West Country style, with steep-sided wooded and winding little valleys, and occasional flat-topped plateaux. Although we were pretty well on course, as evidenced by the appearance of the old, disused airfields of Culmhead and Upottery (another ex-US Navy base), we had come upon them with little warning partly due to the hilly terrain and partly due to our low altitude. Although, as we left Culmhead, we were only some four miles from Dunkeswell, we could not pick it out of the suddenly thickening murk backing up the next line of hills in front. Even as we passed over

Upottery and were by now practically in the Dunkeswell circuit I could only guess where it would appear!

Also, I suddenly had something else to think about; after several minutes at full throttle there was a peculiar and unusual 'hot' smell penetrating my thoughts. This, together with a temperature gauge reading of 90 instead of the normal 70 quickly assumed serious enough proportions to cause me first to ease back the throttle to cruising revs, and consequently our speed and climb, and then to think seriously about shutting everything off altogether. By this time we were up to about 1,500 ft a.s.l., i.e. still not to circuit height which, at Dunkeswell's elevation would be 1,650 ft a.s.l. Dunkeswell was somewhere up on top of the hills immediately in front, and so was the weather!

But weather has a habit of going with you so that as you get closer it seems to open up and is rarely as bad as it appears from a distance; and so it proved this time. As for the 'hot' smell, this gradually lessened once I had throttled back, although I went briefly in my mind over what to do in the unlikely event of any smoke or flames appearing (let's see now: fuel off, stop the engine if black smoke indicates an oil fire, but run till the float chamber empties if a petrol fire, side-slipping steeply to keep the flames off to one side).

Suddenly an airfield materialised under my gaze where seconds earlier there had been nothing but open country – a never-ceasing source of wonder to me though it has happened many times before, even when I know the field well. A lot depends on the light and whether the runway is wet, or the grass just mown, or the hangars and buildings at the near or far end, and probably many other factors as well. Anyway, there it was, at the head of a valley, dead ahead and about a mile distant.

I had about 650 ft over the airfield altitude (plus or minus the difference in barometric pressure between Old Warden and Dunkeswell) but I couldn't climb much more because we were already brushing the underside of the lowering cloud. Keeping our eyes peeled we flew up the line of the runway on the dead side, noting a row of aircraft parked off the main runway, a Luton Minor just landing and nothing else visible in the circuit. Turning across the runway we did a tight circuit within the confines of the airfield and although there was no green "clear to land" light there was no red "go away" either, so we slipped in, landed respectably and taxied up to the end of the line of parked aircraft under the directions of an efficient marshaller. Even as we switched off, another Cub was landing (where did he spring from?) and we could see something else in the circuit as well.

My first desire was to poke around under the bonnet to see if I could find any obvious reason for that 'hot' smell. However, I could find no cause for alarm, and as it had only occurred after some 3 or 4 minutes of full throttle work on an already hot engine, resolved to keep a wary nose open for a repeat performance, but not to tempt its return by using prolonged full throttle once we had cleared the circuit after take-off. It was probably no more than a drop of Titeseal (yes, that really is the brand that Continental recommend in the engine manual!) that had dripped down when Dave installed the engine, and had not burned off at the lower temperatures reached in local flying.

We ambled off to the pilots' Check-in, taking in the scene with some interest. It looked to be a typical Club Air Display, with several dozen assorted visitors varying from a home-built single-seat Luton Minor to the usual run of American single-engined Pipers and Cessnas. There were one or two interesting aircraft, including the Tiger Moth of an old acquaintance who often pops up at this sort of event, and a private Stampe from Yeovilton. The Tiger Club team of five Turbulents was there to give a show and the Navy were scheduled to fly their Swordfish, which was already present, and the Sea Fury, which was not as it would be operating from its nearby base at Yeovilton.

As one would expect for an out-of-the-way spot like Dunkeswell, combined as it was with rather threatening-looking weather, there was a smallish crowd of spectators, numbering probably in hundreds rather than thousands. But there was a Bank Holiday atmosphere about, with gay bunting and ice-cream and hot-dog stalls (all atrociously over-charging as is their wont at Air Displays) and the crowd seemed good-humoured enough, despite a now-chilly temperature, even when a light drizzle set in. What had been different to start with was the attractive scenery to the east, looking out over wooded hills, although the drizzle brought mist with it which soon cut the visibility down to a mile or so.

Airshow proceedings started with a spirited display by the Naval Sea Fury, despite the poor vis. and a cloudbase estimated to be down to 600 ft over the airfield. By the time the Swordfish took its turn, cloud-base was down to around 250 ft, with ragged wisps of cloud below that, causing the 'fish to include a non-scheduled disappearing act in its display. Various light aircraft performed restrained fly-pasts and it became obvious that the rest of the programme ought to be abandoned. Not to be outdone though, the Tiger Club decided to go ahead with their tied-together formation display, and I certainly took my hat off to these gentlemen for their performance.

There were five aircraft in the team, all very similar but with minor variations such as wheel spats, spinners and engines etc., and of course colour schemes. As they took off, cloudbase dropped to less than 50 ft in places and fog was rolling in at the western end of the runway. They entered low cloud several times on their first circuit and by the time they had completed it, visibility was down to several hundred yards. It really was a question of fish-bowl visibility, and they performed some quite remarkable flying in keeping their low-powered, lightweight mounts

155

together in the turbulent conditions. The spectators really got their money's-worth in terms of nail-biting flying, as it seemed time and time again that a collision must be inevitable as these little machines, kicking and bucking, rising and falling, still tied together, disappeared into the rolling underside of the cloud, even at 50 ft or less, all within the airfield boundary. As one wag put it, if they hadn't been tied together they would soon have been lost!

At the conclusion of the Turbulents' display it was obvious that nothing else would be flying for a while and the big question facing the visiting pilots (other than a handful with instrument ratings and a panel to match) was whether the cloud would clear in time for their departure. All that we could get from Air Traffic Control was that conditions were clear in the eastern half of the country and that Yeovilton (just 24 miles east) was reporting a cloudbase of 1,500 ft with reasonable visibility. Although it was expected that the local cloud and mist would disperse towards the evening it was not known when.

I wasn't too worried at the prospect of staying overnight as, although we were well away from anywhere that might offer accommodation, I had been fortunate enough to bump into Noel Collier, who had been with us as a chance passenger on the Land's End flight (Chapter 11, "Land's End and Bust"). Noel suggested we stay overnight with him at Sidmouth, and he would get us back to the airfield in the morning. It happens over and over again that, at even the remotest of airfields, someone will turn up who knows the aeroplane or the pilot and wants to talk over old times or, as on this occasion, lend a helping hand. If anyone had a reason for not wanting to know me again it should have been Noel after I nearly dunked him into the sea off Penzance, although he did say after that little episode that he'd never enjoyed a flight so much!

Whether we left that evening or the next morning, one thing was certain – we needed to refuel while there was still someone around manning the fuel pumps. As is so often the case, immediately I decide to wend my way with the aeroplane over to the deserted pumps so does everyone else so that, by the time we got there, there was a general melée of five or six machines being manhandled into or out of a very small area around the pumps. When my turn finally came I made no mistake about the filling: it was FULL to overflowing, there being no problem of aviating in a fume-laden atmosphere. We weren't going anywhere for a while at least.

In the queue I met Peter Harris, whose Tiger was at that time based at Dunkeswell; he was returning home to Booker in a far more up-to-date aircraft with all 'mod cons' for over-weather flying. He was going to go straight up through the cloud and be back within the hour, though I heard later he had been in the clag all the way back. OK if you must but not my idea of fun-flying. We also met a Turbi (a homebuilt, enlarged, 2-

seat Turbulent) based near us at Hatfield and we agreed that we would attempt to go together if we went at all.

I reckoned that the flight back (still 155 miles), with a 15-knot tail wind, should take 1 hr 55 min, cruising at 75 mph indicated, providing we didn't get too far off track. Allowing half an hour for a fuelling stop if necessary (we really ought to have been able to do it one hop), that meant we should allow 2½ hours from take-off to be reasonably sure of getting back before sunset, i.e. about 21.00. Therefore the very latest we could leave would be about 18.30: this was also the latest that Noel wanted to hang on for us if he was going to take us home with him for the night.

So, after a series of unsuccessful trips to the Control Tower, it seemed too good to be true to be told that the sky to the west of Exeter was now completely clear and it was confidently expected that, if the existing westerly wind continued, we should be clear by 6 pm. When safely on the ground one tends to place an almost pathetic trust in the Met. men when they pass on the sort of forecast one wants to hear, thrusting firmly to the back of one's mind the number of times that they have turned out to be hopelessly wrong. The fact that one remembers the latter only too well immediately after take-off hardly compensates for this! Anyway, not only did they tell us what we wanted to hear about weather clearing from the west, they also assured us that the clearer conditions existing at Yeovilton would be maintained and we would find things getting progressively better as we proceeded further east. Marvellous!

It was about 5.20 that we heard this news. Just time for a quick cup of coffee before the restaurant closed at 5.30, then a rush round to say cheerio to friends, sort out track, speed and time check points, make final arrangements with the Turbi pilot, start up and join the queue for take-off. A Luton Minor going in our general direction and another Cub were taking a more southerly course via Compton Abbas but I remembered this as a very hilly area and decided to stick to my original track. The Turbi could not match our new-found cruise performance but had a longer range, so we decided to stick together as long as practical and, if I had to detour for fuel, for him to press on alone.

Of course, things rarely go to plan; although we got started immediately (the visibility began improving at just after six o'clock), the Turbi refused to start. I had joined the queue and decided, when my turn came for take-off, to get off and see what it looked like from above. There was now a great improvement as cloudbase was up to circuit height and visibility had improved to 3 or 4 miles, but the anticipated clear sky had still to materialise. Once airborne it looked as if there was another line of murk moving in from the west, and if I was going at all it would have to be then.

We did one circuit of the field to see if the Turbi was moving, but he was still swinging the propeller and there was still a long queue to the take-off point, so I reluctantly decided to leave without him. A Cessna 172 had just taken off, which I knew was heading back in our direction, so when he overtook us a mile or so from the airfield I resolved to try and keep his flashing light in sight for as long as possible. Conditions now were very gloomy; behind us the airfield was quickly swallowed by the murk and ahead was a considerable bank of cloud, right down to the deck, which I assumed was hanging over the escarpment, and which hopefully was the last obstacle to the promised clearer weather at Yeovilton and all points east. A sudden change in direction by the Cessna, now probably half a mile in front, confirmed the poor visibility ahead and he flew off to our port side, pretty well at right angles to track.

Normally I would have let him go, trusting my own judgement, but he had radio and perhaps he knew something we did not, so I changed direction to converge on him about a half mile ahead of his present position, gaining a little by cutting across. Eventually he found what he was looking for, a gap in the hills to his right, and turned to go through it, now heading roughly north. The gap, whilst not very large, revealed brighter conditions on the other side, and I naively thought that this must be the edge of the Blackdown Hills. I didn't dare risk taking my eyes off the Cessna's flashing light for fear of losing sight of him but we must have been flying for at least the 10 minutes necessary to take us to the escarpment marking the end of the hills.

The Cessna soon disappeared after going through the gap and I never saw him again. By the time we got there, probably a minute or so later, the cloud had closed in somewhat, but the brighter light on the other side still beckoned us on, so that although we had only about 100 ft clearance at the highest point, the ground fell away rapidly from there and we were through. But now there was another problem, because instead of the anticipated open plain ahead we were flying across a winding valley, in brighter conditions but with no real improvement in horizontal visibility and with the hills on the opposite side topped by low cloud. On my right, in the direction I would have preferred to go, was the head of the valley, also obscured by cloud, and the only way out was to the left, where the valley gradually opened out and curved further round to the left. Apart from a small stream meandering down the floor of the valley there were no distinguishing features, and by now I really had no idea at all where we were, other than vaguely north or north-east of Dunkeswell and obviously still among the wretched hills.

To someone who usually reckons to know his position to the nearest half a mile this was not good, especially as I couldn't afford to eat into my small reserve of fuel by wandering very far off track. To make matters worse, as my map was folded, Dunkeswell lay just under a fold, and because it was a large-scale chart showing little detail along my expected route, I had not refolded it, not fancying the job of unfolding and refolding in the air once we had passed over the fold line. (I often recall with wry amusement the occasion on which a helpful passenger had attempted to do this for me and I finished up with a large unfolded map wrapped round my head, with one end flapping out of the side window and threatening to draw the rest after it – an interesting few minutes followed in which I was glad then to be flying the fairly stable and well-mannered Jackaroo with plenty of height in hand.) I had reasonably well remembered the map details along and immediately either side of track for the 10 miles to the fold, but hadn't catered for my current large departure from track. Now, I reckoned we were flying roughly north-west instead of north-east.

Low cloud kept us well down in the valley until eventually it opened out onto a much wider one. In following the meanderings of the valleys the Mickey Mouse compass fitted as standard to Cubs had got itself quite agitated, and every time I stole a glance at it, it was to find the card rotating quite positively in one direction or the other so that by now I was quite disoriented regarding actual heading. With no recognisable features on the ground and no sunlight to give a rough guide as to which point of the compass we might have been heading, I decided the best thing to do was to keep turning right whenever a choice was offered but not to fly up any small valleys opening up on the right. An obvious decision perhaps but answers don't always seem so obvious in the air, when things are happening, as they do on reflection on the ground!

As with the good things, even bad things come to some sort of end sooner or later, and we eventually emerged from the hills, with the cloud-base now a good 900 ft a.g.l. and visibility opened up to perhaps two miles. Out in the open now, and with less need to concentrate fully on flying, I took the first opportunity that had arisen since take-off to talk to Alan in the back. Not without some apprehension as to the nature of his reply, I asked how he was feeling and what he thought about possibly having to fly through this sort of weather all the way back, even perhaps having to put down somewhere miles out of the way. His reassuring reply indicated that he was enjoying this much more than flying at the normal higher altitudes, where nothing much seemed to happen; as for landing somewhere other than than at Old Warden, if he hadn't been able to trust both myself and the Cub to cope with unusual circumstances, he wouldn't have come. Glancing back, the broad grin on his face seemed to support this, so at least there was one worry I would not have to contend with!

Turning back to our surroundings at first I could see no recognisable features, only flat fields and the odd lane and stream, but after a minute or so, a railway could be picked out off to our left on a roughly parallel course (we were now flying on the planned course heading). This could only be the Bristol-Exeter line and a sizable town looming up in front would tell us whereabouts along it. At first I thought it might be Taunton, but the combination of road, river and railway left little doubt, soon confirmed by some familiar aspects of the town, that this was Wellington, still some six miles short of Taunton and directly north of Dunkeswell. We had been flying for nearly 15 minutes and were no nearer home than when we left, but at least we were now clear of those wretched hills and knew where we were!

Study of the map indicated that unless the weather improved, the best plan would be to follow the railway beyond Taunton to where a main branch line headed towards London. This would take us via Frome to Devizes, safely through the Mendips at the lowest point, and south of Lyneham's MATZ. If we reached Devizes I would be in a better position to decide on a course of action from there on, which would probably be to land at Keevil, or to fly my original course back to Old Warden, or to follow the railway through to White Waltham or beyond.

We were flying at about 750 ft, occasionally popping up to just under cloudbase at 900 ft for a better position fix. I planned to skirt round to the south of Taunton rather than fly over it, leaving the railway lines on the limit of visibility to my left, and rejoin the line about two miles further on. This would help fix my position at the rail junction between Taunton and Bridgewater, which was essential to avoid confusion with various other junctions, and then possibly have to waste time and fuel getting back on course. If flying as usual at 1,500-2,000 ft it is the easiest thing in the world to fix position and heading using a railway as a guide, but at 750 ft with limited horizontal visibility one sees only a correspondingly short length of track which tends to wind about, so that it can be difficult to establish with any certainty the general direction in which one is flying.

Over the years there had been so many track closures and land developments, not always kept pace with on the maps, that junctions shown could be very easily missed or wrongly identified, and I just could not afford to fly up the wrong branch of a line. From the Bridgewater junction, we were to fork right, leading to a second junction where we needed to fork left.

Approaching Taunton, we ran into light rain which further reduced visibility to the extent that I nearly overflew the town. The open country-side suddenly gave way to concrete jungle and ahead I could see goods sidings and a station, and many other buildings. A sharp turn to the right took us clear of the built-up area and I settled down on a heading which should intercept the railway just to the east of the city. Sure enough, after several minutes, there it was, with its attendant rivers, and all seemed well for the next leg. We picked up the Bridgewater fork and were then due to pass a disused track forking to our right some four miles short of Somerton. When I picked out a station ahead I assumed that I had missed seeing the fork (disused lines can be anything from completely ploughed up, built over, converted into roads etc., to something almost indistinguishable from those in current use, so it was no surprise to miss one) and that the station was Somerton. Somerton lies just inside the Yeovilton MATZ, which I didn't fancy blundering into in the reduced visibility, so without overflying the station, I turned onto my original planned course, as we were back on track for the first time since leaving Dunkeswell, albeit 15 minutes behind schedule.

I decided to fly on compass headings only, as the railway would be out of sight at our low altitude for about 10 minutes. If conditions did not improve I would turn right and follow the line of either a disused railway, or the edge of the Mendip Hills if I missed it, to get back to the main railway line which I knew would take us through the Mendips on the flattest possible gradient at the lowest point.

We had reached Somerton earlier than anticipated so it seemed that the tailwind was a little stronger than expected. This was good news indeed as it might enable us to catch up on that 15 minutes and not need to refuel *en route*. It would also mean reaching the disused line in perhaps 8 minutes. So, off we went, across flat, featureless, open country. There was a river to cross, and a stream by the side of the disused railway. Sure enough, a river hove into sight at about the right time, followed by a second, which was bigger than I had expected, but no disused railway. Also, we should have crossed some low hills just before reaching the river, so it seemed I must have drifted well north of track. As the time was about right, I couldn't be that far off so I turned to follow the river, expecting it to peter out before long. But it didn't, and to my surprise it was still going strong when, after following it for several minutes we found a railway coming in from the right. What was more, we soon came across a trailing fork branch line on the right (which according to the map should have been on the left) and then to a small town complete with an obviously used station (there were several people waiting on the platform) and a busy main road. Where the hell were we?

Circling the station we lost height until we could read the name – Castle Cary. How the heck had we got back there? At first there seemed to be no way we could have taken 15 minutes to travel the 12 miles from Somerton, at an air speed of 70 mph with a following wind! However I hadn't at first noticed a little white dot on the map at the disused fork before Somerton, and what I had taken to be Somerton must have been Langport, some four miles short. So the next feature was four miles further on and my high tailwind was not as high as I had gleefully reckoned – instead of reducing that 15 minutes, we were probably now 20 minutes behind schedule!

Still, it pleased Alan that we had reverted to 1920s-style navigation in earnest, and amused the passengers on the station who followed our gyrations with interest and gave us a cheerful wave.

There seemed little meaningful alternative other than to press on and see how conditions developed, although now it was almost certain that we would have to land somewhere to refuel, as that 20 minutes was not just lateness, but effectively a 25-mile shortening of range, which had been tight to start with. There were still plenty of options open as long as conditions got no worse. So we followed the railway up into the hills where we slowly caught up with a train pulling up the gradient from Castle Cary. Throttling back a little, we stayed with him for a mile or so, just for company, the train weaving from one side of our course to the other as it wound its way up through the hills. We dropped down occasionally to have a closer look and judging from the upturned faces at the carriage windows must have occasioned some comment: "Cor Mum, look at us racing that aeroplane, do you think we'll beat him?" or more likely: "Damn fool flying in these conditions." Inevitably, the train came to another steeper gradient with some sharp curves and he gradually dropped behind until we lost sight of him; the driver was possibly blissfully unaware of our presence but I swear I saw him flash his lights at us as we left him.

Shortly after leaving the train it became evident that we were through the pass, as the high ground either side fell away, and the cloudbase which had come down to 600 ft a.g.l. started lifting. Conditions were no worse as the lowering cloud had been due to the higher ground over which we had been flying, but there was no sign of the hoped-for improvement in visibility. Frome came and went and now we had to keep an eye open for a 400 ft-high obstruction at Westbury, which eventually turned up in the shape of a tall factory chimney. The moment of decision for landing at Keevil was now upon us. At this time of evening (around 7.15), on a miserable clagged-in Bank Holiday Sunday, from what we had learned in the morning, there would be no one there.

On the other hand, we still had fuel sufficient at least to get us to Hannington or even to White Waltham, either of which promised better facilities, and the weather had not worsened for some time. I obviously was not going to make it back to Old Warden without landing somewhere, and the weather and the lack of a suitable alternate to Keevil on my original track, plus the MATZ maze around Abingdon, left no doubt that if we were to continue, it must be by following the River Avon through the Vale of Pewsey.

Following the argument that the devil you know is better than the one you don't, I fell easy prey to the 'press-on' philosophy, so we did, not that we saw Keevil anyway as the airfield was some two miles distant from the railway. Immediately ahead was what I expected to be the last hurdle before reaching one of the London area airfields of Booker or White Waltham, that is, a narrow ridge of high ground just past Pewsey. This was shaded on the map as a 500-1,000 ft contour area. I guessed that the railway and canal which we were now following would find a valley through the ridge so that we would still have the ground level at around 500 ft below.

And so it proved, but to offset our good fortune in that respect we found a lowering cloudbase which for the first time forced us down to less than 500 ft as we crossed the ridge. What was more, it didn't lift much once we got past the ridge, in fact the latter appeared to be associated with a general further deterioration of the weather. By the time we reached Hungerford, located on the busy A4 trunk road to London, the general gloom was such that the cars had their headlights on, though the light was still more than adequate for flying. We were now passing over fairly open ground which gradually dropped away to the east as we approached the low-lying Thames Valley, but the cloudbase was lowering with it, so that at Newbury we had just about 500 ft clearance, with misty conditions cutting horizontal visibility to barely acceptable.

At Newbury we were very close to the big USAF base at Greenham Common, which I believed was temporarily housing an all-weather fighter wing normally based at Upper Heyford. Had it not been for the fighters' presence I would probably have landed there, but these were just the sort of conditions one could imagine an enthusiastic CO treating as ideal for practising bad-weather operations. I even thought of landing on the racecourse (occasionally used as an airfield) as I had once before for a Fly-In, but that suggested complications in getting off again in the morning, lying as it does practically within the Greenham Common circuit. We could in fact dimly make out the big black hangars on the airfield as we passed over the racecourse.

We were now just 25 miles from White Waltham (which is so easy to locate, with the main railway line now beneath us running along one side of the airfield) and 30 from Booker. The bobbing wire fuel gauge still protruded about half an inch above the filler cap which, in conjunction with the tailwind, indicated sufficient to get us safely into either. Now the big question was, would the weather hold out or not? So much for the forecast before we left! I couldn't face the cross-country detour to Hannington which, although only 8 miles away, was directly behind Greenham Common, was on high enough ground to probably be enveloped in cloud, and had no easily recognisable features to find it by in poor visibility other than a 1,250 ft-high aerial mast. Thank you, no, I would keep going east for now.

The next question was, what to do about the City of Reading, straddling as it does the river, rail and road complex we were still following. The very last thing I wanted to do was fly over Reading, and as my alternate destinations both lay north-east I decided to to skirt round the northern edge of the city. However, as with so many other little schemes on this trip, the plan did not work out in practice. As we got closer to the city the cloudbase dropped even lower and my concern became one of keeping an eye open for the massive grid pylons and cables in this area, and a spare eye to look again at the map. The plan seemed simple enough, to turn north as we approached the city, fly round the northern edge until we recrossed the River Thames, then along the railway to White Waltham, there now seeming little prospect of getting into Booker with its airfield height of 500 ft.

What I hadn't allowed for was the peculiar shape of Reading, which at that time sprawled out in a north-west to south arc, and in following the railway and the river, we were well into the centre of the arc before I realised it. Now we were down to 350 ft and dodging about keeping our eyes peeled for cables criss-crossing the approaches (there may only have been one line of pylons and cables for all I can recall now but in my mind's eye there must have seemed hundreds!). There certainly was a sub-station forming a focal point for the beastly things to the south, which otherwise was the easiest way out, whereas to the north and north-west, which was the way I wanted to go, lay the bulk of the city's urban areas. Straight ahead I could see open ground beyond a narrow ribbon of houses, so we kept going. On our left was a fresh hazard in the shape of towering blocks of flats, which seemed higher than we were flying, fortunately well-spaced out, and perhaps half a mile distant but still too close for comfort. This seemed to go on for an eternity, though probably within two minutes we were clear and on the eastern side.

We were now only 7 miles from White Waltham, but in front of us, the cloud seemed to reach right down to the ground, and another line of pylons marching over a slight rise ahead convinced me that we had to land in the first open space available. Swinging round to the left we passed over school playing fields with two Rugby pitches and two football pitches – ample room to land but a game in progress put me off attempting it. I guess that if I had kept circling and made some low passes they would have eventually cleared enough space, but conditions were not yet quite that desperate that I wanted to take chances on landing near people or of unnecessarily ruining a game.

Turning to the right I could see ahead a line of poplar trees, suddenly familiar as the course of the old A4 trunk road east of the city, with a big nursery that I recognised as a landmark from my cycling days as a youngster of 15 or so. Strange how heartening are such little flashes of something familiar in the midst of surrounding gloom, and though not aware of any air of despair or despondency (indeed there simply was not time for such thoughts), I sensed a feeling almost of relief that I knew exactly where I was. Not that that helped overmuch, because what I needed now was a clear open space and I couldn't rely on 35-year-old memories to find one. Beyond the poplars I could see the broad sweep of the River Thames which offered some hope perhaps of adjacent recreation grounds, hopefully deserted in these miserable conditions.

Banking around to the right, I flew along the southern side of the river, but could see below and ahead only small fields criss-crossed with hedges and fences, and with many large trees about. We had by now been forced down to 200 ft or less, and at this altitude it was becoming more and more difficult to pick out open spaces. Off to the left, on the other side of the river, I suddenly spotted a long stretch of green which looked amply long enough, so banking sharply in order not to lose sight of it, turned and flew over it. It looked depressingly narrow, and the approach would take us between two large trees. Was it long enough? What direction and strength was the wind? Would I be able to get out of it again once I had landed?

For the first time a sudden shaft of fear penetrated my subconscious. This was for real. I was actually considering putting an aeroplane down in a field that looked smaller than any I had ever landed in before, and previous light airy thoughts about "You can put a Cub down anywhere" were now to be put to the test! Strangely enough, the fear was firstly about damaging Dave's Cub which he had entrusted to me, assuming that I had enough sense not to get into this sort of situation, and secondly that my unfortunate passenger had placed a similar trust in me and now I was putting him at risk. As far as I personally was concerned the old "it won't happen to me" syndrome allayed any fears other than my scrambling out of a wrecked Cub dragging an injured Alan!

Fortunately there was no time to dwell on such thoughts. A low run down the field, skimming the trees, showed the surface to be fairly even with no ditches, but the long dark grass could have been hiding marshy ground. At such a low height I found it difficult to accurately assess the length and could only muster a feeling that it looked long enough but with no absolute conviction of this. One thing was sure, it was definitely marginal! A compass reading showed the field to be roughly east-west, and the wind, unless it had veered, should have been south of west but I could see no visual evidence of this. Swinging round to the left on as large a circuit as I dared to make without losing sight of the field, so that we could get properly lined-up, throttled back and nicely positioned to side-slip down into the field, we crossed back over the river. The only sign of life was a lone cabin cruiser going in our direction with a solitary black oil-skinned figure at the helm, who gave us a cheery wave as we flew over at about 100 ft.

Flying back parallel to the strip it looked no bigger than before and just as I started entertaining my last doubts about using it, whilst realising that the weather was now closing in more rapidly, we passed over a much bigger field but with a fair number of cattle in it. Making a careful mental note of where the original field lay, so that I could find it again if necessary, we started off on a circuit over the new field wondering how many passes it would take to persuade the cattle to move! And then we saw the adjacent field which looked as big as a respectable airfield. I could hardly believe my luck!

There were cattle in this field also, but all huddled down one end, and I could see no obstructions such as cables etc., except for a line of trestled piping across the end where the cattle were. A low run up the field showed no ditches or hedges or barbed wire fences obstructing a good 2,000 ft of flat green grass, well-cropped. Turning short of the end, and noticing high lamp standards along the adjacent road and some low-voltage 3-wire cables, we circled back to position for an approach from that end. With many an anxious glance over my shoulder to make sure we didn't lose sight of the field we passed low over a road, a house with several startled-looking figures with upturned faces, trees, a busy main road, more trees, the edge of a housing estate of detached houses with wooded gardens, now only 50 ft below us, and then banked sharply into the approach. The scene ahead seemed suddenly chock-full of high, elegant lamp standards clutching up at us with those ominous low-voltage cables across the threshold, causing me subconsciously to give a burst of throttle to maintain speed and height, just when a more rational approach would have had me chopping the throttle and side-slipping in. The result was that the A.S.I. was still showing 60 mph when I wanted to touch down, and we seemed to float for ever, consuming a prodigious amount of precious space, skimming the grass, before the speed bled off sufficiently to allow the Cub to settle. The cattle, as inquisitive as cattle ever are, had elected to hurry up the field to greet us, and the last part of the run looked as if it might be to take avoiding action, though this proved unnecessary.

Barely had we switched off, taken a breath and clambered out of the machine, than people and small children materialised in some numbers from the side of the field bordering the road, and dozens of cattle descended on us from the other side. Fortunately the people were very understanding and soon shooed the cattle back in the direction they had come (cattle love to lick fabric aeroplanes and lean against them, and can do some quite expensive damage very quickly). Very soon a car drove up containing the farm manager and the Head of the Agricultural Facility of Reading University, on whose land at Sonning we had alighted. Brushing aside my apologies for having landed in their field and disturbing their cattle, they said how glad they were that it had turned up at just the right time to be of help to us, and how fortunate we were that they had only just moved most of the cattle out of this field into the adjacent one, which was a good deal smaller, rougher and hemmed in by trees. That was of course the field that I had spotted whilst circling for the strip on the river bank. I was not surprised when they said the field we had landed in was the only really suitable one within quite a large radius.

It was by now noticeably raining, but that did not dampen the enthusiasm of the folks rounding up and moving the cattle, and the farm manager soon organised the driving of the cattle into another field. He showed us where best to park the Cub out of view of the main road, and then went back to the farm to return complete with picketing blocks and rope so that we could tie down for the night. Whilst he was away, the police turned up in the form of a very green young constable and policewoman to make the first of their enquiries. Who were we? Where from? Where destined? Had we any illegal immigrants aboard (in a Cub?!)? And finished by virtually asking us whether there were any more questions to which they ought to have answers! Understandable, as it is fortunately not every day that someone force-lands on their 'patch.'

We had apparently caused not a little excitement and interest on the main road we crossed over in landing, as a number of cars then detoured down the lane alongside the field. The inevitable happened as at least one motorist, 'rubber-necking' just a little too long whilst still moving, ran into the back of another who had wisely (or unwisely as it it turned out) stopped. This at least diverted the attention away from us for a short while, and even someone gathering facts for the local newspaper deserted us.

While all this had been going on, and as we got our breath back after the initial excitement of getting the cattle moved away, a very pleasant couple introduced themselves, the man proving to be an ex-Naval fighter pilot. From that moment all our other little problems like where to phone our wives, where to stay the night, where to get something to satisfy the inner man etc. etc. all evaporated, as these two laid everything on. They in fact turned out to be two of the startled-looking faces in the garden of the house next to the road that we had flown over on our last circuit. Realising that we were in some sort of trouble they had foreseen our landing in the field and came dashing over to help, having first phoned the farm manager to get him organised. They couldn't do enough for us and what had threatened to be a chill and gloomy evening proved just the opposite, in the warmth and cheer of their hospitality, yarning well into the night.

There was a further visit from the local constabulary that evening, as it seemed that another aircraft was reported overdue and there had also been unrelated reports of an aircraft crashing somewhere in the Thames Valley area. It turned out to be a low-wing monoplane and of a different colour, but they still had to ask their questions all over again to make sure that we were not the subject of the reports. Had we been, they could thankfully have closed the enquiry, but as it happened they had to go on searching for a possible crashed machine for some hours, before it was finally located at an alternate airfield, where it had landed without reporting a deviation from its Flight Plan. As we had not filed a Flight Plan, we had nothing to go missing from!

Morning dawned golden bright and clear, a typical English late spring, gloriously sunny day, so there were no worries about getting away. We had observed the night before that our bobbing wire fuel gauge had expired altogether so, after an excellent breakfast, the lady of the house kindly offered to go and buy three gallons of 2-star petrol from the local garage, found a chamois-leather and funnel, and then transported us to where the aircraft was tied down. What more could one wish for? No damage to the aircraft, a quick refuelling to put the bent wire back into a more reasonable frame of mind, and with heartfelt thanks for all that had been done for us, we took off, the Cub requiring only a tenth of the space available to get airborne. We flew a low, tight circuit to exchange waves before setting course for Old Warden and the end of a memorable 'day out.'

As a sequel to the happy ending at Reading, I was later able to fulfil a promise to take the couple's two young boys flying in the Jackaroo from Old Warden, which they visited at the next 'Open Day.' It turned out to be something of a birthday treat for young James, the older boy, who brought along several of his friends. Dad took the opportunity to get airborne again though in a vastly different way to his earlier Navy flying, and it needed no second prompting to 'throw it about a bit.'

As a second sequel, when a microlighter from up north had, many years later, to put down in one of the fields near my home, under precisely the same circumstances, I knew exactly how he was feeling and exactly what we had to do. I count myself fortunate in being on the spot and able to help him in the same way that Alan and I had been helped by that charming family at Sonning.

Oh! I nearly forgot: what with not being absolutely full at the start, not knowing exactly how many gallons we put in at Keevil, spilling some at Sonning when refilling, and not being able to top up on return to Old Warden, we were no wiser as to the Cub's true fuel consumption than before!

We heard afterwards that the Turbi did get started, got away some five minutes after us, and got back into Hatfield nearly two hours later. Not needing to refuel, he had stayed on track and thereby missed traversing the Thames Valley, well-known for its notorious clag. Had I not followed the Cessna when it turned north among the hills, I just may have found a way out whilst staying on track, and just might have got back also – on the other hand, I might well have not!

But, as they say, "all's well that ends well" and another bank of experience was added to the store, and more lessons learned about flying (and I do mean "learned"). What were they? Well, they have to be so obvious that I leave readers to draw their own conclusions! In mitigation, and in expectation of a sound drubbing from GASCO (General Aviation Safety Council) for exhibiting what would be labelled these days as an extreme case of 'pressonitis,' I can only add that flying a Cub in such conditions was a far different cry from most of the cases brought to light nowadays in the GASCO Safety Bulletin – also, when I learnt to fly, everyone was taught how to safely cope with just such a situation.

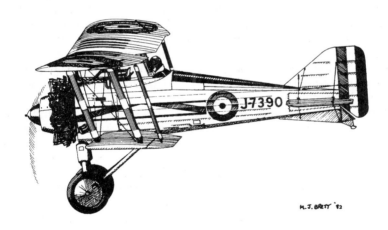

H.J. BRETT '92

CHAPTER 14
TAKKA-TAKKA-TAKKA

Ambling quietly along over familiar ground, deep in thought, my reverie was rudely interrupted by a spine-chilling sound, seemingly right on top of me – "takka-takka-takka-takka" – and I knew I had fallen foul of the local ace. Fortunately I was in the Clubhouse, heading for the CFI's office to get my Log Book signed up; the sound was not that of a synchronised machine gun but merely the Club wag loosing off orally at me, having just seen *"The Blue Max"* and needing to get it out of his system. It was a long time before I was on the receiving end of that sound again, but then it was in far less amusing circumstances.

We were on our way to Blackbushe, to fly in to one of the early meetings of the Warbirds Association, not that we thought that the Jackaroo could be even remotely considered as a warbird, but merely out of interest to see what was. There were four of us aboard, two of the passengers being old hands at flying with me, whilst the third was on his very first trip in a light aircraft. It was a pleasant, sunny, summer morning, with scattered cumulus, a light breeze and excellent visibility. Taking off from Old Warden our track took us over the large static ring aerial at USAF Chicksands, and we circled round at about 500 ft to let our first-time passenger view this rather unusual installation from the air. He was thoroughly enjoying his new experience and drew our attention to the fact that there was some sort of Open Day being held there with roundabouts and traction engines etc., so we circled some more for his benefit.

We had been late getting away and I realised that if we didn't get on with it we would be too late to land on arrival. So, getting back to the business of A-to-B travel I set course, opened up to full bore and started climbing up to the required altitude to take us over Booker, clear of their gliding fraternity. With four up and carrying maximum allowed fuel load this was a laborious climb, the full heat of the day not helping any either. We settled into a steady climb, stick back, nose well up, heading toward the sun, which was now glaring in at us through the clear perspex windscreen, and it, along with the monotonous roar of the engine, induced a fat and contented, soporific sense of well-being.

Apart from intermittent scanning of the surrounding airspace to ensure that we remained in sole possession of our piece of sky, similar perusal of the instruments, and an occasional glance at the map and the ground below to make sure they stayed in accord, there was little else to do but wallow in the sheer contentment of flying. BANG! Takka-takka-takka-takka – a vicious cacophony of alien sound burst suddenly into being, shattering the idyllic scene; just for a fleeting instant of time I must have experienced the same sort of feeling as an early pilot under his baptism of fire. Startled, momentarily helpless after registering that something nasty was beginning to happen, but not yet able to assess where the danger lay and what was the best course of avoiding action to take. The continuous, staccato clatter was beating in time with the engine and was obviously connected in some way, so shut the throttle, at the same time push the stick forward to avert a stall.

The racket died down considerably, and the noise was replaced in my mind by my instructor's old adage – "slow down to gliding speed, converting excess speed to height (gaining an extra 60 ft or so will give you a little extra thinking time and may make the difference between getting into a field or not)". But that flashback was a useless thought in the circumstances – climbing speed and gliding speed are identical on the Jackaroo! Airspeed still about 50 kt, trim to hold it at that. Oil pressure is OK so she is not about to seize up. What is our height now? Just under 900 ft (ye gods, is that all?); are we still flying over open ground? A glance over the side reveals we are; what is the wind direction? No answer, quick, look around for smoke on the ground – nothing – think, what runway did we take off on? Ah! yes, but what was its heading? Damn, we never use the numbers, but it was roughly north; where was the windsock then? Slightly across from the right, so let's say wind direction was about 020 degrees; what heading were we on? Forgotten – then get it from the compass; 225 degrees – so let's turn on to 200 degrees and start looking for a field with a run roughly in that direction and a clear approach from the opposite end.

Nothing good enough below us but that looks a likely pasture over there; I vaguely remember seeing some pylons last time I looked out, where are they now? No sign of them, where the devil are those blasted pylons? Ah! there they are, well clear of our run; any low voltage lines about? Can't see any; can we get in from here, remember we are four up? Yes, I reckon so, using that clump of trees as a turning point; turn through 90 degrees towards it – take a deep breath – relax. Height, 650 ft, speed 50 kt, trim nose up, shall I switch off fuel and ignition? I think not, nothing worse seems to be happening, the propeller is still turning and despite the subdued 'tak-tak-tak,' the engine is still ticking over, oil pressure is still there and who knows, I might need a burst of power if I am foolish enough to undershoot.

Time now to see how my passengers are faring. Time to show more confidence than I feel, and with as casual a voice as I can muster I turn and grin at them and say something to the effect that we seem to have some sort of problem with the engine and that we are going to make a precautionary landing in that large field down there. Two of them have accompanied me during spot landing competitions and need no reminding that this was what they were all about; our third passenger doesn't realise at all what is happening and still seems to be enjoying his flying. So be it.

Let's have another look at that field – I always feel a complete dummy when trying to estimate the length of run available, but this one looks reasonable. We might face a problem if we get too far in as the opposite end of the field now appears to be sloping downwards. The surface still looks reasonable, there are no animals about and, apart from a cart track and wire fence marking the near boundary of the field, the approach is clear. We are now flying at right angles to the landing run, about 300-400 ft from it, enough to be able to slip off height if I have too much in hand when I line up. My god, she comes down fast when fully loaded. Height now about 150 ft and nearly in line. Start turning now – "hold on everyone"; looks as if we may be a little high, can't afford to go too far in – sideslip to lose just a little height, speed still 50 knots. Should be OK at this – but, I don't know, looks as if it is going to be a little tight – shall I open up? I certainly don't want to risk any further damage to the engine. No, we'll make it. Stick back now and at 45 knots we sail over the barbed wire fence, a little too close for real comfort but I am more worried about that now-obvious downhill run at the far end of the field than anything else ; 'crack' as something behind us presumably contacts the wire fence and then we are safely down, stick hard back as our speed drops off rapidly and we roll to a stop, bouncing and banging on the uneven surface. What a satisfying feeling – we made it!

The engine was still ticking over so, I left it running but turned off the fuel and called to everyone to get out as quickly as possible. We checked for anything visibly wrong externally, then, still with the engine running, lifted the cowlings. There was nothing to see either internally or externally, but despite a fairly even tickover there was an obviously unusual noise from one of the cylinders although it was not possible to tell which. All the externally visible plugs were in position, so a cracked cylinder head or damaged valve rocker gear was suspected. Reasoning that an early phone call to base might catch someone before they all went to lunch, and so prove successful in getting a spare head run out in time to replace it, and thus be able to fly out before dusk, we started looking about us for some sign of life.

The track ran towards a cluster of buildings about half a mile distant, beyond the next field, from which a car was seen to head in our direction, so it would seem to be simply a matter of waiting. Meanwhile, I was concerned about that 'crack' from the rear end. Fortunately, a close examination revealed no damage at all, not even a scratch on the painted tailskid arm, so it seemed that we must have caught the very bottom of the tailskid pad on the top wire; half an inch higher and we would probably have heard nothing, but even so it was food for thought, no one really likes being that close! Pacing back to the fence gave us a distance of roughly 450 ft, which was something of an eye-opener, as we had been little above stalling speed at touchdown, and certainly the broken top strand of the wire fence bore mute testimony to how closely we had scraped in. This was a good demonstration of how much longer the landing run is when fully loaded. The ground was typical, close-cropped, grazing land, hard and dry in that parched summer, fairly level though rough, wind was probably no more than 5 knots, about 15 degrees to port. Had I cut the engine the run would undoubtedly have been a little shorter as, even at tickover, the airscrew is contributing something to the forward speed. Later we paced out about 400 ft remaining before the slope would have taken us uncontrollably down to a very solid-looking brick wall.

The farmer turned out to be a good-natured soul who freely made his phone available and eventually, successful contact having been made, a spare cylinder head and tool kit arrived from Old Warden. It did not help your scribe's peace of mind to discover that the trouble was not a cracked cylinder head but the port sparking plug on No. 4 cylinder having blown out. This is located at the rear end of the cooling air duct and the early cursory examination had shown all the others in place but this one pretty well out of sight. What was more, several other plugs were no more than finger tight.

A later *post mortem* revealed that two people had carried out the previous 50 hr check, and each was certain the other had tightened the plugs. It was poetic justice that the pilot on this occasion was one of the two! As a result of this we tightened up our checking procedure and subsequently worked to an initialled check list.

All was well that ended well; we didn't get to Blackbushe, and two of the passengers had to return to base with the crew car – I didn't fancy an unnecessary risk in taking off on a short run with full load, light wind, high temperatures and a rough surface – but it was a memorable and not uncomfortable experience for all of us, including the man on his first flight who said he thoroughly enjoyed it and when could he come again? Moral of this episode for me was to make sure I would remember the wind direction and to re-acquire the habit of looking constantly for possible reachable landing areas so that a minimum of time would be lost in decision-making. Oh! yes, I nearly forgot – from then on I always checked the plugs as part of my pre-flight inspection, including the difficult-to-get-at LH one in No. 4 cylinder, at the far end of the cooling duct!

CHAPTER 15
THINGS THAT GO BUMP IN THE NIGHT

Somewhere back in the mists of time I must have heard or read of "things that go bump in the night," but certainly I cannot now think where; I have most probably misquoted some entirely different phrase anyway. But it is a saying that every now and again fits some particular activity and was very topical on one occasion that brings a wry smile whenever I think of it, although at the time it was more puzzling than amusing.

Following an unwitting taxying excursion into a wire fence we had been involved in a fair amount of work on our favourite Jackaroo. This required minor repairs to both lower wings, the starboard aileron (damaged by helpful onlookers), a complete strip of the engine in order to have the crankshaft removed and Magnaflux-checked for cracks, and a replacement metal propeller. A thorough check round the rest of the airframe with a competent engineer revealed no other damage. She had looked a forlorn sight for some 9 months while the crankshaft was being worked on; with the engine and cowlings removed the nose looked positively indecent and, relieved of the engine's weight, she sat high on the uncompressed, sprung legs of the undercarriage. In fact, so long was she out of action that the next annual check became due on the airframe, so we did the bulk of the work on that whilst we were waiting to complete the engine rebuild. Among other things, this entailed removing the seats and thoroughly checking the controls for free movement and no undue play, jacking up so that the wheels were clear of the ground and similarly checking the undercarriage, opening up wing panels etc. etc. All this work had proceeded smoothly and with no problems.

Came the great day when we were ready for the first flight test, after seemingly endless ground runs of the engine, running-in, checking performance and fuel consumption, and adjusting carburetter and magneto settings etc. These runs had gone well and we were very pleased with the way the engine was performing, the only trouble experienced being during the first two minutes of running when a sizeable cascade of oil was traced to an ill-fitting, new-type gasket; this had been promptly dealt with by replacing the old gasket!

Nine months is a long time not to have flown a well-loved aeroplane and the first moments of re-acquaintance can be as moving as in greeting any other old and long-lost friend; as good an excuse as any for carrying out the first test flight solo, though perhaps safety aspects sound more convincing as the reason. There was virtually no wind that evening, so taxying was confined to about 100 feet across the field to the main grass runway and, with little load, we bounded lightly into the air after a run of probably less than 100 yards.

It was great to be flying the old biplane again and, after quickly checking the power-on and power-off performance and general handling, I brought her in for a "touch and go," i.e. land on, but as soon as flying speed is lost, open up and take off again. This first landing was a most satisfying and very smooth three-pointer, the sort with which I occasionally surprise myself but am rarely able to repeat in front of an audience. It also indicated that the engine tickover speed with the throttle closed was a little too slow for comfort and would have to be adjusted. Just to prove that the first featherlight touchdown was a fluke, the next one was correspondingly heavier, and I simply could not leave on such a sour note, so, despite the now rapidly fading light, I went on round for one more quick circuit.

Climbing out, we had reached about 300 feet when I both felt and heard what seemed to be an almighty bang. I felt the vibration shudder through the stick, the rudder pedals and the throttle lever, and heard it above the flat-out roar of the engine. For a moment I froze on the controls, waiting for something really nasty to materialise, whilst all manner of dreadful possibilities flashed through my mind; catastrophic failure of the crankshaft or propeller, impending collapse of some vital part of the airframe, even fire, none seemed too extreme for the extent of what I had just felt and heard. Long before exhausting all such dire misfortunes I realised that the aeroplane was blandly climbing as before, steady as a rock and quite unperturbed by what may or may not have occurred. Easing the stick gingerly forward, I reduced the power, peering anxiously over the side to see whether I could get into the airfield if the engine suddenly stopped. Hesitantly I tried all the controls, found everything working and scuttled back onto the ground as quickly as the circumstances allowed. Despite the haste, or perhaps because of it, this landing was again like the first so, in that aspect at least, the mission had been accomplished, but now I had other things to worry about.

Those watching on the ground had seen and heard nothing untoward during that last climb out, but listened attentively whilst I went over what had happened. Nothing looked obviously wrong and nobody could offer a serious suggestion as to what it may have been, so we started a systematic search for anything that might offer a clue; we went all over the outside of the airframe, poked around in the cabin and peered down the back end of the fuselage, under the engine cowlings, removed the panels covering the aileron controls in the wings, jacked up the tail and vigorously pushed and pulled anything and everything. Not a thing appeared wrong – nothing!

We turned the propeller over slowly and listened for anything unusual amidst the normal Gipsy Major clackings and sighings, and when that produced nothing untoward, started the engine and listened again. Still nothing!

By now, serious doubts were being expressed as to whether I was actually awake when this real or imagined big bang occurred, or was it that due to the lateness of the hour I had nodded off and was awakened by the Gipsy banging back in the exhaust, which it does occasionally when the throttle is closed. Well, I knew that it had happened alright, but could not proffer any really likely solution. The possible answer that finally sent us off to our beds that night was that perhaps something had been picked up by one of the wheels and had been thrown off by the still spinning wheel during the climb out, striking the underside of the wing or fuselage. But although I could think of nothing better, I felt sure that was not the reason, especially as there was no evidence of this happening.

The following evening found us clustered around the Jackaroo, discussing what to do next. In the end, as we could find nothing amiss anywhere and as the aircraft had continued flying as if nothing had happened, I decided to take it up and try again. We had a test programme to fly to check out the new propeller, and the next hour or so of flying went off without further incident. In fact it was several nights later before anything happened to disturb our peace of mind, by which time even I was beginning to wonder whether or not I had imagined it all. Several other people had flown the machine without experiencing anything untoward, but fortunately this time I had a passenger aboard. Take-off and flying around proceeded as usual until on the approach to land we both felt and heard a distinct thump; it shook the machine like a hammer blow and seemed to echo up into the back end of the fuselage, easily audible above the throttled-back engine. I thought it not as bad as on the first occasion, but it was something that could no longer be ignored; again the aircraft had carried on flying as though nothing had happened and again, during the thorough inspection that followed, nothing could be found amiss. At least this time however I had a witness to the fact that I was not dreaming!

We all went away to sleep on it and to see if we could come up with some sort of inspired guess as to the probable cause. I was half convinced it was something inside the engine, having visions of loose bolts intermittently trapped between gears or crankshaft and conrods, but had to admit that the severity of the shock felt through the airframe would reflect more obvious damage if it had originated in the engine department.

When we next met, the Jackaroo had been moved to a different spot in the hangar, and whilst kicking our heels, despondently chewing over the alternatives open to us, someone noticed that she was sitting one wing low. On closer inspection this proved due to the uneven floor; when moved she regained her normal level composure but this started a fresh train of thought. With one of us pumping the port wingtip up and down we noticed that the port undercarriage leg movement was rather jerky.

Rocking the opposite wingtip produced a much smoother movement of the starboard leg. This was followed by more vigorous rocking of the port wing, with several bodies acting as ballast in the cockpit, until we managed to get the leg to stick momentarily in the compressed state, the ensuing thump as the leg sprang back telling us all we needed to know.

It didn't take long to jack up the undercarriage, remove the leather boot covering the sliding strut end and see the very slight bend in the strut. This at a point corresponding to almost full compression travel of the strut, so that when lightly loaded, the strut functioned normally. A heavy load, such as a slightly heavier landing, would compress the strut to the point where it jammed. As the bend in the strut tube was so slight, vibration from the engine would eventually shake it free. Hence on the first occasion it freed very quickly after my harder second landing, and the next time it freed after taxying and taking off with the added load of a passenger. The reason we had not found it during our earlier inspections was because with the aircraft on jacks and the leg fully extended, it was quite free, and the degree of bend was so slight as to be not noticeable unless you were specifically looking for it. We had not suspected any trouble with the undercarriage as we thought that only the propeller and wings had contacted the fence.

This last item puzzled us a little at first as it was still not obvious how the leg had become bent. So we went and had another look at the spot where the accident had occurred. Measuring up the distance between the point of impact of the starboard wing and one of the fence posts soon showed that once the propeller had chewed its way through the wire, the port wheel would have been in line with another post, the final impact being sufficient to just bend the leg. When dismantled, we found that the tube was bent back about 1/16th of an inch at the bottom, which accounted for why we had not seen it before. In flight, the sudden release of the kinetic energy of the jammed-up compression springs, hammering the unrestrained lower leg against its retaining bolt, was certainly enough to shake the airframe and, left to its own devices, would quite quickly have sheared the bolt. This would have resulted in the lower leg dropping away, the resulting configuration interfering more than somewhat with the normal process of landing. Considering the prospect, one can quite readily appreciate why the Aussies fit restraining cables to the lower legs of their Tigers. Perhaps the most annoying aspect was that we had just accepted final settlement of our insurance claim! So, all you Tiger owners, if something unexplained goes bump, even if not during the night, first have a good look at how well your favourite pet might do in a knobbly knees contest!

CHAPTER 16

A FLYING WEEKEND – BLENHEIM & WOBURN

It all started early in 1980 with an invitation to "tea on the lawn" at Woburn Abbey (although it didn't work out quite like that) for members of the de Havilland Moth Club, which yours truly accepted without hesitation. The opportunity to land in that beautiful park was one not to be missed, and Sunday August 31st was far enough ahead at that time to book unreservedly.

So it was with some horror that I heard in July that the Vintage Aircraft Club was to participate in the Transport Trust weekend at Blenheim Palace, and I was required to take part in a formation flypast on the Saturday and Sunday of that same weekend. After frantic phoning around to check on flight timings I had to decline the Sunday flypast when I found that I could not make both that and the Woburn meeting. It was with even more horror that I found that the Jackaroo would be at Bex in Switzerland over the previous weekend, when I had been asked to present myself complete with aeroplane at Finmere for mandatory practice sessions.

Fortunately Dave Elphick made my presence possible with the loan of his Piper L-4H Cub, which has somewhat similar performance and handling characteristics to the Jackaroo, and the Saturday practice was duly carried out with that instead. However it transpired that 'OIR was not the only essential ingredient at Bex that weekend as Tiger 'NFM had also followed the migratory instinct by returning there that year, leaving our team captain Tony Harold wingless at a vital time. Moreover, apart from Jerry Mead with his 90 hp PA-18 Cub, no one else at Finmere that Saturday had all the necessary accoutrements such as aeroplane, current licence and the required degree of recent practice. So the Saturday practice was carried out in rather blustery conditions with only two aeroplanes, the L-4H trying very hard to look like three aircraft, dodging from one side of a now-imaginary 'vic' to the other, but mostly staying in the 'box' position which 'OIR was to adopt on the day. A box formation had been decided on as being the best we could do with only four aircraft promised.

Came the following Saturday (August 30th) and by 10.30 we had five aeroplanes on the ground at Finmere, all raring to go in conditions which were far more turbulent than the previous week, to such an extent that Tony was seriously considering calling it off for something less hairy. Apart from Tony (now complete with familiar Tiger 'NFM) and myself with 'OIR, there was Allen Clewley in his Auster, Chris Proffitt-White in his Cessna 170 and of course Jerry with the Cub. The formation pattern and sequence had already been formulated the previous Saturday from the timings with the two-aircraft formation. Two "race-track" circuits and two figure-of-eights should take 12 minutes out of a total 20-minute slot, with Tony and Alan Chalkley both taking four minute solo slots each with the Tiger and Alan's Comper Swift respectively.

Although on the previous Saturday there had been only two of us, things had improved by Sunday and Chris and Allen had got in some practice, with David Elphick in the L-4H making up the number, so all of us had had one previous practice session, though not in such windy conditions. There was time for two practice sessions before departing for the display base at CSE Kidlington, and these went off fairly successfully, with my passenger Den Willett staying on the ground to act as observer, timekeeper and critic. Final practice was the trip from Finmere to Kidlington, though formation-keeping under such conditions was relatively simple compared with the left- and right-hand turns of the display pattern. Even so the 20-minute flight helped considerably in practising rapid and accurate repositioning when we were blown out of place by the increasingly gusty wind.

Briefing at Kidlington was minimal, bearing in mind that the display was actually taking place several miles away from the airfield, with none of the display organisers present. Tony had given us a fairly thorough briefing during our practice session and it only remained for the formation leader to orientate himself with the display axis. We were due to be over the display area at 16.00, so 'engines running' time was 15.50 and take-off 15.55, allowing five minutes for climb to 500 feet, form up and run in. We were preceded by John Fairey, in his beautiful Fairey Flycatcher replica, and a display team put up by CSE and, as usual, the final minutes dragged whilst we waited for the moment to start engines.

By now, the wind was blowing hard (reported later as 25 knots) and gusting quite considerably, but we decided to give it a try – if things were too bad we had planned a loose, line-astern formation giving a form of tail-chase which, with four or five aircraft, is always attractive provided the participants keep a fairly even spacing and the leader keeps the team constantly within sight of the crowd. Until we took off I had not appreciated just how bad things had become – even with Den's extra weight on board a particularly nasty gust threw us into the air just before I would normally have expected to fly off, and then did its best to hammer us back onto the ground. As we turned over the airfield boundary at about 200 feet I could see the other three aircraft ahead, with Jerry and Chris above us and Allen at about our level; just then we hit an up-gust that took us up to 400 feet as we cleared a small wood. If this sort of gusting was present over the display area, the next quarter-hour was going to be an interesting session!

By the time Jerry turned onto the line of the run-in to the display area we had all formed up into our box at about 500 feet. We were a little loosely spaced at first but as the formation approached the crowd line we closed into approximately the grouping we had practised earlier, the only difference being the relative vertical see-sawing of each machine. Our aircraft all varied slightly in terms of wing-loading, lift/drag characteristics and control reactions so that the gusting would affect them in different ways. One would follow minutely every variation in the wind strength and direction; at the other extreme another might be relatively unaffected by minor changes but, once started moving off the flight line by the bigger gusts, take more airspace and time in getting back into position.

It seemed that the Jackaroo was less affected by the gusts than the Cub and would respond more quickly to aileron control but, being directly behind it, would occasionally rock very violently when too close to its slipstream. The Auster, on the left, seemed to have adequate lateral control and positioning but was slow to counter the retarding effect of some gusts, whereas the Cessna on my right had very good 'penetration' but, if it started sliding inwards on a turn, that was a good time to drop back out of its way because, when it did start, it kept going!

What had been pleasant fun in practice became very hard work in these conditions, with occasional anxious moments. Like when hit by a downdraught on one occasion I lost some 50 ft and slid forward to a position almost between the two wing men, who then disappeared behind my top wing. For a few seconds, normal control response was sadly lacking; with the stick hard back, throttle closed and only 45 knots showing on the A.S.I. (stalling speed 35 knots) I was still closing on the Cub and losing height. Suddenly, everything reversed as we shot up and back, and I had to ram the throttle open and the nose down to regain position and safe air speed. I know the other two were also engaged in a similar consistent battle against the elements to stay in position.

We did our first two plain circuits and set off on the first figure-of-eight. At some point between the first and second figures, I lost track of where we were in the sequence, not that it made any difference anyway as I was simply following the leader. On one of the diagonals we hit another extreme gust that had Jerry scudding along almost vertically on one wingtip whilst the Jackaroo was going in the same general direction on full opposite bank, with controls and fingers crossed. At this point Jerry wisely called it a day and, when sanity returned to the formation, made a deliberate wing waggle to signal change of formation so that we all dropped thankfully into line astern, or nearly so. Very quickly afterwards I saw Jerry turn abruptly off and up to the left – "1, and 2, and 3, and 4, and 5" and away went Chris who was next in line. After a similar interval

TOP: For every hour in the air, at least two working. I take a break during an annual inspection in the open blister hangar at Old Warden, c. 1977.
Photo: The author's collection.
BOTTOM: A fortunate loss of the Jackaroo for two months in mid-winter 1979, when John Crewdson hired the aircraft for filming *"The Curse of King Tut"* in Egypt for television. We would loved to have flown it out for them but they had to have it there pronto so it went by a Tradewinds CL-44 freighter.
Photo: The author's collection, from an unknown Sussex newspaper.

TOP: 'XHR with myself and Alan Whittaker taking off from Dunkeswell. The 90 hp Continental installation looks just the same as the standard A65. Photo: Noel Collier.

MIDDLE: John Bygraves' first Turbulent (VW 1600-powered), shortly after he finished building it. Somewhat faster than the Jackaroo and definitely twitchy in comparison, it was great fun to fly. Colours were white with light blue & black trim. Photo: The author.

BOTTOM: Whitsun 1971. The Oaks at Welshpool, home to the MULFC, whose Tiger is in the background. The field sloped down 1 in 10 to the left. Photo: The author.

TOP: The end of one of many happy joyriding days at Finmere. Daughter Wendy, myself and Peter Murton.
Photo: By courtesy of the Vintage Aircraft Club.
BOTTOM: Ladies' Day at Sywell (10th June 1973) with wife Irene and daughter Wendy.
Photo: The author.

TOP LEFT: Flying is fun – but? Here I'm busy sandblasting 'PAL's sideframes.
Photo: The author's collection.
TOP RIGHT: All the components of a Tiger Moth's front fuselage frame and engine mountings, sandblasted, etched and painted, ready for assembly.
Photo: The author.
BOTTOM: The end result of many hours of love's labour – rebuilt 'PAL at the PFA Rally at Cranfield, 1984. It was very hot, hence my bare bony knees.
Photo: The author's collection.

TOP: 'PAL was rebuilt from the wrecked Jackaroo over some 12 years by Dave Elphick, myself and son Alan. Finished in the prewar RAF colour scheme and wearing its serial N6847. This was one of the few Tigers that served in France in 1940 with 81 Squadron and got back to England. Photo: Les Smith.

BOTTOM: Despite the drag of the parachutist's bulk sitting on the edge of the front cockpit, the Tiger pretended not to notice. The one and only occasion I launched a "jumper." Shotteswell, 29th June 1986.
Photo: The author's collection.

TOP: One of several DHC.1 Chipmunks I ferried for Bill Fisher, G-BCBF (WD309) still proudly carried its UAS heraldry in October 1974 when flown from Kemble to Elstree. Photo: Bill Fisher.

MIDDLE: A highlight of my US trip in 1986 was to co-pilot the beautiful DH.90 Dragonfly G-AEDU from Antique Field. Later, I was involved with fitting new wheels and brakes from a Pucara when the a/c was returned to the UK. Photo: The author.

BOTTOM: Myself (Chairman of the East Anglian Aviation Society), with Laurie Taylor's Magister 'KPF, before its rebuild in 1971. Photo: The Royston Gazette.

Allen banked away, and then I was counting for my turn and away we went.

So ended our display and for me not a moment too soon. I wiped the beads of perspiration from my brow, because, despite the cold wind outside, it was quite warm in the cabin and it had been unusually energetic work. We had not quite finished however, as we had arranged a photographic air-to-air session with Alan Chalkley in his Comper Swift "The Scarlet Angel." Climbing up to 1,500 ft, we cleared the gusty surface conditions and emerged into a layer of comparatively calm air, in which Alan had little difficulty in tucking in close for the photographer.

Conditions were not too bad, though there were a few isolated squalls about, and we landed easily enough even though the wind was still quite busy at 500 ft and below. Arthur Mason (now of Pietenpol Air Camper fame) came haring back to the airfield to say that he had been down to Blenheim to see the display from the ground, and he reckoned it had looked quite reasonable, considering the conditions, so at least it sounded to have been well worthwhile.

We topped up with fuel and at 17.00 said our goodbyes to everyone, taking off to return to Finmere where we were due to drop off a second passenger, Mike having come along for the ride in the morning. Despite our good intentions, we merely did one circuit! As we climbed up to the 1,000 ft level and set course roughly north-east, I could see, at a distance of about three miles, a solid wall of white extending from the clouds to the ground, all along the northern horizon, from as far as I could see west to a point just east of our track. The wind, which was still gusting well over 25 knots, was from the west, blowing the clouds along at about 45 degrees to our course and, after a very brief run on our selected heading, I decided that I would not be able to outrun the front; still within easy reach of the airfield, I turned back, wondering whether we would get back on the ground before the rain and mist now sweeping in from the west. In fact, although it did start raining after we got back, the murk stayed to the north of the field and Tony Harold took the opportunity to get back home on his more southerly course to Booker.

Going back to the tower, to enquire from the Met. man what he thought might be happening, we found it closed and the weather man on his way home. Although he could not add anything positive, we all agreed that it looked like a passing squall and that given time for a cup of coffee it would probably clear completely. We gathered up Jerry, who was also returning in our general direction, and sure enough, after coffee, the sun came out again.

This time when we got off, although there were plenty of dark clouds about, each attended by its curtain of rain, we could see a way through and duly scurried off back to Finmere. Our route took us along a main road, past Bicester airfield and with the clag all closing up again ahead, beyond Finmere, it was a comforting thought that if it beat us to it, and blotted out Finmere, at least we would find Bicester easily enough again. The sun was shining brightly as we passed over Bicester and Jerry's Cub looked well in its brilliant golden evening light as he tucked in close for more air-to-air photographs. We made Finmere OK and quickly got off again after dropping Mike.

Back in the air we could see we had another race on our hands as the low cloud and mist crept in towards our track, and this time they won. At Buckingham visibility was at a minimum and the cloudbase as such was not observable, but at 500 ft we still had about half a mile visibility; although it was very dark and misty, it suddenly brightened ahead just as I started looking for possible fields to put down in. Sure enough, in another minute or two, we could see we were getting clear and by the time we crossed the long straight ribbon of the old Roman Watling Street (or A5 in modern parlance) we were out of it and trundling along once more in bright evening sunlight. The latter did not last for long as the sun quickly dipped behind the gathering line of clouds astern of us, and with the sun gone, we suddenly became conscious of how late it had become. The evening mists associated with the stubble-burning days of late August were forming up and ahead we could see another bank of low-lying cloud running across from the north. However, by the time we reached Old Warden it was still comfortably daylight and Jerry would have had ample time to turn right at Biggleswade to fly down the A1 to Panshanger. The wind was still turbulent and blowing hard, and left us wondering what the next day would have in store for us.

To my surprise it dawned bright and clear, with not a breath of wind to stir the leaves. A bright golden morning with little haze, such as VFR non-radio aviators dream of. Opening time at Woburn was 10.00 so we had arranged to meet at Old Warden at 09.30, the flight time being of the order of 15 minutes. Daughter Wendy and Den Willett were joining me and for a change I arrived more of less on time. It being a Shuttleworth Open Day, the Jackaroo was out in the flight line and we had left it fuelled and oiled the night before. Being such a beautiful morning and the flight such a short one, we could afford to not hurry, so it was no surprise to see Air Commodore Wheeler take off in his Tiger Moth at about 09.50, to be the first in at Woburn, while we were still ambling around on the ground.

We got off at about 10.10 by which time puffy little cumulus clouds were forming up, inviting us to go up and join them. Cloudbase level was about 2,500 ft, and by 3,500 we were over the tops, the brilliant white cloud wonderland holding its usual never-ending fascination. Delighted squeals from Wendy indicated that the conditions were right for a rainbow-haloed shadow on the gleaming white faces of the clouds and we played around briefly with our shadow as we climbed through the gaps;

Woburn appeared beneath us all too soon and we came down through the breaks in the clouds in a series of long, swooping, sideslipping, gliding turns and wingovers, with the Park always below us, looking like a beautiful bright green oasis in the midst of light corn stubble and dark green woods.

There was very little activity below: just a Chipmunk in the circuit and several Moths parked to one side of the mown grass runway. The latter looked quite long (700 yards according to the briefing sheet) and extended from a small lake on the threshold up to the main through road in the Park. As we came lower, we could see that the strip ran along the bottom of a valley with a steeply-rising grassy slope on one side and a small wood along the other. Dotted around the lake (and a second, larger lake behind it) were more trees, and it became obvious that there was no straight line approach if one wanted to land near the start of the runway.

I chose a long curving approach from a base leg which kept us easily clear of the trees and which was quite acceptable while there were no other aircraft on long finals. Sideslipping off the last few feet we skimmed over a gravel road that ran between the lake and the grass, a white-coated marshal on the road holding back a line of cars to give us a clear run in. We dropped in fairly short onto grass that was smooth and flat where we landed and we turned off at about one-third along the runway to position at the end of the row of parked Moths. With the longish grass in this area combining with the uphill slope it was easy to position the aircraft accurately in line without the aid of wingtip marshals, always a satisfying end to a flight.

We could now see that there were four Tigers and Tim William's familiar red and yellow Jackaroo 'PAM (Sheila Scott's old "Myth II") in the line-up, whilst on the other side of the runway, in the non-Moth park, were several other aircraft including the Chipmunk we had seen in the circuit and Jerry Mead's Piper Cub. Jerry had dropped in on his way to Finmere for the Sunday performance at Blenheim Park and was not stopping. Walking down the line, we found a refreshment tent and a marquee, a small truck pumping scarce 80-octane (!) fuel from 45-gallon drums, and Stuart McKay dispensing his usual warm welcome plus various handouts, the most interesting being vouchers entitling one to purchase precious 80-octane fuel at a special low price. The sun shone from a beautiful blue and white skyscape, it was warm, there was no wind, the birds were singing, the grass was green and there were more Moths in the circuit, including a nice tight little box of four Tigers from Little Gransden. What more could a Mothist ask?

While we were wandering round the now-growing line of biplanes, seeing many old familiar faces and being introduced to new ones, a man and his wife approached and asked if I had come in 'OIR. When I nodded, he produced a copy of a local Gatwick newspaper which had a short feature and photograph showing the Jackaroo, *en route* for filming *"King Tut"* in Egypt, being loaded aboard a CL-44 freighter at Gatwick, with wings, tail and undercarriage removed. It was very good of him to take the trouble to bring the paper along just on the offchance that the aircraft would be there, so that he could pass it on – typical of the spirit of members of organisations such as the DHMC and the VAC. I thought about this after he had moved on and it occurred to me that we might do the same sort of joyriding for DHMC members that we usually did at the Vintage Club meetings. On mentioning this to Stuart, he thought it a good idea so we instituted a list of members to fly after the main programme finished at 16.30.

In the meantime though, there was a navigation exercise to enter and complete before the aerobatic competition started in the afternoon. As usual we were late getting away, with little time to spare to study the questions first, and this was to cost us marks later. These events are usually great fun if not taken too seriously, something like a Sunday afternoon Car Treasure Hunt from the air. This was approximately 75 miles round with five legs, identifying the answers to various *en route* questions as we went. This particular one involved no complicated route plotting as the course was already marked up for us on a local 250,000 map, it simply being a question of copying it over onto one's own chart. There was no time limit but one was confined to opening the envelope only when aboard the aircraft to prevent, it was said, too obvious a swapping amongst crews of clues and answers, not that there was much likelihood of that amongst the competitors.

Den Willett, just back from his successes in a similar event in Ireland, had the map, Wendy had the list of questions and all I had to do was take off and fly in the direction I was told. We took off immediately behind a Tiger, with Mike Vaisey's Tiger running up on the ground behind us. We swung into line behind the Tiger, now perhaps a mile ahead but, his cruising speed being higher than ours, we soon lost him. It took a little while to evolve a positive method of sorting out the route, checking we were on track, deciding when the next clue had to be answered, and just what the answer should be.

One of the early clues was "What is the colour of the bridge?" at a point at which there were about three bridges in a quarter-mile radius, road, rail and river. I settled for a grey-painted steel road bridge over, I believe, a railway, this seeming the most likely as far as position and colour were concerned, all the others being nondescript concrete colouring. By the time we had got to the end of the first leg, we could see Mike's black and yellow Tiger G-AIRI catching up fast. At the turn we were supposed to sketch the shape of a service road and, of course, there were two service roads of different layouts about ¼ of a mile apart. We circled once, trying to decide which one was more likely, and were somewhat disconcerted to see Mike steaming past slightly to the east and heading off past the turn – this always makes one wonder where one has gone wrong, assuming the other fellow to know precisely what he is doing and to be doing it correctly.

The next clue was the only one we had any real doubt about, as we were to state how many church spires there were within one mile each side of the track over a distance of five miles. This one really needed a little quiet study to pinpoint where the five miles started and ended and what villages lay within the band width, and this we had not taken the time to do, so we almost certainly got this wrong.

One of the turning points was a windmill tower, and through misreading the question, we counted all the windows in the tower instead of how many we could see from the direction of approach, but this we corrected on the ground before handing in our sheet. We were almost the last to finish but, after seeing Mike overshoot the end of his first leg, we saw no other aircraft until near the end of the last leg but one; then we were suitably worried to observe a Tiger, some hundreds of feet below, rushing along with his nose to the ground on the reciprocal to our course. This looked to have been the Tiger that took off ahead of us and, sure enough both it and Mike's Tiger landed some 10 minutes or so after us.

Having checked our papers to make sure we had not overlooked something, we handed them in and more or less forgot all about the competition from then on, not anticipating having done well enough to get a placing. There was more urgent work afoot in the form of an excellent cold buffet lunch and we proceeded to look after the inner men (and women) until the aerobatic competition started in the afternoon. Not being officially agile enough to be classed as aerobatic (though I am sure she holds her own views on that), the Jackaroo had to sit this one out, so her crew also sat back and enjoyed the show. Extra interest was added when one of the competitors "lost his prop" on the final stall turn and, being too low to restart by diving and turning, elected a glide back to a 'dead-stick' landing. He judged this very nicely, being positioned upwind of the strip initially and gliding back parallel to and to one side of it, turning in when lined up with the runway threshold. Barry Tempest of "Barnstormers" fame was competition judge and commentator, and was able to continue his running commentary on the finer points of aerobatics with a "for-real" description of a forced landing. It took place right in front of the crowd and there would have been no hiding the consequences of any errors!

After the show came the presentation of awards, starting with a pleasant surprise for each 'Moth' captain in the form of an elegant blue glass dish bearing a Tiger Moth engraving and commemorative wording. These were presented by the Marquis and Marchioness of Tavistock. Then followed a presentation of awards for the Navigation Exercise

('OIR's crew gaining second place to their eternal surprise) and the Aerobatic Competition, with a special award for the 'dead-stick' landing.

There remained only the joyriding for several of the Moths; we had agreed to take up five groups of three passengers, each trip lasting approximately 15 minutes including loading and ground manoeuvring. First we had to fuel up and, by the time we had completed this and loaded our first group, departure of the other aircraft was well under way. With so many Tigers in the circuit it was only natural that some of them would form up into *ad hoc* formations; there was one magnificent one in particular with six assorted Moths in Vic behind a Chipmunk!

We got up in time to formate on Ron Souch's lovely Gipsy Moth G-ABEV and then on the second trip had a little excitement with Henry Labouchere. On this one we had on board a couple of youths of fifteen or so (one trying to look like a present-day Hell's Angel!) and an older man who was learning to fly gliders. This prompted me to let him take the controls for a few minutes during which time I caught sight, out of the corner of my eye, of Henry's yellow Tiger, on a skidding, climbing turn on our left, pointing straight up at us. There was nothing else about, so I yelled to the chap behind that I was taking the controls and jabbed a finger towards the rapidly-closing Henry. I guessed that the latter was aiming to fasten on our tail and felt that conditions were right for a little friendly dog-fight.

Banking hard left, I turned sharply towards the Tiger which had now curved round on a pursuit course. Seeing us swinging round towards him, Henry tightened his turn and so did I. Within a few moments, we had settled into opposite sides of a tight circle, each trying to tighten his turn in order to close onto the tail of the other. If anything, the Jackaroo, perhaps by reason of its slightly greater span and longer tail movement arm, seems to turn just slightly more tightly than a Tiger, but with four up needs more power than it possesses to maintain height in a very tight turn. Gradually, as we carried on circling, I started to lose height even though I was turning inside the Tiger, and this more than offset the turning advantage. With that little extra height, Henry could break off whenever he wished without me being able to do anything about it, whereas if I had turned off before getting close behind him he could have dived on my tail immediately.

Before I could close sufficiently, Henry tired of circling and pulled up in an opposite turn, intending perhaps to loop over and come down behind me. Once I saw him move out of the circle I followed and observed him pull up over us, following through to keep him in sight, with my head craned right back, watching him through the cabin roof panels. As he came over, I turned in towards him so that, had he continued, we would have finished up in the same circle that we had started from, with him probably at or below my height. If this had been his intended manoeuvre, he abandoned it and pulled back up above and ahead of me, slowing right down so that I could climb up to him. I quickly slotted into a starboard echelon position and exchanged waves with a broadly-grinning Henry, with much arm-wagging between his and my passengers. We formated thus for a minute or two then Henry indicated he was going down and I broke away to our right.

Out in the clear once more I turned to see how my passengers were faring. "Hope you didn't mind that," I yelled and the delighted grins from all three were sufficient answers, though my "Hell's Angel" answered that it had been just great. I make no apologies for agreeing with him – it was!

We did several more trips, formating on Mike Vaisey's black and yellow Tiger on the last one. Mike and I were the last to leave and when I called it a day, Mike was still trundling around in the gathering dusk. We only needed 10 minutes' flying time to get back to Old Warden, there being no clouds in the sky to divert us on the way back. We were last in at Old Warden and I smiled as I ticked off the entry I had made that morning in the Flight Log – "Back by dusk"; it was just that!

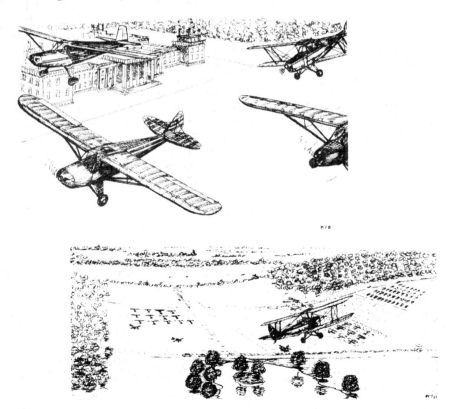

CHAPTER 17

HOW OFT THE PLANS OF MICE AND MEN . . .

One of my tasks in the Jackaroo Group was to run the flight booking list, so I knew all about the plans my old friend George was making to fly down to Salcombe to pick up his younger daughter 'Becca. He had filled me in on the background when booking the aircraft, though there were still some details to sort out.

It was going to be quite some trip, involving reconnoitring a likely landing strip near his elder daughter's cottage at Blandford, landing at a now-defunct private airfield at Haldon (south of Exeter), then using that as a base to look at the possibility of landing on the site of the old wartime RAF airfield up on the cliff top at Bolt Head. He had been in touch with the owner of Haldon (an enterprising character who converted an undulating stretch of open land into a very adequate airfield by filling in the hollows with many tons of earth from cuttings made locally for new roads) and obtained permission to land and refuel there. As for Bolt Head, he had written to the local police station and asked if they could suggest who to contact to find out whether it was still possible to land there, and to obtain permission to do so.

To his surprise the local (Salcombe) 'bobby' rang him one evening to tell him that, although the old aerodrome was now divided up into small fields, there was one which would probably be suitable, and gave him the name and phone number of the farmer. Following that up, George had talked to the farmer, who said he would lay some white markers in the field if George would tell him when he was coming and had given instructions on where to look for the field, "about three fields east and one south of the old airfield buildings," which could be identified by the presence of a radio mast. "How big was the field?" Oh! he didn't know off-hand but he seemed to recall someone else landing on it many years earlier, so it should be big enough (where have I heard that before?). Its heading was roughly east-west on the line of the main grass runway of the old airfield, so that should cause no crosswind problems.

George still had a few minor details to work out, like laying on some cans of two-star petrol at Bolt Head and Haldon, which entailed stationing his daughter's Minivan at some convenient point, full of cans and funnels and filters, chocks, picketing gear etc. I made envious noises about how much I would have liked to go with him but he was planning to go from Tuesday to Thursday and I had insufficient leave left to be able to do that.

The first hitch in the plans came on Monday evening when George was due to ferry the aeroplane from its base to a local airstrip near him at Eaton Bray, so that he could load up ready for an early departure next day; as he lived some 25 miles away this would save time in the morning motoring over, and because it was *en route* would also save flying time. But old aeroplanes (and their owners) being the perverse creatures that they sometimes are, some servicing which should have been done by then wasn't finished; the upshot of this was that although, with George's help, it was completed that evening, it was too late for him to fly out.

Now, despite the fact that an England v. Australia cricket Test Match had been going on since the previous Thursday and, by all normal standards, the weather should therefore have been raining cats and dogs, it had in fact been gloriously sunny right through, with initially very good visibility. According to another weather man's Basic Law, England is not allowed to have more than three fine clear days on the trot, which meant that by Sunday a distant heat haze had started to develop and by Monday evening the haze was a definite mist. So Tuesday morning dawned with thick fog which persisted long enough to ensure that the unfortunate George had to abandon his plans to fly down to collect his daughter and ignominiously go by car (it couldn't be put off as she was required at her sister's wedding). By Wednesday pm the weather man, having observed George departing by car, felt it safe enough to roll back the mist so that Thursday was once again a fine, bright, clear sunny day.

Fortunately for me, George, once having got this bee in his bonnet, was not to be so easily put off and phoned one evening soon afterwards, launching off with a now-familiar "I've been thinking . . ." As a result, I found myself drawn (albeit enthusiastically) into George's scheme as an essential counter to the weather man's wiles, with a 4-day trip planned for Friday to Monday a couple of weeks hence. Monday being August Bank Holiday, it required only one extra leave day from me, which I could manage.

Meanwhile, George completed his plans which, as always, were organised to an incredible degree of detail with alternatives to altern-atives to cater for almost all eventualities. What was now planned was for me to fly over to Eaton Bray on Friday morning to top up with fuel and load up with baggage etc. 'Becca was to accompany us down to Salcombe, with George flying the first leg to Compton Abbas. There he had already stationed the Minivan, complete with necessities, and we would then all drive the short distance to his newly-married daughter's cottage at Blandford, to look at an adjacent field to see if it was suitable for landing in. After lunch we would drive back to Compton and perhaps have a go at landing in the field, in which case 'Becca would drive the Minivan to the field. I was then to fly 'Becca to Haldon, George driving the van, and we would meet up again for refuelling before I took the aircraft on to have a look at Bolt Head. If it was OK then I would land at Bolt Head and phone George to bring the van. If it wasn't suitable, I would fly back to Haldon and we would all go down to Salcombe in the van. Yes, it was as complex as that!

Beyond that, no further arrangements for the rest of the weekend or the return had been made, except that an essential part of the proceedings involved joyriding trips for people like the farmer and the policeman who had made it possible.

For the whole of the week preceding Friday, the sun had shone brightly, though my 3-day rule brought thick hazy conditions on the Thursday. Sure enough, on Friday morning I could not see across the road from my front windows, and it was not until 13.00 that it looked worth visiting Old Warden in the hope of the haze lifting. Visibility never improved to as much as a mile for the rest of the day, but when carrying out the D.I. on the aircraft, I found an exhaust manifold gasket blown. I'm not sure which was worse, finding that the weather had stopped us going, or discovering that even if it hadn't the gasket would have done.

There was nothing for it but to fit a new gasket, which generally entails a couple of hours of work at most. This time it was much worse than usual, the reason for the gasket having blown being a cracked flange on No. 3 cylinder pipe. It was half past midnight before I had tightened the last nut and finally locked the cowling in place. This had entailed chasing around to find a replacement manifold which, when tightened down, was found to be too distorted to effect a gas-proof joint on each face. Fortunately, our engineer had a manifold jig and by heating and stretching, the distortions were eliminated sufficiently to achieve the desired seal.

Saturday did not dawn bright and clear and, whilst not as gloomy as the early scene on Friday, was no better than Friday at its best. There was little improvement through the day, but I did venture into the air around midday, remembering other occasions when I had found it possible to see through the haze at over 3,000 ft. This time it was not to be, with horizontal visibility again being less than a mile, and clouds forming in the haze at 1,600 ft, despite the sun shining fitfully on the ground from occasional patches of thin blue sky. Non-flyers would have been quite satisfied with the fine, warm, hazy day that was Saturday and a phone call to Blandford brought forth a corresponding response, with the rider that it was very hazy. Flying can be so frustrating at times!

And so on to Sunday which, if not presenting a clear sunny morning, at least was flyable. An earlyish start saw me arriving at Old Warden at about 08.00 to find the place astir with people pushing aircraft out of hangars and generally preparing for a Shuttleworth Open Day. This alone was enough to ensure reasonable flying conditions as I can remember very few occasions on which an Open Day had been abandoned due to bad weather. One thing about flying on an Open Day was that usually the tiresome and tiring business of uprooting the heavy oak airfield fence, hauling three quarters of a ton of aeroplane up the slope to the airfield and re-erecting the fence, had already been done by the ground crew responsible for moving all the aircraft out of the hangars. However, on this occasion I wanted to be off as quickly as possible and without waiting, hooked the aircraft tailskid dolly onto my car and trailed it up to the airfield. By the time I had chocked and loaded the aircraft and found somewhere to park the car, the groundcrew had moved all the other aircraft in the hangar, so I didn't save much time and expended a lot of effort into the bargain.

At least there were plenty of people around to swing the propeller, and after a quick D.I. we got started, and by 8.30 I was off. There was almost no wind, there were no aircraft in the circuit and as yet no air traffic control to worry about, so take-off entailed taxying some 50 yards to the nearest grass runway, lining up and opening the throttle. With only myself on board, the tail came up immediately and we were airborne on reaching the infamous hump on that runway.

By now the sun was shining strongly from an almost clear sky overhead, but once up I could see a distant menacing bank of fog to the south, the top looking like the upper surface of stratus clouds. In between, there were strands of mist hanging in the hollows and Stevenage looked, from a distance of some 15 miles, to have its usual low-lying band of fog, with protruding tree-tops and buildings – "usual" because in conditions of fog and mist one can almost guarantee that if it is going to be foggy anywhere in the area, it would be at Stevenage. Overall, a truly beautiful scene with the early morning sun reflecting brightly off the low-lying layers of scattered mist.

Turning on course to Eaton Bray I could see ahead what appeared to be thick banks of mist but to which I noticed, as on many occasions, we never seemed to get any closer, and this indicated that it was more likely to be normal haze. Certainly, overhead at Eaton Bray, the weather was much as it had been at Old Warden. No sign of George on the airfield, so I carried on to the village at Slapton to circle his house, but without any apparent effect. As he was expecting me, it was reasonable to assume he was on his way. Nevertheless, though I flew over the roads he would have driven along, I could see no sign of a familiar car. Landing at the strip, which can sometimes be awkward, depending on wind strength and direction, was a 'piece of cake' as I was able to select the most favourable approach, i.e. towards the apple orchard and not over it! Surprisingly, George was not there either, but he soon turned up, having found a friendly neighbour to bring him and his gear in her car, which was why I failed to see his! No 'Becca, as she had gone down to Blandford by road with her sister on Friday evening, having seen what the weather could do to George's plans!

Our private fuel store at Old Warden had been empty on Saturday and I had not bothered to get any more, thinking that George was laying on a supply at Eaton Bray. He, in turn, had only brought enough to top up, so that was the next hitch, requiring George to go haring off to obtain another 9 gallons. By the time I had given his neighbour a quick 'thank you' circuit over Slapton on their return, and filled up etc., we had taken some 90 minutes more than planned, and the weather man had sneaked in some more thickening haze to the west.

George now took over the driver's seat and I sat in the back to help out with the navigation. Ahead now, as we flew south-west over the Thames Valley area, the mist up-sun was giving George some problems in picking out landmarks, but we got down to Compton Abbas pretty well on ETA, with enough time to fly over the field he was hoping might prove useful to land in. We couldn't make up our minds from the air as I was not too happy about the downward slope at the end of the landing run. Nearby, however, was a large green field which we determined to look at from the ground.

Back at Compton we found the wind gusting hard and swinging through 90 deg, giving George plenty to think about on the approach. Apart from one of the Club's two Tigers standing outside the hangars, there was nothing of interest amongst the line of metalware in front of the public enclosure, and in no time at all the Jackaroo's arrival brought forth a little knot of interested onlookers. As was often the case, this produced a nostalgic ex-RAF pilot who had trained on Tigers and, surprisingly, a couple of VAC members making their way to Finmere and hoping to hire a Tiger in which to fly there. These, alas, were not operating as the wind conditions were considered too rough (a Tiger Moth is much more of a handful in crosswinds than a Jackaroo, owing partly to the narrower-tracked undercarriage).

We made our way by road to Blandford where we had a closer look at the two fields and decided reluctantly that the stubble field would probably be eminently acceptable in an emergency but not good enough to want to deliberately set down in. The surface was furrowed and liberally sprinkled with large and vicious-looking flints, there was what looked like a large bomb crater on the line of best approach and, with the current wind direction and strength, the landing run would have finished perilously near a steepening downhill slope. On the other hand, the second field had a good covering of thick grass and, even though surrounded by trees on the approach, had an ample length. The only snag to landing at that point in time was that the good thick grass was being munched contentedly by a fair-sized herd of cattle.

After lunch, we drove back to Compton Abbas, filled up the fuel tank and, leaving George to drive the van down to Salcombe, 'Becca and I took off into the now not-so distant and noticeably gloomier haze. It was around 16.30 that we left and George expected to be in Salcombe by 19.00. Routeing via Blandford we had another closer look at the two fields from the air, reinforcing my earlier feelings. Making a very enjoyable low slow pass over the grass field, with the wheels flicking the tops of the long grass, I was almost tempted to land, as the cattle had all moved down to the far end of the field; but the thought that they might wend an inquisitive way back to my end of the field and thus stop me taking off again proved all-powerful and I reluctantly pulled up and away.

As we turned west, the haze appeared to be thickening more rapidly but still not enough to cause any real concern. All we had to do, if in doubt about our course, was to fly due south to the coast and then turn right to regain track, which followed the coastline westward from Bridport. We found the pornographic chalk "giant" at Cerne Abbas – to confirm our track – and then enjoyed an idyllic coastwise trip from just west of Bridport right round to our destination at Bolt Head. The sun was bright enough on the coast to dispel the inland gloom and the stiff on-shore wind was whipping up the white horses in sharp contrast to the deep ultramarine blue of the sea. We skimmed along the cliff tops from Lyme Regis to Budleigh Salterton, keeping a respectful distance from beaches and towns, then crossed the wide estuary at Exmouth and gazed down on the broad sandy stretch from Dawlish to Teignmouth. Up again to 1,500 ft over the urban sprawl of Torquay and Paignton, before dropping down over Dartmouth estuary almost to sea level for the final run in to Bolt Head.

The tide was halfway out, uncovering wide, flat, sandy beaches along the length of Start Bay, interrupted only by rocky promontories and jutting cliffs. Here, we enjoyed the rare privilege of flying along just off the water's edge, at times down almost to wave-top height, at others gaining a little altitude to keep within gliding distance of the shore whilst flying round headlands at below cliff-top height. The cold, gusty wind off-shore kept all the would-be swimmers huddled in towels or top coats wherever shelter could be found, leaving the beaches almost deserted except for a few of the hardiest or the youngest. Mostly they waved at us, one of the exceptions being a man and a boy who were flying a small kite and who thought it prudent to haul it down before we got there – they were not to know that I would have given it a wide berth had they left it up.

On past Stoke Flemming, Strete, Slapton Sands, Torcross and Bee-sands until we lifted up inland over the looming cliffs of Start Point and Prawle Point, then down again for the run-in to Salcombe estuary. Bolt Head is at an altitude of just under 500 ft and we climbed to 1,000 ft to look for the field we were supposed to land in. On top, the aerial mast and some of the old airfield buildings were easily visible; "three fields this side of the mast and one south" and sure enough, there in a small, grass, rectangular field was a line of white markers, with a Land Rover tucked in against a hedge.

Small was the operational word – it looked just about long enough to be safe but everything would depend on the wind direction. A first low run over showed no power lines around, a good level surface with a slight upward slope from the low threshold hedge, and a 3-strand wire fence as the boundary at the end of the landing run, with a fine flat field beyond. But where was the wind? As we crossed the cliff edge we experienced severe buffeting to demonstrate its presence and strength but that was all. Gaining height for a circuit over the town, I looked all around for some indication of wind direction; smoke or flags would have been useful but all we saw was smoke from a large bonfire on the lee side of the hill. This, though swirling in all directions, indicated a general drift at some 90 deg to that expected. Not much help as I could not believe it would be true as close to the cliff edge as our field was.

Pressing on over the site of the main airfield I looked longingly at a lengthy strip of mown grass alongside the squat concrete buildings now forming all that was visible of the underground installation, but we had been advised that it was taboo to go onto the Ministry site. Lining up with our field I tried again from about 50 ft to estimate the direction of the wind over the surface, but we were swung about in all directions, culminating again in extreme turbulence at the cliff edge, this time further round at some 45 deg to the landing line. Still no help, so round again for another run, this time down to between 5 and 10 ft above the surface. I got the impression that the main direction was from the left but again the swirling eddies seemed to be from all directions. This was a pity, as the field was wide enough to give perhaps 10 deg either side of the main direction by running diagonally from corner to corner. In the end, I decided to line up on a straight run in: at least the low pass had indicated that there was enough room. In the event, the touchdown was an anticlimax, the landing run finishing some 150 ft from the wire fence despite a faster than normal approach in deference to the gusty wind conditions.

Swinging round to meet the approaching Land Rover at the side of the field, there was little time to enjoy the warm glow of satisfaction at having accomplished what at first sight had appeared to be a somewhat marginal operation. Gusts of wind were rocking the wings and it was a question of cutting the engine and getting out to manhandle the aircraft nose to wind, close to the hedge, as quickly as possible. Helped by the farmer, a young man in his early twenties named Simon, this was soon accomplished, the chocks we carried with us pushed firmly behind the wheels to stop the old Jackaroo from being blown backwards. On the ground, it was easy to establish that the general direction of the wind was, as thought, about 45 deg to the left of the line of the hedge. It was a good field, with a firm surface and lush, over-long, green grass which had helped slow our landing run; I just hoped that on our next flight the grass would not also be soaking wet, otherwise the help on landing might be too much of a hindrance on take-off.

Now we needed George with the van and its picketing gear to secure the aircraft, but at least close up to the hedge it seemed steady enough. We accompanied Simon and his girl friend down to the farmhouse for a welcome cup of tea. In the course of conversation it transpired that he had several holiday chalets which were not currently let and, if we were not already fixed up, we were welcome to use them overnight. 'Becca had originally booked for three nights in Salcombe but when it was obvious we were not going to make it on Friday, she had cancelled the bookings and wasn't sure whether or not accommodation was still available, so this offer was very welcome.

Time ticked past and no sign of George, so we went for an exploratory walk round the field and along the cliff edge. On the way out Simon showed us the farm pets, unusual in being a group of five red deer, including at least one stag and three does, and very attractive they were, one of the does being tame enough to feed out of our hands. The wind showed no sign of abating, if anything it was getting stronger, and I had no desire to tempt providence in flying again under those conditions, though I would have liked to offer Simon and his girl friend a joyride round the farm (which extended over a scattered 800 acres). Neither of them had flown in a light aircraft before and these blustery conditions were far from ideal for a first flight.

Back at the field, I paced out the length to see what we had and also to see how much difference using a diagonal would make. We made it about 450 yards by 100 yards, and the effect of the diagonal was no more than an additional 10 paces, not that we needed any more. What was much more useful was that using the diagonal took us 10 deg more into the existing wind. Also the south-westerly corner, i.e. that on the approach to the most favourable diagonal, dropped away quite steeply to a gateway, and in conditions of no wind the up-slope could help shorten the landing run considerably.

Still no sign of George, so we explored the path along the cliff top and here, even on the ground, the wind turbulence was severe. We decided to walk along the farm entrance road to meet George on his way in, but after about a mile we got to a public highway and had still not found him. By now it was dusk and we reckoned that he might be having difficulty in finding the road or farm entrance, having not been there before, so we carried on a bit further, and a bit further and a bit further until, at a junction where he could have come from either direction, we called it a day. At which point he materialised out of the gloom and stopped to ask us the way.

Suddenly, we were running out of time. Back to the farm to arrange to use the chalets, rush down to Salcombe to find somewhere to eat before it all closed up for the night, back up to the field to picket the aircraft and then to bed to try to catch up on sleep. The meal in Salcombe, by mutual consent in view of the time of night, turned out to be take-away fish and chips, to be consumed at the quayside in the harbour. Perhaps because we suddenly realised that we were hungry, having not eaten for some 7 or 8 hours, or because Salcombe harbour on a mild late summer evening in the dark was an ideal place to be eating take-away fish and chips I know not, but I can say that I cannot recall a more enjoyable fish supper – fresh fish, properly deep-fried, really takes some beating in such circumstances!

Picketing the aircraft turned out to be quite a laugh. George had a carpenter friend who had made up for him some wooden pegs, to be driven into the ground as tie-down points. Unfortunately, they were too blunt and there was no way that we were able to drive them into the unyielding ground. Eventually, George tied the aircraft down to complex arrangements of fuel drums, oil cans, spare Minivan wheel etc. etc. The wind seemed to have increased in strength, and was still gusting, the resultant rocking of the aircraft wings giving us cause for misgivings about any possible increase during the remainder of the night. We finished up by turning the machine tail to wind and securing the stick fully forward; this certainly helped, with the van parked in front of the tail to shield that as much as possible. We eventually got to bed at around half past midnight.

Next morning we awoke to the sound of flurries of rain spattering against the windows, with the wind still gusting noisily. By the time we had got up and cleared up behind us the rain had gone, but there were low clouds scudding past under a continuous higher overcast. Making our way up to the field I observed gloomily to George that we might find that any flying was out of the question, as the wind looked to have swung to a 90 degrees crosswind, but the direction was deceptive and in fact it was still at about 45 degrees.

George was keen to have a look at the field and its approaches in daylight, so we did just that. By the time we had returned to the aircraft with the intention of driving the van down to Salcombe for breakfast, the local 'bobby,' now off-duty, had arrived with his wife and two children for the promised joyrides. We could hardly ask him to wait until we had had some breakfast, which would have taken at least an hour before we returned, so we untied the aircraft, fed it some fuel and oil and started up.

Meanwhile, the sun was making spasmodic attempts to shine through gaps between the scudding blobs of low stratus, but all around us the higher hilltops were lost in a general sort of murk. At this time the possibility of not getting back home that evening was not to be dismissed, but the day was young as yet.

Taxying downwind to the far end of the field it was pleasing to note that the thickish grass compensated for the effect of the gusty following wind, in that the tailskid had something to bite on and provided an adequate measure of control. Although it had rained earlier, the wind had kept the grass little more than damp and the big, fat, Tiger tyres squashed the grass flat and rode smoothly over the firm surface. George loped along at the left wingtip and when just in front of the hedge, with a burst of throttle from me, pulled us smartly through 180 degrees to face up the field. We quickly loaded up Bob (the policeman, who else?), and the younger of his two children, a boy of about 13, needed no second bidding to climb aboard, though his older sister preferred to wait and see. Whilst Bob and his son could think of nothing other than the joyful prospect of flying, his wife, as with all mothers, could see danger at every turn – the scudding low clouds, the strength of the gusts of wind and the shortness of the field (not even a proper aerodrome!); there was no mistaking the look of doubting apprehension on her face which only the safe return of husband and son would remove. I guessed that she would be unlikely to be flying with me that day.

But now the sun, already high, drifted into a large clear patch of misty blue and brightened the scene with its friendly warmth as I opened up for take-off. Before we reached the gate marking the mid-point of the field, the wheels were tapping lightly at the ground and, with more than the usual amount of left aileron to compensate for the swirling wind rolling in from that side, we were airborne. Once up, I headed into wind and gained as much height as possible before we reached the area of extreme turbulence at the cliff-edge. With 100 ft of altitude at this point, although the gusts rocked us violently through some 60 degrees of bank, we lost no height and were quickly through into calmer air. Now I had time to see how the other two were faring – no questions were needed, they were obviously enjoying it tremendously. Bob had only been up once before, in a police helicopter, and his son never, so as is often the case this was a new experience to them.

We flew past Salcombe 500 feet above the estuary, continuing up one of the quiet little backwaters to the north, then turned west. It was now mid-morning but the world below seemed barely awake, with little traffic on the roads and very few people about. A fairly weak sun was sufficient to bathe the misty countryside in a warm, yellowish light and, as we turned, we could see ahead the buildings in Kingsbridge, some 5 miles distant, standing out clearly from the surrounding greens of the fields and woods. It was a delight to be flying low and slow over what must be one of the most attractive areas of scenic beauty in England. Turning again over the outskirts of Kingsbridge we came down almost to surface level to fly back over the still near-deserted estuary, waving to the occupants of any small boats we passed. Lifting up as we approached

Salcombe again we circled over the town, so that Bob and his son could pick out their house, the school, and various other points of local interest. All too soon it was time to return to the field and I flew round the edge of the cliffs, staying high enough to avoid any turbulence, until lined up with the strip.

For this first return to the field I aimed at the low corner on a diagonal run to get as much into wind as possible. Keeping a trickle of power on and an extra five knots to counter the gusts, the run-in was surprisingly smooth until just short of the boundary, when, at a height of about 20 ft, we were rocked violently by a nasty swirling eddy round some tall bushes. No matter, we were back on an even keel by the time I chopped the throttle and we settled smoothly into a three-pointer on the slope up from the corner. This slope gave us a surprisingly short landing run and we were soon unloading Bob and his son and persuading his wife and daughter to climb in; Bob's enthusiasm and delight with the flight quickly brushed aside her last misgivings and we were soon under way again.

This time we visited a different creek to the north-west of Salcombe, circling a small waterside hamlet with a fine old stone church, from the tower of which fluttered a clean white and red cross of St. George. A stronger sun gave more positive tones to the colours of the fields, the woods, the creek and the old buildings in the village, and any apprehensions Bob's wife might have had appeared to have given way to an intense interest in the beauty of the scenery below. By the time we flew back over Salcombe she was as excitedly picking out familiar landmarks as had been Bob and his son. Retracing our previous flight-path on the approach to the field I decided to make a straight run in, this time keeping to the windward side of the bushes. Sure enough we missed the turbulence experienced on the previous approach and still had a comparatively short landing run, even without the assistance of the slope at the corner of the field.

With the duty flights out of the way we could now refuel, hopefully both the aircraft and ourselves. George was a little concerned that his daughter had not yet appeared, she having stayed overnight with friends in Salcombe. However, as we were deliberating what to do, a car came bouncing across the track and she was soon introducing her friend Ian. 'Becca of course wanted Ian to have a flight round the town as well, and thoughts of breakfast were beginning to merge into thoughts about lunch. We refuelled from what George had with him and it was arranged that Ian and 'Becca would collect another 5 gallons or so after we returned and at the same time find us something to serve as both breakfast and lunch.

Ian was yet another to have his baptism of flying that morning, having never flown at all before. It is always something of a relief when first-timers obviously enjoy their first essay into the air and Ian took to it like a duck takes to water, even when, at his request, we did some very tight circles over a building he wished to photograph. On our return, in which we nudged unexpectedly into the base of some very low cloud at 800 ft above the field, he was so impressed with the experience that he was even talking about learning to fly himself.

While Ian and 'Becca went shopping for petrol and food, George and I sorted out our plans for the remainder of the day. George did not want to land at Compton in this turbulent wind and, in view of the way we were using up time, and with the weather worsening if anything, felt it might be wise to give Haldon a miss. In the end, we decided to see how things developed after phoning both Haldon and Compton and finding cond-itions rather better than we were enjoying.

Brunch turned out to be rather large and enjoyable Devon pasties which filled us up in a satisfying manner, and we were soon happily on our way. 'Becca was driving the van up to Compton with instructions to fill up the now-empty drums and we were to meet her there, hopefully around 16.30 though George privately felt she would not be there much before 17.00. Such was George's urgency I quite forgot to fly him round our field and instead headed out eastward along the coast, skimming past a coastguard, in his dark tie and white shirt, in his lookout where the estuary joins the sea. Again, the coastal scenery viewed from just offshore, comfortably above the top of the cliffs, was breathtaking.

Though still overcast with a thin, translucent, broken layer of low stratus, the light was bright and the sea was blue. Inland, there was thick haze on the higher hilltops but the fields in the foreground were bright with green grass or the yellow of corn stubble. Mostly the cliffs and foreshore were almost deserted but now and again we would come to a little coastal hamlet, or a fishing village with a harbour, and then there would be a fair sprinkling of people. George pointed out a ghost village (Hallsands) at the foot of the cliffs near Torcross. From the air the ruined walls and foundations of the buildings that had slipped into the sea in 1917 could be seen quite clearly.

We flew along the coast past Shaldon and Teignmouth (on opposite sides of the Teign estuary), lifting briefly to 1,500 ft over Torquay, now basking in warm sunshine, having left the stratus behind us. George had planned a foolproof way of finding Haldon, by flying along the railway where it hugs the coast past Dawlish and Dawlish Warren to Starcross on the west bank of the Exe estuary, turning left at Starcross Station to follow the only westbound road, winding up through the hills to Haldon, located by a major dual carriageway road. George had previously visited Haldon by car so he knew what he was looking for but I had no idea what to expect. The hills were covered in large forested areas of what looked to be tall, dark green conifers and the road and any small clearings were well masked by them. From our low altitude we could not pick out many features further than about a mile ahead, and so we happened upon the airfield suddenly and rather unexpectedly. It was a roughly triangular-shaped patch of bright green grass, surrounded by the dark of the trees on the near sides and edging on the far side to a steep ravine.

We crossed the field at about 500 ft, having seen no aircraft in the air or on the ground, and circled just over the edge of the escarpment encountering, as expected, noticeable buffeting from the wind turbulence over the valley. I had already started climbing, so carried on up to circuit at 800 ft, so that I could make a steep side-slipping approach from the valley to counter the turbulence. To my surprise, there were three clearly marked grass runways of quite respectable length with a nice bright orange windsock to confirm the wind direction. The steep approach ensured we had no wind problems and the resulting touchdown was satisfyingly feather-light on the smooth short grass. The wind was still very strong so I taxied no further than necessary to save turning across it, and parked roughly tail-on, tying the stick forward to lock the controls in the safest position.

We spent perhaps an hour and a half just talking aeroplanes and airfields and models to the owner and to some radio-controlled aircraft modellers who were now the main users of the field. The owner was such an interesting character to talk to that we had the greatest difficulty in tearing ourselves away. It was a good half hour after saying we must go that we finally got away, with a promise to come back the following year.

Our next leg, to Compton Abbas, was uneventful, picking up and retracing our outward course from Exmouth. As we progressed eastward along the coast the visibility over inland Somerset and Dorset reached a new low for the day but was still sufficient to cause no serious misgivings. Turning inland near Weymouth we flew straight over the beautiful little village of Milton Abbas, its straight main street packed with visitors – but there were no car-parking problems when viewed from the air! As we circled over the airfield at Compton Abbas we looked for 'Becca's little buff-coloured Minivan, and to our surprise it was sitting by the fence in the spectators' car park. We were later than anticipated and she had had a good trip with few hold-ups for traffic. After refuelling and booking out, George flew the last leg back to Eaton Bray.

We went up to 3,000 ft to clear some of the MATZ (Military Air Traffic Zones) and at this height our range of visibility at ground level was down to between one and two miles for much of the way. However, George's navigation was spot on and we arrived back on time at Eaton Bray. Here, to his horror, he found that the wind that had been playing games with us all weekend had not yet finished with us, so that the windsock, stiff from the strength of the wind, was nodding at around 90 deg to the direction of the field. Eaton Bray is not an easy field to tackle under such conditions, being narrow and allowing no leeway for angling across the wind on landing but, despite not having a great deal of recent practice in such extreme crosswinds, George got us safely down in one piece.

It was now getting late and dusk was not far away so I bade George a quick farewell and departed for Old Warden. Crosswind take-offs are always much easier to handle than crosswind landings, and the now lightly-loaded Jackaroo leapt quickly enough into the air, aided by a 30-degree offset into wind. Although on roughly the same course, I flew much lower and the effects of the strong headwind were, if anything, more apparent. By halfway, sufficient lights were appearing on cars, streetlamps and occasional houses to make me glad to be back over familiar territory. There were still a good few minutes of reasonable daylight remaining when I touched down but, although flying for the day was finished for me, there was no respite for the Jackaroo. One of our Group members had been waiting, hoping to get in a quick circuit or two before sunset, and the Jackaroo was quickly airborne again.

All in all a good, satisfying weekend, and one which demonstrated that even in the early eighties one could still fly safely and legally, without radio or elaborate flight plans, on a 'take-it-as-it-comes' basis – true freedom of the air!

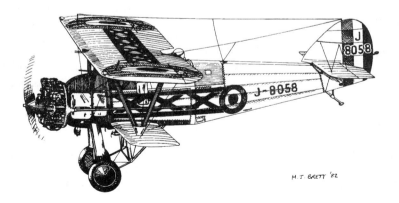

M.T. BRETT '82

CHAPTER 18
THOU SHALT NOT

Despite the best intentions to remain always within the written (and unwritten) rules of the air and after taking what seem at the time to be all the necessary precautions, it is only too readily possible to find oneself in a situation, not only wherein the letter of the law may inadvertently be broken, but which is potentially lethal as well.

Apart from the rules, most pilots have their own limits beyond which they will not willingly proceed, and to exceed such limits, however lofty or lowly they may be, becomes something of an adventure.

There was an occasion on which I found myself beyond perhaps the most important (to me) of my own limits. It was, and still is, a "Thou shalt not" commandment and I am still just a little surprised at how easily I came to break it.

In June of each year, dating back as far as the sixties, or possibly even the fifties, the Tiger Club organise an all-comers Dawn-to-Dusk competition, the main object of which is to put in as many hours as possible, flying over a non-repetitive route, between dawn and dusk. The rules have been changed in recent years to reduce the number of hours flown although, since competing once in 1967 (see Chapter 6) I had not had the opportunity to sample the new arrangement first-hand.

So, when a phone call out of the blue requested my assistance for one of the competitors, it needed little persuasion for me to agree. Charles (although unknown to me at the time) needed someone to position a Jackaroo at Thruxton to fly his father from there to Middle Wallop as part of his project. Charles' father had carried out the very first test flight of the prototype Jackaroo in 1957 and 1982 saw the 25th anniversary of the flight.

I should explain, perhaps, that the competition now requires entrants to support their flight plan with a theme of their own choosing and he was linking historic events with places he landed at. There would be a number of aircraft flying with him over various legs around his planned route and this, together with the combination of opportunity, and reason for landing at a number of exotic places such as Longleat, Blenheim Palace, Woburn Abbey etc., was too tempting to turn down.

Even the fact that it meant taking off at the crack of dawn was a reason for doing it rather than not. It had been denied to me in a previous attempt due to adverse weather conditions delaying our planned take-off at 04.30 to around 05.30 and never, since then, had there been sufficient incentive to actually arrange with someone else to help push out and start up at that time of morning.

So it was agreed, and Charles and I met one Monday evening at Hatfield to discuss arrangements for the next morning. He was to take off from Hatfield at 04.30 and I would do so from Old Warden at 04.15, for us to arrive at Thruxton around 05.45. Charles thought that the weather forecast was good enough for the flight to be on.

Returning home I worked backwards from 04.15 and decided that, with the aircraft all fuelled up and ready-to-go in advance, I should arrive at the airfield at 03.30. Leaving home at 03.10, up at 02.30 – two thirty?!? Ignoring the question "Was this a good idea after all?" I rang Den Willett, who was coming with me to try out his new video camera on some air-to-air shots, to give him the final details, and retired relatively early.

Peering out of my front bedroom window at 02.30 next morning, I could see the lights of Letchworth some three miles distant and I seem to recall (somewhat blearily) that a full moon was only partially obscured by high thin cloud. At that moment I could have wished for a thick blanket of fog to send me scurrying back to bed.

With the weatherman's forecast not obviously incorrect, I left for Old Warden pretty well on time but before going very far, ran into thickening mist lying in the hollows. Comforted by the observation that it was neither very thick nor very extensive, I pressed on only to find that the closer I got to the airfield the more persistent was the mist.

Den, as usual, had beaten me to it and in the pre-dawn half-light was moving barriers and fences when I arrived. We were OK on fuel but needed some oil and, what with this and various other things, by the time we had the aircraft positioned on the airfield, all the fences put back and the cars parked etc., 04.15 had come and gone. However, I had been in no hurry to depart earlier; keeping a wary eye on the mist, which dawn's early light had first indicated was creeping up on us and then alternately receding and returning, I kept finding excuses not to start the engine. Once its noisy clamour had drowned the dawn chorus, I wanted to be away without any delay for fear of waking the entire neighbourhood.

Inevitably, there came the point at which there was no reason, other than the visibility, for not starting. Looking at the distant line of trees I always used as markers for assessing horizontal visibility, I had to admit that it was marginal; vertically it seemed acceptable, with large areas of sky showing through patchy low cloud whose base I estimated as around 1,000 ft. Weighing local knowledge of the effect the River Ouse has, in the way of mist in low-lying areas, against established criteria suggested that, if the weatherman's forecast was good, we would be alright once we cleared the area; after all we could stay up there for three hours and it would surely clear before then. Minutes ticked by and my marker trees came and went, though the overriding impression was one of steady improvement; but the air was so still and quiet that the mist would have to burn off with the sun rather than disperse with the breeze. 04.30. Go now or abandon!

Let's go! If conditions look worse from above than from on the ground I could turn back immediately, as I have on one or two previous occasions. The engine started at first swing and the Gipsy's clatter echoed noisily back from the hangers, seemingly ten times louder than normal, shattering the early morning peace. After the usual four-minute warm-up, engine checks showed no problems and the trees had obligingly stayed constantly in view, indicating surface visibility of over one mile. There was no wind so we lined up on the adjacent downhill (mainly) runway and opened up just before the top of the rise. Up came the tail straight away and we were quickly off the ground, the aircraft as stable as if running on rails, so calm was the air. Climbing out past the brook at the north-east corner of the airfield, I noticed, out of the corner of my eye, a low-lying swath of white ground mist spread across the adjacent road, but there was no opportunity to see more – at a height of around 150 ft and without any warning we entered cloud and lost all visible reference to the ground.

Reaction was immediate and instinctive – throttle back slightly, nose down slightly in an attempt to get back below cloudbase, which thankfully we did within seconds though not completely clear of thin patches and streams of cloud mist. Circling sharply left I aimed to line up with the crossing runway and get back onto the ground as quickly as possible. Alas, I had been too eager, the patchy cloud had disorientated me slightly and my 270 deg turn was too tight to give me time to lose height for a landing. A succession of snapshot glances showed the road beneath with, of all things at that time of the morning, a car with its headlights on and its driver craning out of the window; the runway lined up too nicely below and in front of us; the A.S.I. indicating some 70 knots and our height still about 150 ft – too high, too fast and too close to the runway to land. In normal circumstances I believe I could have landed from that position but I was too shaken to think constructively just then.

Looking to the left, the far end of the main runway was still clear but it was impossible to tell how close or high was the cloud bank we had just left. Whipping round left to circle and line up with that runway took us over the adjacent farm buildings and a copse of tall trees. Now, to my horror, I realised that the trees were very indistinct, with the tops disappearing into the cloud again, this time with no certainty of what lay ahead – no nosing back below cloudbase now! This was a mug's game, as foolish as Russian Roulette, and I had no stomach for lurching into and out of cloud at tree-top height in an area with numerous woods and isolated tall trees. Again, once back in the cloud and knowing that it should be only a thin layer, there was no real doubt as to the next move. Throttle wide open and climb up out of it, eyes now switching constantly between A.S.I. and turn-and-bank, conscious of the need to match climb angle to a safe airspeed, and to keep the turn and slip needles central like never before. This was blind flying for real!

In probably no more than a minute or two, which seemed nevertheless like many times more, we emerged into another world, from the all-enveloping whiteness into the crystal-clear, cold light of dawn. There was a feeling of finality about the situation we were now in. I had broken my prime "Thou Shalt Not" rule and had done one thing I had vowed never to do, i.e. get above continuous cloud with no certainty that there were any breaks in it, and worse, in the knowledge that the cloudbase was measured in tens rather than hundreds of feet.

Rather like being on the wrong side of the road round a blind bend – if you are lucky there will be nothing coming. In this situation, if I was lucky we would find a break in the clouds before we ran out of fuel. At least, we could now take stock of the situation whilst circling and continuing to climb. Above, there was a high, thin layer of alto-stratus which probably accounted for why the sun was noticeably still abed. Immediately beneath us was a solid carpet of white but to the south-west, dark horizontal streaks were soon identifiable as the tree-covered tops of high ground. I had little idea of exactly where we were but, reasoning that the Sandy aerial mast should be protruding above the cloud, this was soon spotted several miles away to the north-east. This meant we were still roughly in the vicinity of Biggleswade/Old Warden and the high ground would be somewhere in the Clophill area. As we climbed higher it was possible to see larger stretches of dark, beyond the high ridges, which meant that in the general direction of our route we should expect to find reasonable ground visibility.

Setting course for Thruxton at about 1,500 ft and knowing that we were flying into clearer conditions, the worry of finding below us an unbroken blanket of cloud now a thing of the past, we could take in the beauty of the scene unfolding before us. The mist cloud below was a pure, cold, shining white of the sort that washing powder advertisers love to boast about; as we flew over the high ground the trees seemed to emerge from the mist, at first just blurred tops, till finally complete woods and small open spaces were sharp and clear. Beyond the ridge, the mist had a much less tenuous hold and was confined to low-lying patches, and strands of opalescence, with just a thin veil elsewhere below the high ground. In the distance ahead, further successive ridges stretched across the scene, each a shade lighter than the one before, to finally merge into a distant greyness that marked the line of the Chilterns. At least we would be able to pick out a field somewhere amongst that lot, and preferably a known strip such as Eaton Bray or an airfield such as Halton.

It was almost eerie, flying over a landscape so changed by the mist patterns as to be virtually unrecognisable, to see miles and miles of roads with no movement on them, and small towns and villages with no sign of life. Not till the M1 motorway came into focus was there any indication of normalcy and even there the traffic was thin and scattered. We were literally in a world of our own.

Off to the south, there appeared to be a solid wall of cloud down to the ground, much as now lay behind us, over Biggleswade, and beyond to the north and east. How then would Charles be faring, starting as he was at Hatfield, some 25 miles away due south? It seemed highly unlikely that he would have found better conditions than we had encountered and it was almost certain that he would still be on the ground. No matter, if we got to Thruxton before him we would just sit and wait.

Meanwhile, landmarks on the higher ground came and went and soon we were turning over the airfield at Halton, visibility here being quite good with very little ground mist or cloud cover. But, somewhat blocking our route over the Chilterns, lay a thickening bank of cloud with tops at about 1,000 ft. As we got closer it could be seen to be well broken, with largish holes through which the ground was visible; ahead the large radar aerial mast near Stokenchurch (just off the M40), with its complex of dishes and antennae, could be seen protruding through the cloud, marking the line of the still-invisible Chilterns.

Should we press on or hold over at Halton? It was mainly a question of whether conditions at Halton would worsen, or elsewhere get better. I knew that over the Thames Valley area, from Reading to Newbury, conditions were always worse than to the north or south, and that there would be a good chance of clear visibility beyond Thruxton as forecast. Let's give it a whirl but keep a wary eye on conditions behind us. If the cloud closed up over Halton we could be in trouble.

Thames Valley lived up to expectations and the cloud below gradually filled in until there were virtually no breaks at all. To make matters worse, there was now an intermediate layer of cloud forming, with its base at about 2,500 ft, and we were beginning to feel like the meat in a sandwich. We had been flying for 15 minutes with no identifiable sight of the ground and things still looked worse ahead rather than better. Just as I decided I would cut and run back to the safety of Halton, a sudden clear break in the cloud off to the left showed a familiar sight – the runways of the old airfield at Aldermaston readily identified by the unusual shapes of the research buildings now erected upon them.

That meant we must be just about over the old Bath road and Newbury would be within spitting distance to our right. Newbury spelt two large areas to land on; the huge complex of the airfield at Greenham Common on a ridge some 400 feet above the town, or the Racecourse nestling at the foot of the ridge. One of these two ought to be visible through the small breaks in the cloud below. Things were looking more hopeful now, and through a fairly large gap in the cloud I could pick out beneath us a road, railway and river running side by side through a small hamlet. The road was obviously a main trunk road with sections of dual carriageway and I felt sure this was the A4 Bath Road. It was impossible to see what the cloudbase was, but with a hole this size I could perhaps get below it and, if the base was high enough, follow the main road to Newbury. If not, I would climb back up.

For the second time that morning, theory was one thing, practice another, and try as I might, I could not get beneath the cloud (this was very fortunate as it later transpired) as the hole kept closing in and re-opening elsewhere. We dropped below cloud top level at about 1,200 ft and I got down to around 800 ft but was too worried about the hole closing up on me to drop any further. Just as well, because by the time I got back above the cloud tops the hole had virtually disappeared.

Continuing westward, circling over breaks in the cloud with occasional tantalising glimpses of the main road beneath, we got to what I considered to be Newbury but could not see enough at any time to be certain, and reluctantly decided to go back to Halton. So near, yet so far – continuous cloud cover extended south-west to the horizon, with a possible merging of the two layers, and there was no certainty that Thruxton would be clear. If it was not, then in the additional time it would take us to get there and back, we could have lost Halton as well.

Turning back on the reciprocal we headed towards where I hoped Halton would be. Every now and again there would be an extra large gap in the clouds showing a number of navigational features but I was not stopping to pinpoint them. Way off ahead the cloud thinned to the point where darker streaks showed the ground to be clear and at about the time I reckoned we should be beyond the Chilterns I saw what I took to be the chimney stacks of the big cement works at Pitstone. By now, a thin sun was beginning to light the scene below but there was still much haze and ground mist.

As we got closer I felt there was something odd about the cement works, and after circling several times, realised this was not Pitstone. But I knew of no other cement works in what was a fairly familiar area. Was I too far west or too far east along the ridge? If too far east, and I turned east, I would blunder into the Luton Control zone so it had to be a westerly turn. The edge of the hills was still completely obscured by cloud but suddenly the top of the radar mast at Stokenchurch again stood out clear and sharp. So we were west of Halton, placing the cement works at Chinnor. Heading eastwards again it was all plain sailing. Picking out Halton's hangars ahead through the haze, I cut the throttle and side-slipped straight in. No need to join the circuit at this time of the morning, nothing was astir below.

Taxying over to the line in front of the deserted control tower I switched off and sat for a few minutes, enjoying an unexpected feeling of relief at being safely back on the ground. Time was just after 06.00 and we clambered out expecting to see a Land Rover approach us at any minute, bearing members of the guard demanding to know what we were doing there. We were still waiting at 08.00 before any real sign of life materialised, by which time we had had a little walk and a little nap and had attended to Nature's needs.

During this time, there had been no noticeable improvement in the visibility. So much for the Met. forecast! We had also taken the opportunity to top up the tank from the two Jerricans we had brought with us. This had been a good point at which to refuel, allowing time for the chamois leather filter on our funnel to dry out – there is nothing worse than a wet filter in the cabin from either comfort or safety aspects!

The RAF people were most helpful, though they extracted, albeit very apologetically, a landing fee from us. With their help we got an update on the weather and were able to establish that Charles had not progressed beyond Thruxton to his next port of call, Middle Wallop (who seemed to know nothing of him at all) or to Yeovilton, though the latter gave us a clue that they thought he had forced-landed in a field near Newbury. It seemed a good idea to try and locate him in case we could be of any help in any way; perhaps the best thing to do would be to go to Thruxton, to see if anyone else expecting to meet him there was either there or had left a message. It was too early in the morning for anyone to be adequately awake at Thruxton to answer the telephone, so we flew there as soon as it cleared sufficiently at Halton.

At 09.00 we left Halton, knowing that it would be clear all the way, though conditions were much hazier than we expected. No problems now in finding Thruxton but the place showed little sign of life when we got there. In the ops room we found two people who looked like air traffic control staff, but they knew nothing of Charles' plans for landing at 05.30 though they knew him. They eventually linked him with an earlier enquiry from the local radio/newspaper for details of an aircraft that had crashed near Newbury, and established for us that he had made an emergency landing in standing corn, had turned over, but that no one was hurt.

There was little more we could do but it seemed worth trying to call in on Tim, who was fairly local and had been going to participate, and thus perhaps was in contact with Charles. Alas, no one knew the location of Tim's airstrip but air traffic suggested that if we could get into Cliff Lovell's place he would know. Cliff had an interesting field near Kingsclere, located by the adjacent aerial mast about half a mile to the north. The field slopes very steeply from his workshop and hangars down to the southern tip, which solves all problems with wind direction; regardless of the latter you land uphill and take off down.

Here we were in luck as one of the engineers on his way to work had passed the field in which Charles had crashed. Once he had got over his surprise at seeing an upside-down Tiger in the cornfield, he had lent a hand in dismantling it, and had left when they had got the wings and tail off and the fuselage the right way up. He confirmed that neither occupant was hurt but that the fuselage had broken its back and several wing spars would need replacing. Armed with the location both of the cornfield and Tim's house and strip (but not, unfortunately, his phone number) we tried again. We found the field easily from the directions given us and there, sure enough, was a camper van or similar, with several Tiger wings loaded on to its roof rack, and several more lying alongside. We couldn't recognise anyone on the ground but exchanged waves and pointed in the direction of Tim's strip in the hope that someone would realise what we meant. Charles had been unlucky that this otherwise excellent field, one of the few in the area, had green standing corn which at 5.30 a.m., shrouded in mist, would have looked like grass – had it been grass his 'arrival' would simply have been a precautionary landing.

Departing first for Tim's house, which we circled, and found that either everyone was deaf, or asleep, or out, we pressed on to Tim's airstrip, about four miles or so from Charles' cornfield, and landed to sit and wait to see if anyone would come. Adjacent to the airstrip was a beautiful country house belonging to the owner of the strip but neither the house nor the locked hangar or the field showed any sign of life.

By now the sun was hot, the sky was blue and it had turned into a glorious English summer day. Den and I demolished the remainder of what food and drink Den had brought with him, and then sat and basked in the sun, with the sleep-inducing background song of birds and buzz of bees.

We gave Tim about half an hour and then decided that if he was coming he would have been there by then and, in view of an ominous-looking build-up of cloud, left for home without further delay. There was now quite a breeze rocking the trees, blowing across the field and causing me to take off at an angle to the run of the field in order to gain what advantage I could of the resulting headwind component. This was not very clever as our climb-out path then lay across some tall trees, over which there was noticeable turbulence, fortunately not enough to cause a problem. The rest of the journey back was uneventful and we landed just after two o'clock.

It was some weeks before I saw or heard from Charles, finally encountering him again on the DH 100 Rally. He had had good clear visibility at Hatfield at 04.30, running into thickening conditions in the Thames Valley area, and finally finding himself forced down by rising ground meeting lowering cloudbase. With no time for search and no room for manoeuvre he was relieved to find a large, open green space under his nose with the results that we now know. A dawn neither of us will forget and for me, a case of "There, but for the Grace of God . . ." – a sobering thought!

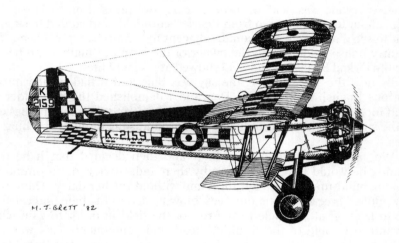

M.J.BRETT '82

CHAPTER 19
CLOUD FANTASIA

Saturday September 21st, 1975. Old Warden–Holbeach St. John–Fin-mere–Loughton–Old Warden. Jackaroo G-AOIR.

From an overcast windy start in the morning, the weather had tailed off to give a fine clear afternoon with high cumulus. Fully loaded with three passengers aboard, and *en route* to Finmere, where we were to join the defenders for a VAG Tea Patrol, we climbed steadily up towards great towering banks of cumulus, the sort that beckon one on to enjoy their delights. Cloud cover was now about 5 oktas with great gaps between the larger clouds, the bases of which were at about 3,000 ft. All aboard agreed that we should accept the challenge and see if we could top these giants, two of the passengers having never before been above the clouds. What a treat awaited them!

Close to the cloudbase, the large gaps between the clouds appeared to have narrowed considerably and the clouds themselves seemed much larger, darker and somewhat forbidding. It became necessary to skirt wide of the clouds to avoid penetrating them which, apart from being illegal in VFR, with our low rate of climb, and the height of the clouds, was definitely to be avoided. Even when some hundreds of feet below the cloudbase level, noticeable turbulence was encountered which reinforced the necessity for keeping well clear of them. Although there was no rain about, the clouds at close quarters looked black enough to drop some on us at any time, and with the sun completely blotted out by the dark grey mass above one felt that even flurries of snow could not be discounted. Before having to ease off our climb to avoid entering the cloud we reached the far side and, like sea lanes through pack ice, could see avenues opening up between the clouds ahead. None lay in our direction of travel however and we diverted left through a narrow gap between two mountainous giants.

Climbing hard we topped several of the smaller outcrops at about 5,000 ft, but were still left with an even higher and seemingly unpassable bank ahead, which stretched unbroken across the end of our now-widening avenue. The two cloud masses on either side still loomed hundreds of feet above us and I felt sure we were not going to get above them this time. At the end of the avenue we emerged into a great lake of clear air, when the bank in front of us could be seen to be broken at either side. As we had turned left last time I now turned to the right. The ground was still visible directly beneath us in another detached, unreal world, but the height and proximity of our cloud banks shut out most of the direct sunlight, although there were great patches of blue sky above.

As we skirted round the end of the bank that had confronted us there were yet more avenues opening up, but somewhat narrower than before, and seemingly without openings at the far end. The clouds, though cloudscapes are never the same, were more irregular in shape than any I had noted before, leaving an impression of vertical cliffs and chasms, with gloomy narrow gorges and skeins of mist. Bright shafts of sunlight pierced the shadowy valleys and it struck me vividly that here, if anywhere, was a visible interpretation of Grieg's "Hall of the Mountain Kings"! We were now under another layer of cloud and climbing hard for a narrowing stairway between two sun-dappled monsters. Altitude 6,200 ft and severe doubts now as to whether our winding, ascending path would peter out in a cul-de-sac, or our ever-richening mixture keep us climbing much longer (as with most Tiger Moths our mixture control was disconnected so that student pilots would not accidentally put the mixture to lean when closing the throttle). The engine sounded a little different (it always does when you least want it to, such as when flying over water!) but kept us boring steadily upwards.

At 7,000 ft we were skimming over a patchy, lacy, white 'ground mist' as our pathway threatened to close in on us, but miraculously our climb matched the gradient of the cloud top directly beneath us – and then suddenly, unexpectedly and breathtakingly, we were out above the entire layer of broken cloud, flying above a snowscape so dazzling as to bring tears to the eyes (whether through the contrast or just being immersed in such grandeur it mattered not) with shadowy valleys and cliffs stretching in brilliant sunshine to the deep blue horizon. There is just nothing to match the glory of such a scene, familiar only to flyers, mountain climbers and jet passengers. This emergence from the cloud layer must be 'old hat' to many airline passengers, but far too quickly the jet leaves the cloud far below and, away from its proximity, the sheer beauty of the scene is lost – blink and you will miss it!

Out on top at 7,300 ft, and soon well clear at 7,500 ft, we just ambled around for a few carefree minutes, drinking in the exhilarating scene stretching around us, chasing our shadow on the cloud tops beneath, looking for the rainbow halo surrounding it. The cloud layer looked unbroken to the horizon in all directions but below we could still see the ground through many adjacent gaps. As we had to cross under Airway Amber 1 East to get to Finmere we had to be below 4,500 ft before we got to it. Back then, down through the gloomy caverns some 4,000 ft, engine throttled back, popping and banging as only an old Gipsy Major does in protest at the indignity of being driven by the airscrew. Now standing on our nose and diving headlong under an overhanging cloud shelf, now pirouetting on one wingtip in a hemmed-in valley, hauling back to zoom over a sudden outcrop of cloud; then pulling a Rate 4 turn and tying the knot whilst circling and deciding the next avenue to follow, reluctant as ever to leave this cloud wonderland. Before very long we were back below the cloudbase in comparative gloom, and scurrying back onto track so as to not miss our Tea Patrol duties (we perhaps need not have bothered as we spotted no attackers, but our absence would have been noticed!).

And what of my passengers? As always the first-timers could scarcely believe that such a scene was waiting there on the top of every cloud; now they had seen, first-hand, that even the blackest of clouds really do have a silver lining!

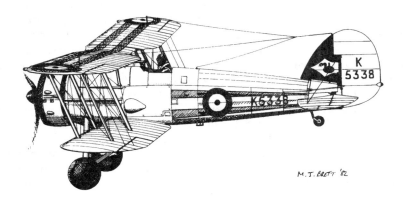

M.J.BRETT '82

CHAPTER 20
DEAD STICK

It was one of those weekends, as had been most of the others that September, where frustration was rife, for a whole variety of reasons. Over the previous weekend the main activity had been to try and resolve a persistent and seemingly illogical tendency to fly one wing low on the part of our (my son Alan and my) recently rebuilt Tiger Moth 'PAL.

On that occasion, after the time-consuming process of removing the wing bracing wire tie-rods and adjusting the wing incidence angles, there had been opportunity for only one flight to check the effects, which proved unsuccessful. Having taken the next step of altering the lengths of the aileron operating crank arms it had proved impossible to observe in flight the results of so doing, because the weather man, having tried and failed to stop flying with blustery, gusting winds, dug in his bag and produced a thunderstorm and continued heavy rain. I had retired temporarily defeated.

So the following Saturday afternoon saw me airborne, once again in very turbulent conditions, to see whether altering the aileron arms would enable the Tiger to be flown 'hands-off.'

With such a long gap between flights it was difficult to be sure whether there was an improvement or not, but the result was sufficiently encouraging to continue the same treatment until the point was reached where either the cure was found or things became noticeably worse. This time, though very windy, the blue sky was scattered with puffy cumulus clouds and there was no resisting the temptation to hop up to 6,000 ft to get above them whilst testing the controls. It was still difficult to be sure whether there was any improvement, so another turn on each aileron rod would be called for, and after 20 minutes aloft I was back on the ground, but with a noticeably fluffy-sounding exhaust.

A glance at the manifold confirmed my worst fears of a blown exhaust gasket – there would be no more flying until that was fixed. As the afternoon merged into evening the wind died away and the sun sank into a glorious red sunset, almost the best evening of the month. Everyone else was flying but my Tiger had chosen this precise time to blow a gasket! That evening I had the manifold off and had tweaked the aileron control arms in preparation for the next flight.

Sunday dawned to the patter of heavy rain and blustery winds on my bedroom window, but the overcast quickly broke up and by the time the manifold and new gasket had been fitted, the sky had cleared, though the wind was still blowing fitfully at up to about 20 knots. The next flight would have to be a short one as fuel was getting low and I would need at least one more after that. As is often the case, one of the other pilots wanted a flip in the Tiger and though it was not going to be much of a joyride, what with the front stick removed, no intercom and its just being a check for the effect of the latest adjustment to the ailerons, he still came along.

This flight showed that the last adjustments were having an adverse effect, so something else would have to be tried next, but that is another story. Part of the downwind checks is to look at the fuel level sight-glass and the level indicator appeared to be still bobbing about the low mark, which experience told me indicated about 4 or 5 gallons still left in the tank, so I would be OK for at least one more short flight.

On this trip I decided it was time to get back into the habit of power-off glide approaches when coming in to land, which I had rather neglected to do of late. With the strong wind it was surprising how much height one needed in hand and I was disgusted with myself in having to use a trickle of power to get in. Maybe the extra weight of a passenger had upset my calculations, or perhaps it was just that I had lapsed into mentally lazy ways; whatever the reason I would have to remember to allow a little more height next time.

Back on the ground I spent a lot of time going over again the adjustments we had been making to wing incidence and aileron arm settings before deciding what to do next. We had made a number of alterations to the aileron rods without curing the problem, so there was no point in simply resetting them to what they had been before. Perhaps having taken the adjustments to a worsening situation the next move should be to make another minor change to the wing incidence angles. It should be said that all these changes were very minor ones of no more than a half turn of either the aileron arms or the bracing wires at a time – it was not a question of curing a dangerous situation but merely of getting it as good as possible. I was reluctant to go to the next step of taping a length of cord on the aileron trailing edges (the age-old solution to curing wing-drop) if it could be cured mechanically, because that would have entailed a paint-spray job!

Looking at the fuel gauge, the top of the indicator could still be seen, confirming my calculations that, taking account of what fuel had been put in and how much flying had been done, there should be enough for perhaps 45 minutes, so another 10-minute flight (one circuit) should be OK.

Once again there was an eager would-be Tiger joyrider in the form of the son of an old friend, he being there for just the weekend and then away at college until Christmas – there could be no refusing this one either!

By now the wind had dropped completely, the sock hanging limply on the mast. The engine was not cold, so only the briefest run-up was necessary, and on taxying out I didn't bother to go through the tiresome business of backtracking to the end of the grass strip for the sake of the extra 50 yds – there is insufficient room to turn the Tiger without someone on the wingtip.

Taking-off was a joy in the calm conditions and despite the lack of wind on the nose we were off in about 100 yds. Climbing out I could sense that the ailerons felt a little better and I turned as soon we got to 300 ft, noting that the roll control was good. Still at full bore, climbing steeply on the crosswind leg, I was just about to check aileron/stick positioning when there was a noticeable miss on one cylinder. Just the one, once. This puzzled me and I forgot about the ailerons while I went quickly through what might have been the cause.

Nobody near the switches, throttle still wide open, fuel cock full ON, and the engine had not missed more than the once; but it should not have done that, something was not right. I turned short onto the downwind leg, looking down at the ground about us. Plenty of places to put down now that all the crops were in but a fair number of fields had been ploughed already. As we completed the 90 degree turn, there it was again, this time several short bursts of two cylinders at a time.

Now there was no doubt in my mind. This was fuel starvation and yet as I looked up at the fuel gauge I could swear the indicator was still bobbing. There was 800 ft showing on the altimeter and it seemed best to throttle back and conserve what little was left. If the engine would keep going at about 1,600 or 1,700 rpm for another minute or two we should have no difficulty in getting back into the field.

Turning short again onto base leg, the engine coughed and spluttered briefly before lapsing into silence as we completed the turn. This was for real, with no possibility of opening up to stretch the glide; this had to be right first time. I was suddenly very thankful that I had tried just such an approach on my last flight and that now the wind had dropped almost completely. We were running in closer to the field than on the previous occasion with initially plenty of height so I had no real worries. Looking around I could see no better bet than to continue on back into the airfield, all the other fields within reach now being ploughed.

Nevertheless we did seem to be losing height very much faster than was usually the case when throttled right back. Turning onto finals, where I had anticipated slipping off height, there was now no question of that. The road and the low hedge in front of the strip suddenly looked very unfriendly and it seemed a good idea to let the speed build up to 80 mph instead of the customary 60-65 mph, so that if it appeared to be too tight I could turn through 90 degrees at the last moment, without fear of stalling on the turn, to land in the field in front of the road; ploughed or not it would be preferable to dropping onto the hedge. With that extra 15-20 mph I could safely pull up over the hedge or, if necessary, make the turn.

The propeller was still windmilling silently and it suddenly struck me that that was why we were descending so much faster than normal – instead of contributing to our speed as it would, even at tickover, the propeller was now acting as a brake, absorbing power rather than delivering it. On the descent I went briefly through any other actions I should take – it is amazing how instructions given once, light-years in the past, come back at such times: "Close the throttle and switch off – you don't want a sudden burst of power at the last moment when you are committed to scraping into a small space." Well, I was scraping into an ample space and would have welcomed a brief burst of power at any time, so deliberately did not switch off or close the throttle, not that this invoked any response from the very dead engine at any time.

The last few seconds of the approach were in no hurry to pass. For long agonising moments it seemed that we were not going to make it. The last point at which I could have made a 90 degree turn came and went and only that comforting 80 mph reading on the A.S.I. let me continue. At the last moment, with perhaps six feet clearance over the road I was able to pull safely up over the hedge and float across the 150 or so feet of ploughed ground between the hedge and the start of the grass runway. The propeller flickered to a stop as we lost speed and we touched down on the very edge of the grass (the skid actually furrowed the ground about six feet before the grass!), coming to a halt a few feet beyond our starting point. This was the shortest landing roll to date for me in the Tiger and the first time I had managed to land short on this runway and not be thrown back into the air by the Gransden bump (because we never reached it!). But it was not an exercise I intend to repeat!

This was one flight on which I was relieved not to have any communication with my front-seat passenger. There was nothing he could have done, there was nothing obviously wrong and there would have been no point in worrying the life out of him by telling him we were out of fuel. As it was, when we stopped he was completely unaware of what had happened and thought I was showing off by deliberately cutting the power on the base leg – even when the prop stopped he assumed it was due to me being too clever and losing it accidentally. When it finally sank in, he too agreed that he was very glad he had not been aware of the true situation!

So how did this come about? How could a normally reasonably sane (I hope) individual come to be caught out in such an ignominious way, after 20 years of flying? Obviously, carelessness in not looking in the tank before flying to make sure this Tiger fuel gauge gave the same under-reading as did the other one I knew so well (in Jackaroo 'OIR). In the latter, when the float indicator sank out of sight there was still some four or five gallons in the tank – a sort of reserve that I confess to having relied on, on more than one occasion.

So, at the conclusion of the last flight prior to refuelling, when the indicator was still visible, I had assumed there were some four gallons in the tank (because of the shape of the tank and the tail-down attitude, these are not visible through the filler). Then I had put in five gallons to do a couple of rigging test flights, after which the indicator started bobbing again as expected confirming, I thought, the amount of fuel in the tank; that is when I should have looked through the filler – nine gallons would have been easily visible, five barely so. Now I knew that overall fuel consumption on circuit flying was a shade under six gallons an hour, therefore the five gallons would normally give 50 minutes flying, over and above the 40 minutes or so from the four gallons thought to be left in the tank. Thus it should have been OK to fly up to about 45 minutes leaving a safety margin of at least 30 minutes. When I took off on that last flight I had flown 10, 20 and 10 minutes respectively since putting in the five gallons.

On reflection I remembered that during the 20-minute flight I had climbed to 6,000 ft, and on full power in the climb would have used much more fuel than normal. The three flights had been from cold starts, in which the engine has to be warmed up and then run up to full power before checking the mags, all of which use more fuel than cruising flight. Even so that should still not have accounted for the difference. Fuel stains on the underside of the tank and on the front cockpit cover pointed to a slight leak and though not at any time obviously dripping would, over a period, have accounted for an unknown amount.

The final answer came when I put more fuel in. Firstly, with the tank empty, the top of the float was still visible, unlike the other one in 'OIR. Secondly, it started moving only after three gallons were put in, so it must have been very nearly empty when I put the previous five gallons in.

Two things came out of this little episode. The first was guilty awareness of the unnecessary risks to which I had exposed my passenger, with the possibility of writing off or badly damaging the Tiger, or at least of the extensive time and trouble it would have taken to retrieve the aeroplane had I successfully landed in an adjacent ploughed field. Secondly was the satisfaction of finding myself able to deal with such a situation and having the luck to pull it off. Luck? Had there been an extra 50 ft of height to slip off on the approach it would have been as a result of good judgement – with literally no feet to spare it was a matter of good luck!

Luck also in how long the engine kept running. Take-off to touch-down was about 3½ minutes and about half this time was with power off. Rate of consumption at full bore is about 8 gallons/hr, so 1¾ minutes running would require just under two pints of petrol. Had I needed a full four-minute warm up, or back-tracked to the start of the runway the engine could have stopped at a very, very embarrassing point. Definitely LUCK!

CHAPTER 21
PINPOINT NAVIGATION

In 1984 George and I were finalising plans to ship our Jackaroo and my Tiger Moth to the USA, there to fly over the 2,010 miles route of the old Oregon Trail from east to west across the Rockies, returning via Canada, and completing a double coast-to-coast crossing of the States (to find out how we got on read *"Flying the Oregon Trail"*). The Oregon Trail route is now well-documented, and we planned to film the main route and the major historic sites along the way. There remains an estimated 300 miles of wagon-wheel ruts, and in order to locate those we reckoned we had to fly within 100 yards of the defined Trail route. Neither of us had any experience of flying that accurately, or even any idea of whether it was possible to do so.

Initial route planning had been based on motoring maps, which showed the principal Trail routes, but these of course were at such a small scale as to be useless for what was planned. What were readily available were the US Sectional Aeronautical Charts (Sectionals) at a scale of 1:500,000 (roughly 1/8 inch to a mile), and a book of Oregon Trail maps at a scale of ½ inch to a mile.

Perhaps the most pressing job, whilst waiting for delivery of the Trail maps, was to establish how well-suited the Tiger would be to following the Trail at low level and acting as a camera platform. It was obvious that unfolding and refolding a large chart in the draughty, open cockpit of the Tiger would constitute a major hazard, so the first need was to draw a small sample map showing comparable features. An old Roman road near Brent Pelham was chosen because it consisted of stretches of both visible and invisible sections of road. By invisible, I mean where the roads are not shown but their original presence could be inferred as connecting adjacent marked sections. This first small test chart covered just a five-mile stretch, drawn at 0.8 inches to the mile, mounted in a transparent waterproof cover.

The test chart was based on the popular 1-inch-to-the-mile OS maps. The Roman road was drawn in red, oriented from bottom to top ignoring the compass bearing. Solid lines showed where it lay over existing roads or tracks, and dotted lines where it was not marked. Major roads were in brown, minor roads in black, woods in green and all other features such as houses, farms, tumuli, moats etc., were shown – I needed all the help I could get! On Saturday August 11th 1984, with George acting as navigator in the front cockpit, we finally got airborne on our first real Oregon Trail exercise.

Both of us carried standard 1:250,000 Aeronautical charts (roughly ¼ in to a mile); in addition George had an OS map and I my special map. One difficulty we faced on this (and on many later flights in the Tiger) was that I had not yet managed to arrange any form of intercom between the cockpits, so that communication was by hand signals or written notes, or shouting with the engine throttled back! Before taking off, I set the altimeter to height above sea level. This enabled me to determine height above the undulating ground over the section of Roman roads, using spot heights from the chart.

It was about 16.15 when we took off, in ideal conditions with good visibility, little wind and hardly any turbulence. Over the Roman road, we flew at 800 ft and 70 mph, and had no problems with orientation (using the compass to check direction when over open ground where there was no sign of the road). There were no real snags in eye-switching between ground, instruments and the map when the latter was held at eye level. Over open ground, it was possible to see several miles ahead to where the next visible section would be, helped by identifying small woods shown on the map.

After the initial run over the section, we had a look from 500 ft and decided that a ground speed of 70 mph was as fast as it would be desirable to go, 60 mph being much better. From this height it was also obvious that one could pick out signposts etc., and that therefore it would be possible to see the occasional Historic Marker boards and stone markers along the Oregon Trail.

We tried again at 1,500 ft and could see the whole five-mile stretch very clearly, but at none of these altitudes was it possible to pick out any sign of the old road over the unmarked sections. The only thing that bothered me about keeping on course over an invisible section was that I found myself using the locations of woods as one of the most prominent aids, and by now I knew that such were not shown on the US Sectional charts and would probably not appear on the Oregon Trail maps.

It also confirmed that any aircraft used for route finding had to have tandem seating rather than side-by-side, as it was essential to be able to look out to both sides. Hence we would have to use the Tiger Moth and not the Jackaroo as the lead aircraft. This was a pity in that peering over the side in the slipstream meant goggles had to be worn, which restricts vision to a certain extent, especially if wearing spectacles, as did both George and myself. This could prove tiring if carried out for any length of time; we would have to do a full day's dummy run as soon as possible to assess the effects.

So much for the practicality of viewing and identifying the trail from the open cockpit of the Tiger Moth. What I was not happy about was how one would manage the maps. Trying to hold the map with one hand and fly with the other was acceptable as long as I had no need to adjust the throttle setting. The ideal position for the map was about one foot from my eyes, at eye level. Anywhere else and it was difficult to focus on it for the detail needed.

The major problem seemed at first sight to be near-insuperable. It was necessary to keep track of position simultaneously on the map and over the ground in order to match the two. Peering from the map to the ground, seeking identifiable features to confirm that we were on course, presented no real problem. But locating the last known position again on the chart in order to ascertain what to look for next, even after merely taking a quick glance at the instruments, consumed so much time that we had flown past the next ground feature even before I had found it on the chart.

The Tiger could not be trusted to fly hands off long enough for me to keep my right index finger over our location on the map while holding it at eye level with my left hand. At 500 feet above the ground, in only slight turbulence, there is insufficient margin to allow a playful Tiger to look after itself for more than a few seconds!

I searched in vain for something to rest the map against so that I could pin it down with a finger over the required spot and still read it. Placed on my thigh, it skulked in the dark, too far away. Held against the only vertical face available, the instrument panel, it then covered up vital instruments!

Trying to hold both the map and the control column with my right hand, and my left index finger pointing to the position, failed equally miserably. The map was again so far away, deep in the gloom of the cockpit, that I could not easily read the details. In any case I could not keep my finger in position whilst making the necessary continuous, corrective movements of the stick. In turbulent air, these are almost intuitive, neither I nor my left hand knowing what my right hand would do next! Even a few seconds concentration on the map soon resulted in the realisation that it had gone awfully quiet outside (which indicated that if I didn't do something quick we would stall in), or a rising crescendo of wind noise suggested the Tiger was intent on making an unpremeditated and early return to the ground!

Even if I could find a solution for the tiny sample map, there was still the problem of what to do about a chart large enough to show the distances we would be faced with in the States. Another need was to highlight any important features to look for or to photograph, and to name them so that I knew what I was looking for on the ground, e.g. a grave, a marker, a log cabin, a series of ruts or whatever.

At least I now knew what was needed, even if it did look to be impossible to provide. It should be located at the cockpit rim, in full daylight to avoid contrasting levels of light, as near eye level as possible, requiring the absolute minimum of eye movement between map and ground, and it was going to demand something like 125 feet of map at the scale we had just used, with no folding or unfolding. Most importantly it had to allow the last known position to be positively and continuously marked so that, when I looked away and then back to the map, I could instantly locate it. A tall order!

I returned from this sortie more than a little dismayed, knowing that this could be the smallest of the difficulties we had yet to face! Such problems are not normally encountered in flying light aircraft by visual navigation, because one then tends to be following straight line tracks, primarily by compass, merely using ground features to confirm position at fairly infrequent intervals. Also because one is flying that much higher, very much more of the ground can be seen, and there is far more time to relate map to ground, etc.

Initially, it had seemed possible that we could use something like the loose-leaf approach that author Greg Franzwa offered with his book of Trail maps – until I actually had a copy in my hand. Then I realised that, while this might offer an ideal solution when driving around in a car, it would not be practical as a means of aerial navigation in an open-cockpit Tiger Moth! In a car, one could pull into the side and stop whilst sorting out the relationship between the non-overlapping top left corner of one sheet with the bottom right corner of the next, whilst comparing them with a local Highway map to fill in the gaps.

At one time I had felt that perhaps we could create separate maps to match the individual legs of each stage. This would have required about 17 maps, giving a maximum coverage of around 160 miles per map. That approach argued against using the ½-inch scale of Franzwa's Trail maps on size alone (80 inches-wide charts?). On that basis it would be better to use the 1:250,000 scale we generally flew by at home (¼ in to the mile), giving 40 inches maximum per map. Even that looked too enormous a task if we had to draw the charts manually, resulting in a minimum of 42 feet total length! What a pity there was not complete coverage to this scale in the USA.

There was no way I could see that any larger scale, such as the 1:500,000 scale of the Sectional charts, could give the detail required. Even at the preferred ¼-inch scale, the thickness of a readily visible line on the chart would represent a strip on the ground of over 100 yards width. If we displaced putting that line on the map by its own thickness we could be 200 yards adrift in pinpointing a location on the ground! I felt we could just about live with that but certainly not any greater margin of error. So, that really settled the scale at 1:250,000.

What if we were to draw the charts double-sided onto stiff card, so that they could be drawn as a narrow strip of 20 inches length, then folded concertina-fashion? That would be better but was still not the answer as it would require two hands, and time, to find the right fold. And what if we had to change the leg at the last moment? Then we would at best have to use two adjoining charts on one stage, and so on until we got back to the original plan.

It was a natural progression from that line of reasoning to the idea of a continuous roll, mounted in a weatherproof case. It got round the problem of defining leg start and finish points, but even more importantly, it completely solved the real bugbear of any previous scheme, that of locating position on the map. By rolling the map under a fixed cursor line to match our progression over the ground, the cursor would instantly show our last known position where it crossed our planned flight path, i.e. the route of the Trail!

The more I thought about it the more I realised that a roll map could solve all the operating problems. But we were still left with one – how to make it? Even that gradually resolved itself when I recalled that plastic draughting film came in 60 ft-long rolls and was waterproof. George came to the rescue by supplying the necessary roll of film, 6 inches wide, obtained by sawing off that amount from a standard-width roll.

Experimenting with various pens and inks finally provided a multi-coloured set of fibre-tipped pens, capable of drawing a solid, coloured line of ½ mm thickness in quick-drying, waterproof ink. The resulting map was almost indestructible, and certainly bore immersion in water, and even scrubbing, without loss of clarity. This meant that I would be able to write on it with a soft pencil and rub off the marks if required – this might prove useful for making notes in the air.

A case width of 6 inches was settled on after experimenting with a cardboard model, intended initially to be strapped to my left thigh. This was the greatest width I felt able to accept in the space available, but sitting in the cockpit soon determined that strapping a box that size to my leg was not going to be the solution. For one thing, a case for a 42 ft roll of film would have to be at least two inches deep, with some form of handle or knob at the side to enable the roll to be wound on. Such a box would limit the free range of sideways travel of the control column; with the degree of manoeuvrability required, that would be unthinkable. Not only that, but the map would be down in a dim area of the cockpit and just beyond the comfortable limit of vision for close scrutiny.

The only acceptable position was above the left-hand top longeron, and that only with the side entry flap permanently open. Not that that would cause any concern – Tiger pilots often choose to leave it down in order to take advantage of the extra elbow room it offers! But that meant that at 6 inches width, the box would protrude way out into the slip-stream and whatever weather came our way!

The winders would have to be inside the cockpit because it proved impossible to get my left hand into position on the outside for winding in either direction. This meant winding with my left hand in a very awkward position if the knobs were inside, or of flying left-handed and winding with my right. Still awkward, because that meant reaching across with the right hand, in effect crossing arms. It seemed that perhaps the only solution would be to have the roll motor-driven, but the thought of the extra complexity and greater possibility of having something going inextricably wrong prevailed, and I determined to keep it simple.

Up till now, I had not devoted too much thought to what the chart would actually look like, assuming it would be a longer length of the sort of thing used on the initial trials. Normally, in laying out a flight route, one simply connects up start and destination points with straight lines, dog-legged as necessary to avoid Restricted Areas, etc.

After plotting the Trail route in detail on one of the Sectional charts I realised how different a problem I was faced with – even when tracing old Roman roads they normally went more or less in the same direction for dozens of miles. But nowhere on that Sectional was the Oregon Trail straight for more than a few miles! Typically, it would wind its wandering way perhaps 20 miles roughly north-west, then turn west for another 15, then north for maybe 25 miles, and so on. To lay out the route in a straight strip to fit my 6 inch-wide roll was impossible.

The motoring solution of drawing a route as a straight line with all the navigation features at the scale distances and locally at the correct angles was also considered, briefly. As a solution to low-level, visual air navigation, which depended so much on pattern recognition, it was a non-starter!

As is often the case, the final solution was simple, and seemed so obvious once determined that I wondered afterwards how it had taken so long to arrive at. At 500 feet above ground I established that I rarely needed to look further than two or three miles either side to establish position. So, the width of the chart was reduced to 3½ inches, a scale width of 14 miles. This would leave me a strip on the left side of the map of 1¼ inches in which to note any Trail features that I should look out for. A corresponding strip on the right of 5/8 inch left room to make any other notes, such as distance from start or compass headings etc. These dimensions added up to 5½ inches, which would enable the external width of the case to be kept down to 6 inches.

Trying this idea out on the Sectional chart, the Trail route was split into a series of sections which would fit between parallel lines spaced 14 scale miles apart. As soon as the route wiggled outside the lines, one straight section ended and another began, angled to suit the new heading. It worked! As most of my identification of the route would be by reference to surrounding visual features, the compass heading would normally be unimportant. Of far greater significance was the fact that the route always headed up the map, no matter where it went in practice. This entirely eliminated the bad habit of turning the map through 180 degs when heading south and then not being able to read the names!

Only when there were no local features with which to identify the route would a compass heading be needed. This would be written on the

RH side margin with the distance from the start so that bearing and times elapsed would fix location. Or so the theory went! Each straight section would end in the Trail route diving off to one side or the other, the next section starting with an overlap sufficient to identify the new orientation.

Now all that was needed was to find a workable, practical solution to the problem of actually drawing the map on the plastic film. I was almost surprised to find that I had begun to accept that it would have to be drawn by hand in the end, a task that appeared so daunting in the early thinking that it had been rejected as totally unacceptable. I have always been haunted by the fear of embarking on a task so time-consuming that no matter how long is spent on it, it will never be completed, and that had been how this one had initially been viewed. Perhaps the realisation that it was the linchpin on which everything else depended had something to do with it – no map, no flight and there was no one else who would do it for me!

Franzwa's maps were at ½-inch scale, so if I could reduce them by half, they would come down to the required ¼-inch scale. Nothing I possessed would enable me to create a reduced print other than by the costly and time-consuming process of photographic copying and printing. Some local office copying machines would produce prints reduced to roughly 70%, but that was all. George came to the rescue once again, offering reduced prints of 71% or 82%, and we discovered that by copying twice at 71% we got almost exactly a 2:1 reduction. Once the first production batch came through I was at last able to make a start.

This of course introduced more problems. The first thing to do was to tape together a string of adjoining sheets, which immediately highlighted enormous gaps where adjacent sheets butted together corner to corner. Also, there were gaps sometimes where the Trail ran along one bank of a river which formed the boundary between adjacent survey sheets. For instance, for miles along the Platte River, there was full and detailed information along the south bank but nothing at all on the north side. Good enough for people driving along the highway but not exactly suitable for aerial navigation, where the north bank features would be needed for confirmation of position.

Enlargement of the Sectional charts was no problem, as a friend of mine had a high-power epidiascope which he willingly lent me for the job. With this I could project the Sectionals onto the reduced Trail maps at the required enlargement, and both fill in the vital information missing from the latter and add the important air navigation features. These were primarily the location of airfields, Special Rules Zones and any Restricted or Danger Areas.

Another important aspect was the location of overhead power cables. Up till then, flying in the UK, I had only been aware of the necessity for knowing where they were in order to avoid them like the plague, but I suspected they were detailed on the Sectionals for another reason as well. In areas of open sage desert where there were few roads etc., the power lines were an important and sometimes sole aid to navigation.

Another shock awaited me on projecting the Sectionals onto the reduced maps. The two sources did not always agree, due either to proven differences in the data shown on the maps, or in distortion in any of the various copying stages (e.g. during the initial reduction when printing the book maps from the Survey charts, our further reductions through two copying stages or my 2:1 enlargement of the Sectionals). This was most noticeable on river courses. Later, I learnt these were, in some areas, subject to massive changes over the years as a result of serious flooding on major rivers such as the Missouri and Snake.

There were differences in the ranking of roads (sometimes one map would show a road as nothing more than a track whilst the other indicated a metalled highway over the same course). Even railroads were subject to major discrepancies! What made it difficult to decide which to believe was that the elderly Survey maps were drawn to a much greater degree of detail, but the Aero Sectionals were reviewed and reprinted every six months! In the end I decided to trust the Sectionals, and practice proved me both right and wrong at different times in so doing.

Perhaps the biggest surprise in comparing the two was the realisation that, in having to print the basic charts in monochrome, Franzwa's maps lost many of the rivers and streams. These tended to disappear into the background, possibly being printed in light blue on the original charts, this colour not copying very well. On the Sectionals, these showed very clearly as a major navigational feature, and gave quite a different picture of the terrain over which the Trail ran.

Neither chart showed the topography very clearly, the Sectionals having coloured bands for differing contours, but understandably on the scale used these were so widely spaced as to show only major variations. Lack of contour shading was the feature I missed most on my map, and I had to manage with only spot heights to show the ground altitude. No problem normally, but there were a few areas in which the Trail route could have been more easily located had I known whether it was following the top of a ridge or wandering along a valley bottom.

Gradually, by a process of elimination, a rapid and reliable method of working evolved. Eventually I could estimate fairly accurately how long a given section was going to take, based on a mapping speed of about 12 map miles per hour, whereas originally it was taking five times that long. The method used was to tape together a string of reduced Trail maps until the Trail route wandered outside the 3½ inch-spaced parallel lines. The prints, trimmed to the angle of the lines, were taped onto a single large white sheet of paper.

The Sectional chart was then projected onto the prints and enlarged to the same scale. All additional required information was drawn onto the prints, or the backing paper where there were gaps between the prints, adjusting any conflicting shapes to the most likely pattern. The resulting master was secured on a long flat working surface and the plastic film taped over it. The translucent plastic was prepared in advance by washing with soap and water, to remove the slightly oily film which would prevent the inks adhering. The side margins were drawn on at this stage. Producing the finished chart was a simple matter of tracing in the required lines, using seven different coloured pens; straight lines were drawn against a ruler but curved lines were freehand. On the Sectionals, obstructions such as masts, smoke stacks etc. are always drawn vertical, i.e. pointing North, and this orientation was kept on the map, providing a useful rough indicator of North.

Although the mapping soon settled down into a matter of routine, there was still one little horror in store for us. By the time my map had reached Oregon, George had produced all the final reduced copy prints, and the end looked to be in sight. But as I projected the Sectional onto the first string of maps in Oregon, nothing matched. The shapes seemed to be similar but consistently larger. By reducing the size of the projected Sectional I could make it fit, but the resulting scale was smaller than ¼-inch.

I hoped it was an error in copy printing, but a check against the original sheets in the book revealed that the discrepancy lay there. This was disastrous – without a recognisable scale I would not be able to measure distance accurately nor calculate the time it would take to fly over it. Perhaps not too important over areas where there were plenty of landmarks, but this section was going to take us out over featureless desert and alongside the Boardman Bombing Range, so accuracy there was going to be important!

All sorts of ideas came and went with no real solution in sight other than to rescale the Trail maps, which would have taken an immeasurable amount more time. But one thought kept nagging away – if Franzwa or his printers had arrived at an odd scale, it should be through one of the standard reductions available. Remembering that George could obtain 82% reductions as well as 71% prompted me to try reducing by first one then the other instead of twice at 71%. Miraculously it worked! All we had then to do was to make a further set of second copies and all would be well. It cost us much valuable time, 20 waste copy sheets and some real worries, but nothing worse.

Looking back on the period in which I was producing the map, and the 200-odd hours spent in making it (not to mention as much again in planning how to), I recall the intense interest which the route held over all those miles. If at first, one of the compelling reasons for travelling over the Trail was in order to discover what the terrain was like, I guess that by the time I had finished drawing it I had a pretty good idea. Certainly I knew where all the important features and landmarks were. It was just as well that I found it so interesting; at that point, confidence in raising sufficient funds to be able make use of the map was at its lowest ebb.

With the map completed there was still a major task of making a case for it. I knew well enough that I could too easily embark on a job with no foreseeable end. So rather than design in all sorts of niceties, the simplest solution that would work was the one to go for, no matter how crude it might look. By then, in April 1985, we had taken the decision to delay the flight until the following year, and I had decided to visit the 1985 OCTA Convention at Scottsbluff in August. Part of the necessity for doing so was to try flying with that map over the Trail, to see if I really could pinpoint locations down to 100 yards or so with the detail I had on it. So I had to have some sort of case ready before then, even if I could subsequently get a better one made professionally.

Remembering that the Meccano construction set used by my sons was still around somewhere at home, that seemed a good starting point. It provided me with spindles, pulley wheels, a couple of plastic model road wheels to serve as winding knobs, and various perforated strips. Most of all it was a convenient way of trying out ideas.

The finished article was a simple, wide, U-section case of thin sheet steel, the map being wound over two lengths of broom handle with sawn-off woodscrews as spindles. The rollers wound the map over the outside of the case, with thin plastic card providing a smooth white backing surface so that the map details showed up clearly. Tension on the rollers to prevent them unwinding was provided by rubber bands passed over the pulley wheel. It all worked well though there was no time to make a suitable mount for attachment to the airframe; for the trial in the air, someone else would have to fly so that I could have both hands free to hold and operate the map!

Later, I was able to get a case professionally made, courtesy of British Aerospace, who were anxious to see that those of their employees embarking on this exercise, using an aircraft designed by one of their constituent companies over 50 years earlier, were properly equipped to do so. Again, I kept the design as simple as possible, employing a universal mounting enabling the case to be tilted in three planes, so that it could be mounted upright on the Tiger Moth upper side longeron (where it passed through the rear cockpit) and at precisely the required angle. The lid was hinged and secured closed by a strap and dot-fastener so that it could be opened in the air for making notes on the map. Another important feature was that it was possible to change the map roll, because by now we had decided that it was vital to carry out a dummy run in the UK, using an equivalent map roll.

The route started near my home town of Baldock, following the Icknield Way, then the Ridgeway and finally Offa's Dyke to its northern end. The return journey was to follow mainly disused railway lines. A map roll, identical in concept to the Oregon Trail route, was created for this purpose. Chapter 22, "Dress Rehearsal," describes how we got on.

One final thought. In these days of magic electronickery, I have been asked if GPS would not have provided a better, faster, more accurate solution. I am inclined to think not, as the vagaries of the rambling Trail would perhaps have demanded too many waypoints to be determined and fed in; but then, I have never used GPS so how can I say? Bearing in mind that my first thoughts on finding a mapping solution was that it was impossible, had GPS been generally available then, a way may have been found had it been necessary.

CHAPTER 22
DRESS REHEARSAL

As mentioned in Chapter 21, during preparation for the Oregon Trail flight it was decided that with so many unknowns it was essential to carry out a full-scale dummy run in the UK, to check the practicality of as many of our planned arrangements as possible.

We really had little choice as to when to attempt the full dress rehearsal flight. By the time all the necessary preparations were complete – the route, map, aircraft, intercom, cameras and mounting, and pre-flight air tests – there were only two weekends left before we planned to dismantle the aircraft for shipping. With the weather being what it is in these islands, the five days available over these two weekends (including Spring Bank Holiday Monday) could be reckoned to give a 50:50 chance of just one day having acceptable conditions. That meant standing by every day, ready to go on the first that was flyable.

There was an added complication. Paul Chapman, our member in the Gulf, had come home on leave especially to put in some Tiger flying time before the big flight. Since purchasing a third share in my Tiger, the weather in our part of Cambridgeshire had been so poor throughout the time that he was home that he had only been able to fly an hour or so. Prior to his last weekend, he had only managed some 90 minutes flying. Even so, he had agreed without reservation to John Elbourne (who was to crew the Tiger with me on the Oregon Trail flight) and I having the Tiger standing by for the first flyable day of that weekend.

When that first Saturday was forecast to be very windy, with showers and low cloud in the west, sufficient to preclude any attempt at the rehearsal flight, Paul was able to put in some more dual Tiger time with me. We carried out some additional camera trials, at the same time both of us gaining more experience with the Tiger in much stronger cross-winds than we had tried before. Even that was a two-edged sword! It would give us useful practice in marginal conditions but, if they became too bad and we found out the hard way the limits beyond which we could not operate, there was very little time left to put right the results of even a minor excursion into Little Gransden's notorious ditch!

All went well, however, despite a wind strength of over 20 mph, gusting to 30 mph, angled at some 35 degrees to the runway, i.e. a crosswind component of around 15 mph. Paul flew eight circuits and a little cross-country work while we shot off a full 36-exposure film on the fixed camera, to check the mounting and the remote shutter control.

During the week, I had attempted to contact the operators of the airfields we planned to use. Because we needed grass runways (unbraked Tigers with tailskids are unmanageable in crosswinds on hard runways), preferably nearly into the prevailing wind and with fuel available, these fields were mostly small private strips. So far I had drawn more blanks than successes. Hawarden, conveniently near the northern end of Offa's Dyke, was a British Aerospace company airfield and was not open over weekends. Badminton welcomed us, with a promise of fuel, but the owners of three private airstrips along the route could not be contacted.

On Saturday I tried again, this time having some success with the owner of a field near Oswestry, about three-quarters of the way along Offa's Dyke. He was not too optimistic about Sunday's forecast weather and neither was the Met. Office, with Force 8 gales off Shannon and Lundy! So Sunday was declared a day of rest and we would try again for Monday. Two down, three to go.

Sunday evening's forecast looked just acceptable for Monday. There would still be strong winds, but these down now to 17 mph in the south-west, though with a possibility of rain or fog in that area. So a quick phone around roused all the stand-by people – John for the Tiger, with Les Smith and Andy Watson in the Jackaroo. We were all to meet at Gransden at 08.00 for an 08.30 start, with both aircraft fuelled, oiled and ready to go. Hope forever springs eternal but by Sunday night I had not had time to get back to the Tiger to top up the last few gallons of fuel; neither had we been able to get Andy's chart marked up with the route we were to follow.

Les and Andy got over to Old Warden early (07.00 said Les) and in fact made it to Gransden by the appointed hour, circling overhead just as I arrived. But that 08.30 start really stood no chance. There seemed a hundred and one more things to do than we had allowed for, including a new 'baby' whose needs had to be carefully attended to – a very expensive Leica camera mounted up on the Tiger centre-section struts.

We were nearly an hour late in getting away. The wind seemed much stronger than forecast. When I had woken, the sun was shining and there was the lightest of breezes. But now a half-gale was drawing strength after covering the sun with a low layer of grey clouds. The tops of the trees were bending before it and the corrugated iron hangar doors were rattling noisily on their runners. What now passed as a windsock was streaming its tattered strands like some demented weather-vane, swinging wildly through some 60 degrees, first nearly in line with the main runway but more frequently with the shorter one that crossed it. Not just swinging but flapping vigorously up and down.

Normally I would have looked at this display of strength and gone back home. It should improve, if the VOLMET transmissions which Andy picked up on his radio were to be believed – I just hoped that whoever was responsible for the off-stage wind machine knew that!

Using the short runway at Gransden with an unbraked, tailskid aircraft is always a time-consuming exercise, as it is a little too narrow to be sure of turning round in its width unaided. Someone either has to be at the end of the runway, or a passenger get out of the aircraft, to hang onto a wingtip and heave the aircraft round so that it faces back down the runway. In this case Les drew the short straw, the Jackaroo being the second aircraft away and easier to get out of and back into, but it still entailed extra delay.

At 09.20 we were airborne in the Tiger and circled once to check that the Jackaroo got off as well, before setting off following the imaginary green line representing the Icknield Way etc., as marked on my roller map (our 'track'). There was, of course, nothing to see corresponding to that line (neither would there be when flying over some 80% of the Oregon Trail). All one could do was to check that other features on the map appeared as expected, to confirm that one was actually flying over that imaginary line!

The first moments of orientation in visual low-level (500 ft above ground level) contact flying are vital. Unless one concentrates on establishing exact position, and maintaining course, one can soon be miles off track. This time was no exception. John was having communication problems with the intercom – I could hear him easily but he could not hear me. During the first few minutes, in which we tried to resolve that, I lost the thread and we were quickly blown a mile east of track. We soon retrieved the situation but it left me wondering how much this was helped by my local knowledge of the area, and whether I would cope as well over unfamiliar ground. I was soon to find out!

The first stretch of Icknield Way proper came at Ickleford, but we saw no evidence of it even though we were exactly on track at that point. Nor did we see anything of the next section at about 25 miles out, where we crossed some open, featureless hills to the north-east of Luton. Very few roads were shown on the map at this point and such as there were crossed our track at right angles, thus giving no indication as to whether we had strayed to one side or the other.

Beneath us, numerous farm tracks showed chalky ruts through the grassland, criss-crossing from one small huddle of farm buildings to another, none of which related to anything on my map. These had an almost mesmeric effect as I tried and failed to identify them. Neither did an inquisitive Cessna 150 help, when it was spotted just above our level heading towards us, finally crossing in front. No doubt it was *en route* for Luton and probably thinking no one else would be daft enough to be out in such conditions.

When eventually a metalled road did appear I had lost count of time and was no longer certain which one it was – in any case, the way it wriggled about had no counterpart on my chart. This period of uncertainty can have lasted no more than two or three minutes but it seemed very much more. It meant we had no chance of identifying the

Icknield Way even if there had been anything to see. The lesson was striking home – keep better track of time.

Soon, a sharply defined knoll half a mile to our right was identifiable as a marked 601 ft spot height – we were on the wrong side of it so I thankfully turned towards it, picking up other matching roads as we neared it. A few miles further on and more familiar terrain came into view as we skirted the site of the old Eaton Bray Sportsdrome and shortly after that the village of Slapton where team member George Cull lived.

A disused railway appeared as expected and led us straight towards Aylesbury, which we skirted to the south, finally picking up the course of the Icknield Way again. But for all the evidence we saw of this, it might never have existed.

After some five miles of non-existent Icknield Way, we came to what I had expected would be the first real test of how well I would be able to follow an imaginary line. I had to admit to myself that I had not done very well up to that point over what should have been quite easy sections. At this point, the last mile of marked Icknield Way entered a MATZ (Military Air Traffic Zone) round RAF Benson (home of the Queen's Flight). Here, I planned to follow the circular edge of the zone over a stretch of ground where navigation features came thick and fast.

Now, in following ground features as a means of establishing and maintaining track, especially at very low altitude, there is only one aspect worse than having none to relate to, and that is in having too many! A bewildering array of minor roads, screened by trees so that their pattern could not easily be discerned, soon lost coherence. With my attention occasionally distracted by other air traffic from Booker airfield, I was drifting too far east and very quickly became disoriented with my map. I could not even make use of compass readings as the required track was on a continuous curve. I made a mental note not to try that again.

After some four minutes flying, initially south-easterly, swinging round to south-westerly, a large river, unmistakably the Thames, came into view. A small town to the west of a U-bend looked familiar and John soon identified it as Henley-on-Thames. We were obviously too far south-east, drifted there by the strong westerly wind, my compensating corrections for the latter being insufficient. My strip map was too narrow to reach out to Henley, and it needed another eight minutes before we got back on to it, regaining track at Goring, due west of Henley. It was obviously vital that both crew members had a copy of the standard air chart as without mine (left behind because of the difficulty in stowing it and unfolding it in company with the route sheets) I had been completely lost once off my strip map.

So far we had not done too well; if this was to be typical of how we would fare over the Oregon Trail, we might as well give up there and then!

But from here our south-westerly course became westerly and we were heading straight into wind. Dropping down from over the high ground east of Goring, we could easily pick out the first of the real landmarks we were to follow, the Ridgeway Footpath. Here it climbs the western slope of the Thames valley, up out of the town of Streatley, one of the world's most ancient paths, used by wandering tribes and traders from prehistoric time.

Although the sky was still fairly overcast and the wind was blowing and blustering as strongly as ever, we saw our first Ridgeway hikers at the top of the hill. As with many others later, they waved their greetings to us as fellow travellers along the Way. Here also was set a pattern that was repeated throughout most of the length of the footpaths we followed; wherever there was a road access to the path, there would be a little cluster of parked cars and a signpost or small white obelisk marking the way. These features were to help in identifying the course of the path whenever there was any doubt as to which of several alternatives to follow.

Generally, the path stood out starkly in chalky-white contrast where it crossed the grass-covered Downs, but as often as not it coincided with a farm road or track. As it was, the combination of these features and the clear marking of the route on my chart left us in little doubt as to the location of the Ridgeway Footpath, all the way from Goring until we left it where it joined the great Wansdyke earthworks near Devizes.

We had to make two detours to avoid the Restricted Area surrounding the Atomic Research Establishment at Harwell, and the Lyneham Special Rules Zone around the RAF Transport Command airfield, but these caused no problems and we could see the route of the path a mile or so to our right in both cases. We could also see clearly why it was called the Ridgeway: for most of its length it wandered along ridges or escarpment edges, always on the high ground.

Our first real thrill of discovery (even though it was of the obvious) came as we approached the site of Uffington Castle. At this point, the Ridgeway wandered close to the first of five White Horses cut in the turf on the sides of the hills along the Vale of the White Horse. As it turned out, it was the only one we saw, all the others being a little too far off track to be seen from our low altitude; this is the oldest, dating back 2,000 years. At first it was difficult to recognise the 375 ft-long chalk lines as a horse from the angle at which we approached it. We drew off a little way, it then being recognisably of the form of the older cave drawings of animals.

Even from the cockpit of our noisesome Tiger it was impossible not to feel an aura of antiquity about the place. Here, legend has it, is where St. George slew the dragon, the very essence of English mythology. Other antiquities, which could be very clearly seen and much better appreciated from our bird's eye view, were the defensive earthworks of various camps, hill forts or castles along the route.

Our stage length was originally calculated as being about 120 miles which, at a ground speed of 60 mph, would give us a flight time of around two hours. After nearly an hour of flying, at the point where we changed to a westerly heading, we had not covered as much ground as expected. John's rule-of-thumb check (literally – he had dropped and lost his scale somewhere in the depths of the cockpit) suggested we had covered seven inches on the map, i.e. 56 miles. Nevertheless, at the two-hour point we had still not reached the Wansdyke. It was patently obvious that the wind was much stronger than expected, our ground speed now being down to less than 45 mph! At least that aided route-finding!

Although previous flights to the West Country had taken me over this area in the past, they had mostly been at altitudes of 1,500 to 2,000 feet above ground or higher. On those occasions I would have been looking for White Horses only as confirmatory landmarks and never sufficiently aware of the location of the Wansdyke to look out for it. Now that I was proposing to fly along it for some eight miles I was most curious as to what we would actually see.

As we approached the edge of the hills along which the great ditch was dug, expectancy was running high. But neither John nor I were prepared for what now came into view. Time had rounded the contours, and softened with a cloak of green grass what must originally have been a starkly contrasting scar. Here and there, bushes and small wind-blown trees grew on the banks, but nothing could hide the extent of what, in those early days of our history, must have been a gigantic undertaking on a hitherto unknown scale.

We joined the Dyke, a great furrow with material removed from the trench piled each side to form high banks, where it crested a hill, the folds of which lay at right angles to a steep escarpment. It ran east-west and could be seen in either direction, loping off down from the crest of one ridge and up over the next and the next, always on the very edge of the escarpment, burrowing through younger coppices and woods and out over open ground.

As a defensive earthwork, it could not have been better sited, located as it was on the very edge of the Lambourn Downs, overlooking a steep, high drop to the wide floor of the valley hundreds of feet below. Any force attacking in strength from the valley would have been visible for miles whilst forming up. Having climbed the steep slope they could have had little reserve for fighting their way across the double banks and ditches of the dyke, although one theory has it that the dyke was a defence against attackers from the top of the hill! Though centuries younger and more primitive than the corresponding stone wall built by the Roman Emperor Hadrian along the Scottish Border, it is at least as impressive.

For ten exhilarating minutes we flew above and alongside the Dyke as it wandered westwards, as clearly definable now as the day it was dug. We were not the only ones determined to gaze in awe at the works of our ancestors; the path running along the Dyke was busy with groups of two, three, four or more walkers, defying the cold, blustery wind and the now threatening clouds forming our western horizon.

Reluctantly we turned south-west, past Devizes, to skirt the lower corner of the Lyneham Special Rules Zone, the broken line of walkers marking the path and the Dyke as they meandered off on our right towards Morgan's Hill.

Now we had another concern. The clouds to the west were hanging ominously low over the valleys of the Avon, their lower tendrils stretching down for the tops of the 800 ft-high hills to the north of Bath. Plans to fly over the disused RAF airfield of Charmy Down, to skirt westwards of the parachute dropping area of RAF Colerne, were hastily abandoned. It looked likely to be a race against the clouds to take a direct route to Badminton before they closed in our only remaining way through.

Ahead, Melksham was still clear but there was no sign of the 10-mile-distant City of Bath, lurking behind its encircling hills and canopy of mist and low cloud. Thankfully we turned north-west towards Colerne – no need to worry about parachutists in this wind. The question now was, would Colerne still be clear? Just in case it was not I asked John to look out for an alternate that we could escape into if conditions forced us back. Fortunately, in an emergency, we could have sought haven at the gliding field at Keevil (another disused wartime aerodrome), as I had done once before under similar conditions.

Still skirting Lyneham's Zone we picked up the River Avon, with the railway line emerging from its two-mile tunnel under the Mendips pinpointing our position. Peering out into the buffeting slipstream on the right I could not at first understand why I was getting 'pins and needles' on my forehead, until it dawned on me that it was a light drizzle, confirmed by the tiny rivulets running down the windscreen. This was it then – any moment now and those clouds might reach down to us. Time to turn back for Keevil while the way was still open and before we got trapped in the valley? At which point the airfield and hangars of Colerne stood out starkly on the western rim, the black runways glistening dully in the rain.

If necessary then, we could go in there and wait for the clouds to blow through. So was this as far as we were going to get? Now the valley which would lead us to Badminton turned north and after cautiously following it round, anxious not to lose the newly-acquired Colerne, we saw the murk open up and the way through was clear, the clouds lifting and the visibility brighter and more extensive ahead.

With similarly lightened hearts we sought and soon spotted the M4 motorway, the road leading to Badminton crossing it at the crown of a long northward curve. There it was, dead on the nose, followed by the Great House of Badminton and its beautiful grounds. A bright shaft of sunlight reached down and pointed to the airfield, lighting up the Dayglo windsock to show the wind exactly aligned with the runway.

No need to circle, there was nothing else in the circuit and we were nicely positioned off the end of the runway. Closing the throttle I expected to have to slip off a little height, but the wind shortened the glide so much that we almost needed power to get in, and the aircraft would probably have stopped within 100 ft of the threshold. So we finished our flight with a long, tail-high taxy the whole length of the grass runway. By the time we had wiggled our way past two parked aircraft and politely declined a marshaller's invitation to turn in our own length (impossible without wheel brakes or someone hanging onto a wingtip), the sun was blazing fiercely down from an almost cloudless, brilliantly blue sky. Unbelievable!

When we switched off we had clocked 2 hrs 35 minutes, an average ground speed of only 46 mph. Although we had gone off course round the Benson MATZ we were never more than two miles off and could have covered only a little more distance than planned, indicating a wind speed of nearer 30 mph than the expected 17!

The Jackaroo soon joined us in the parking area and in no time at all a little knot of watchers had materialised from nowhere. After the usual exchange of views and experiences about the flight, it was back to work. Wipe off the streaks of warm engine oil reaching blackly down the fuselage (where does it all come from?); check the oil level, top up the petrol and oil tanks and change the film in the camera.

Here we received a rude shock – the lens of the fixed camera looked like a piece of frosted glass, the inside being thickly coated with condensation. Peering through the viewfinder confirmed the worst; if that had happened before flying under the low wet clouds we would have little to show for our filming efforts. Hopefully the warmth of the sun would dry it out before we were ready to leave, so we turned the Tiger to face directly into the sun.

Parched throats could wait no longer, so off to the little cafeteria-cum-Clubroom for coffee and sandwiches after washing from our hands the surplus black oil transferred from the aircraft. More time was consumed in settling the bill for fuel and landing fees; like, they could not use my credit card and had we got enough cash between us to settle not only this bill but the next two as well? Andy finally resolved all by paying for the lot on one cheque, which we would sort out later.

Before we could leave we needed to phone Oswestry, to check that there would be someone there, and to get an observation on their weather. My first attempt produced no more than an endless ringing tone. At least there was an alternative number given in the Airfield Directory. That produced a charming lady's voice telling me that the owner had sold up to her and she knew not of his whereabouts.

Consternation! I had spoken to the owner earlier in the weekend and he was quite adamant about wanting us to phone our ETA (Estimated Time of Arrival) before we left. In any case I needed an 'actual' weather report from him of local visibility, and wind strength and direction relative to the single grass runway. A second call brought no better response than the first.

Plan B was brought into play, to phone one of the alternates. One of these was an old favourite, Long Mountain, Welshpool, offering two grass runways and emergency fuel. Further delays ensued after the first call was answered by the farmer's wife, who said her husband was out and that she knew nothing of the airfield state. She gave us another number to try.

All our 10p coins had now gone but we were saved by the airfield manager, who had obviously met this situation before and was better prepared than us. With a handful of 10p pieces we finally made contact with a man who knew about these things. "What's that? You're coming in a Tiger Moth? Oh! marvellous." He told us that the wind was very strong and gusty but straight down the long runway. Visibility was perfect with not a cloud in the sky and there would be all the petrol we would need! Fantastic! The hoped-for drying of the condensation on the camera lens had not happened, though it had reduced to a broad ring rather than a solid disc. No matter, we would still get further experience in operating the camera even if the resulting slides were imperfect.

By now we had been on the ground for two hours, though it had seemed much less. This in fact is one of life's greatest mysteries – why time flies so fast in such circumstances, no matter how frugal one seems to have been in spending it. Time to climb aboard and get going again. Filton (Bristol) Air Traffic Control was seemingly not operating today so we could have gone straight to the Severn Bridge instead of round their zone, but it seemed prudent to stick with the original plan.

Both engines started easily and, exchanging farewell waves with the onlookers, we moved out onto the runway, wings rocking with the wind, for the long taxy to the far end. The wind was as strong and blustery as ever, making turning in the runway width without a man at the wingtip a questionable business, more so in the Tiger with its narrow track undercarriage. Just at the point where I wanted to turn, a small marker on a stout post was positioned at each side of the runway, making it imperative not to swing wide. In my anxiety to turn tightly I went too sharply and the wind forced the outer lower wingtip to brush through the grass as we turned – a close thing!

As we climbed away we could see just how perfect the visibility had now become. At 500 ft above the 500 ft hills, we could see the 40 miles-distant, 2,700 ft-high Black Mountains as clear and sharp as if they had been only 10 miles away; beyond and beyond ranked range after range of hills into the distance – it would not have surprised me to know that the 130 miles-distant Mount Snowdon had been one of the blue-grey bumps on the horizon. But there was no time for such conjecture, with work to be done. Right now it was essential to get a positive fix before we got too far from known features. At least the towers of the Severn Bridge stood out clearly even though 14 miles away.

John had been having trouble in hearing me clearly on the intercom on and off throughout the first leg. We found that when turning my head to the right, my throat microphone picked up no sound when I spoke. So I had to remember to look ahead or to the left when talking to him. But that in itself was not the whole answer, though occasionally he could hear me very clearly. Going up and down in tone and volume, we had eventually settled on a low pitch and loud but not shouting. But here we were at the start and already John was not receiving me, despite my looking to the left and speaking out of my boots. I had learnt the lesson from the first leg and concentrated on where we were on my chart rather than whether John could make sense of what I was saying.

It still took too long to settle down but by the time the first railway line came into view, six miles west of Badminton, we were comfortably on track. Ahead the Bridge was reassuringly close, but from our level the mud flats of the Severn looked intolerably wide, and I remembered the tragic loss of the prototype Bristol Britannia airliner, which made a successful wheels-up landing on these flats and then could not be dragged clear before becoming engulfed by the incoming tide. No chance then for a little Moth if the engine should die on us when out of gliding distance of the shore!

Many of man's greatest engineering achievements are virtual works of art, and never was this more true than when applied to the Severn Bridge. It is a work of art and a thing of beauty, and never more so than when viewed from 500 ft with the sun shining brightly along its length, a picture of form and light and shade. As we swung out over the water I glanced down to see the wind whipping up the surface into great rolling white horses – it was difficult to relate the size of the waves with the height at which we were flying, remembering we were in a sheltered estuary. The wind turbulence kept the Tiger constantly busy but the bridge looked as steady as a rock, as if no force of nature could possibly have an effect upon it.

Up behind us the Jackaroo had closed in nearly to our level and I guessed that Les would be busy shooting off some shots of the Tiger framed by the bridge – it would have made an entrancing picture with

239

the sun reflecting off the polished wings. Alas, he had run out of film at that point!

Back to sterner stuff. Somewhere along the Sedbury cliffs above the far shore, we should see the first signs of Offa's Dyke. The guide book had said that it ran right up to the cliff edge. Well, I could see the 100 ft-high cliffs but no earthworks resembling anything such as we had seen along the Wansdyke.

Circling back we searched carefully along the edge again, this time also looking further inland to try and spot anything making a broken straight line. There was a hedgerow at the western end of the cliff and sure enough this lined up with an unusual formation in a small housing estate, the line pointing to a small sewage plant. That was it then, exactly as mentioned in the guide book, the Dyke now so overgrown with bushes and trees as to look at first glance like an ordinary hedgerow. Circling out over the estuary again, we flew in along the line of the hedge and could now see the massive ditch and banks hiding under the bushes.

Turning to skirt north of Buttington Tump and Pennsylvania Village on the Beachley Peninsula (between the Rivers Wye and Severn) we rejoined the route of the footpath above Tutshill, with Chepstow and its magnificent Castle and bridge over the Wye on our left. Again, although the map shows here the next section of Offa's Dyke, clear sighting of it from above was thwarted by the trees which covered it.

Besides, over the next several miles, the very feature which adds so much grandeur to the scene, the steep cliff side to the gorge, was, in combination with the strong, gusty, westerly wind, giving me plenty to think about. The turbulent wind off the cliffs varied with the snake-like shape of the gorge. It would toss us on an updraught then, dropping away with the descending ground, catch now one wing then the other, so that the Tiger was like a living thing, possessed of demons, fighting and bucking the air currents.

The Dyke obstinately lurked under the trees all along the edges of Dennel Hill, Worgan's Wood, Shorn Cliff, the Devil's Pulpit (how aptly named this day) and Caswell Wood. But we picked it out clearly enough as it descended Madgett Hill, opposite Tintern Abbey, my main regret being that I forgot to take a good look at the latter, so much concentration did all the other factors demand.

And so we proceeded along the breathtaking beauty of the lower Wye valley, the Dyke leading us to Lower Redbrook, where suddenly it was no more. Ahead, the gorge opened out into a wide forked valley, at the bottom of which sprawled Monmouth. The last hilltop before the town was surmounted by the curious Naval Temple at Kymin, where visitors thronged the well-kept grounds. This was virtually our last readily identifiable landmark for some 10 miles or so, when our correct course would be confirmed by the presence of White Castle.

TOP: One good turn deserves another. When Mark Jefferies required a crest of a horseman killing a snake painted each side of the fuselage of his newly-restored Yak C-11, I was able to help. In return Mark offered me an eagerly accepted flight into Duxford on one of the Display Days, and use of his heated workshop for spraying the Taylorcraft cowlings in mid-winter. Photo: The author.

BOTTOM: Mark formating on 'PAL in 1984. In return for a painting of the Yak C-11, I gained an exhilarating hour's dual with Mark in sister Jungmann G-BIRI. Photo: The author.

TOP: The unfortunate Turbulent G-ARTF ("The Artful Dodger"), with Geoff Thompson at Gransden, which I reduced to a black smudge in an adjacent field when the engine seized just after take-off. Photo: The author.

MIDDLE: August 1981; G-AOIR sheltered from the wind by George's Minivan in a field that had once been RAF Bolt Head, near Salcombe. Photo: The author.

BOTTOM: The end of the line: my 1941 model Taylorcraft BC-12D G-BRPX after a 2½-year 'basket case' rebuild – the aircraft had sat mouldering in a hangar for 21 years, losing various items. A real pussycat to fly. Photo: The author.

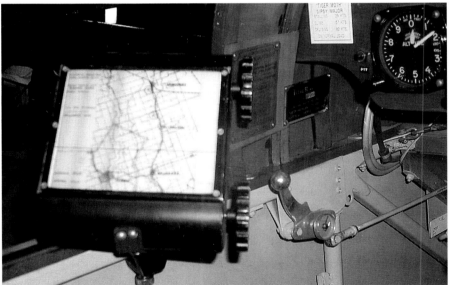

TOP: G-APAL, with Den Willett in the front seat, formating on Mike Vaisey's Gipsy Moth over Melbourne, Herts, during the DH Moth Club's 50th Anniversary re-enactment of the start of the MacRobertson London-to-Melbourne (Australia) Air Race in October 1984. Photo: Mike Vaisey.

BOTTOM: The roller map case mounted on the upper left side longeron of a Tiger Moth and protruding into the slipstream. The two knobs at the side are for positioning the map under the fixed cursor line. Photo: The author.

TOP: Southern Martlet G-AAYX standing proudly on its new legs in the Shuttleworth Collection's workshop at Old Warden. Andy Presland machined all the components and built the u/c from scratch.
Photo: The author.
BOTTOM: 'AYX as it was in 1932 during a rebuild in the workshops of Reading Aero Club.
Photo: By courtesy of the Shuttleworth Collection.

We kept our height to take us clear over Monmouth, the feature most catching my eye being the bridge carrying the now dismantled railway over the Wye, the sweeping course of the railway bed standing out sharp and clear. It was difficult to pick out the footpath route once it had left King's Wood, and in fact I gave up trying for several miles. Once disoriented, nothing seemed to fit. Now steering by compass, we passed over beautiful wooded valleys and farm meadows with not a single distinguishing feature until Llantilio-Crossenny came into view.

At least we would soon be back on track, the River Trothy forming an easily recognisable landmark. Above the hamlet, a moated, medieval castle site, Hen Cwrt, was clearly discernible as we swung first westward, then north along the Trothy valley. The substantial ruins of the 12th century White Castle stood out starkly, the neatly-mown lawns dotted with visitors. Now the ground was rising to over 800 ft before dropping into the broad valley of the Afon Honndu. Here we had another clear fix where the A45 road and the railway converge at Pandy.

Up to this point, we had seen very few people on the footpath to confirm route-keeping, but as we located the path from Pandy the situation changed. From here the ground rose steeply from 350 ft at the valley bottom and we had to climb hard as ahead loomed the bulk of the Black Mountains. The path was more readily visible now and, as on the Ridgeway, at convenient access points, little clusters of parked cars showed where the walkers had started out.

In the lowland valleys, the contours had been soft and subdued, with small farms and meadows draped over the folds. But now there was an angry ridge forming up ahead. Past Pentwyn and its Iron Age fort, at the head of a 1,000 ft-high spine rising steeply from Pandy, and suddenly, the ground below and ahead was climbing faster than we were. On each side of the ridge, the valley bottoms were dropping further below. My interest at the steepness of the hillside was giving way to concern that I might yet have to swing away, to avoid an unpremeditated landing on its narrowing back.

Still it went up. Now I was at full throttle, climbing as steeply as I dared, yet having to keep the air speed high enough to cope with the buffeting from the wind curling down over the ridge. Ideally I should have been on the windward side of the ridge, riding the up-currents, but from the start I had been caught wrong-footed and inexperienced in this sort of flying. Now the Tiger could not climb fast enough to gain sufficient height to swing safely through the turbulent downdraughts to the other side.

The Jackaroo, initially some 500 ft above and behind, rode serenely upward, clear of the swirling currents over the ridge, now climbing higher and faster than the trapped Tiger. I refused to turn back and be outdone by this aggressive stretch of mountain and its windy alley, and continued to do battle. The struggle continued over 1,750 ft-high Hatterrall Hill, 2,000 ft Loxidge Tump, past the 2,300 ft summit until the Tiger shook itself clear, breathless but triumphant. We swung out over Pen-y-Beacon, with its breathtaking scenery, towards Hay-on-Wye, nestling in the deep-set valley, some four miles ahead.

The view was impressive across the complex pattern of ridges and valleys and broad hilltops – small wonder that so many people put on their hiking boots and toiled up and up the long steep gradient. For once the reward would have been sufficient for even me to try it sometime. The well-trod path was easy to see, recognition reinforced not only by occasional walkers, but also by small white markers, perhaps a mile or less apart. What I did lose out on, in my battle with the wind, was that I forgot to look out for the remains of Llanthony Priory, at the bottom of the valley on the other side of the ridge. But we were, in any case, probably too low to see over the ridge into the valley.

At Pen-y-Beacon, the frenzied tossing of the wind had abated somewhat, the narrow, steep ridge broadening out to form a plateau. Here the wind, though still very strong, seemed almost to pause for breath while it decided from which direction to attack next. I expected to run into severe downdraughts as we headed out over the escarpment, running like a steep cliff at right angles to the ridge we had just flown along, but our passage was no more turbulent than elsewhere.

Now we dropped down to the valley below, past the awe-inspiring, craggy cliffs of the Beacon and of Wenallt, turning over the A438 just south of Hay-on-Wye. We were reminded it was a Bank Holiday Monday by the long queue of stationary road traffic, tailing back over the old bridge, where the B4351 joined the main road.

The path followed the River Wye through the pleasant, broad green valley for several miles, past the old Roman Camp on the west bank, before turning up the tree-lined Bettws Dingle to follow the Cabalva Brook for half a mile.

There was a profusion of tracks over the open moorland but one pointed unerringly past the site of the ancient Pen-twyn Camp and from there past another camp site on top of the 1,200 ft-high Little Mountain. But from there I lost the track and could not find the little hamlet of Newchurch, turning up the wrong valley past the scatter of houses at Michaelchurch instead. Thus we missed also Gladestry and Hergest Ridge, approaching Kington from the south-west instead of the west and becoming totally confused into the bargain.

We had great difficulty in positively identifying Kington, as it could equally well have been Presteigne, four miles north. I was beginning to appreciate the difficulties of following a nebulous green line on my map as compared with normal visual navigation from the air. After circling twice round the town we picked out the course of the old disused railway, which finally clinched its identity, and with relief set out to locate the first sign of Offa's Dyke since leaving Monmouth.

Heading north, we climbed up past Bradnor Hill on our left, picking out what we took to be a tree-lined section of the Dyke, though this is not marked as such on the OS (Ordnance Survey) maps. On our right, a better-marked section ran up and over Rushock Hill and Herrock Hill, before plunging 700 ft down the steep side of the latter and crossing the flat bottom of the Vale of Radnor. We lost any signs of the Dyke beyond Hindwell Brook crossing, but were impressed by the size of the ancient Camp on top of Burfa Bank.

The Dyke was visible again halfway down the opposite side of Burfa and now stood out quite clearly as it marched across the open ground to Evenjobb Hill and beyond. Along this stretch we came across more groups of walkers than we had seen for some time, proving perhaps that the known sections of the Dyke are more popular than the footpath named after it.

So the Dyke unrolled before us, now sharp and well-defined, then visible only because adjacent sections pointed to where it must lie, such as where it crossed the River Lugg valley. Furrow Hill, Hawthorn Hill, Cwm-Whitton Hill and Ffridd, across all of these we navigated by following the clear course of the Dyke. The town of Knighton came up unexpectedly as I realised, with a feeling of guilt, that I had been so preoccupied with what was revealed below that I had not been winding on my roller chart.

Knighton lay in a triangle, bounded on two sides by the Rivers Teme and Wilcome Brook, and on the third by Offa's Dyke, with the 1,100 ft-high Ffridd, Garth Hill and Panpuncton Hill towering steeply above it. Westward beyond Panpuncton, the Teme Valley opened out into a broad, flat-bottomed vale with the river meandering aimlessly through it. Three miles up the valley lay one of the off-Dyke landmarks I had been waiting for, the long railway viaduct at Cnwclas, which I spotted as we crossed Panpuncton Hill. That sight compensated for the fact that there was no sign of the Dyke climbing the 1-in-4 slope of Panpuncton, though north-ward from the top of the hill the winding line could be spied for miles ahead.

From here, for the next 25 miles, we were following the best preserved section of the Dyke and also the highest, where it furrowed the crest of the 1,400 ft-high Llanfair Hill. It was also noticeable along this stretch how much this Dyke differed from the Wansdyke in its role. While the latter was a natural and formidable defence line, at least in long stretches, Offa's Dyke can have formed little more than a token on many stretches of low-lying or rolling, hilly countryside. It must have been an impossible task to man it constantly and sufficiently to always be able to repel invaders, and it was more probably intended to act only as a frontier marker between the more defensible camps and hill forts.

Although the route of the Dyke was easy to follow, it was not so obvious where exactly we had got to, unless I religiously checked off features such as roads and villages as they appeared. So fascinating was the Dyke itself that again I found myself neglecting to wind on my map. Past Llanfair we followed the Dyke over Graig Hill, looking for the prominent right-angled turn at the base of Hergan. From here the westward-facing defence works changed to an eastward slope before reverting to form over Edenhope Hill. Still the Dyke marched northward, now in fine form with a deep narrow ditch and high banks over undulating parkland.

We and the Dyke skirted east of the old fortified town of Montgomery, the Dyke here being little more than a shallow depression but still easily discernible. Ahead now we could see the old town of Welshpool with Long Mountain, on top of which and to the east, lay our destination airfield. On we went, past the prominent Castle Mound at Nant-cribeau, following the line of the A490 before sweeping off to the northeast where the road curved north-west.

Now we had one eye on the Dyke and one on the rising bulk of Long Mountain on our right. We swung up and over The Stubb, picking out Offa's Pool and beyond it the unusual square pattern of Moel-y-Mab. Reluctantly, we turned our back on the Dyke and started a search for the cunningly concealed airstrip.

It was not that the airfield was intended to be concealed. But even when in regular use by the Montgomeryshire Ultra Light Flying Club (MULFC), with frequently-mown grass runways, THE OAKS prominently mown out of the long grass at the side of the strip, and the corrugated steel covering of the blister hangar shining newly in the sun, I had sailed straight over the top of it on my second visit, without spotting it. Now with two-week-old grass on the runway, the name long since swallowed by the hay grass, and the hangar dulled with age, it might just as well have been deliberately camouflaged!

Now I needed to recall the local geography and the position of the strip relative to the roads in order to locate it. No wonder Andy in the watchful Jackaroo failed to pick it out until I had circled and settled into the approach.

It was probably some four years or more since I had last visited Long Mountain. But it still looked much the same and, though the friendly little Club had closed, the welcome by the half-dozen or so people there was as unrestrained as ever. There were enthusiastic hands to pull on our wingtips, as they walked us up the last few yards of the 1-in-10 gradient in which the runway ended, and to swing us into position by a visiting Jodel. First the Tiger, and very shortly after, the Jackaroo, were parked nose into wind, their crews wiping off the streaks of oil trailing back from the engine cowlings and exchanging stories about the flight.

The old Clubhouse, still proudly claiming to be MULFC, was opened up for tea or coffee and somewhere to sit out of the wind. There followed the usual discussions about where we had been, what the conditions were like and where we were going. Which led me to wonder whether it was worth going on up to the end of the Dyke, or to head back for home. After all, having flown for 4½ hours, we would have been up for 6 hours at least by the time we got back. By now, we had proved the technique of using the roller chart for following visible or invisible tracks: we had already learnt a lot about our team procedures; had no properly working still cameras and no video cameras on the Tiger; and leaving that last stretch unflown would offer incentive to try again, when we had video equipment available.

Andy was a little disappointed that we failed to go on, but we decided to return home from there. Our excited chatter had in any case sped us through an hour or more, and the thought of high-tailing it back home, with the still strong wind behind us, was suddenly very attractive. So, tanked-up and refreshed, we took off and headed south-east instead of north, and prepared to find and follow the course of a series of old railways, the tracks of which had long since been lifted. Compared with what we had just done up to then, the return was a pleasant doddle.

Back home, the lessons learned had to be absorbed and acted upon. At least I now knew that I could stand up to 6 hours concentrated navigating and flying in the Tiger Moth. This aspect had been causing me not a little concern when I realised that I had never done anything quite like that before. Crewing in a Dawn-to-Dusk competition flight in a Tiger some 19 years earlier was not really comparable – although we had flown for over 9 hours in a day on that occasion, the navigation was straight-forward, was shared between two of us, and bore no comparison with what we had just been doing.

Something would have to be done about the intercom in the Tiger and to improve communication between the two aircraft. Leitz would have to be approached for their views on condensation on the camera lens. We still had to look at the slides we had taken, even though they would probably have been ruined by the condensation, which had persisted to the end. There should be much to learn from these slides as to whether the remote control was now as reliable as it had appeared, and whether we had got the angle of the camera set up correctly.

Finally, flying over the ridges and slopes of the Black Mountains in such strong winds had taught me a valuable lesson. I resolved to never again get myself as badly positioned as I had that day now that I knew what to look out for, and it was good to know that the Tiger could cope with such conditions, even though they were probably nothing like as bad as the worst we might encounter in the States. All in all, Whit Monday 26th May had not been a bad day's work and definitely more encouraging than not.

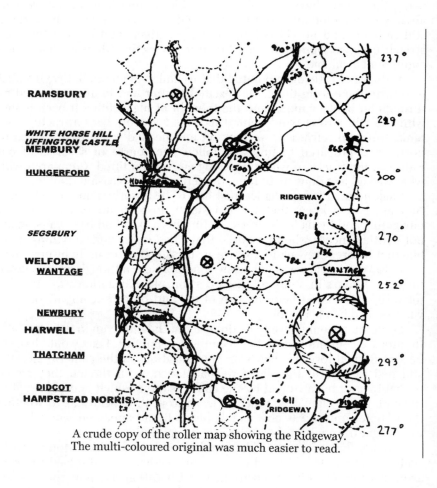

A crude copy of the roller map showing the Ridgeway.
The multi-coloured original was much easier to read.

CHAPTER 23
A SUDDEN SILENCE

It was a very nice little Turbulent. Perhaps quite the nicest I have come across. Airframe-wise it was difficult to fault; no slop in the controls, all surfaces neat and true, no obvious excess weight, fabric taught and clean with the minimum dope so that it didn't betray its years. Engine-wise it was a different matter.

When my friend had bought it some 15 years earlier it was fitted with a well-behaved, converted, 1200 VW engine, quite adequate to propel its trim female owner comfortably about the skies. When I first flew it I also felt quite happy about the power, but then (as now) I weighed in at less than 11 stones whereas John, its new owner, was a little more than that. Despite its comparatively low power, it handled quite superbly, the controls providing a feeling of perfect balance, with a top speed approaching 100 mph and a stalling speed a little over 40. But John felt it needed more urge and eventually fitted a 45 hp Stamo from a Tipsy Nipper, which admittedly gave it just that. This entailed making mods to the cowlings and controls (which added to the weight), and a continuing spate of carb. and magneto changes and adjustments, and it was a long time before I flew it again.

I had been suffering Jackaroo and Tiger withdrawal symptoms, and my Taylorcraft post-rebuild first flight date was not yet in sight. John had kindly offered to let me keep my hours up in his Turbulent, which he had kept for local fun flying as distinct from more serious family flying offered by his Robin. I accepted his offer with alacrity, remembering just how enjoyable it had been to fly.

The replacement engine and installation was a little heavier and personally I thought that although it now displayed an impressive turn of speed it had lost just a little of that near perfection of handling, and the stalling speed was now over 45 mph. What was more, one had to be very careful about braking – when taxying with a tail wind, even braking on just one wheel for turning would, despite the stick being held hard back, too readily bring the tail up as I later found out.

My first flight in the new configuration passed very pleasantly, but on almost every subsequent occasion there was some sort of glitch – always related to the power plant. The modified throttle control had a habit of slackening at the lever after a number of hours of running – nothing serious but when slack it needed adjusting before flying, and it seemed to save up its slackening for when I was about to fly. Correction entailed removing the entire throttle lever assembly as it was impossible to adjust it *in situ*, which always set one back an hour or so (the size of the cockpit prevented any work being done whilst sitting in it, so it was a case of removing any bulky items like the seat etc., and working head down inside, kneeling on the wing root or standing behind it – oh! my aching back!).

Another series of work details occurred when the cylinder holding-down bolts (on cylinder No. 3) worked loose, which they had a habit of doing after some hours of running. Tightening and locking the bolts was a labour-intensive operation requiring the removal of quite a number of intervening parts! Eventually John had to have thread inserts fitted, which solved the problem for a while, but these soon gave up and something more positive had to be done.

The answer was to have the engine completely overhauled and entailed locating a number of difficult-to-find replacement major items e.g. a new crankshaft, which as can be imagined involved a considerable amount of time. But eventually the engine was returned by the overhaul organisation, who specialized in Porsche racing car engines (the Stamo is based on the Porsche engine). With that background I had a clear vision of the engine, plugs out, running in on the bench for the requisite number of hours. It looked great and John, with a little hands-on help from me, soon had it back in the airframe and running. I wasn't there when John first flew it but when next I saw him he was 'over the moon' with it.

The Stamo had always been a difficult starter and when overhauled it was no better, which probably placed the problem squarely in the court of either the carb. or the single-drive dual magneto. So I nearly gave up on the occasion of my first intended flight with the overhauled engine. I had been swinging for around half an hour, with not a pop from a single cylinder, and was somewhere near a state of exhaustion when suddenly it burst into life, and into my dimmed senses came the realisation it was running somewhat faster than usual! I ran frantically round the wing with the slowly rising tail foremost in my sights. I lunged at the fuselage at the nearest point, just aft of the cockpit, and draped myself across it, halting the forward-tipping movement.

But now I was in an insoluble predicament – the throttle lever was just out of reach, a tantalizing inch beyond my outstretched fingers. The aircraft was balanced on its main wheels with the tail off the ground and me literally over a barrel and battered by the slipstream. Before I had worked out how to slide my weight towards the tail (something on my jacket was snagging on the rear of the cockpit) I realised that the now warmer engine was running faster and the tail slowly but inexorably lifting again; there was nothing for it but to make a grab for the throttle. This time I got it first go and with the throttle closed everything returned to normality, the tail took its usual position on the deck and the engine obediently ticked over like a sewing machine. Had I caught it in time? There was no evidence from the spinning propeller that there was anything amiss. Although reluctant to switch off, and face another period of prolonged swinging if there was nothing wrong, I could not believe that the tips had not contacted the ground.

It took another couple of months to get a new prop made; the old one had not only chewed up the outer half inch of each tip (which was probably repairable) but had also cracked one blade down to the hub (which was definitely not). Apart from the cost of the new prop (there was never any question of who should pay for that!) the new prop hub was a ½ inch thicker which meant new prop bolts, and a 30-minute job became one of several days. There was no provision on the hub for locking the bolts which meant that like the old ones, the heads of the six new ones had to be drilled so that they could be wire-locked – have you ever tried that? But it was eventually fitted, and John pronounced himself happy with the new prop in the air, and I was clear to have another go, this time with a very large weight tied to the tailskid before starting the engine!

By now I was in danger of running out of time in which to complete my requisite annual hours, so I planned to fly in the morning and afternoon. With John's help I got the engine started in the morning with no more than the usual exertions (John's stock plan for starting from cold was to 'suck in' 36 turns before switching on!). There was a fairly strong and gusty crosswind on the main 30/12 runway so I used the 1,600 ft 21. All went well and the engine performed just as John had said it would – smooth and responsive.

Came the afternoon, and the engine totally refused to start. I know some engines don't like starting when warm but this was ridiculous. Here it was, late February and the engine was to all intents and purposes as cold as I was. After nearly an hour of swinging, on and off, I had more than somewhat warmed up and decided to give it a miss. It was now obvious this engine just wasn't very kindly disposed to me and this was equally not a good day to do any more flying. I was just preparing to return it to the hangar when John popped in and insisted on having another go.

Of course, the wretched device started almost straight away for John (its a bit like one-arm banditing – just once more and you'll hit the jackpot; if you don't fall for that line someone else always comes up and gets the payout).

So, off I went for another happy hour, practising circuits and bumps. I was reminded that on closing the throttle for a glide approach, the Turbulent tended to come down like a brick, a feature common to many small-wing ultra- or micro-lights. This together with the strong wind gave very little penetration once the engine was throttled back, and on the first couple of approaches I needed to get the nose well down to keep flying speed, with a late burst of power to clear the hedge on the approach. It all quickly came back and after a few more circuits I found I could judge a power-off approach to put it 'on the button' without having to open up.

The fifth circuit started off well enough. About halfway down the runway the aircraft lifted off, but almost immediately I noticed a short period of vibration, so faint I could almost have imagined it. By now it was too late to abort; 21 ends in a high hedge, a clump of tall trees and a spider's web of power lines, so I reduced power by about 100 revs as the vibration ceased, and continued climbing at about 55 kt, anxious to gain height as quickly as possible. A quick glance at the oil gauges showed both normal. Whilst still mulling over what might have caused the vibration (could have been a clump of mud on a spinning wheel?) and what to look for when I got back on the ground, there was, unbelievably, a sudden, shattering, spine-chilling silence.

Unbelievable, almost, because there had been no real prior warning apart from the brief vibration some 5-10 seconds before, no loss of power, no popping and banging; one moment the engine was at full bore, the next stopped. As if to emphasize the point there was a stationary prop blade pointing mutely to the sky. In these circumstances one is allowed a moment of shock, but no more than a moment!

I don't remember any immediate thought of action; what followed was on automatic, as if I had made no mental contribution to the action my right hand took in pushing the stick well forward. The nose dropped quickly to reveal that we were at about 70 ft up and heading towards a long, low farm building stretching from centre of vision to the right and a farmhouse to the left. Both had tall trees on either side and in front of them was a road bordered by a high hedge on the near side and power cables on the far side. From the experience of the previous circuits there was not enough speed and height to get over the buildings and yet too much to get down in front of the hedge.

I noticed that the port wing was a little low and, without pausing to see if it was dropping further, instinctively, rightly or wrongly, ruddered into it; the thought also then was that I had to turn away from the insurmountable heap of trouble that lay dead ahead, and I was too busy assessing the new situation on my left to turn my head to look to the right and down to remind myself what lay on that side. The main priority was to maintain flying speed and not enter a spin, so I dropped the nose still further into a steepish diving turn. The road that crossed our path initially, turned through a 90 deg bend some 150 yards to the left, so that now I was facing it and the high hedge once more. Right where I might have attempted to put down in the paddock in front of it, another power line crossed my path, so I continued turning.

At about 180 deg into the turn I was facing the runway I had just left with, in between it and me, the hedge, trees and power-lines I had just cleared on take-off. But to the left was an invitingly large, open field, the only obstacle being yet another high hedge, topped by yet another set of 11.5 kVA power-lines. A quick glance at the A.S.I. showed I had just enough speed in hand to try flattening the dive sufficiently to pass over the cables. Straightening out as the field appeared under the nose I held my breath – with an ounce of luck we might just clear the lines. But I hadn't allowed enough for that brick-like glide angle (compounded by the drag of the stationary airscrew blades and the loss of the trickle of power normally provided by the tickover revs) and, teetering on the brink of a stall, the bottom of the lower prop blade clipped the top cable.

That broke off the blade close to the hub and snapped the cable, one end of which (unknown to me at that point) wrapped itself round the prop shaft. This roughly halved the airspeed and slewed and tipped the aircraft so that from a height of about 20 feet it dropped onto the right wingtip with considerably reduced forward momentum. The wing broke off at the root, in so doing absorbing most of the remaining energy, with the result that with hardly a bump the fuselage slid along the ground on its right side for about 6 feet and stopped. It took very few seconds to release the harness and wriggle out of the cockpit to put some yards between myself and the wreck.

It was not really much of a wreck. True the starboard wing had snapped off but the rest of the airframe looked otherwise virtually undamaged except for the prop. Looking back up at the cables, the lower two were intact, which suggested that we had caught no more than the lower tip of the prop otherwise the undercarriage would have taken them as well; just a couple of inches more height and I would have been standing by a complete aeroplane! On the other hand if the prop had stopped other than vertically it is probable that the wheels would have caught the top cable and the machine would have somersaulted with a vastly different end result! Although I still had on my helmet, my goggles and spectacles had fallen off and when I realised that there was no immediate danger of fire I went back and retrieved everything loose from the cockpit including the goggles, though there was no sign of my glasses anywhere. Walking round to the front I could smell petrol and then noticed the cable wrapped round the prop-shaft.

I had a feeling of having been here before (see Chapter 8, "Flash, Bang, Wallop") and slowly followed the cable as it lay in the grass. Just a few yards on there was a puff of smoke where the restored power (on breaking the line, the overload protectors would have tripped and reset after a short delay) was arcing to earth and, as I watched, it moved steadily towards the aircraft like a burning fuse. Rushing back to the tail I tried to pull it clear of the cable but the latter was too tightly wrapped round the shaft, and a minute or so later the arcing reached the petrol. Within 10 minutes the resulting fire had entirely consumed the airframe;

all that the firemen, who had by now arrived on the scene, could do was to toss the starboard wing on the blaze before I could stop them.

The time that elapsed between the engine seizure and arriving back on the ground had not seemed unusually short whilst in the thick of the activity; there was time to judge distances, height and speed, to decide on some courses of action and reject others, but later, taking into account the height and speed of the aircraft and the ground distances, I worked out that it could not have been more than 7 or 8 seconds. Time must be a wonderfully elastic medium!

Observing how quickly a wood and fabric aircraft can burn out I thanked my lucky stars I had not been knocked out in the crash! As it was I got away with it without even a scratch. But I have never taken off from runway 21 since.

John turned up to find that, apart from the engine and a few pathetic bits of metal and cables, his beloved Turbulent was now just a black smudge on the grass. It helped that his main concern was that I was OK with a feeling almost of guilt on his part that the crash had been due to the engine seizure; he was also thankful that his newly-qualified son had not been flying it when it seized! Wandering disconsolately around in the by now half light of dusk, amazingly he found my undamaged glasses which had incredibly survived the trampling of many feet around the crash scene.

As a postscript, the subsequent PFA enquiry established that the reason for the seizure was the incorrect assembly of the dowel pin locating the crankshaft rear bearing shell, which had led to the dowel failing to engage and distorting the shell against the journal. The overhaulers had not done any bench running-in – there has to be a moral there somewhere!

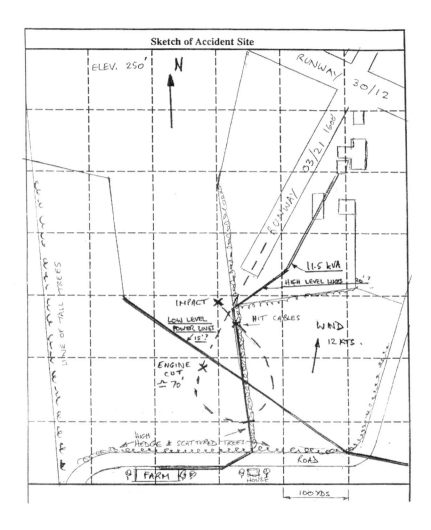

Sketch of Accident Site

ELEV. 250'

N

RUNWAY 30/12

03/21 1600'

RUNWAY

11.5 kVA
HIGH LEVEL LINES 20'?

IMPACT ✗

LOW LEVEL
POWER LINE
15'?

HIT CABLES

WIND
12 KTS.

ENGINE
CUT
≃ 70'

LINE OF TALL TREES

HIGH
HEDGE & SCATTERED TREES

ROAD

FARM

HOUSE

100 YDS

253

CHAPTER 24

TALE-END MISCELLANY

The LVG

In mentioning the work carried out for Shuttleworths on the LVG restoration I commented on the lozenge camouflage, which entailed dying many yards of fabric in ten different colours. There was another factor of the overall finish that was just as important, if the end product was to look as it would have done in 1918, namely the highly-polished, varnished, plywood-covered fuselage. When the RAF had restored the LVG to flying condition for the 1936 Hendon Pageant, they had applied a non-standard camouflage scheme which entailed brushing standard red shrinking dope onto the fuselage as a primary filler. When we came to clean off the paint from the fuselage prior to varnishing it, we discovered that the dope was so ingrained in the plywood that it was impossible to remove it completely. The solution was found by gluing a very thin, paper-backed wood veneer (total thickness around ·01 in) over the entire fuselage, rather than reskin the semi-monocoque structure. The late Wally Berry, a Shuttleworth staff member, completed this by overlaying a whole series of approx. 1 in-wide strips each of about 6 in length around the gun ring support structure laminations, a really messy job but which looked superb when finished.

With the veneer covering, it became possible to varnish the fuselage, which then took on the authentic, highly-polished finish of the original aircraft. As with so many of the jobs associated with aircraft restoration, an alternative solution sometimes has to be found if the costs are not to escalate out of all proportion.

Other tasks, requiring a visit to Brussels to view the only other LVG C.VI known to exist, were to establish the cockpit layout, fittings and instrumentation; the dimensions of the interplane struts and their end fittings so that new ones could be made (the steel end fittings were drawn up by the author and made by the apprentices at BAC Stevenage); the air intake and cooling air ducting for the Benz motor; the radiator design and water piping layout; and to establish how the observer's Parabellum machine gun was fitted, so that a new mount could be drawn and manufactured. This was all very well but to gain access to the aircraft, which was suspended from the ceiling of a vast exhibition hall, the author initially had to make a perilous ascent of a long and very wobbly ladder – mercifully a tower platform was erected later. The search for this vital data was not helped by the discovery of a 1/16 in-thick layer of grey dust over all the upper surfaces, which at least explained why they had been quoted as being of a 'uniform grey'; with the dust brushed away the fabric was found to be standard 5-colour upper lozenge fabric with bluish-grey rib tapes. The other anomaly in the colour scheme was that the 'dull red' fuselage was a standard varnish finish in which the red component of the stain had become dominant; where not exposed to direct light in the cockpit, the varnish was the normal golden-yellow hue.

The final upshot for the author, as a sort of mark of Shuttleworth's gratitude for the effort involved, was the offer by Air Commodore Wheeler of a flight in the gunner's cockpit at a Display staged by *"Flight"* at Cranfield in September 1973. Alan Wheeler was to fly the Bristol Fighter and Neil Williams the LVG, so the resulting dogfight was more than somewhat interesting. What I discovered in the course of this flight was a whole new understanding of what rear gunners went through when fighting in WW1! At first, I was amazed at how comparatively comfortable the observer's position was during the very short duration of the flight. Sitting down on the seat positioned one's head in a relatively draught-free area; standing up, protruding well into the slipstream, placed one in a boisterous blast of warm air blustering down from the centre-section radiator, further enlivened by occasional spouts of scalding water from the vent! But when the Bristol swung round into an attacking posture it became a different matter altogether when I tried to swing the Parabellum round onto it.

The gun ring is released for rotation by a squeeze-grip handle on the ring: squeeze with the left hand and the ring can be moved, helped by leaning one's body against a pair of cushioned blocks on the inside of the ring. The gun, when its rifle butt-type stock is not clipped in a U-shaped holder on the ring, is free to pivot vertically in a cradle mounted above the ring. The cradle is free to rotate horizontally and can also be swung up and down by a handle on the left, when released by a lever (like a cycle brake lever). If that sounds complicated it is, relatively speaking, the complication being that no human yet found has two left hands as well as a right! So the procedure for using the gun was to place the right hand on the pistol grip and unclip the gun from the ring, swinging it round to position the butt on the right shoulder; release the gun ring using the left hand, and swing the ring and gun in the direction of the attacking aircraft; remove the left hand from the gun ring handle (thus locking the ring) and place it on the cradle handle; release the cradle lock to enable it to be moved vertically, then point the gun at the target. If the latter is closing rapidly, the cradle and the ring positions may have to be adjusted alternately using the left hand. Tricky? I'm glad not to have ever been in a position to have to use the gun to save my life!

What made the task one of awe-inspiring proportions was the weight of the gun even without the ammunition, and the fact that releasing the ring lock whilst the aircraft was manoeuvring meant that the ring swung almost uncontrollably in the direction of bank. Bear in mind the fact that in operational conditions the Parabellum carried a seriously heavy belt of hundreds of cartridges on a drum on the right-hand side and consequently would have been much more awkward to manipulate. As if all that was not enough, once a number of rounds had been fired, there would have been an empty, canvas cartridge belt flapping around in the breeze roughly in line with one's face when sighting the gun! If the attacking fighter had little speed advantage and was engaged in a long pursuit course then the task of positioning and sighting the gun may have been acceptable, but in a dogfight with several fast fighters manoeuvring rapidly around, it must have been almost impossible to have returned effective fire. It is notable that many of the more successful fighter pilots had initially served as observers, thus knowing how best to approach a two-seater!

Miles Magister (G-AKPF)

Sometime in 1969 I discovered a thriving local organisation for aviation enthusiasts, the East Anglian Aviation Society. Meeting monthly in a Village College Hall in Bassingbourn they arranged an excellent series of interesting talks on a variety of aviation-related subjects, and I soon decided this was a must. They were very much involved with USAAF Eighth Air Force Reunions associated with the local airfields of Steeple Morden, Bassingbourn (the latter had been home to the 91st BG of "Memphis Belle" fame) and Duxford, and had just started to get interested in 'wreckovery,' having dug up a P-47 Thunderbolt engine. They laid on dances in the College Hall to the music of Glen Miller played by the like of the Sid Lawrence Orchestra, and visits to airfields: all very nostalgic.

Shortly after my joining them they were offered the long-term loan of a very sad and dilapidated Miles Magister if they were interested in rebuilding it. This was owned by Laurie Taylor, who had discovered it languishing in a farmer's field in Suffolk. The story was that it belonged to the farmer, who had flown it until the C. of A. expired in April 1963, at the time of the big scare about failing glue joints in wooden aeroplanes. The wings had been removed and it was simply left standing in the field, being used by chickens as a sort of hen coop. Occasionally the farmer would run the engine and taxy it about. Laurie bought the engine (for £100) and the airframe went with it, the farmer taxying it down the road to where it could be loaded on a lorry for transport to Laurie's father's Garage in Needham Market, where it was stored under cover. The wings were left in the field.

When I first got involved with it, the plan had been to restore it for static exhibition, but I foolishly suggested that as it was an all-wooden aircraft we ought to be able to rebuild it to flying condition. There were no "Maggies" in an airworthy state at that time and I knew that David Ogilvy was looking for one for Shuttleworths (he soon acquired 'JDR). By the time we had reached agreement with Laurie on the loan arrangements we had discovered a spare set of airworthy wings (ex-'HYL) stored at an RAF station and had carried out a preliminary inspection of the aircraft less the original wings. What we found was most discouraging, but not sufficiently so to prevent us going ahead. Seven years of exposure to the elements had rendered virtually all the woodwork unusable and the fuselage only held its shape because of the hundreds of small brass screws securing the ply covering to the basic structure. Not one glue joint remained sound and when the screws were removed the whole lot fell apart.

David Crow, the EAAS Secretary, had a large wooden hut in his garden, big enough to accommodate the fuselage and the building jigs. Laurie had to move the Maggie from his father's garage, and he arranged to transport it to a Nissen hut in a local field belonging to one of the members, so that we could dismantle it sufficiently to get it into David's hut. That was in November 1970, but we assembled a willing team to work on it at weekends through the winter, huddled into one corner of the Nissen Hut; no spare space, no heat and no light – we must have been mad to even think of it!

Eventually we got it broken down into manageable pieces, the biggest job being to separate the fuselage from the centre section, after removing the engine and the undercarriage. At this stage we had no drawings and little else in the way of information about the construction, so we had to take many photographs and make careful notes of the sequence in which things came apart. At last we were able to move it into Dave's hut which now became known as the Steeple Morden Aircraft Factory. A large flat-bed worktable was constructed to use as a jig for building the fuselage sides, using the original ones as patterns for laying out the blocks that would position the longerons and struts etc. It was fortunate that only the screws were holding the fuselage together, so that as they were removed the components separated without being damaged, thus being usable as patterns. Very little of the original structure was usable other than the vital metal fittings and a few blocks in the section positioning the fuselage on the centre section, the latter being made of ash.

Meanwhile, construction of a new tail unit was going ahead, and by the time the fuselage was reassembled we were able to carry out a trial fitting of the tailplane and elevators, fin and rudder. With those in position it began to look like an aeroplane! We had hoped to be able to use the centre section spars with new plywood facings, but the more we dismantled things the more it became obvious that we would need new spars as well, with costly new spruce booms and complex machining. Fortunately, by this time, several years after starting, Dave Ogilvy had rescued the major portions of two more airframes, 'NWO and 'IUA; Shuttleworths had already rebuilt and flown 'JDR, and could offer us 'IUA's usable centre-section in exchange for a serviceable propeller for a Gipsy Moth. We had already been able to make several other items available to Shuttleworths, including new undercarriage oleo seals, of which we had previously obtained the last stock items from Lockheed.

Before work actually started in earnest, an approach had been made to the Popular Flying Association to see if the rebuild could be carried out on a Permit to Fly. The ARB agreed to this and work proceeded under the critical eyes of PFA Inspectors Malcolm Frazer and, subsequently, Carl Butler after Malcolm left for New Zealand.

Whilst the woodwork was proceeding in one part of the hut, work on the engine had started in another corner. Study of the logbooks obtained from Laurie indicated that, despite his thinking that there were several hundred hours of life remaining, the engine had just about run out of hours, no doubt a factor in the non-renewal of its last C. of A. It was all to do with the wretched crankcase mods, which had been such a problem for the Jackaroo group. Again, an unmodded ex-military engine had a life of only 1,100 or 1,200 hours, this one being of an early mod. state and thus only 1,100.

We were keen initially to restore the Maggie to its wartime service markings and had discovered, under the coats of dope applied postwar, a yellow number 27 on each side of the decking between the engine cowl and the front cockpit. What made this number particularly interesting was that it had been brushed on using a stencil, the 'two' being so shaped as to form a 'five' when reversed and inverted! Later, when we discovered that the fuselage was actually that of N3788 (from various components and the manufacturer's plate) and not V1075 as recorded in the logbook, we opted for the prewar all-yellow scheme with polished cowlings.

Alas, for all the work put in by the author and the small team at Steeple Morden, we never got the rebuild finished. Owing to disputes between EAAS and Laurie Taylor over the ownership, Laurie eventually (and rightfully) retrieved it around 1976 and employed some full-time workers to try and complete it. He finally sold it to Adrian Brooks who did at last get it flying; the only real compensation for those originally involved, apart from the learning process, was the knowledge that without our early efforts it almost certainly would never have survived long enough to be flown in the nineties!

DH.89A Dragon Rapides (G-AJHO & G-AKRP)

The EAAS saga continued for a while with the acquisition in 1976 of a Dragon Rapide (G-AJHO) which had been written off by the insurers. Though the C. of A. had only just been carried out, and the damage was slight, the cost of repairs would have exceeded its value, and the insurers were willing to present it free to any recognised organisation prepared to take it on (though the engines would be exchanged for time-expired examples). As usual, there was a slight catch in that it had to be dismantled and removed from Netheravon at very short notice, like next weekend. I managed to raise a small team of about 6 or 7, and by working through from Friday, had it stripped and loaded onto a trailer by Sunday. This was quite a challenge, as neither I nor anyone else in the team had any experience of tackling a machine of this size, but apart from the greater size of the components, it was very much like a big Tiger Moth, the greatest problem being in separating the fuselage from the centre-section. That was transported to the EAAS airstrip at Croydon (Cambs), was eventually rebuilt, but was lost on its first flight when an engine caught fire.

The knowledge gained in stripping the Rapide was put to good use some years later, over Easter '81, when a German friend, Bob Wirth, needed urgent help in removing a partially dismantled Rapide (CN-TTO, ex-G-AKRP) from the docks in Bremerhaven. As with 'JHO, time was of the essence. Bob's stumbling block was in removing the constant-speed props, which required special tools for removing the spinners and the hubs. Before separating the fuselage from the centre-section he needed to remove the engines and was reluctant to do that with the props and nose-cowls still in place. Unbelievably, an ex-engineer colleague of mine just happened to have a set of the tools in his loft, waiting for such an occasion! Armed with these and instructions on how to use them, I sped off to Bremerhaven and helped remove the props, the engines and the centre-section within the required time. Bob eventually had to give up on restoring the Rapide, and subsequently sold it to Rex Ford, who should get it back into the air this year (2000)

Duxford and the RE.8

Around 1970 the EAAS instigated a move to save Duxford airfield and buildings from the County Council's plans to convert the site into a prison. A major tie-up with the IWM saw the prison plans quashed and work was soon started to make the hangars and buildings usable again. At this time the Society had some 200 members and there was no shortage of hands to start cleaning up the site, dozens of people giving up their weekends to carry out filthy and thankless tasks. There was much to be done if the dereliction of the buildings was to be halted – broken glass in the windows to be replaced, hangar doors to be repaired, drains cleared etc. etc. When I first saw the site I felt there was just too much to be done but, amazingly, order began to be restored and eventually the buildings became ready to receive the first aircraft, the IWM seeking EAAS help to move their RE.8 from the Museum in Lambeth and start work on its renovation at Duxford.

As with the LVG I saw this as a heaven-sent opportunity to do some meaningful renovation work on a worthy subject. Accordingly on Whit Sunday 1972 a small team, drawn principally from the Magister group, was locked in the Museum after it closed, with the intention of lowering the RE.8 from its suspension from the roof, dismantling it and loading it on a flatbed articulated lorry for removal to Duxford. All this was to be completed before the Museum reopened to the public the following morning. Pre-planning had arranged for a temporary ramp to be provided onto which the aircraft could be lowered, this serving also as a platform on which to carry out the dismantling. We had one person making notes of the order in which each item was removed and any special comments about the operation, and another filming the work as it proceeded. The whole job went very smoothly with few surprises.

Perhaps the highlight of the whole operation came when the fixed, forward-firing gun was removed for the first time, and hydraulic fluid dripped from the pipe connecting the gun trigger to the synchronization gear pump on the engine. It was a sobering thought that the first World War was still raging when that pipe was filled – the fluid had remained there undisturbed for 54 years! Although the aircraft had been dismantled and removed for safe keeping in 1939, and had been repainted at an RAF MU before being put back on display, it was believed that only the wings had then been removed.

Care had to be taken not to put any weight on the tyres. The rubber had carbonised over the years and become brittle, though still retaining the shape of fully inflated tyres – they looked pristine but were not. I feared any attempt to put pressure on the rubber would have shattered them, as I had seen happen to a pair of Camel wheels and tyres at Old Warden. As it happened, we used those wheels for moving the RE.8, courtesy of Shuttleworths. One really interesting discovery for me was that an original self-sealing, latex-covered fuel tank was fitted, and I had not been aware that any such had been fitted as standard to wartime aircraft. I felt that this was such a unique example that it really ought to have been on show in its own right, with a standard metal tank fitted in its place.

The other exciting discovery was that the drab chocolate-brown dope had been applied when the aircraft was repainted after the second World War. Marketed by Titanine as PC10, this has become the standard colour on virtually all WW1 British aircraft in the UK, both restorations and replicas, in the mistaken belief that this was the true and only representation of PC10 dope. Under the chocolate and in areas where the respray had not penetrated, was what I believe to be the authentic standard finish, a true green-tinged brown with a semi-matt varnish top coat. I have seen a number of examples of original fabric, which varied considerably from a yellow-brown khaki, through green or green-brown shades, to the modern interpretation of PC10, including that on eight SE.5A wings rescued from a barn roof in 1982 – very few equated to modern PC10!

The RE.8 was re-erected for the inaugural Open Day at Duxford held later that year. After that, work was started in earnest on stripping and rebuilding both the engine and airframe, the intention being to restore the aircraft to flying condition so that if the IWM ever relaxed its rule on not flying its aircraft, this one could be ready! If nothing else, we intended to run the engine to enable it to be taxied. Bear in mind that when put into store in 1918, this aircraft had made only its acceptance test flights. With the fuselage fabric removed it could be seen that the wooden structure was indeed like new with the shiny yellow varnish unblemished. Alas, the restoration to flying condition was not to be, and completion of the work was in effect taken out of my hands later, when the IWM and EAAS fell out, the latter's place being taken by the Duxford Aviation Society, formed by dissenting EAAS members. As is so often the case, ambition and politics take over to ruin the efforts of those at the coal-face!

A Sopwith Snipe?

One further interesting little jaunt was occasioned through the EAAS. Through membership of the British Historic Aircraft Preservation Society, to which all the major national and private museums and organisations belonged, we heard of a Bentley BR2 rotary engine, still in its original packing case, available for the taking from a museum in Ulster. It appeared that it had been wished on them after the last war, having been discovered on a dockside in Belfast, with no one claiming ownership and the only paperwork relating to an aero engine identifying it as a Bentley, delivered sometime in the thirties. The Port authorities wished to have it removed and virtually dumped it on the Ulster Museum. They had never had any use for it, and now wished to use the space it was taking up – please, would someone take it away before they sent it to the local scrapyard. This was unbelievable, were they sure it was a Bentley? Yes, they had looked in the case and it was a rotary engine, which had always been identified as a Bentley.

This was too good to be true, but even if not a Bentley, any sort of rotary surely must be worth collecting. We soon established that it would be possible to obtain a set of manufacturing drawings for a Sopwith Snipe, and if it really was a Bentley, building a Snipe from scratch was not deemed beyond our collective capability! Accordingly, Dave Elphick and I set out for Belfast one Friday evening. Dave's big Volvo estate towed a close-coupled four-wheel trailer thought to be comfortably capable of carrying the 490 lb weight of the engine, plus the packing case. We enjoyed a smooth ferry crossing to Belfast and set off with high hopes for the Ulster Museum, being careful to avoid any likely trouble spots.

At the Museum, we were shown around their impressive collection (which if I remember correctly included at that time a Miles Whitney Straight, though we were too impatient to view the Bentley for that to register firmly). Eventually, with the arrival of the appropriate official, we were taken to see the engine in the storeroom. Immediately we set eyes on the packing case, my heart sank. The case was enormous, something like 5 feet square and 4 feet long – much, much bigger than would be required for a Bentley! The heavy wooden planks were black with coal dust and oil, and several were missing, leaving a great gaping hole on one side. Whatever was in there would certainly not have been protected from the elements over all these years, and would probably have been subjected to much corrosion.

Plucking up the courage to peer inside revealed an enormous radial engine, soon identified as a Bristol Pegasus, unprotected and consequently well corroded. A Pegasus weighs something of the order of 1,100 lb, and the packing case possibly half as much again. First thoughts, of turning round and running for home without it, were quickly superseded by the realisation that a Pegasus such as this might yield some usable parts for the Navy's Swordfish, then grounded with engine problems. We discussed the possibility of removing the engine from the packing case in order to lighten the load. However, the realisation that this would leave us with no means of supporting the engine, or stopping it rolling around on the trailer, left us considering whether our little trailer could actually be persuaded to carry the weight.

The Museum quickly produced a mobile hoist and, not without some trepidation, we hoisted the case and engine onto the trailer to sit transversely between the wheels, where it towered over us. The suspension (which consisted of four Mini rear suspension units, two in tandem each side) sagged alarmingly but held. Dave and I jumped energetically up and down on the trailer to see if the arms would bottom, but they didn't. Securing the case with ropes, we drove as fast as we dared around the car park, and though it leaned alarmingly it stayed put.

The journey home was fraught with alarms about how the trailer was coping. It didn't help that the sea crossing was accompanied by a force-too-many gale, during which a vehicle was reported as having broken loose on the car deck. Dave and I just knew it was ours but fortunately it wasn't. Miraculously we got it back to Duxford by mid-afternoon, only to be met with a refusal to let us in, on the instructions of the IWM, who had finally broken off diplomatic relations with the EAAS. We got round this one by stating that the engine was a Pegasus destined for the Navy, and left it there for someone else to sort out. The Navy gratefully collected it but later informed us that it wasn't a lot of use to them as it was the wrong Mark for the Swordfish and was very badly corroded anyway. Oh! well, at least we saved it from the scrap man (we hope).

The Southern Martlet (G-AAYX)

After retiring in 1986, I became very much involved with Shuttleworth's Martlet rebuild. Staff engineer Andy Presland had the main task of rebuilding this aircraft, which had last flown in 1949/50 when owned by Butlins. As with the LVG, many vital parts were missing and there were no manufacturing drawings available, but in this case no other examples to look at. Andy was faced with sorting out a great heap of minor fittings and we spent many an enjoyable hour trying to work out what they did and where they went. The biggest problem was that the complete undercarriage was missing, but we did have many sharp, detailed photographs to work from; however they revealed that almost every one of the six Martlets built differed in some form or another. Eventually, it was possible to determine from the photographs the major dimensions and geometry of the undercarriage, but at first lack of details of the shock struts was a problem.

We knew that the springing was by external coiled springs with oil and air dampers, and that they had been designed and built by Basil Henderson, designer of the Hendy Hobo and Heck. These struts were similar in principle to the shock struts fitted to the Armstrong Whitworth Siskin, the springs in that case being enclosed, and in the end we designed new legs based on the Siskin struts, scaling up from a sectional drawing of the Siskin leg. To ease manufacture of the swivel joints it was found possible to modify Tiger Moth strut-end and axle fittings. Wheel rims of the right size but later design enabled motor tyres to be fitted in place of the original beaded-edge tyres, and these were fitted to new hubs. It all looks pretty authentic, and if nothing else I am confident the dimensions are very close to original. At last I had good cause to appreciate what I had learned about stressing during five years at night school back in the fifties!

DH.90 Dragonfly (G-AEDU)

On the strength of assisting with the Martlet undercarriage I was approached to help with the rebuild of G-AEDU, which had suffered a major accident in the USA. This had been put down partly to a well-known hazard in operating Dragonflies, namely the Bendix cable-operated brakes. Even when new these gave trouble, and they are believed to be the main reason why so many Dragonflies suffered take-off or landing accidents; drag from binding brakes, or unequal application, could cause an uncontrollable swing to develop, or the brakes were not effective when required to correct a developing swing (either on accelerating or decelerating at low speed with the tail on the ground). In the resulting ground-loop, the tubular metal centre-section spars would be bent and the cost of repairing or replacing these was more than the aircraft was worth. That is, until there were only one or two left, when their scarcity factor made them worth repairing!

Back in the late seventies I, and many others, had believed that they had become extinct. In 1979 I discovered that G-AEDU had survived and was lying dismantled outside a private museum near Boise in Idaho. After some complex string-pulling by an old pen-friend in Idaho, I eventually managed to view the pathetic heap of parts. It had been bought at the auction of Frank Tallman's collection after the latter's death, and not being airworthy had been dismantled in order to transport it from California. The owner insisted he was going to restore it to an airworthy condition, but he had so many other projects on the go and it looked to be in such a poor state that I really couldn't see that happening. I returned to England with pictures of it, only to discover that another non-airworthy Dragonfly had been discovered in South Africa and had been shipped to BAe at Hatfield; whilst there for the start of the DH Moth Club's 'Famous Grouse' rally to Strathallan I found it still in the packing cases in which it had arrived. Suddenly, from none there were two, with a good chance of once again seeing in the air one of the most beautiful biplanes ever built!

'EDU was eventually brought back to England and rebuilt, only to be sold back in the States again, where it won the AAA Grand Champion Award. This was more fortunate for me than I at first realised! In 1986, whilst on the home run on my Oregon Trail flight, a visit to Antique Field at Blakesburg (where my 1946 Aeronca Champ slotted in nicely as a 'classic') revealed Mike Simpson and the Dragonfly engaged on joyriding activities (free to any genuine enthusiasts). Here my wildest dreams came true, not only to get a flight in such an exotic beast but to be allowed to handle the controls for a meaningful period! All this was magic stuff, and included flights in Tom Hayes' Stearman C-3R and a Brunner-Winkle Bird.

Shortly after that, 'EDU was badly damaged when, guess what, a swing developed on landing, and at first no one seemed inclined to take on the rebuild. Henry Labouchere bought it on behalf of Torquil Norman and shipped it back to the UK for rebuilding, and eventually in 1992 it reappeared, if anything better than ever. I became involved in the rebuild when it was decided to replace the cable brakes with hydraulic ones. Henry had discovered that Pucara main wheels were the same size as those fitted to the Dragonfly, and with minor modifications might just about be squeezed into the undercarriage legs without redesigning the entire undercarriage. Accordingly, a pair of new Pucara wheels and tyres obtained from stocks captured in the Falklands was located, and I was given the task of designing, drawing and stressing the modifications both to the undercarriage and the rudder bar to accommodate the heel brake pedals. Further proof to me that life begins at sixty!

Wet Boots

From the earliest days I have always been fascinated by seaplanes, from the elegant Supermarine S.5s and 6s on, considering that some aircraft look incomparably better on floats than wheels (Moth, Swordfish, Seafox to name just a few). So when the opportunity was presented to sample floatplane-flying it was eagerly accepted. This came about when driving up the Pacific coast in Oregon in May 1979, where a roadside notice board at Woahink Lake advertised joyrides and dual tuition flights.

Inquiries indicated that the owner of a Cessna 180 floatplane riding at the dockside had nothing better to do at that moment than give me some hands-on experience. For the princely sum of $30 he agreed to give me 30 minutes of tuition, with my wife coming along for the ride. It was unfortunate that we could spare no more time, being bound for Wenatchee in Washington State that evening, and already behind schedule.

Having established that I had a current UK licence with around 350 hours on Tigers and Jackaroos he saw no problems with me flying the Cessna. After a little demonstration on how to 'sail' a floatplane on the water, he took off and landed it once to show how, and then said: "OK, you take it, fly it and land it just like a Tiger Moth and you should have no problems." Exactly true, and I did two glorious circuits to prove it. Only after we had left did my wife realise that I had flown the last two circuits; it was probably just as well she hadn't known at the time as she probably wouldn't have enjoyed it as much! Where else but in the States could you do this?

A Tin Goose

Another old aircraft which I have always been interested in was the Ford Tri-motor, and in 1979 I finally got to view a 5-AT-B (N9651) at Morgan Hill in California. Although this was airworthy it was not at the time available for joyrides, so all I could do was to stand and admire it (and not for too long as there were so many other exciting aircraft there, even including an old friend G-ADDI, a DH.84 Dragon last seen at Rush Green). In 1986 I was able to view another 5-AT-B (N9683) suspended from the ceiling of the Smithsonian in Washington DC. In 1988 I found two more, one at Oshkosh (a 4-AT-E, N8047) and perhaps the most famous of them all, Admiral Byrd's 4-AT-B, N7584, at the Ford Museum at Dearborn. The latter, along with the earlier Fokker FVII/3m "Josephine Ford" also on display, was used by Byrd for his Polar Expeditions. The pace was hotting up!

Finally, in 1993 after my second Oregon Trail flight, I was able to actually fly in one! This was a 5-AT-B (N9645) on a positioning flight from Independence OR to McMinnville OR, the home of the Evergreen Air Venture Museum. The Ford is the 'Queen' of the Museum, which also boasts ownership of the Hughes HK-1 Spruce Goose. Even to see or hear one in flight was a momentous event but to actually ride in one . . . !

I was pleased to find that, despite all the contrary reports penned by chic young present-day journalists comparing Fords with 747s, it was no noisier in flight than any modern light aircraft. Indeed, I found it very comfortable, with only slight vibration through the floor panelling and seat armrests (countered completely by using the footrests on the seat in front, and by removing one's arms from the armrests). I could quite cheerfully have contemplated several hours flying in it! Also impressive by any standards was the fairly sprightly performance. Penn Stohr Jr, the son of a Tri-motor back-country pilot with the Johnson Flying Service, climbed quite steeply from take-off to swing round in a 45 deg bank, tightening up to 60 deg to line up with the taxiway adjacent to the runway from which we had just departed, in order to make an impressive low, fast run past the public enclosure.

From my seat in the second row from the front, carefully chosen so that both sets of outer engine instruments (mounted externally above the nacelles) were easily visible, I could see that in all flight conditions, Stohr kept the port engine running faster than the starboard, 2,000:1,800 rpm at take-off (despite a full passenger load) and 1,900:1,600 in cruise. This was presumably to save an aching right foot from applying continuous right rudder to counter engine torque.

I had read *"Fly the Biggest Piece Back,"* the story of the Johnson Flying Service, who operated a fleet of Tri-motors continuously from 1934 until 1969, principally flying awkward loads to mining operators and dropping Forest Service Smokejumpers to fight forest fires in the mountains in Montana. The connection with Evergreen and Penn Stohr Jr was that they took over Johnson in 1975. Bob Johnson had certainly made a reputation as a mountain flyer with his Tri-motors and this was presumably why a tall brake lever in front of the throttle pedestal was known as the 'Johnson Bar' (not fitted on N9654 which had heel brakes).

Before the flight I asked Penn how the Johnson Bar was used, when you needed the left hand on the control column and the right on the throttles etc. He demonstrated that you twisted slightly to the right and hooked the right leg round the bar, pulling it towards you to apply left brake, or pushing it away for right braking, or straight back for both, leaving the rudder control to the left foot! Even for a tall man, as Stohr is, it sounded a bit of a tall story to me and juggling all those controls simultaneously was a bit like operating as a one-man band! Of course, if flying with a co-pilot, the latter applied the brakes by hand. I suppose it's not really that much different to driving a rally car with one hand on the wheel, one changing gear, left foot operating the clutch and right foot heel-and-toeing for braking and blipping the throttle, often all at much the same time – though not with one leg stretching behind!

Taylorcraft BC-12 (G-BRPX)

When the Jackaroo was sold and Stevenage Flying Club disbanded in 1988 I was left with no immediate visible means of airborne support. A year or so later, on one of my occasional visits to Little Gransden to fly the "Artful Dodger" (Turbulent 'RTF), I spied a forlorn-looking heap of bits in the back of No. 2 hangar. The principal item was a light-blue-painted fuselage vaguely reminiscent of an early Auster, which I soon recognised as an American Taylorcraft, of which the early Austers were licence-built versions. I had come across a number of Taylorcrafts in the

States at various times, regarding them as little different to a Piper Cruiser, i.e. a side-by-side two-seater version of the Piper Cub. With my new-found respect for 65 hp Continental A-65 engines, one of which had performed so reliably and economically for me in the Aeronca "Champ" (see *"Flying the Oregon Trail"*), I realised that this could well be just what I was looking for to replace the Jackaroo.

This one was really in a desperate state, the cowlings battered well out of shape, the windscreen cracked, fabric in tatters, leaning to one side and with a flat tyre: it was just what I was looking for. I had been to various auctions and viewed several 'airworthy' Taylorcraft, "Champs" and Cubs. Invariably I found that if they were in my price range they were universally in bad shape, with crazed doped fabric, battered cowlings, translucent window perspex, stiff or slack controls, dripping oil and worn tyres etc. etc., in other words in need of a complete overhaul, but priced as airworthy. I wouldn't be content to fly anything in such a condition, so I might just as well buy a 'basket case' and go the whole hog, knowing that at the end of the day I would have a sound aeroplane looking the way I wanted it.

This one came from the States as part of a job lot, bought by Mark Jeffries in 1989 when seeking Boeing-Stearman PT-17s for rebuilding. The story was that it had been taken in part-exchange for a Grumman Ag-Cat and had sat deteriorating in the back of a hangar since 1970, losing minor parts in the process – unloved and uncared for. Mark had started work on it in a small way and had registered it with the CAA. I negotiated a deal with him, paying half as much again as what I considered was its market value, mainly on the basis that the engine looked sound and there were not exactly too many of these little planes around at that time – and I wanted it! The big attraction was that it could be operated on a PFA Permit to Fly rather than a normal C. of A., which meant I could do all the work myself, at home in my garage.

My original work estimate was that it would take a year to rebuild and, had all the information and parts needed been readily available, that may not have been too far out. As it was it took some six months to gather up enough of the information needed (manuals, parts lists, sources of supply etc.) to be able to order the materials and parts from the USA before starting work in earnest. The first work had been to strip and remove the engine whilst at Gransden to ease the task of transporting it home. This had been a terrible job as it proved difficult to remove the cowlings without further damaging them, because the fasteners refused to yield. The propeller hub had to be left in place because I could find no one who knew whether the securing nut was a left-hand or right-hand thread, and it did not want to undo either way. With the cowlings eventually removed the entire engine was found to be covered in a thick coating of dried oil and Mississippi mud which had set like mortar. Hidden in the dark depths the securing arrangement for the engine cooling baffles, which fitted closely round the cylinders, at first defied all attempts to find out how they were secured. Even they yielded in the end and, with ever-willing helper Den Willett, I was able at last to reduce the engine to handleable-weight components.

At last I got hold of a service manual for the engine and almost wished I hadn't. It was quite a shock to discover that virtually every part that moved was worn outside the acceptable limits, including the barrels, requiring the replacement of every bearing, a full rebore with new pistons and rings, regrinding of the crankshaft and camshaft and new valves! Even the magnetos needed a complete overhaul. At least in fitting sodium-cooled valves I could hopefully avoid the problems of having to use 100-octane fuel. It was fortunate that my old friend Mike Vaisey had, with Paul Shannon, just formed VinTech (Vintage Engine Technology Ltd) so that I was one of their first customers – they helped enormously with the machining and professional advice.

Otherwise, everything went well. Den found me a good 'tin-basher' to smooth out the wrinkles in the cowlings, and I discovered that the brakes and wheel bearings did not need replacing, even the tyres proving to be OK once new inner tubes were fitted. Most of the control cables were replaced, but several of the original cables were still usable, with neatly spliced cable ends rather than the pressed copper sleeves widely used in later years. Some of the woodwork needed replacing, as did the seats and canvas hammock carrying them, but overall the condition throughout was quite remarkable with virtually no rust. One of the biggest problems was in fitting new undercarriage bungees, the task of easing the loops into place while stretched seeming an insuperable one. Trans-Atlantic correspondence solved this one with advice on how to use a car side-lifting jack and a rope loop to stretch the bungees, cutting the rope once the bungees were in position so that they sprang into place. Easy when you know how!

One of my aims was to restore the aircraft to as near as possible its original state, keeping it light so as to reproduce the original's performance. Most Taylorcraft owners I have spoken to reckon the empty weight of their aircraft extends to well over 800 lb and it is too easy to add spats, lights, radio, extra instrumentation, carpets, soundproofing, luxury upholstery etc. etc. My only concession was to fit rear side windows and clear roof panels, similar to the factory-fitted ones, in the interests of safety – I don't like having any blind spots that can be avoided. Consequently, the empty weight is 777 lb, though even this is higher than some sources quote as original. I also wanted to adopt a colour scheme as close as possible to factory schemes. Unfortunately the two-tone colour breaks revealed under the top layers of dope on the fuselage indicated a rear fuselage horizontal break on the centre line, just too low to fit in CAA regulation-size registration letters in the lower colour, so I raised the break line just sufficiently to allow this; it barely shows. The original colours on N39208 were black lower/red upper on the fuselage with red wings, but I changed the red for cream for better visibility, still, I believe, a standard factory combination. The nose paint scheme came from adverts in some old 1945 copies of *"Flying,"* obviously kept by me for all those years for just such a purpose!

Came the day for the first engine run. Wheeling the fuselage out onto the front lawn, making sure there were few neighbours around to disturb, Den and I chocked the wheels, put some fuel into the tank, primed, sucked in, switched on and swung the prop. "Chuff," went the motor. "There's life in the old girl yet – switches still ON, try again," from me, at the same time advancing the throttle 1/16 in. This time the motor burst into life. Unbelievable! There can have been no sweeter sound in all my life, as that little motor sat there ticking over smoothly and quietly, like a sewing machine. We left it chuckling quietly to itself at 800 rpm for 15 minutes, the first part of the running-in period, watching anxiously for oil or fuel leaks. There were none, other than a very slight weep from two of the rocker boxes, soon cured by tightening the securing screws. The only fault was that the oil pressure was running at 45 psi instead of the required 30, the result of fitting a new relief valve spring, rectified by replacing the old one! Reckoning myself as more at home with airframes than engines, I can recall no greater satisfaction, ever, than at so success-fully re-lifing this little motor, perhaps because it was so obviously completely worn out when I started. If this is how doctors and surgeons feel on completing a life-saving operation, I think they should pay the patients for the privilege!! At the time of writing, the engine has completed some 150 hours of trouble-free running and usually starts first swing.

Work on the airframe continued to completion for another three months, finally getting PFA clearance to test-fly it in June '93. I had managed to get a flight in another Taylorcraft so knew roughly what to expect from mine, and it proved to be every bit as good as I had hoped it would be. I have to admit to just a little feeling of trepidation before opening the throttle for the first flight, much as on my first solo 29 years earlier. This time it was: "Have I really tightened and locked everything?" rather than: "Can I really do this?". It was an entirely successful and joyous occasion, and the only thing I can think of which might be more satisfying would be if one had also designed the aircraft from scratch – that must be the ultimate!

What Now?

Ever since I started flying the greatest fear was always that something would happen to stop me flying for good. I used to try and imagine how I would feel if, for instance, I ever failed a medical. A sudden enforced cessation may have seemed so catastrophic as to make life not worth living – though I very much doubt that any drastic action would have followed.

In actual fact, that situation has approached so gradually over the last 10 years as to be reasonably acceptable. When rheumatoid arthritis was finally identified as the reason for problems throughout 1988, culminating with being provided with a Disabled Driver sticker at the end of that year, it did not in itself stop me flying. The real problem was the after-effects of pulling and pushing aircraft into and out of hangars and swinging props, which would not show up till the evening and could put me out of action for a week.

The arthritis responded well and rapidly to treatment, leaving me with a slightly 'dicky' right hand, and I quickly gave up my Disabled Driver badge. For any others similarly afflicted the good news was that it did not stop me rebuilding the Taylorcraft, or flying. Since then other factors have made me realise that flying is not so much fun these days: six-monthly medicals; the increasing number of airfields which will not accept non-radio aircraft; the narrowing gaps between controlled areas; the need for PPO at even old familiar airfields; the difficulties of getting a clear, lucid and reliable weather forecast in plain English; the growing anti-social stigma of flying; the ever-tightening Rules, Regulations and Restrictions; insurance companies who add 50% to premiums for older pilots; the dulling effects of the 'safety first' brigade who would take all the challenge out of every 'different' activity mankind engages in etc.! It will no longer seem to be the end of my world when I finally give up flying.

****

At the time of going to press the Taylorcraft has, reluctantly, now been sold and other activities are jostling for the time thus released. Building and flying radio-controlled models is looming large though even that hobby is subject to ever-growing bureaucracy, with licences needed for every facet, and under threat from the 'anti' brigade. I suppose that if nothing else, I can switch on my PC Flight Simulator and wrestle with that, though it is a poor substitute. Perhaps I'll even finish off and have published my Gloster Grebe scale drawings, or the AW Argosy drawings, or even a new set for the Ford Tri-motor series . . . or get out my paint brushes again . . . or? . . . Happy landings!